REAPPORTIONMENT IN THE 1970s

A publication of the
Franklin K. Lane Memorial Fund,
Institute of Governmental Studies,
University of California, Berkeley

Nelson W. Polsby

Editor

REAPPORTIONMENT IN THE 1970s

Published for the
Institute of Governmental Studies by
UNIVERSITY OF CALIFORNIA PRESS
Berkeley, Los Angeles, London
1971

University of California Press
Berkeley and Los Angeles, California
University of California Press, Ltd.
London, England
Copyright © 1971, by
The Regents of the University of California
International Standard Book Number: 0–520–01885–0
Library of Congress Catalog Card Number: 73–142046
Printed in the United States of America

CONTENTS

CONTRIBUTORS

CARL A. AUERBACH, born 1915 in New York City, is Professor of Law at the University of Minnesota. He received the A.B. degree from the Long Island University and the LL.B. at the Harvard Law School. He is co-author of *The Federal Regulation of Transportation* (1953) and *The Legal Process* (1961) and author of "The Reapportionment Cases: One Person, One Vote—One Vote, One Value" (*The Supreme Court Review* 1964) and numerous articles in legal and other periodicals.

GORDON E. BAKER was born in 1923 in Poughkeepsie, New York. He received the A.B. degree from Reed College in 1948, the M.A. degree from the University of Washington in 1949, and the PH.D. from Princeton University in 1952. He is Professor of Political Science at the University of California, Santa Barbara, where he has taught since 1952. He is the author of several books and monographs, including *Rural Versus Urban Political Power* (1955), *State Constitutions: Reapportionment* (1960), and *The Reapportionment Revolution* (1966).

ALEXANDER M. BICKEL, born 1924 in Bucharest, Romania, is Chancellor Kent Professor of Law and Legal History at Yale University. He received the B.S. degree in social science from the City College of New York and the LL.B. from Harvard University. He is the author of several books, including *The Least Dangerous Branch* (1962) and *The Supreme Court and the Idea of Progress* (1970).

WILLIAM E. BICKER, born 1940 in Cleveland, Ohio, is Assistant Professor of Political Science at the University of California, Berkeley. He received the A.B. degree from Western Reserve University and the PH.D. degree in political science from Indiana University.

DAVID BRAYBROOKE, born 1924 in Hackettstown, New Jersey, is Professor of Philosophy and Politics at Dalhousie University. He received the A.B. degree from Harvard College in economics, and the M.A. in philosophy and the PH.D. in ethics, epistemology, and economic theory from Cornell University. He is the author, co-author, or editor of several books, including *Three Tests for Democracy* (1968), *A Strategy of Decision* (with C. E. Lindblom, 1963), and *Philosophical Problems of the Social Sciences* (1965).

MILTON C. CUMMINGS, JR., born 1933 in New Haven, Connecticut, is Professor of Political Science at the Johns Hopkins University. He received the A.B. degree from Swarthmore College, the B.PHIL in politics from Oxford University, and the PH.D. in political science from Harvard University. He is the author, co-author, or editor of several books, including *Congressmen and the Electorate* (1966) and *The Image of the Federal Service* (with Franklin P. Kilpatrick and M. Kent Jennings, 1964).

ROBERT G. DIXON, JR., born 1920 in Canajoharie, New York, is Professor of Law at the George Washington University National Law Center. He received the A.B. and PH.D. degrees in political science from Syracuse University and the LL.B. from George Washington University and was a Ford Foundation Faculty Fellow at Stanford University Law School. A frequent contributor to professional journals and author or co-author of several books, he was accorded the Woodrow Wilson Foundation Book Award in 1968 for *Democratic Representation: Reapportionment in Law and Politics*.

MALCOLM E. JEWELL was born in 1928 in Woonsocket, Rhode Island. He is Professor of Political Science and chairman of that department at the University of Kentucky. He received the A.B. degree from Harvard College, the M.A. from Columbia University, and the PH.D. from Pennsylvania State University. He is the author, co-author, or editor of several books, including *The Politics of Reapportionment* (1962), *Senatorial Politics and Foreign Policy* (1962), *The Legislative Process in the United States* (1966), and *Legislative Representation in the Contemporary South* (1967).

CHARLES O. JONES, born 1931 in Worthing, South Dakota, is Maurice Falk Professor of Political Science at the University of Pittsburgh. He received the A.B. degree at the University of South Dakota and the M.S. and PH.D. in political science at the University of Wisconsin. He is the author of several books, including *The Minority Party in Congress* (1970) and *An Introduction to the Study of Public Policy* (1970).

DAVID R. MAYHEW, born 1937 in Killingly, Connecticut, is Assistant Professor of Political Science at Yale University. He received the A.B. degree from Amherst College and the PH.D. in government from Harvard University. He is the author of *Party Loyalty Among Congressmen: the Difference Between Democrats and Republicans, 1947–1962* (1966).

RUSSELL D. MURPHY, born 1934 in Boston, Massachusetts, is Associate Professor of Government at Wesleyan University in Middletown, Connecticut. He received the A.B. degree from St. John's Seminary in Brighton, Massachusetts, the M.A. from Boston College, and the PH.D. in political science from Yale University.

NELSON W. POLSBY, born 1934 in Norwich, Connecticut, is Professor of Political Science at the University of California, Berkeley. He received the A.B. degree from the Johns Hopkins University and the M.A. and PH.D. in political science from Yale University. He is the author, co-author, or editor of several books, including *Community Power and Political Theory* (1963) and *Presidential Elections* (with Aaron Wildavsky, 1968).

CHARLES PRESS, born 1922 in St. Louis, Missouri, is Professor of Political Science and chairman of that department at Michigan State University. He received the A.B. degree from Elmhurst College, the M.A. and PH.D., from the University of Minnesota. He is co-author of *The American Political Process* (1965) and co-editor of *Democracy in Urban America* and *Democracy in the Fifty States* (1966).

DOUGLAS W. RAE, born at Indianapolis in 1939, teaches political science at Yale University. He received the A.B. degree from Indiana University and the M.S. and PH.D. degrees from the University of Wisconsin. He is author of *The Political Consequences of Electoral Laws* (1967) and *The Analysis of Political Cleavages* (with Michael Taylor, 1970) and of articles published in the *American Political Science Review, Comparative Politics, Comparative Political Studies, British Journal of Political Science, New Republic,* and *Polity*.

ALLAN P. SINDLER, born 1928 in New York City, is Professor in the Graduate School of Public Affairs at the University of California, Berkeley. He received undergraduate and graduate degrees from Harvard University in political science. Among his publications are *Huey Long's Louisiana: State Politics, 1920–1952* (1956), *Political Parties in the United States* (1966), and, as editor, *American Political Institutions and Public Policy* (1969).

PREFACE

Early in the academic year of 1969/1970, my colleague Professor Eugene Lee approached me with the proposal that we collaborate on a conference that would bring together on the Berkeley campus of the University of California some of the leading figures in the study of reapportionment and some of the people in state government who would be most concerned with the actual job of reapportioning state legislatures and congressional districts after the 1970 census figures became known. As director of the university's Institute of Governmental Studies, Lee regularly engages in interpreting the findings of political and social science to governmental officials and in interesting scholars in problems that public officials must face in the course of their work. The 1970 census would have both practical and scholarly relevance to reapportionment, Lee thought, and would serve as an excellent occasion for the application of diverse perspectives to a single problem.

The present volume is the stepchild of that original idea. It proved impossible to find adequate financial support for a conference on "Reapportionment in the 1970s." Instead, drawing upon the Franklin Lane Fund of the institute, we determined to put together a set of papers that would open up some of the lines of conversation which we might have pursued had we been able to come together. It is, as books often are, more theoretical and less circumstantial than our conversation might have been. We have maintained the symposium format in the hope that a part of our original intention, which was to stimulate interchange, would be preserved.

As editor of the symposium, it is my pleasant responsibility to thank each of the contributors for his interest in this project and for the remarkably high quality of his work. Reviewers are always justified in referring to collections of essays as uneven, but, to paraphrase George Orwell, some collections are more uneven than others, and in my opinion, this one is far less uneven than most.

I am grateful to Kathleen Peters, for helping me keep track of this project as it percolated along, to William McClung and Judith Quinn of the University of California Press for their quick and skillful cooperation, to Darwin R. Leister for preparing the Selected References, to his colleagues Nancy Kreinberg, Harriet Nathan, and Stanley Scott of the Institute of Governmental Studies for their encouragement and assistance, and, most of all, to Eugene Lee, who was all carrot and no stick.

My services were brought to you through the courtesy of Linda O. Polsby, Lisa Polsby, and Emily Polsby.

NELSON W. POLSBY

Berkeley
October 1970

INTRODUCTION

SOME DIMENSIONS OF A
NEW POLITICAL ISSUE

Nelson W. Polsby

Alexis de Tocqueville is often quoted as saying that "scarcely any political question arises in the United States that is not resolved, sooner or later, into a judicial question." [1] It must not be supposed, however, that resolution into a judicial question necessarily contributes to the expeditious or just settlement of any and all political questions. This, after all, is a matter best determined by the outcomes of particular cases and the values of observers. A rather substantial body of experience, which judges of a certain persuasion not infrequently cite, argues that political questions cannot in the nature of things be settled by judicial institutions.

Whether or not we come to agree with this view of the matter must depend in some substantial measure for our generation upon what we make of the political question of reapportionment. There is nothing more political than how the boundaries are drawn which determine who represents whom in Congress, state legislatures, and other governing bodies. This political question, the drawing of these boundaries, became one particular kind of judicial question in the early 1960s by virtue of a series of Supreme Court decisions which held, first, that the Court could determine whether these boundaries were drawn in accordance with commands of the Constitution and then interpreted these commands as forbidding ever-smaller inequalities in the numbers of persons enclosed by the boundaries of congressional, state legislative, and other districts.

This is the political issue that is the subject of the present symposium. Because politicians found it inconvenient to disturb increasingly archaic and manifestly unjust political boundaries, and because the Court declined

1. *Democracy in America,* vol. I (New York: Knopf Vintage Books, 1954), p. 209.

to disturb them before the 1960s, reapportionment had never been a major preoccupation at all levels of American government. To be sure, each decennial census took a few congressmen away from a few states and gave a few to a few states, and this meant tinkering with the district boundaries in the affected states. But, as a central preoccupation of state governments everywhere, reapportionment is a very young issue as issues in American politics go, and we have by no means learned all we will need to know to make sense of the way it unfolds in future years.

When the nation was younger, and still expanding into new territory, problems of apportionment and representation, tied as they were to the question of slavery and the delicate balance of power in the U.S. Senate, were central to American political life. But this has not been true since the end of Reconstruction, and few of the lessons of American politics in the turbulent middle of the last century are likely to help us unravel the complexities of reapportionment in the next decade. The one big thing the events of those years teaches, of course, is that what the boundaries are and how they are drawn can matter enormously in the conduct of politics. There is a sense, however, in which we can say that we know less about modern reapportionment than about the nuclear arms race, problems of pollution and conservation, and even urban blight and unrest. All of these have, in any event, been much studied and pondered, as they should be. This symposium is an effort to focus the energies of political and legal analysts upon reapportionment as it reappears as a central issue in American politics.

Following the official report of the 1970 census some time in the early 1970s, and then again after the censuses of succeeding decades, nearly all congressional and state legislative boundaries will have to be redrawn to reflect geographic shifts of the restless and growing United States population. Three main political institutions will impinge upon—and be affected by—how this is done. One of these is the United States Supreme Court, which sets the standards to which boundaries must conform. The Court may or may not rest upon its current interpretation of the Constitution, which forbids virtually all deviations from mathematical equality in the populations of legislative districts. It may or may not take up future cases affording it an opportunity to recede from that position and give weight to desiderata other than strict numerical equality, such as the representation of natural communities and the recognition of historic boundaries. Essays in this volume by both Robert Dixon and Alexander Bickel, and the commentary by Carl Auerbach, speak rather sharply to this point. Both Dixon and Bickel propound legal theories by which the Court could in the first instance have avoided intruding itself so far into the politics of reapportionment, while at the same time honoring its responsibility to see that the acts or failures to act on reapportionment by legislatures did not violate the Constitution. Dixon suggests rather optimistically that a new political institution—bipartisan reapportionment agencies—might provide an acceptable device by which the Court could ease away from its current inclination to monitor reapportionment schemes rather closely. Auerbach makes a spirited defense of the theory under which the Court acted and challenges critics of the Court to show that the consequences of the one man, one vote, formula have been as deleterious as they had feared.

Douglas Rae and Gordon Baker had the assignment of looking at the consequences of reapportionment under the Court's present formula. Rae concludes that an increase in political democracy has resulted from reapportionments thus far accomplished, though the benefits from future reapportionments are likely to diminish. This is not, of course, a defense of the legal theory by which reapportionment was compelled, and so it does not contradict Baker's findings on gerrymandering, echoed also in the articles by Bickel and Dixon. So long as numerical equality is the only standard, these three essays argue, reapportionment may well violate criteria of democracy that reflect other standards. Baker's discussion of the gerrymandering that is not only permitted, but encouraged, under the present law helps to make this point.

State legislatures will also be much concerned with reapportionment in the 1970s. They must draw the boundaries of congressional districts, and both houses of each state legislature also must conform to the one man, one vote, standard set by the Court. We know very little about how this affects the politics of state legislatures. Unfortunately, we were not able to attract to the symposium the participation of an author who could deal directly with this problem. Because each of the states has a history, a demography, and a politics of its own, an enormous amount of detailed knowledge would be involved in making generalizations that will stand up about the impact of reapportionment on state legislatures. Filling this gap in our knowledge ought to be a first priority of future research on reapportionment, because the legislatures are the workshops in which the reapportionments of 1970 and later years will be forged.

Some work has been done on a state-by-state basis in discussing the political outcomes of reapportionment. On the whole, this work treats state legislatures as black boxes which produce policy outcomes. The latter have been measured under a variety of circumstances, and inferences have been drawn from them about the effects of apportionment.

William E. Bicker's essay summarizes and criticizes this literature. Its significance derives in part from his questioning of the conventional wisdom that apportionment makes no difference in policy outcomes within the states.

Congress is the third major American institution that reapportionment touches in a major way. Owing to the explicit language of the Connecticut Compromise, the apportionment of the U.S. Senate is beyond the reach even of a constitutional amendment enacted in the ordinary way. But the House of Representatives is another matter. Milton Cummings, Charles O. Jones, and David Mayhew take up the consequences for Congress of the population shifts reflected in the 1970 census. The picture Cummings draws is, from the standpoint of the policy concerns of Congress-watchers, quite ambiguous, since the greatest growth in population has been in the suburbs. If the suburbs get the number of congressmen they are entitled to, in the doughnut-shaped or wedge-shaped districts the Court's inattention to gerrymandering permits them to have, the people who live in cities—who were traditionally shortchanged, in comparison with country-dwellers—may well be shortchanged again. Of course, they may not be; it all depends on whether the issues of the 1970s are more likely to ally city and suburban congressmen or to split them. On many local issues relating to such questions as control of police and schools, city-dwellers and suburbanites have not always seen eye-to-eye. Not all such questions come regularly before Congress, but the federal presence has been increasing in what used to be purely local issues.

David Mayhew argues that a major possibility of reapportionment is that it could prevent congressmen from entrenching themselves in safe districts. Mayhew points out, however, that congressmen have, in fact, been using reapportionment to dig themselves in. Readers may or may not be impressed with his recitation of Huntington's argument about the virtues of new blood in Congress. Many grizzled congressional scholars take the view that whether or not one enjoys the sight of new blood depends upon whose ox is being gored to produce it. The counterargument runs this way: That the real problems Congress faces have to do with oversight of the bureaucracies, that effective oversight is only possible when congressmen know their way around, that familiarity is only possible when a representative's service in Congress is sufficiently long to permit it, and that therefore having a Congress consisting mostly of persons enjoying continued service is a good thing.

Sensible men will undoubtedly want a little of each: responsiveness in Congress through party competition, and responsiveness in the bureaucracies through effective congressional oversight. It is not easy to get either without sacrificing some of the other. This does not, of course, dispute Mayhew's observation that, on the whole, there are fewer and fewer marginal congressional seats and that reapportionment efforts have favored incumbents.

In addition to strengthening the hand of Congress vis-à-vis the executive bureaucracies, the increase in the number of safe congressional seats contributes to the independence of Congress from the President. It does this by increasing the number of congressmen whose chances of survival are not tied to the turnout or the results of presidential elections. Presidential landslides—and midterm recoveries for the out-party—take place mostly in marginal seats. As seats of this kind diminish in number, the amplitude of the swing from presidential year surge to off-year decline will attenuate.

Observers are bound to contemplate this trend from more than one point of view. As Mayhew and his discussant, Allan Sindler, point out, there is a strong norm in American political theory favoring party competition that here conflicts with another norm—the separation of powers. Of course, it is by raising such issues directly that scholarly discussion can assist practical men in seeing the consequences of the choices they make.

It is clear, I think, even from these cursory observations, that reapportionment has important effects on our political institutions and, through these institutions, on public policies that quite likely will substantially affect the lives of American citizens. There has been considerable debate over whether apportionment affects the value of equal protection of the law as it is set forth in the Constitution, but none over the proposition that there are intimate, if complex and little understood, relations between representation and the responsiveness of government, between representation and the public policies enacted by representative institutions, and between representation and the ways in which we go about the difficult business of governing ourselves. It is to these relations that this symposium is addressed.

1

THE COURT, THE PEOPLE, AND "ONE MAN, ONE VOTE"

Robert G. Dixon, Jr.

The 1960 decade gave us a new slogan—"one man, one vote." It remade the political map of America, albeit inconsistently because of the accordionlike quality of the initial requirement of "substantial equality" of legislative district populations and its lack of correlation with the total complexities of political representation. It will do so again as legislatures, litigants, and courts react to the 1970 census. In the Simplistic Sixties our legislative reapportionment and congressional redistricting efforts—like all we did in racial integration and the War on Poverty—was accompanied by a deep sense of assurance of purpose and optimism about results.[1] "One man, one vote," would return politics to the people, reinvigorate state legislatures and the national House of Representatives, and open the path to rational solutions for all political problems. As Chief Justice Earl Warren said on retirement, the reapportionment rulings were

[1]. There is no agreed usage for terminology in this field. Some persons speak of revision of state legislative districts as reapportionment and of revision of congressional districts inside a state as redistricting, but frequently the two terms are used interchangeably. The Supreme Court cites the precedent cases in these two kinds of revision interchangeably, even though the former is under the Fourteenth Amendment's equal protection clause and the latter is under Article I, Section 2, concerning allocation of congressional seats to the states. Both kinds of revision, and all other changes inspired by the one man, one vote, concept are covered in this chapter.

Logically the one man, one vote, upheaval has made it improper to use the term *reapportionment* regarding state legislative seats, because the tight population equality now required makes it legally impossible to "apportion" state legislative seats to existing units such as counties or cities. With no fixed districts, the whole process is simply redistricting. In deference to custom, the old terms have been continued in this essay; occasionally the phrase *apportionment/districting* is used as an all-inclusive term.

the key decisions of his era, because they nourished democracy at its roots.[2] It was a grand age—in retrospect, perhaps our last age of innocence.

As we move into the Sober Seventies, the dominant spirit is one of innocence lost, with a sense of negative return on the efforts of the past. Reapportionment has transferred political power to the suburbs, but minority representation is undervalued or precarious under the predominantly majoritarian cast of the rulings. Gerrymandering opportunities may be enhanced under the Court's newer "precise" equality standard, developed in 1969 and seemingly continued in an early 1970 ruling.[3]

In educational integration, neither suits by the Attorney General nor the power of the federal purse remade southern school systems in the sixties. In northern cities, where creative mixing and innovative programs have been the greatest, the educational return has been modest or negative. In welfare we have been unable to spend ourselves up to middle-class standards for all, but we have created a new class of well-to-do professionals —the poverty consultants. Segregated housing patterns have yielded neither to President Kennedy's promised "stroke of the pen," nor to the more inclusive fair-housing law of 1968.[4] Although the overall United States birthrate is down, there is unequal restraint in various groups of the population—and little restraint abroad; and yet population control is the ultimate pollution problem, as well as being an aspect of welfare and international relations, too.

In domestic politics federalism has again become the "in" word, with obvious implications for the role and responsibility of state legislatures in the 1970s as effective representative and decision-making institutions. (And, of course, state legislatures will also create our new congressional districts after the 1970 census.) Revival of popular faith in federalism

2. New York *Times,* June 27, 1969, p. 17, col. 6.

3. *Kirkpatrick* v. *Preisler* 394 U.S. 526, and *Wells* v. *Rockefeller,* 394 U.S. 542 (1969); *Hadley* v. *Junior College District,* 397 U.S. 50 (1970). The ambiguities in the latter ruling are discussed in text, *infra,* notes 50–67.

4. In his 1960 presidential campaign against Richard Nixon, John Kennedy promised to end housing segregation with the "stroke of a pen." After a series of "freedom rides" in the South, the "stroke" came in November 1962 in the form of an executive order forbidding use of mortgages insured by the Federal Housing Administration or the Veterans Administration in support of segregated housing, but the order did not cover conventional mortgage activities of federally assisted lenders. Exec. Order No. 11063, 27 Fed. Reg. 11527 (1962); 1963 Report of United States Commission on Civil Rights 95–103. The 1968 law, based on the commerce power, purports to be all-inclusive except for owner-occupant transactions where no broker is used and no discriminatory preference is indicated. 82 Stat. 81 (1968), 42 U.S.C. §§3601–3619 (Supp. IV, 1969).

and downgrading of the national government as the chosen instrument for solving our domestic ills was the theme of a report filed early in 1970 by the United States Advisory Commission on Intergovernmental Relations. "Historians may single out the 1960s as one of the half-dozen periods of the country's history that were most crucial for the survival of federalism in the United States," the report said.[5] The report attributed the death of the concept of an all-powerful federal government to "program indigestion" among state and local governments and to activities such as the antipoverty program, which not only by-passed state governments but degenerated locally into feudalistic community-action programs which were a disintegrative force in city government.[6]

There are some obvious dangers to the cause of civil rights—especially desegregation—in a headlong rush to federalism. But it appears unlikely that any significant dismantling of existing national controls is in the offing. National funds are a large component of state/local expenditures and must be used nondiscriminatorily. Rather, the reaction toward federalism is a matter of tone and spirit, a realization that in the long run the only enduring progress is that made locally, where the people live. Constitutional litigation cajoles, threatens, and points new directions. Full implementation can come only through local political acceptance.

The new maxim of democratic politics for the 1970s may amount to this: That society is best which spreads human fallibility among several power centers so that error can cancel error, rather than one which concentrates fallibility at a central point of maximum power. To be sure, we need central leadership, too—even charisma. But the leaders of the seventies must contend with popular disenchantment regarding all grand national solutions—a disenchantment strengthened by our new learning concerning the external costs of all "good" programs and the sheer diseconomies of large size.

Our new perceptions are forcing us back on ourselves, as it were. We are giving up democracy as merely an elective kingship—in the image of Franklin Roosevelt and his successors in office. We need to embrace democracy again at the elemental level of faction, party, political organization, and legislative representation.

5. Advisory Commission on Intergovernmental Relations, Eleventh Annual Report, 1969–1970 (Washington, D.C.: Government Printing Office, 1970), pp. 1, 3.

6. See Beck, "Organizing Community Action," in Robert H. Connery and Demetrios Caraley, eds., Governing the City: Challenges and Options for New York (New York: Praeger, 1969), pp. 162–178; R. G. Dixon, Jr. "Rebuilding the Urban Political System: Some Heresies Concerning Citizen Participation, Community Action, Metros, and 'One Man-One Vote,'" 58 Georgetown Law Journal 955.

The sixties also were a period which put new strains on judicial review. Conventionally, the outcome of a successful constitutional attack on governmental action is an order to desist. However unpopular the ruling, this sort of judicial review is manageable—for example, the invalidation of New Deal programs in the thirties, state economic legislation earlier, infringements on freedom of expression, and various criminal procedures. Far less manageable are rulings which impose on government affirmative duties to act, as do those in reapportionment cases and recent desegregation litigation. In the former cases the Court has talked frequently of a goal of "equal representation," but in practice it has borne down ever more heavily on the adjective and ignored the noun. With this approach it drove New York congressional districts for the 1970 election down to a maximum population deviation from mean of only 0.12 percent.[7] Necessarily, however, the new district lines cut across preexisting county, city, and town lines with great abandon, creating artificiality in districting. It will be the task of the seventies to put some meaning into the key noun, "representation." In desegregation the analogous term is "equal education." Will the Court again subordinate the noun and make the adjective "equal" dominate the scene?

In short, what is equal education in a system which once had de jure segregation and is now under an affirmative duty to devise a desegregation plan that "works"?[8] And what is equal representation in a system which had unconstitutional malapportionment in the past? Is there any logical stopping point, short of attaining absolute equality under those indiciae which are most easily measured—that is, bare population in apportionment; exact proportionalization of Negro and White students and teachers in education? Or are the key words, after all, "representation" and "education" ? As Archibald Cox aptly phrased it, the equality concept, once loosed, is not easily cabined.[9]

REPRESENTATION: THEORY AND GOALS

Legislative elections and the party system which organizes them are critical parts of the American process of political representation. We ex-

7. Joint Legislative Committee on Reapportionment, Appendices to Interim Report (January 19, 1970), pp. 29–30. The litigation is discussed in text, infra, notes 34–42 and 107–109.

8. Green v. County School Board, 391 U.S. 430, 439 (1968), in which the Court said: "The burden on a school board today is to come forward with a plan that promises realistically to work, and promises realistically to work now."

9. Archibald Cox, "Constitutional Adjudication and the Promotion of Human Rights," 80 Harvard Law Review 91.

pect far more from the election system than mere filling of legislative seats. One essential purpose is to maintain popular faith in government. Another is to avoid instability, which Americans associate with the development of multi-party splinters. We expect the election system to yield both a majority capable of governing and a minority sufficiently cohesive to be both critic and heir apparent. A further goal, more easily stated than achieved, is that there be room in the system for all significant interests to acquire spokesmen—preserving the right of all to be heard, if not to be in control.

Coexisting with formal systems of representation, there is a vital informal structure of governance which is largely beyond the reach of the recent one man, one vote, developments. For most purposes, however, the formal structure makes the final decisions. In the long run, we can check the informal and often hidden power structure only through formal, open systems of political representation.

Since *Baker* v. *Carr*,[10] which opened the political thicket to judicial scrutiny in 1962, we have been much concerned with the impact of apportionment and districting practices on the legislative election process, the maintenance of a competitive party system, and the adequacy of minority representation. These concerns, however, have been more a product of the reaction to the Supreme Court decisions than an outgrowth of the Court's own limited constitutional perceptions. Wielding one man, one vote, like a meat-ax, the Court has not been content only to lop off extreme population malapportionment. It has come close to subordinating all aspects of political representation to one overriding element—absolute equality of population in all legislative districts.

In a series of relatively simple cases in 1964 headed by *Wesberry* v. *Sanders* and *Reynolds* v. *Sims,* which challenged serious population inequality in congressional and state legislative districts, we learned that congressional districts must be as equal as "practicable" [11] and state legislative districts must be "substantially" equal.[12] More recently, in April 1969, we learned that in constructing congressional districts—and presumably state legislative districts, too—there must be a good-faith effort to achieve "precise mathematical equality";[13] hence, even a maximum

10. *Baker* v. *Carr,* 369 U.S. 186 (1962), authorizing judicial entry into what had been treated as a forbidden political thicket in *Colegrove* v. *Green,* 382 U.S. 549, 556 (1946).

11. *Wesberry* v. *Sanders,* 376 U.S. 1, 7–8 (1964).

12. *Reynolds* v. *Sims,* 377 U.S. 533, 568 (1964), and see also the phrasings at 577–579.

13. *Kirkpatrick* v. *Preisler,* 394 U.S. 526, 530–531 (1969).

deviation of only 3.1 percent might be—as in this case—unconstitutional. Additional decisions have extended the rule not only to general local government, but to most special districts, as well.[14]

These decisions represent a sharp break not only with past practice, but with past theory. Our traditional concept, like recent practice in Great Britain,[15] was that some representation of units or communities per se was valuable and that the preeminent "population principle" itself did not require anything approaching an exact census-count equality. More importantly, the new doctrine has in it seeds of inconsistency.

Arithmetic absolutism points toward abolition of districts and the instituting of at-large voting. Or, if districts be retained, it points toward fluctuating artificial boundaries in tune with population shift and out of phase with any considerations of community or of county or city lines. The typical goal of plaintiffs in these cases, however, is better representation—that is, more proportionate representation—of the viewpoints they share with others in their own community and elsewhere in the total area governed by the legislature in question. Indeed, there probably is a widely shared popular feeling that something is wrong, or at least suspect, in any system which frequently fails to give some legislative seats to all sizable political parties or other identifiable voting blocs.

These two developing themes—"arithmetic absolutism" and the "proportional-representation (PR) result"—at times run on parallel tracks; at times they do not. When the task in the early sixties was one of rectifying egregious population malapportionment, arithmetic absolutism did yield a PR result of sorts. Seats were removed from the rotten boroughs in the rural and small town areas and transferred to the suburbs. But when we examine such common practices as at-large voting, or use of multi-member districts, we find that a PR result is usually unattainable except by chance, even though these practices are all right under a simple Supreme Court test of arithmetic absolutism.

Once it is perceived that the reapportionment plaintiff's goal is more proportionate representation, it follows that some electoral instruments not yet declared unconstitutional should be and, conversely, that some electoral instruments which have been declared unconstitutional would help to approach the goals of the plaintiffs in representation cases. For example, a plaintiff wanting a fair representation should oppose: at-large voting for city councils, because of the winner-take-all tendency; all use

14. *Avery* v. *Midland County, Texas,* 390 U.S. 474 (1968); *Hadley, supra,* n. 3.

15. Robert G. Dixon, Jr., *Democratic Representation: Reapportionment in Law and Politics* (New York: Oxford University Press, 1968), pp. 91–94.

of multi-member districts, for the same reason; and gerrymandering of multi-member or single-member districts, whether it occurs by design or by chance. He should encourage devices for minority representation which will ensure that, while the majority rules, the minority will be heard. He also should be willing in some circumstances to combine in one legislature different representation principles, so that the pluralism-in-fact of the populace will not be overridden by a unitary, wholly majoritarian legislature.

A paradox of the one man, one vote, revolution is that we now perceive our goal to be something approaching a proportional result, in terms of group access to the legislative process, while retaining the district method of election. But the district method itself, when combined with straight plurality election, is the source of many problems. Because parties and interests are not spread or grouped geographically, so as to facilitate legislative elections' having this ideal result, it is obvious that all districting decisions, whether made by gerrymandered design or by chance, will have crucial but arbitrary political effects on such matters as the availability of candidates, the distribution of safe versus swing districts, the number of homogeneous versus the number of heterogeneous districts, the competition between parties, and the representation of minorities. Nonproportional relationships emerge between the degree of party and ethnic-group support in the electorate as a whole and the degree of actual party and group strength in the legislature.

For example, using new single-member districts, the Democrats in California in 1966 elected majorities of 21–19 and 42–38 in the state senate and house, respectively, even though they polled fewer statewide legislative votes than the Republicans. In the same election the Democrats gained a 21–17 edge in congressional seats, again with a minority of the statewide congressional vote. In New Jersey in 1966 the Democrats gained a 9–6 edge in congressional seats, despite a Republican plurality in the popular vote. By contrast, for the state legislature in New Jersey, using a mixture of new single- and multi-member districts, a comfortable but not overwhelming Republican plurality in popular votes in 1967 produced a sweep of two-thirds of the seats in each house.[16] Many other examples could be given of these gross imbalances between popular votes received by a party and the number of legislators elected from that party, both before and after one man, one vote, revisions.

A further difficulty is that representation itself is an elusive concept and can be approached from varying premises, for example, the

16. *Id.* at 339, 378, 462.

delegate model and the free-agent model.[17] The former conceives of the representative as the agent of his constituency, or at least of a majority thereof. The task of the legislator is to record the will of the constituency; legislative representation becomes an additive process. By contrast, under the free-agent model the task of the legislator is to be guided by what he conceives to be the enlightened self-interest of his constituency.

These models, however, tend to push us into an oversimplified either/or approach. A more helpful approach may be to focus on the quality of the representation received by the minority—a minority party or an ethnic minority—particularly if it is a part of a significant statewide minority in a state legislative or congressional election. The minority will receive some recognition simply by being part of the total constituency to which the legislators must look for reelection. But can the minority's allegiance to the formal political system be maintained if the minority continually fails to obtain some direct representation, as well?

Complicating all analysis is the flexibility of lines of partisan division and allegiance in the American party system, both intra-state and nationally. From the standpoint of consensus this may be a virtue, but it blurs the actual function of representation. For the very reason that loose party organization outside and inside legislative halls results in many issues' being resolved by shifting bipartisan coalitions, it is all the more critical that the electoral system yield for the minority party a more-or-less proportionate share of seats. Only thus can the minority party, and minority interests generally, participate meaningfully in the process of forming cross-party coalitions and gain a stake in the decision-making process.

The attainment of a goal of fair and effective representation for all citizens is a large order. The reapportionment revolution has focused our attention on the problem as never before, by forcing a revision of all legislative district lines—and many peripheral political arrangements, as well. In the increasingly simplistic approach of the Supreme Court, however, there is a real danger that this revolution, too, may devour its own. Some opportunities for creative experimentation in forms of representation have already been lost.

It is beginning to appear that, just as the political process needed the prod it received in *Baker* v. *Carr* in 1962 to reform patterns of representation, the judicial process now needs aid from the political process in

17. On this old and familiar problem, see essays by Hanna Pitkin and Robert G. Dixon, Jr., in J. Roland Pennock and John W. Chapman, eds., *Representation* (*NOMOS X*) (New York: Atherton Press, 1968), pp. 38 and 167, and H. Pitkin, *The Concept of Representation* (Berkeley: University of California Press, 1967).

civilizing and institutionalizing the one man, one vote, revolution. We need to build fairness into the initial process of constituency formation, to expose gerrymandering, to give minorities a fairer share of the seats, and to achieve finality sooner, both by clarifying apportionment standards and by warding off the endless suits brought against reapportionment plans by a few disgruntled voters (*any* voter has standing to sue). To these ends, should we amend our state constitutions, as some states have done recently, so that the reapportionment function is transferred to a bipartisan commission with a tie-breaker? A plan by a bipartisan commission might be deemed to be entitled to a judicial presumption of constitutionality, thus increasing the challengers' burden of proof. Should we adopt cumulative voting or similar devices to guarantee some minority representation? Should we even consider amending the national constitution, in simple fashion, to state the degree of population equality required? Recent experience teaches us that without an agreed *de minimis* rule litigation is endless; and a pursuit of absolute population equality creates both complete artificiality in district lines and a gerrymanderer's paradise.

THE SUPREME COURT: PRISONER OF ITS OWN LOGIC?

The largest issue in discussing the problems and prospects of reapportionment in the 1970s is the role of the Supreme Court. Put bluntly, the picture is not as encouraging as it should be. The question is not of returning to the pre-*Baker* era in which the judiciary avoided the political thicket. It is rather simply a question of being clear-minded about the breadth of judicial responsibilities which arise upon judicial entry. Seeing the problem, Justice Felix Frankfurter wanted to back off. Not seeing the problem, the majority wanted to plough ahead.[18] Frankfurter was right in perceiving the dimension of the issue. The majority was right in taking action. And the tragedy, mixed with some early joy, is that since then we have had judicial action without judicial wisdom in the field of political representation.

The Golden Mean Which Might Have Been

Baker v. *Carr* can be justified without jumping all the way to the rule of arithmetic absolutism which emerged in 1969 and which seemed to be

18. The last eight years of reapportionment litigation belie the comment in *Baker* v. *Carr, supra,* n. 10 at 226, that: "Judicial standards under the Equal Protection Clause are well developed and familiar . . . ."

confirmed by the Court's 1970 decision in *Hadley* v. *Junior College District*[19] despite some ambiguities in Justice Hugo Black's majority opinion. In a dozen states in 1962 at least one state legislative district was more than 500 percent deviant from average (arithmetic mean). Deviations of congressional districts were somewhat less extreme, but exceeded 50 percent in a dozen states. Such deviations are unjustifiable under conventional conceptions of democracy, even if the extent to which the political process actually was distracted by this factor and the boons which reapportionment brings are still debatable.[20] There was frequent critical comment in the press, and malapportionment seemed to be undermining popular faith in our system. Political avenues for change had become dead-end streets; some judicial intervention in the politics of the people seemed necessary to have an effective political system.

To rejuvenate the political system by forcing major reapportionment effort, it would have been sufficient for the Court to rule that egregious population deviations were per se unconstitutional, as a violation of due process. This is the spirit of some other recent cases, such as the 1965 invalidation of Connecticut's anti-birth-control legislation[21] and the 1969 invalidation of one-year-residence requirements for welfare eligibility.[22] The spirit here is substantive due process, which still lives as an operative constitutional doctrine in some fields, despite the Court's disposition no longer to use it to police legislative policy choices on economic matters. The concept is that the Court can invalidate legislation or operating governmental practices if it feels that the law or practice has no reasonable relationship to a valid governmental end and that "fundamental liberties" are at stake. Invalidation of malapportionment on grounds of due process would focus on the reasonableness of the legislative choice and the practical effect of its implementation, thereby leaving some room for consideration of the complex representation values at stake in the

19. *Hadley, supra,* n. 3.

20. On the policy impact of malapportionment and reapportionment, see the subsequent essay in this volume by Douglas Rae; see also the materials discussed in Dixon, *Democratic Representation,* pp. 574–581.

21. *Griswold* v. *Connecticut,* 381 U.S. 479 (1965).

22. *Shapiro* v. *Thompson,* 394 U.S. 618 (1969). Although nominally resting on a new "right of travel" concept plus the equal protection clause, the basic ground for the decision was a conclusion of gross unreasonableness in the legislative policy— directly analogous to the old "substantive due process" ruling in *Lochner* v. *New York,* 198 U.S. 45 (1905). For recent rulings reflecting a similar spirit, see *Williams* v. *Rhodes,* 393 U.S. 23 (1968), directing Ohio to place George Wallace on the presidential ballot in Ohio, and *Kramer* v. *Union Free School District,* 395 U.S. 621 (1969), invalidating a restrictive school board electorate law.

manner in which a state's population clusters were arranged into electoral constituencies. The degree of mathematical perfection required could be related to the existence and cohesion of political communities. The census figures themselves are not accurate enough nor, except momentarily, recent enough to justify minute equalization. Professor Malcolm E. Jewell has observed that "existing political subdivisions do have some sense of community and community interest," and he offers this hypothesis: "It can also be argued that legislators are less likely to be visible and identifiable to their constituents if legislative district boundaries are completely independent of other existing city and county boundaries." [23]

A due-process approach would not create, as the Court's rulings based on the equal protection clause have, a never-ending affirmative duty to try to equalize representation on the basis of census figures alone. The Court could have said that apportionment plans escaped the rule of per se unreasonableness if they were within some unannounced but hinted at rule of thumb, such as a 10 to 15 percent maximum deviation, easily supported by reference to social-science testimony, similar to the approach of the Court in *Brown v. Board of Education*.[24] In these lower ranges apportionment plans still would be carefully reviewed, perhaps invalidated, but only if plaintiffs could prove unreasonableness and harm in terms more realistic and relevant than the mere showing of minimal differences in the census populations of the districts. There is ample precedent for such a judicial adjustment of proof relevant to an ultimate finding of harm. In the antitrust field the courts for years have worked with a concept of a per se violation in certain instances, supplemented by more stringent proof requirements for the borderline areas where conflicting values come into play.[25]

The Equal Numbers—Equal Representation Fallacy

These 1960 might-have-beens suggest that we could have had our cake and eaten it too. At the beginning of the seventies, however, it is simplistic equal protection under the Fourteenth Amendment which rules

23. Correspondence with author, August 1969.

24. *Brown* v. *Board of Education*, 347 U.S. 483 (1954). In *Brown* there was some social-science testimony on the effect of segregation on learning. For a representation suit, political-science testimony was available for the proposition that complete equality was impractical but that a 15 percent maximum deviation was a reasonable rule of thumb. American Political Science Association Committee Report, "The Reapportionment of Congress," 45 *American Political Science Review* 153.

25. Harry A. Toulmin, *Antitrust Laws of the United States*, vol. 6 (Cincinnati: W. H. Anderson Company, 1951), pp. 34–75, 85–86.

the field of state and local legislative representation and one man, one vote. Congressional districts are covered by a similar rule derived from Article I, Section 2, of the Constitution. Any lingering doubts about the mathematical rigidity of the Supreme Court approach were substantially undercut by the 1969 congressional districting cases, *Kirkpatrick* v. *Preisler* and *Wells* v. *Rockefeller*,[26] and the 1970 federated college district case, *Hadley* v. *Junior College District*.[27]

The Court still characterizes reapportionment cases as mere right-to-vote cases, and focuses on something called individual voter weight, which is measured solely by the equality of district populations. In other words, it transfers a concept of voter equality which neatly fits the single-constituency election situation over to the multiple-constituency election situation, where it is only one of several elements of fairness and effective voice. Hence, Justice Hugo Black wrote as follows for the Court in 1970, echoing what the Court had said in 1964:

> [T]he Fourteenth Amendment requires that the trustees of this junior college district be apportioned [in subdistricts] in a manner which does not deprive any voter of his right to have *his own vote given as much weight,* as far as practicable, as that of any other voter in the junior college district.[28]

Inside a single constituency—to elect a governor or to elect the President under a direct popular-vote plan, or to elect one legislator—voter equality simply means uniform voter qualification standards, an honest count, and a straight plurality (or majority) rule for determining the winner. If each voter has one vote, there automatically is equal voter "weight" in the final outcome—that is, opportunity to link with fellow partisans and win.[29] In a multiple-constituency election for a legislative

26. *Supra,* n. 3 at 542.

27. *Supra,* n. 3.

28. *Id.* at 52. *Reynolds* v. *Sims* was full of similar language, for example 377 U.S. at 554–556, 560–563. Occasionally there was evidence of a realization that the supposed "personal" right at stake was intertwined with group dynamics, for Chief Justice Warren also wrote that "achieving of fair and effective representation for all citizens is concededly the basic aim of legislative apportionment." *Id.* at 565–566.

Until the Court clarifies this ambiguity in its own approach by abandoning the superficial "right to vote" characterization and by coming to grips with the knotty concept of representation, apportionment litigation will continue to have a distressing shadowboxing quality—and political equity may elude our grasp.

29. *Gray* v. *Sanders,* 372 U.S. 368 (1963), in which the Court voided Georgia's county-unit system of vote weighting in statewide elections, is an example of this simple situation.

assembly, the factor of exact population equality among the districts does *not* automatically yield equal voter "weight" in the analogous sense of opportunity to link with fellow partisans and elect a majority of the legislators. Equal weight will depend in important part on how the various partisans are scattered through the districts. Happiness in this kind of election situation (and this *is* the reapportionment field) turns on our fellow partisans' being a bare majority in as many districts as possible— enough, we hope, to control the assembly, or at least to be a force to contend with. This also is the "right to vote," functionally viewed.

Insofar as the Supreme Court's logic brings in representation at all, it is done by a forced marriage of two distinct terms: "equal numbers" of persons in districts, which is an objective concept; and "equal representation," which is a wonderfully subjective concept.[30] Writing for the Court in 1969, Justice William Brennan rephrased this concept as follows:

> Equal representation for equal numbers of people is a principle designed to prevent debasement of voting power and diminution of access to elected representatives. Toleration of even small deviations detracts from these purposes. Therefore, the [constitutional command] permits only the limited population variances which are unavoidable despite a good-faith effort to achieve absolute equality, or for which justification is shown.[31]

On close analysis the subtle phrase "equal representation" either has no meaning or is an awkward way of calling for the abolition of districting and the substitution of proportional representation. Similarly, it makes little sense for the Court to say, as it did in *Reynolds* with districts of unequal population in mind, that, "weighting the votes of citizens differently, by any method or means, merely because of where they happen to reside, hardly seems justifiable." [32] All districting discriminates on grounds of residence, even if population be equal—that is, it arbitrarily qualifies the right to vote at the payoff level, by discounting utterly the votes of the minority voters. We necessarily accept this when we accept districting plus a simple plurality rule. The true issue of representation in a district system is not exhausted by looking at equality of numbers, but includes: (a) where the districts are put, (b) what right-to-vote interests are thus maximized or minimized in each district, (c) what con-

30. For detailed discussion see Dixon, *Democratic Representation*, pp. 17, 267–271, 437, 443, 449, 582–583.
31. *Supra,* n. 13 at 531.
32. *Supra,* n. 12 at 563.

straints are imposed on districting choices (strict equality of population or some allowance of unit representation, or a mixture) and how those constraints relate to the effective exercise of the right to vote; (d) how the districts, taken collectively, relate the right to vote of like-minded *groups* of voters to a fair share of seats in the legislative house—the functional or payoff approach, again.

An astute member of an apportionment commission phrased the matter this way a few years ago:

> Every plan has a political effect, even one drawn by a seventh grade civics class whose parents are all nonpartisans and who have only the United States census data to work with. Even though they drew such a plan with the most equal population in districts, following the maximum number of political subdivision boundaries and with the most regular shapes, it could very well result in a landslide election for a given political party.[33]

In short, the basic issue for one seriously devoted to one man, one vote, is how a given set of legislative districts filters the popular will on its way to the legislature.

Doctrinal Touchstones for the Seventies

THE MEANING OF PREISLER AND WELLS. As long as the Court was merely voiding the rotten boroughs from which many legislators were formerly elected, as it was in the early sixties, few persons were concerned about the niceties of the Court's reasoning and the precision of its standards. But in the *Kirkpatrick* v. *Preisler* and *Wells* v. *Rockefeller* decisions of 1969 [34] from which the above quotation by Mr. Justice Brennan is taken, the Court nullified Missouri and New York congressional districting plans in which the maximum deviations from "ideal" [35] were only 3.1 percent and 6.6 percent, respectively. And yet at the very time the Court ruled, the 1960 census figures themselves were estimated to be inaccurate by from 10 to 20 percent or more for some parts of those states. In neither case was there meaningful proof of any significant unfairness in actual representation results.

33. A. Robert Kleiner, Democratic member of Michigan Bipartisan Apportionment Commission, National Municipal League speech, 1966.

34. *Supra,* n. 3.

35. By ideal is meant the arithmetic mean. For example, if a state with 100,000 population had 10 senators, each elected from his own district, the ideal district would be 10,000. A 9,000-person district (and an 11,000-person district) would have a 10 percent deviation from ideal; and if no other district deviated by more than this figure, 10 percent would be the maximum deviation.

Most surprising of all, the New York plan was the negotiated, bipartisan product of a legislature in which each party controlled one chamber, and the case was brought to the Court as a solo appeal by one voter. While the case was pending, the Republicans captured both legislative houses, and they already had the governorship. In its April 1969 ruling, therefore, the Court was in the position of overturning a quite equal bipartisan plan which apparently all except one voter were prepared to accept and of ordering a partisan replacement under a newly phrased mandate to "make a good-faith effort to achieve precise mathematical equality." [36] Mr. Justice Abe Fortas expostulated that this new standard exceeded the "boundaries of common sense" and suggested the absurdity of "running the congressional district line down the middle of the corridor of an apartment house, or even dividing the residents of a single-family house between two districts." [37]

Justices John Marshall Harlan, Potter Stewart, and Byron White also objected to the Court's phrasing and underscored two key points which should have been perceived earlier in representation litigation: They stated, first, that tight reapportionment arithmetic increased the freedom to gerrymander by providing not only an excuse but a mandate to ignore traditional political subdivision lines; and, second, that a computer was no answer. With population equality preeminent and all other parameters subordinated, a computer could spew forth hundreds or thousands of equally equal "computer plans," whose political effects would vary wildly.[38] As Justice White put it:

> In reality, of course, districting is itself a gerrymandering in the sense that it represents a complex blend of political, economic, regional, and historical considerations. . . . If county and municipal boundaries are to be ignored, a computer can produce countless plans for absolute population equality, one differing very little from another, but each having its own very different political ramifications.[39]

36. *Wells* v. *Rockefeller,* 394 U.S. 542, 546 (1969) (quoting *Preisler, supra,* n. 13 at 530–531).

37. Concurring opinion, *supra,* n. 3 at 538.

38. Neither of these points was new. Regarding the districting process, it already had been pointed out that in "a functional sense . . . all districting is gerrymandering" and that there would be "some gerrymander in *result* as a concomitant of all district systems of legislative election" because of the winner-take-all feature operating district by district. Regarding use of computers, it had been observed that a simple computer program based only on census tracts to achieve maximum equality "will produce not one set of districts but several, each with different political implications—and who is to choose?" See Dixon, *Democratic Representation* 462, 533 (1968).

39. *Supra,* n. 36 at 554–555, 556.

Justice Harlan, in an opinion joined by Justice Stewart, focused on the relationship between equality and representation as follows:

The legislature must do more than satisfy one man-one vote; it must create a structure which will in fact as well as theory be responsive to the sentiments of the community. . . . If the Court believes it has struck a blow today for fully responsive representative democracy, it is sorely mistaken. Even more than in the past, district lines are likely to be drawn to maximize the political advantage of the party temporarily dominant in public affairs.[40]

The majority of five, however, thought otherwise.[41] And before closing his opinion for the Court, Justice Brennan went on to list and negate virtually every conceivable "rational" basis for stopping even slightly short of an arithmetic absolute. The following were all rejected: (1) deviations made to avoid fragmenting areas with distinct economic or social interests; (2) deviations which were the product of the legislative process of negotiation, compromise, and adjustment; (3) deviations caused by attempts to follow existing county, municipal, or other boundaries, as a check on gerrymandering; (4) deviations produced by an attempt to discount the presence of large nonvoting populations (such as students or military) in some districts; (5) deviations produced by attempts to recognize projected population shifts, unless subject to a high degree of accuracy; (6) deviations resulting from policies of geographic compactness.

The third negation in this list is particularly surprising because it expressly runs counter to Chief Justice Warren's warning in *Reynolds* v. *Sims* that "indiscriminate districting, without any regard for political subdivisions or natural or historical boundary lines, may be little more than an open invitation to partisan gerrymandering."[42] And yet in these *Preisler* and *Wells* rulings Chief Justice Warren not only did not demur; he provided the crucial fifth vote which made the Brennan opinions a majority viewpoint.

Some lower courts were quick to apply the stringent *Preisler* and *Wells* congressional district rulings to other areas. Thus the Illinois state legislative districts, which had been reconstructed and approved in 1965 within a narrow 7 to 8 percent maximum-deviation limit, were voided afresh.[43]

40. *Id.* at 551, 552.
41. Technically *Preisler* and *Wells* were 6–3 decisions because Justice Fortas, despite his vigorous objection to the majority opinion's absolutism, did vote against both Missouri and New York plans on special grounds. But on the key issue of the phrasing of the equality standard, they were only 5–4.
42. *Supra*, n. 12 at 578–579.
43. *Skolnick* v. *Ill. St. Elec. Board*, 307 F. Supp. 691 (N.D. Ill. 1969).

A county board in Alabama with a maximum deviation from average of only 5 percent (approximate—the figures are in dispute) met the same fate.[44] An occasional court tried to suggest that congressional districts were different and that the Court's original "substantial equality" rule still lived for other kinds of districts. For example, on March 2, 1970, the New Jersey Supreme Court concluded a long sequence of state legislative reapportionment litigation[45] by upholding the reapportionment provisions of the state's new 1966 constitution, even though they permitted a potential maximum deviation of 20 percent and a population variance ratio between the largest and smallest districts of 1.5:1.[46] The New Jersey court harked back to the *Reynolds* v. *Sims* dictum[47] that in order to deter gerrymandering and in order to recognize the relevance of local governmental entities to state policy-making, the states could use the lines of political subdivisions in districting so long as the resulting population deviations were not excessive. The court admitted that the *Preisler* and *Wells* rulings might cast some doubt on the justification of population deviations as deterrents to gerrymandering (Brennan's third negation, above), but felt that the state-policy-making justification might survive. Noting that *Preisler* and *Wells* concerned congressional districting, the New Jersey court suggested that different considerations concerning political representation were at stake in state legislatures:

> Nonetheless the county and the municipality are the meaningful units in state-local relations in many . . . situations, and elections from districts are the more worthwhile if the county and the municipality are reflected in drawing the district lines.[48]

44. *Driggers* v. *Gallion*, 308 F. Supp. 632 (M.D. Ala. 1969).

45. *Jackman* v. *Bodine*, 55 N.J. 371, 262 A.2d 389 (N.J. 1970), and the earlier ruling in the same case, 53 N.J. 585, 252 A.2d 209 (N.J. 1969). See also *Abate* v. *Mundt*, 25 N.Y. 2d 309 (1969), in which the New York Court of Appeals in ruling on a local government case suggested three levels of one man, one vote, stringency —congressional, state, local.

46. The population variance ratio compares the extremes—the largest and the smallest district. With reference to New Jersey, the state constitution seeks to preserve local units as bases for districting, but specifies that no "district contain less than eighty per cent nor more than one hundred twenty per cent" of the norm. Thus, if 100,000 were the norm under a given census, there could be an 80,000-person district and a 120,000-person district, yielding a population variance ratio of 1.5:1. In practice in New Jersey, deviations from the norm and the variances between the largest and smallest districts are not this large. The court was ruling only on the question of whether the state constitutional formula was "inherently intolerable." 262 A.2d 389.

47. 377 U.S. at 578, 580, discussed by the New Jersey court at 252 A.2d 210 and 262 A.2d at 393–394.

48. 262 A.2d 394.

In the light of the general trend of Supreme Court decisions from 1964 to 1970 and the Court's tendency to make no distinction between state legislative and congressional districting cases and not to consider realities of representation, the New Jersey court's ruling may have no more strength than summer ice. It does evidence a developing restiveness with arithmetic absolutism which is shared by some in the academic community.[49] Indeed, a more important part of the New Jersey opinion by Chief Justice Joseph Weintraub is its preliminary discussion of the basic proposition already set forth in this chapter—that is, the lack of a close correlation between arithmetic equality in districting and effective representation of identifiable groups of voters. Without this correlation, there is no reason to push population deviations down to the vanishing point at the cost of all other elements of districting. If the Supreme Court of the 1970s, with its somewhat changed membership, should wish to retain the basic one man, one vote, decisions of 1964, but implement them with more sophistication than the Warren Court, the New Jersey decision of 1970 would provide a respectable intellectual foundation on which to build.

THE MEANING OF HADLEY. The first Supreme Court reapportionment decision of the 1970 decade, *Hadley* v. *Junior College District* (at least as seen through the eyes of the dissenters) produced no easing up on the Court's apparent passion for "mathematical nicety."[50] The vote was 5 to 3 (Justice Fortas's seat still being vacant), with the new Chief Justice Warren Burger joining Justices Harlan and Stewart in dissent. The surprising vote was that of Justice White, who rejoined the majority despite his sharply worded dissent from "precise mathematical equality" in *Preisler* and *Wells* a year earlier. He gave no explanation.

In view of these recent close divisions, a question naturally arises: is there now an incipient 5–4 majority for a return to the concept of "substantial equality" with which the reapportionment revolution began in Chief Justice Warren's 1964 opinion in *Reynolds* v. *Sims*? The tentative answer may be yes, provided that two assumptions may be made. The first is that Justice White's vote in *Hadley* can be explained away on some special basis, leaving his views in his *Preisler* and *Wells* opinion unmodified. The second is that the new Justice Harry A. Blackmun will take an

49. See comments of Gordon E. Baker, William M. Beaney, William J. D. Boyd, Malcolm E. Jewell, Robert B. McKay, and David Wells (successful plaintiff in *Wells* v. *Rockefeller*) in Dixon, "The Warren Court Crusade for 'One Man-One Vote,'" 1969 *Supreme Court Review* 219 at 231–233.

50. *Hadley, supra,* n. 3 at 62. *Hadley* was decided February 25, 1970, a few days before the New Jersey decision of March 2, 1970, discussed in the preceding paragraphs, but is not mentioned in the New Jersey opinion.

approach toward one man, one vote, like that of his predecessor Justice Fortas, with a disposition to focus on realities of representation and to shy away from pat formulae.[51] Much depends on the caliber of briefing and oral argument, which throughout the reapportionment revolution has been weak on the side of the states. The states have presented unimaginative defenses and have failed to think—or to help the Court to think—in terms of the larger issues of political representation.

In *Hadley* the Court voided the representation system in a federated junior college district in Kansas City, Missouri, because it was based strictly on the "equal numbers" rule for legislative districting. The long-range significance of the case, discussed later in this chapter, was its apparent negation of the possibility of achieving regional metropolitan government by federation formulae which gave some representation on the basis of political units as well as on the basis of population. In other words, although our national Congress still rests on the Connecticut Compromise, this device cannot be repeated at the local level as a means of local union. The immediate significance of the case was its indication of how firm the current majority of five was on the equal-numbers rule.

The facts were somewhat complicated, as is often the case at the level of local apportionment. The defendant junior college district was one of several organized under Missouri's Junior College District Act. The act authorized high school districts to federate for the purpose of superimposing on themselves a junior college district. The election giving initial consent was at large in the total area to be served, an area-wide majority vote being sufficient. Once past this stage, the constituent high school districts were given recognition in the apportionment of six trustees of the junior college district under a statutory formula keyed to percentage of school-age children. (The non-use of total population as the apportionment base was not in issue.) If one or more component school districts possessed more than one-third (or one-half, or two-thirds) of the population between the ages of 6 and 20, it elected two trustees (or three, or four) at large in the high school district, and the remaining trustees were elected at large in the remainder of the junior college district. Under such a formula the larger constituent units are always somewhat underrepresented, on an arithmetic basis, unless they fall exactly on the one-third, one-half, or two-thirds percentage line. In the junior college district at issue in *Hadley,* the Kansas City high school district with 59.59 percent of the school-age population had three trustees; seven suburban high school districts elected the remaining three trustees.

In invalidating this arrangement the Supreme Court, through Justice Black, phrased its ruling in broad terms, as follows:

> We therefore hold today that as a general rule, whenever a state or local government decides to select persons by popular election to perform governmental functions, the Equal Protection Clause of the Fourteenth Amendment requires that each qualified voter must be given an equal opportunity to participate in that election, and when members of an elected body are chosen from separate districts, each district must be established on a basis which will insure, *as far as practicable,* that *equal numbers* of voters can vote for *proportionally equal numbers* of officials.[52]

The key phrase in this formulation is "as far as is practicable," which derives from Justice Black's prior opinion in 1964 in the original congressional districting case, *Wesberry* v. *Sanders,* and which is analogous to the "substantial equality" concept of *Reynolds* v. *Sims* and the other state legislative apportionment cases in the same year.[53] For, while absolute population equality may be possible—and this is the goal mandated in *Preisler* and *Wells*—it may not be practicable, if the realities of district voting and political representation be considered.

It may be significant that Justice Black's opinion, in addition to the uncertainty about "practicable," contained several other observations which would be inconsistent, or at least unneeded, if equal numbers were the sole rule. First, on the facts of *Hadley* itself, he stressed the point already noted in the factual summary above that the Missouri percentage formula necessarily produced a "systematic discrimination against voters in the more populous school districts." [54] Hence, a somewhat ad hoc policy of attempting to follow boundaries of political subdivisions in districting might be all right.

Second, he reintroduced the 1964 substantial-equality concept by stating that "mathematical exactitude is not required." [55] And he did not cite the *Preisler* and *Wells* ruling anywhere in his opinion, let alone try to ex-

52. *Hadley, supra,* n. 3 at 56 (emphasis added).
53. *Supra,* n. 11 and 12.
54. *Hadley, supra,* n. 3 at 57.
55. *Id.* at 58.

plain it, although he did cite virtually every other Supreme Court one man, one vote, case since 1964.

Third, Justice Black said "there might be some case in which a State elects certain functionaries whose duties are so far removed from normal governmental activities and so disproportionately affect different groups that a popular election in compliance with *Reynolds* . . . might not be required." [56] The thought here, difficult to square with a simple equality concept, is that voters may have "unequal interest," particularly if the function at issue is not traditionally "governmental." Justice White had introduced this thought earlier in the context of local special-purpose districts, where it did not seem to fit at all, because in special districts there is, by definition, an unusual homogeneity centering on one function, and not "unequal interest." [57] A better example of what might fit Justice Black's formulation is the variety of devices for "citizen participation" and "community action" which have been developing under the impetus of the Model Cities program of the Department of Housing and Urban Development and certain programs of the Office for Economic Opportunity. [58]

Fourth, Justice Black even suggested that in "certain cases," not defined but surely rare—even exotic—a state may "limit the right to vote to a particular group or class of people." [59]

Fifth, he indicated that some population deviations might be excusable if they resulted from the "inherent mathematical complications in equally apportioning a small number of trustees among a limited number of component districts." [60] This point is quite mysterious. The basic thrust of one man, one vote, has been to make "apportionment" in the traditional sense per se unconstitutional (although we still use the term by force of habit) and to reduce the problem to one of equal "districting" on a clean slate. [61] Also, apportionment in Black's sense is exactly what

56. *Id.* at 56.

57. In the basic case applying one man, one vote, to local government, Justice White, who wrote the majority opinion, added this caveat: "Were the Commissioners Court [county board] a special purpose unit of government assigned the performance of functions affecting definable groups of constituents more than other constituents, we would have to confront the question whether such bodies may be apportioned in ways which give greater influence to the citizens most affected by the organization's functions." *Avery* v. *Midland County, Texas,* 390 U.S. at 483–484.

58. *Supra,* n. 6.

59. *Hadley, supra,* n. 3 at 58–59. *But compare Kramer* v. *Union Free School District,* 395 U.S. 621 (1969); *Cipriano* v. *City of Houma,* 395 U.S. 701 (1969).

60. *Hadley, supra,* n. 3 at 58.

61. *Supra,* n. 1.

Missouri attempted, and yet Black struck it down. The justice's statement, nevertheless, may give some comfort to proponents of local federations as a device to solve the metropolitan muddle, if it means that the real vice in *Hadley* was simply that under the formula used the range of possible inequality was too high and always favored the smaller units.

Sixth, he reindorsed the "flexibility" and "experimentation" language in some earlier local government cases,[62] two of which produced rulings inconsistent with a theory of arithmetic absolutism. In one case the Court had upheld gross population inequality (with a range of from 733 to 29,048) in candidates' residence districts simply because the elections were at large.[63] But this unequal residence device restricts political candidacy and also permits the larger districts to control by electing "patsy" residents from the smaller districts. In the other case, the Court had upheld a pyramidal system of electing a county school board, in which grossly unequal subdistricts each sent one delegate to a convention which, in turn, elected the county board. The Court said this was really an appointive system (but so is a presidential election on this theory), and that the central school board's functions were not legislative in the classical sense because the central board had less policy control than the subdistrict boards.[64]

What is left of Justice Black's "general rule" in the light of this sequence of amplifying explanations? It would seem that *Hadley* is an exercise in how to turn the whole cloth into Swiss cheese. Small wonder that Chief Justice Burger, fresh to the reapportionment wars (this being the one kind of case his District of Columbia Circuit never received), should expostulate:

> The failure to provide guidelines for determining when the Court's 'general rule' is to be applied is exacerbated when the Court implies that the stringent standards of 'mathematical exactitude' which are controlling in apportionment of federal congressional districts need not be applied to smaller specialized districts. . . . Yet the Court has given almost no indication of which nonpopulation interests may or may not legitimately be considered by a legislature in devising a constitutional apportionment scheme for a local, specialized unit of government.[65]

As Justice Harlan, also dissenting, perceptively observed, the Court's concern about "built-in discrimination" really bars the legislature from

62. *Hadley, supra,* n. 3 at 59.
63. *Dusch* v. *Davis,* 387 U.S. 112 (1967).
64. *Sailors* v. *Board of Education,* 387 U.S. 105 (1967).
65. *Hadley, supra,* n. 3 at 70–71.

establishing "*any* formula of general application for apportionment." [66] This is so because a general rule, merely by being general, produces predictable, consistent patterns of different treatment. It favors one defined group more than another—hence yielding a built-in discrimination. And yet, before a legislature proceeds too far with this thought that some unplanned, ad hoc deviations are all right, it should remember that one ground for nullifying population deviations in the past has been the inability to justify them as the product of a rational plan! [67]

APPORTIONMENT/DISTRICTING VARIABLES
AND GERRYMANDERING

The basic reality, often overlooked, is that generically all districting is gerrymandering.[68] We commit ourselves to inexact correlations between popular voting and legislative representation when we opt for districts plus a plurality rule in each district as the basis for electing legislators. The alternative of a wholly at-large election would ensure against minority control of the legislature, which occasionally can occur with a district system, but minority representation would then be wholly submerged. The alternative of using a system of proportional representation would better proportionalize popular voting and legislative representation, but would jeopardize the two-party system and governmental stability. Hence, with the British, we traditionally have embraced the district system. Our history of governmental stability vindicates the choice. But we should not be shocked when gerrymandering also results.

There is no agreed definition of gerrymandering, but there are several misleading ones. Many attempted definitions of gerrymandering focus too much on shape, too little on substance; they are too precise, and hence too narrow. Gerrymandering is simply discriminatory districting which operates unfairly to inflate the political strength of one group and deflate that of another. It may be associated with oddities in the shapes of the districts but has no necessary relationship to these distorted shapes. And

66. *Id.* at 68.
67. *Swann* v. *Adams,* 385 U.S. 440, 444 (1967); *Kilgarlin* v. *Hill,* 386 U.S. 120, 122 (1967); *Reynolds* v. *Sims,* 377 U.S. 533, 579 (1964); *Baker* v. *Carr,* 369 U.S. 186, 254 (Justice Clark concurring).
68. This section and the following section on bipartisan apportionment method are adapted from my article in the 1969 *Supreme Court Review* (University of Chicago Law School) 219, at 246–268, "The Warren Court Crusade for the Holy Grail of 'One Man-One Vote.'" See also the more detailed treatment in Dixon, *Democratic Representation,* pp. 310–313, 333–340, 358–362, 380–384, 456–543.

an accidental gerrymander can be just as devastating as one which emanates from a secret chart room. In short, the test of a gerrymander is to be found in the degree of partisan fairness in the election results under a given districting plan and not in its population equality.

A nearly infinite number of sets of "equal" districts may be drawn in any state, each set, however, having a quite different effect in terms of overall party balance and minority representation. This fact is the primary reason that it is not possible simply to turn the districting problem over to "the computer" and that it is grossly misleading to speak of nonpartisan districting techniques. To the extent that important political data is kept concealed, the districting process will take on the quality of Russian roulette. At the same time, computers can be very helpful when used as analytical tools. They can be most safely used in conjunction with bipartisan apportionment agencies.

The Problem of "Standards"

Attempts have been made, with minimal success, to specify in advance some criteria for districting, supposedly in the hope of channeling and limiting partisan discretion and accidental blundering. A concern for districting standards is likely to continue even though the Supreme Court's 1969 and 1970 rulings in *Preisler* and *Wells* and *Hadley* put in doubt the extent to which any criterion other than near-absolute equality of population can be followed in districting. The primary difficulty in forming standards is that the familiar criteria, even including that of equal population, tend to fail at the outset by not recognizing the complexity of the ultimate goal of fair and effective political representation for all significant groups.

For example, contiguity and compactness, which often are viewed as touchstones of proper districting, whether they are specifically required or not, are really pseudostandards. Given the modern realities of rapid communication and the lack of close association with one's neighbors, particularly in metropolitan areas, modest departures from contiguity pose no intrinsic problems of representation unless gross partisan purposes are present. At the same time, a requirement of contiguity does not block gross partisan purpose. The requirement of compactness is usually interpreted to mean that districts are to be as symmetrical as practicable. (An alternative approach would be to stress the population's "center of gravity," drawing lines so as to minimize the distance of each citizen from the district center—which could be a quite symmetrical arrangement.) Achieving symmetry by drawing districts as perfect circles is obviously impossible. A symmetrical pattern of square districts, while practicable, could well operate to submerge significant elements of the electorate because of the variant factor of residence patterns, a factor which is also crucial in educational desegregation. More important, a benign gerrymander, in the sense of some asymmetrical districts (which is the analogue of busing in educational integration), may well be required in order to assure representation of submerged elements within a larger area. This same consideration casts doubts also on overly rigid requirements of adherence to natural boundaries or those of political subdivisions, even though most of these boundaries may well coincide with actual communities of interest.

Further, an attempt to delineate detailed districting standards in advance may run into a requirement of uniformity of application, imposed judicially via the equal protection clause of the Fourteenth Amendment. At this point equality in form may defeat equality in substance, in terms of the basic interest in fair representation. To paraphrase Walter Bagehot's comment that gross appearances are great realities, it may be said of political districting that neat appearances conceal gross realities.[69]

The factor of safe versus swing districts for the two major parties and the corollary factor of homogeneity versus heterogeneity, generally, may have a decisive effect on the practicalities of representation. All persons receive some general representation, whether their district is swing or safe. However, only in swing districts do the members of both opposing parties have an opportunity for "control representation," that is, the election of a member of their own party. Intrinsically, a district system of legislative election is weighted in favor of the voters who are members of the majority party in the safe districts. Ideally, there should be a large number of swing districts, in order that both parties be responsive to a broad spectrum of interests. And the safe districts for each party should be scattered, rather than grouped in regional patterns, in order to maximize opportunities for political expression by all voters. All of these practical elements are present whether the design is for single-member or multi-member districts. However, because there are more seats at stake in each multi-member district, the suggested effects are exaggerated.

The Supreme Court and Gerrymandering

The thorniest nettle in the political thicket is gerrymandering, both racial and nonracial. Understandably, the Supreme Court has yet to grasp it

69. Walter Bagehot, *The English Constitution* (New York: Oxford University Press, 1900), p. 217.

firmly. The Court seems to have hoped that policing the simple concept of equal numbers would be enough and that the political forces would somehow work out the other problems. Although *Baker* v. *Carr* was more than eight years old when the Supreme Court reconvened in October for its 1970 term, the Court had yet to indicate unequivocally that nonracial gerrymandering issues were even justiciable. Detailed judicial policing of gerrymandering would be a herculean task bordering on the impossible. Whatever the Court does in this area, it can be expected to move cautiously. Logic, as well as experience, tells us, however, that there can be no total sanctuaries in the political thicket, else unfairness will simply shift from one form to another.

The plaintiffs in all apportionment/districting cases, like the plaintiffs in *Baker* v. *Carr,* are concerned about political representation in a personal, partisan sense. The aim is to force a reshaping of legislative districts so that they and their fellow partisans will have a better opportunity of electing like-minded legislators. This goal is not only natural but proper. The focus is substance, not form. In a functional sense the gerrymandering issue is the same whether the districts are single-member or multi-member—and whether or not a racial factor is present, because racial gerrymandering is simply a particular kind of political gerrymandering. Anomalously, there do seem to be differences in judicial perception of the gerrymandering issue when it appears in these nominally different guises.

The greatest uncertainty surrounds challenges to unfair single-member districts, where no racial factor is alleged. Although the Supreme Court has not addressed itself to the issue, some lower courts have suggested that the issue is not even justiciable, relying on an early, solo dictum of Justice Harlan[70] and the dismissal in 1966 of an appeal in a Michigan case.[71] Since then the Court has twice avoided the gerrymandering issue in the New York congressional districting case, *Wells* v. *Rockefeller.* The first time it had the case, it nullified the districts, as discussed above, by creating a stringent population-equality rule.[72] After the districts were redone by the New York legislature with a maximum deviation of only 0.12 percent, the Court affirmed a favorable district court decision in 1970, despite renewed allegations of gerrymandering.[73]

Despite some uncertainty concerning the precedent value of dismissal

70. *WMCA* v. *Lomenzo,* 382 U.S. 4, 5–6 (1965).
71. *Badgeley* v. *Hare,* 385 U.S. 114 (1966).
72. *Supra,* n. 36.
73. 398 U.S. 901 (1970).

of an appeal,[74] neither the Michigan case nor the New York case furnishes solid ground for concluding that nonracial gerrymandering of single-member districts is nonjusticiable in the Supreme Court. In each case the issue presented was a novel and crucial one in the area of constitutional law and the record of actual inequity was meager. Some lower courts, perceiving the inconsistency in a judicial policy of intruding on the political thicket and then disclaiming responsibility for the results, have engaged in what might be called backdoor invalidations of gerrymandering. After making a bow to the Supreme Court's hesitancy to act, they have granted relief on extra tight arithmetic equality grounds, thus nullifying an alleged gerrymander without saying so.[75]

There is far less doubt concerning the justiciability of nonracial gerrymandering challenges to multi-member districts. In a series of dicta in cases from Georgia,[76] Hawaii,[77] and Texas,[78] the Court or individual justices have expressed concern regarding the dangers of submerging minority political interests in large multi-member districts operating under a winner-take-all rule. As Justice Brennan phrased it, writing for the Court in a suit unsuccessfully challenging the election of seven state senators at large in Fulton County (Atlanta) Georgia:

> It might well be that, designedly or otherwise, a multimember constituency apportionment scheme, under the circumstances of a particular case, would operate to minimize or cancel out the voting strength of racial or political elements of the voting population. When this is demonstrated it will be time enough to consider whether the system still passes constitutional muster.[79]

This concern has been echoed in some lower courts.

In a case which was argued before the Supreme Court in December of its 1970 term, *Chavis* v. *Whitcomb*,[80] a federal district court nullified

---

74. Review by the process of certiorari is discretionary, and denial of a petition has no precedent value. Review by the appeal process is supposedly mandatory, and there is some uncertainty on the meaning of a dismissal for "want of a substantial federal question." Dixon, *Democratic Representation*, pp. 488–490.

75. See, for example, *Jones* v. *Falcey*, 48 N.J. 25, 222 A.2d 101, 105–106 (1966); *Long* v. *Avery*, 251 F. Supp. 541 (D. Kans. 1966).

76. *Fortson* v. *Dorsey*, 379 U.S. 433, 439 (1965).

77. *Burns* v. *Richardson*, 384 U.S. 73, 88 (1966).

78. *Kilgarlin* v. *Hill*, 386 U.S. 120, 122 (1967).

79. *Supra*, n. 76 at 439.

80. 305 F. Supp. 1364 (S. D. Ind. 1969). This case has had a complex subsequent history and may become moot without a Supreme Court decision on the merits of the racial-representation issue. When the Indiana legislature failed to replace the

a mixed single-member and multi-member apportionment plan for the Indiana legislature. Among the several arguments presented by the plaintiffs was the contention that *any* legislative districting system which mixed single-member and multi-member districts or which mixed different sizes of multi-member districts could be shown on mathematical grounds alone to overrepresent the residents of the larger districts, in terms of their ability to influence policy outcomes in the legislature.[81] The analysis turns on the fact that residents of the larger districts have a larger number of representatives who may be in a position to cast a deciding vote in the legislature. And the exaggerated influence may occur even if the populations of the different sizes of districts are arithmetically proportional, for example, a 10,000-person district with one representative and a 90,000-person district with nine representatives. If this "higher math" analysis of one man, one vote, is adopted, the mixed or "disuniform" districting system would be irrebuttably unconstitutional—a gerrymander per se.

The Indiana federal district court, although impressed with the plausibility of the argument, chose to rest its decision on the primary ground asserted by the plaintiffs, namely, the submergence of Negro voters in the large Marion County (Indianapolis) multi-member districts. Because the fifteen state representatives and eight state senators in that area were elected at large, Negro victors were rare; whereas, if subdistricting had been required, the principal Negro ghetto area should have elected approximately two house members and one senator.

As the *Chavis* case indicates, there is no doubt at all regarding the justiciability of political gerrymandering where invidious racial intent or effect is alleged. The challenge may be directed to a multi-member districting plan or to a single-member districting plan, as the Supreme Court

---

nullified districts, the district court in December 1969 adopted the plaintiff's plan for the 1970 elections, 307 F. Supp. 1362, but this order was stayed by the Supreme Court 396 U.S. 1064 (1970). Thus, the 1970 elections will be held under the old plan, and impending reapportionment under the new census figures may moot the issue, even though a challenge to the district court's replacement plan was to be on the Court's fall 1970 docket. 397 U.S. 984 (1970).

81. This can be called the "higher math" of one man, one vote, to distinguish it from the "sixth-grade arithmetic" of only equalizing (or proportionalizing) gross population figures. See J. H. Banzhaf, III "Multi-member Electoral Districts—Do They Violate the 'One Man, One Vote' Principle?" 75 *Yale Law Journal* 1309; Riker & Shapley, "Weighted Voting: A Mathematical Analysis for Instrumental Judgments," in J. Roland Pennock and John W. Chapman, eds., *Representation* (*NOMOS X*) (New York: Atherton Press, 1968); Dixon, *Democratic Representation*, pp. 535–543.

itself indicated in *Wright* v. *Rockefeller* in 1964 [82] in its handling of an unsuccessful attack on the four congressional districts on Manhattan Island. In the *Wright* case the Court found it difficult to ascertain what fair representation is for a racial minority which may have one safe seat if its votes are massed (the Harlem district) or no safe seat, but a possible balance of power in several districts, if its votes are spread.

It can be predicted that in all gerrymandering cases proof will be difficult and alleged instances of discrimination will be susceptible to alternative explanations, some supporting a conclusion of gerrymandering, others suggesting a chance outcome in a complex process. For this reason, although the Court *must* treat the issue as justiciable to hold true to the spirit of *Baker* v. *Carr,* actual invalidations can be expected to be rare. Judicial review in this part of the political thicket is a last line of defense. Our primary concern should be to find means of building fairness and equity into the districting process at the outset.

THE BIPARTISAN COMMISSION
FOR APPORTIONMENT/DISTRICTING

The choice of the reapportionment agency has special relevance to the nearly insoluble problem of political and racial gerrymandering associated with the use of a district system.[83] Traditionally, apportionment and districting have been a legislative function dominated by the party in power at the moment. With such an agency, no present standards—or standards likely to be articulated—can guarantee avoidance of gerrymandering, in the invidious sense of a planned disproportionate relationship between votes cast and seats gained. The Supreme Court's tendency to increase the stringency of the standard of equal population even operates to maximize gerrymandering opportunities by permitting (or requiring) all traditional alignments to be ignored in favor of arithmetic equality. The idea of a so-called nonpartisan or neutral commission offers no certain path to representational virtue. Indeed, it is essentially a "three monkeys" policy: speak no politics, see no politics, hear no politics, and hope that men are angels, after all.

Nor is the judiciary likely to offer much help here, even though courts have played a near-dominant role in the reapportionment revolution so far. The central problem is one of proof, which becomes even more difficult once the easily identifiable factor of race drops out. Even worse, in

82. 376 U.S. 52 (1964).
83. *Supra,* n. 68.

order to avoid too overt an appearance of political litigation, there is the danger that courts may adopt the logically unsatisfactory but naïvely appealing principle that all overt recognition of political data and political interests in the redistricting process is impermissible. Such a policy would have the effect of making it virtually impossible for state legislatures to retain the function of legislative apportionment or congressional redistricting, except on a "blind-man's buff" basis.

The problem is how to institutionalize a process for avoiding one-sided partisanship at the outset of redistricting, while preserving political realism. The answer is the bipartisan commission with tie-breaker, which has been considered or adopted by several states since 1966.

Use of such a bipartisan commission for the apportionment/districting function solves several problems at once:

1. It permits a focus on the realities of political representation in all proposed plans, thus avoiding a process of shadowboxing with pseudo-standards such as contiguity and compactness;

2. the commission can adjust to any given rule of equal-population stringency, although, as with any districting agency, its task will be harder if there is no agreed minimum of acceptable deviation;

3. the redistricters will know or will have access to the relevant political and social data bearing on representation needs and the degree to which alternative redistricting plans would satisfy them;

4. the unavoidable, overweening element of partisanship, which is simply a sign of a politically alert populace, will be formally recognized and will be ameliorated institutionally within the redistricting agency itself;

5. invidious gerrymandering detrimental to either party will be checked at the outset rather than being left to uncertain correction in the judicial process, which is not well adapted to this kind of litigation;

6. there could be some gain for ethnic minorities, for, although it might not be advisable to attempt to conduct all commission business in open session, the commission's existence would bring the process into the open and provide a responsible focal point for making known the interests of particular groups concerning representation;

7. a plan devised by a bipartisan commission, although still subject to judicial review, could be undergirded with a strong presumption of representational fairness, unless particularized "unrepresentativeness" could be shown.

This last point is especially important. Burden of proof is crucial in apportionment litigation. For years plaintiffs enjoyed a virtual presumption of unconstitutionality whenever they could bear the easy burden of showing that a plan more "equal" than the state's plan was conceivable.

Now that we are dealing with tiny population deviations, it does not make sense to require the state to "justify each variance, no matter how small." [84] Such a rule flies in the face of life and the legislative process. Whenever a legislature or a commission seeks to incorporate competing values, it is foredoomed to be irrational—that is, inconsistent and lacking in full logical symmetry. Yet it may well produce a reasonable accommodation which is far more satisfying than pushing a single value to its logical conclusion. This is so regarding tax legislation, zoning legislation with its variances and exceptions, the difficult area of educational policy, and many other areas.

The point is especially pertinent regarding gerrymandering claims. There is no single "right" set of districts which will yield fair and effective representation. Rather, there are several different kinds of combinations which may yield fair and effective representation (this concept itself being a goal and not a self-defining term). Thus, there never can be a clear-cut standard against which the judiciary may review challenges concerning the gerrymandering or nongerrymandering qualities of any plan. With the proposal of a bipartisan commission, undergirded by a presumption of constitutionality, the judiciary would still be an important backstop against gross unfairness, as proved by the plaintiff. But it would not have to attempt an affirmative definition of political fairness on an uncertain record.

Bipartisan redistricting already does occur, informally, in those situations where control of the two houses of the state legislature and the governorship, with its veto power, is divided between the two parties. This fortuitous circumstance of divided government did permit some bipartisan procedures in some states in the period after 1964, when state legislative districts and congressional districts were overhauled on a massive scale. However, this factor cannot be counted on, and such informal bipartisanship has no provision for a tie-breaker.

Since 1966 New Jersey (1966),[85] Pennsylvania (1968),[86] and Hawaii (1968)[87] have amended their state constitutions to authorize bipartisan commissions with tie-breakers to perform the function of state legislative apportionment. Draft constitutions for Maryland[88] and New York[89] and

84. *Kirkpatrick* v. *Preisler*, 394 U.S. 526, 531 (1969).
85. N.J. Const. Art. XI, §5 (1966).
86. Pa. Const. Art. II, §§16, 17 (1968).
87. Hawaii Const. Art. III, §§2, 4, as amended (1968).
88. Maryland Proposed Constitution (defeated May 1968), Art. III, §3.05–3.08.
89. New York Proposed Constitution (defeated November 1967), Art. III, §2.

the Oklahoma revision pending in 1970[90] proposed use of this commission device for congressional districting as well as state legislative apportionment.[91] In December 1970, Illinois ratified a new constitution which retained reapportionment power in the legislature but provided for use of a bipartisan commission with tie-breaker in event of legislative deadlock. The New York and Maryland draft constitutions were defeated at the polls, but the defeats were not attributable to the provisions involving the bipartisan commissions.

The partisan members of the bipartisan commission can be the majority and minority party leaders in each house of the legislature or persons appointed by the state central committee of each party. To curb self-interest, an optional provision may be included to bar from election within a specified period any person who has served on the bipartisan commission. The tie-breaker may be appointed by the entire bench of the state's highest court or by the chief justice of the state or by the governor. The first device, appointment by the entire bench of the state's highest court, may have the special merit of being less partisan than gubernatorial appointment, while at the same time blunting the political onus which might attach to the state's chief justice if he were solely responsible for this selection. One of the plans submitted to the Illinois constitutional convention in 1970 sought to avoid the involvement of either the courts or the governor in the selection of tie-breaker. It provided that one of the nonlegislative members of the commission, chosen by lot, would break a tie by selecting one of the plans considered by the commission.

The commission device does not touch the problem—if indeed it be a problem, in view of our commitment to a two-party system—of consideration of third-party or intra-party factional interests. But neither does our present practice of districting by state legislatures deal formally with this matter. Certainly, the commission device is a clear advance over straight partisan apportionment where many interests—major party, as well as minor party and subgroup, interests—may be sacrificed. Also, a plea of the constitutional right of special interests to representation on an appor-

90. Special Committee on Constitutional Revision (Oklahoma), Report and Recommendations, 10–11 (1968), pending for action in state senate in 1970, as HJR 1022.

91. There is no federal obstacle to shifting the congressional districting function in a state from the legislature to a bipartisan commission. The federal statute speaks simply of redistricting "in the manner provided by the law" of the state. 2 U.S.C. §2a(c) (1964). In the past, congressional redistricting legislation has been subjected by state law to popular referendum and to gubernatorial veto. *Ohio ex rel. Davis* v. *Hildebrant*, 241 U.S. 565 (1916); *Smiley* v. *Holm*, 285 U.S. 355 (1932).

tionment commission would raise the larger question of a right to such representation on administrative bodies generally.[92]

DEMOCRATIZING THE NATIONAL
PARTY NOMINATING CONVENTIONS

Dissatisfaction with the representative character of some recent national party nominating conventions, most notably the 1968 Democratic national convention, has created another frontier of one man, one vote, theory —and a search for enforceable constitutional constraints. The matter was studied in 1969 by two offshoots of the Democratic National Committee: the Commission on Rules under Representative James G. O'Hara and the Commission on Party Structure and Delegate Selection under Senator George S. McGovern. The latter commission issued a report, suggesting guidelines for reform.[93]

In approaching the question of constitutional constraints to be enforced by court action, a sharp distinction must be made between the interstate aspect—that is, the apportionment of delegates to the states under the national party rules—and the intra-state aspect—that is, the varied procedures under state law or state party rule for selecting the state's share of the national convention delegates.

The question in either aspect is a vital one not only for both major parties, but also for the public in general. In the absence of a national primary system, these party processes produce the nominees for the highest elective public office in the land—at least, the "serious" contenders of the two major parties. To be sure, the electoral college system itself, like the now discredited Georgia county unit system, is a far cry from one man, one vote. But this area, too, is undergoing rethinking, as evidenced by the proposed constitutional amendment for a direct popular vote, which was approved by the House of Representatives on September 18, 1969, and was pending in the Senate in 1970.[94]

In delegate apportionment to the states (interstate aspect) indefensible inequalities exist, whether judged from the standpoint of a voter or a

92. George Wallace did prevail in his suit to get on the Ohio ballot in 1968, but that case involved access to the ballot to run for public office, whereas an apportionment commission is a nonelective device to discharge a special pre-election function. *Williams* v. *Rhodes,* 393 U.S. 23 (1968).

93. Commission on Party Structure and Delegate Selection, "Mandate for Reform" (Democratic National Committee pamphlet, 1970).

94. See House Report, No. 253, 91st Cong., 1st Sess., May 16, 1969. The proposal died in the Senate in 1970 and was reintroduced in the Ninety-second Congress by Senator Birch Bayh as S. J. Res. 1, Jan. 28, 1971.

party member. For example, the current apportionment rules for the Democratic party allocate national convention delegate-votes ("delegate-votes" is used because the state party may send more than one person to cast a given "vote") as follows: (1) three convention delegate-votes for each electoral vote; (2) one vote for each national committeeman and each committeewoman (each state has one of each); (3) one vote for each 100,000 popular votes or major fraction thereof cast for the Democratic nominee in the previous presidential election; and (4) a victory bonus of ten votes for each of those states carried by the nominee in the previous presidential election. This formula produces significant disparities; for example, although Humphrey received almost identical popular votes in Tennessee and Oregon in 1968, for 1972 Tennessee Democrats will have thirty-nine convention votes, while Oregon Democrats will have only twenty-four. The disparity would be even greater if Tennessee had a victory bonus of ten; but in this instance neither state is entitled to such a bonus.

Even laying aside the question of justiciability, it is doubtful that these inequities can be attacked judicially under existing reapportionment and voting precedents. The problem is an interstate one, stemming from rule-making by the national party organs. The key aspect of existing reapportionment and voting precedents is that they are intra-state rulings affecting either a statewide political process or a political process in some sub-unit of the state, but in either event controlled by organs within the state. The Fourteenth Amendment's equal protection clause has been the primary reliance for these cases, and its essential rule is one forbidding intra-state discrimination among persons subject to the state's jurisdiction. For congressional districts the Court has used Article I, Section 2, but the result is the same—a limitation on population inequality among intra-state congressional districts. An appeal might be made to the due process clause of the Fifth Amendment. It does operate on national public organs and, since the District of Columbia school desegregation case, also includes within due process the equality idea.[95] It would then still be necessary to overcome the "political question" hurdle and to show that national nominating conventions were public bodies. The latter requirement might not be too difficult, by analogy to the intra-state cases which have held White primaries and special preprimary devices to be an integral part of the process of filling public office, and hence within constitutional constraint.[96]

95. *Bolling* v. *Sharpe*, 347 U.S. 497 (1954).
96. *Terry* v. *Adams*, 345 U.S. 461 (1953).

The intra-state aspects of delegate selection would seem to be more amenable to judicial control, by simple extension of existing legislative districting precedents, treating the delegate as a public officer for this purpose. Lower courts, however, have been loath to intervene in party matters absent a showing of racial discrimination, and some suits concerning intra-state aspects of delegate selection to the 1968 Democratic convention were unsuccessful.[97] However, where the issue is third-party access to the ballot, courts have adjudicated.[98]

REBUILDING THE URBAN POLITICAL SYSTEM

Effective administrative structures require a viable political base.[99] The lack of such a base may be the key to the metropolitan muddle which seems to get worse with each passing year. Three elements worth special study in this regard are: (1) the recent thrust toward requiring citizen participation or community action as an adjunct of certain federally funded programs; (2) the possible use of enlarged city councils elected from many single-member districts in order to continue, but also to domesticate, the goals of the citizen-participation movement; (3) the integrative possibilities in the local Councils of Governments (COG) movement, as affected by the recent *Hadley* case.

Citizen-participation Movement

The newest development in local representation—more recent than one man, one vote, and overdue to be related to it—is the flourishing experimentation with various types of devices for citizen participation. Through their varied local activities, the Office of Economic Opportunity (OEO) and the Department of Housing and Urban Development (HUD) have been major forces in this development, but the phenomenon is spreading to all social service programs. The movement was sparked by the requirement of "maximum feasible participation" of the poor in the Economic Opportunity Act of 1964[100] and the HUD requirement since 1966 of "wide-

97. Note, "Regulation of Political Parties: Vote Dilution in the Presidential Nominating Procedure," 54 *Iowa Law Review* 471. See also *Irish v. Democratic-Farmer Labor Party of Minnesota*, 399 F. 2d 110 (8th Cir. 1968); *Smith v. Democratic Party of Georgia*, 288 F. Supp. 371 (N.D.Ga. 1968).

98. *Moore v. Ogilvie*, 394 U.S. 814 (1969); *Williams, supra*, n. 92.

99. For a detailed treatment of the suggestive comments in this section see Dixon, 58 *Georgetown Law Journal* 955.

100. 78 Stat. 516 (1964), 42 U.S.C. §2782 (a) (3) (Supp. II, 1967). Subsequently, in 1967 the act was amended to enhance the role of state and local governments in designating community-action agencies and in participating in the governing boards. 81 Stat. 693, 42 U.S.C. §§2790(a), 2791(b) (Supp. IV 1969).

spread citizen participation" in the Model Cities program.[101] The result-
ant devices included elected community boards, citizen committees, community corporations, task forces, and the employment of the poor as
trainee-administrators in the programs themselves.

The citizen-participation movement, once created, tended to expand
beyond its OEO poverty-program origins to encompass other programs of
special concern to residents of the inner city, many of which are federally
funded and involve joint federal-local administrative arrangements. Few
functional fields from prenatal care to old-age assistance remain untouched. Logically, the movement may reach all government "client
groups," including the not-so-poor.

In significant respects, the emerging picture is one of confusion and
chaos. Decentralization in order to "humanize" government, even at the
cost of some inefficiency and policy confusion, has become the dominant
theme.[102] The dominant mode is citizen-clientele participation. The
dominant goal of the participant shifts quickly from input to control.
The result is a major political movement with significant implications
for political representation. They must be recognized and dealt with
in terms of representation, if the drive for governmental intimacy is not
to degenerate into administrative anarchy.

Apart from the obvious problems of democratic theory posed by the
citizen-participation movement, there are certain practical dangers.
There is a danger of replaying the already tragic story of exaggerated
expectation followed by dashed hopes. The movement deals with specific
client groups generating consumer self-interest, primarily drawn from
the poor. In one form or another, these groups want to share the wealth
of a larger group which, by its size as well as its wealth, is the dominant
part of the total political constituency which determines wealth-sharing.
Obviously, the citizen-participation movement is attempting the impossible
when its basic thrust is to separate the receiver from the giver, while
at the same time it seeks to put real power in the hands of the receiver.
What is needed is not a special, separatist politics, but a more effective
general politics for more personal representation and mediation.

To the extent that the various community-action groups acquire sig-

101. 80 Stat. 1256 (1966), 42 U.S.C. §3303 (a)(2) (Supp. IV 1969).
102. See Herbert Kaufman, "Administrative Decentralization and Political
Power," 29 *Pub. Admin. Rev.* 3, 11–12; Howard W. Hallman, "Community Control: A Study of Community Corporations and Neighborhood Boards" (Washington Center for Metropolitan Studies Monograph Series, 1969). See also Committee
for Economic Development, "Reshaping Government in Metropolitan Areas" (1970),
pp. 42–44.

nificant power over governmental programs, they will become in effect little legislatures and be subject to one man, one vote, precepts similar to those affecting general government. Relevant questions include: Who is entitled to be enfranchised for a particular functional purpose? If indirect representation through districts is needed, what should be the apportionment base—total population, or something else? Are at-large elections permissible, or should techniques for representation of minority factions within the client group be included?

Reviving the City Council

None of these limitations inspired by the one man, one vote, concept is relevant, however, to the larger question of relating community action to the larger political whole. To achieve this crucial purpose may take a long evolutionary process, but one partial solution is readily at hand. We should seriously consider turning our backs on the traditional theory of urban reform, that local virtue is achieved only through small city councils and at-large elections. There are strong arguments now for going in precisely the opposite direction and creating councils large enough to give pinpoint representation to ethnic neighborhoods and subgroups of all kinds. In form, the councils should be based on many small single-member districts, unless agreement can be reached on specific devices for minority representation.

In function, members of such revived city councils may be viewed both as service and as power brokers, analogous to the former ward and precinct leaders. Unlike leaders in recent citizen-participation systems, district-based councilmen would operate within the framework of the responsible, democratic power system, safeguarded by the secret ballot—the very essence of a free political system.

Local Councils of Governments

The "in" word in the local-goverment lexicon is regionalism, and one of the most promising regional innovations of the last decade has been the rise of the local Councils of Government (COG) movement. Older than one man, one vote, and "community action," the COG movement is still developing and will be materially affected by those still newer forces. The underlying premise of the COG movement is that voluntary action is better than no action at all and that much can be accomplished by developing regularized relationships among the leaders, especially the legislative officials, of the several local governments in all sizes of metropolitan regions.

Unless the COG movement, which thus far has yielded only voluntary cooperation, can be regarded as the building block for the development of federated local government, prospects for true regional government in the near future are not bright. But at this point there may be constitutional complications flowing from the one man, one vote, doctrine and the recent *Hadley* decision[103] invalidating the federated Junior College District of Metropolitan Kansas City. This district, arguably, was based on the very form of representation which may be needed, at least as an interim step, to change COGs from voluntary organizations to local federations with true governmental power. The invalidated percentage-representation formula may have been a necessary incentive for getting suburban districts to join —and thus accomplish the "good" end of creating junior college districts. As phrased in the brief for the junior college district:

> The percentage aspect of the election method encourages individual school districts to join together to form a junior college district—without their being swallowed up and losing all trustee representation to the larger school districts—and promotes the growth and development of the junior college system. Straight elections at large, as advocated by appellants, would do the opposite.[104]

The Supreme Court ignored this "federation concept" argument in voiding the Missouri Act, although it was the only major issue of nation-wide significance in the case. Dissenting from the *Hadley* ruling, along with Chief Justice Burger and Justice Stewart, Justice Harlan viewed the statute as reflecting a "careful balancing of the desirability of population-based representation against the practical problems involved in the creation of new educational units." [105]

Of course, as noted earlier in this chapter, the majority opinion by Justice Black was full of caveats. In view, however, of the Court's actual vote, the outlook is hardly encouraging for the creation of regional governments in which representation is based on a mixture of population and political units, even if the resulting population deviations are quite modest, as they were in the *Hadley* case.

CONCLUSION

We have come a long way since Justice Thomas Clark supported the majority in *Baker* v. *Carr* in 1962 for the limited purpose of releasing the

103. *Hadley, supra,* n. 3. See text *supra,* notes 49–66 for a detailed discussion of the case.
104. Brief for Appellees at p. 23, *Hadley* v. *Junior College District, ibid.*
105. 397 U.S. at 64.

"stranglehold" of rotten boroughs and freeing up the political system to work out its own destiny. Surprisingly, we still have a long way to go toward the basic goal of achieving a fair and effective system of political representation which can operate by regular political action and not by perpetual lawsuit.

Only a handful of states will greet the reapportionment upheaval of the seventies with procedures—such as bipartisan commissions with tie-breakers—designed to accomplish revision of the system of representation with speed, fairness, and political realism. For the rest, political rape may be the fate. Gerrymandering opportunities may actually be increased if the Supreme Court continues to require a near-absolute population-equality rule. Judicial review will be sought, but problems of proof may make court action ineffective in this part of the political thicket. Minority representation is still precarious. The impact of one man, one vote, on political party conventions, on local experimentation with proposals for metropolitan government, and on the requirements of extraordinary majorities (e.g., two-thirds) to pass such things as bond issues,[106] is just beginning to emerge. Scrutiny of the *internal* processes of legislative operation may lie just over the horizon; it can be asked how equal voters are if their representatives are weighted by a seniority system.

"One man, one vote," however, is a slogan, not a political theory. In insensitive hands it can have the quality of a shibboleth or a hatchet, as Justice Fortas observed. A rule of absolute population equality also can have a boomerang effect, as illustrated by *Wells* v. *Rockefeller*.[107] In its final outcome in 1970 this case had almost a quixotic quality. It will be remembered that, after a bipartisan revision of New York congressional districts was accomplished by a split legislature in 1968, Mr. Wells took a solo appeal. Even though the most deviant district was only 6.6 percent from ideal, the Supreme Court voided the plan and announced a precise equality rule. On remand, the New York legislature, then controlled by Republicans in both houses, produced a plan only 0.12 percent deviant at its extreme. This plan was not to Mr. Wells's liking for alleged gerrymander reasons. Accordingly, he returned to the federal district court in 1970 to plead that, if it did nothing else, it at least should restore the very plan which he had successfully contested the year before![108] The

106. *Rimarcik* v. *Johansen*, 310 F. Supp. 61 (D. Minn. 1970); *Lance* v. *County of Roane*, 170 S.E. 2d 783 (W.Va. 1969); *Larez* v. *Shannon* (Superior Court of Sutter County, Calif., Aug. 8, 1969, appeal pending).

107. 394 U.S. 542 (1969), discussed in text, *supra*, notes 34–42.

108. Plaintiff's memorandum in United States District Court, March 9, 1970, p. 29. Anomalously, the Republican-controlled committee may have produced a

court refused, and the Supreme Court affirmed.[109] Certainly, this poignant outcome indicates that it does not make sense for the Supreme Court to treat legislative districting like a process of Immaculate Conception, to require absolute population equality as the sole consideration and to assume that this will bring about the Heavenly City.

The reapportionment revolution caught everyone unprepared—judges, political scientists, lawyers, political philosophers. We now are beginning to perceive that there is more to fair representation than the elimination of rotten boroughs under a simplistic "equal population" logic.[110] The life of the law, as Holmes noted, is not logic but experience—not a Platonic quest for the ideal, but an Aristotelian quest for the viable. This is the message of the sixties to the seventies.

*   *   *

COMMENTARY by Malcolm E. Jewell

Professor Dixon's analysis of the unresolved problems of transforming equal representation from a theory to a reality is as perceptive and provocative as his previous studies on this topic. The purpose of this commentary is not to criticize, but to develop in more detail a few of the points that seem to me particularly important.

As Dixon has repeatedly pointed out, the Supreme Court, in its search for equal representation, has demonstrated an obsession with equality and a neglect of representation. Basic questions of representation are inherent in the major unsolved problems of apportionment: the preservation of county and municipal boundaries in districting, partisan and racial gerrymandering, and the use of multi-member districts. In these brief comments, I will devote attention to these problems.

---

fairer plan than the one then in use under which the Democrats in 1968 gained a 26 to 15 (63 percent to 37 percent) control of the congressional delegation, even though the popular vote was close. In the November 1970 elections, under the new plan, Democrats captured 58.5 percent of the seats (24-17) with a statewide congressional vote plurality of only 50.9 percent. And if the six districts in which there was no effective contest are eliminated, the outcome is even more unexpected: the Democrats with 49.7 percent of the congressional vote captured 54.3 percent of the seats (19-16). *Source:* computations of David I. Wells using initial unofficial figures.

109. 311 F. Supp. 48 (1970), aff'd 398 U.S. 901 (1970).

110. For a provocative review of the slipperiness of the equality concept in other public law areas see Kurland, "Egalitarianism and the Warren Court," 68 *Michigan Law Review* 629 (1970).

REPRESENTATION OF CITIES AND COUNTIES

Probably the most curious part of the Court's opinion in the *Preisler* and *Wells* cases is the refusal to permit deviations in population equality in order to follow county and municipal boundaries.[1] There are at least three reasons why state legislatures should be permitted and even encouraged to base legislative districts on county and municipal boundaries. The first is that the residents of counties and cities have certain common interests and needs, and their local governments must often seek the assistance of their state legislators in sponsoring and supporting legislation to deal with specific local problems. As the Court recognized in the *Reynolds* case, "In many states much of the legislature's activity involves the enactment of so-called local legislation, directed only to the concerns of particular political subdivisions." [2] In addition, the legislature is increasingly called upon to regulate the relationships among local governments. It is important for legislators to represent the voters living in specific cities and counties, and not just those residing in particular census tracts. If the Supreme Court is going to ignore boundaries of political subdivisions in congressional districting cases (*Preisler* and *Wells*), it might recognize that they are more pertinent to state legislative apportionment cases. In the *Reynolds* case the Court suggested that "some distinctions may well be made between congressional and state legislative representation" and that "it may be feasible to use political subdivision lines to a greater extent in establishing state legislative districts than in congressional districting" because of the larger number of seats involved.[3]

A second reason for maintaining political boundaries in apportionment is less often recognized. One reason that state legislatures appear to be ineffective is that citizens seem to know little about their activities and often do not know what their own legislators are doing—or even who they are. If these legislators are elected from districts that are unrelated to familiar city and county boundaries, they are likely to be even less visible to the voters. The visibility of legislators is not a trivial problem, but is central to the functioning of a representative system.

A third reason for maintaining political boundaries remains as valid today as when it was stated by Justice Warren in the *Reynolds* decision: "Indiscriminate districting, without any regard for political subdivision

1. *Kirkpatrick* v. *Preisler, Wells* v. *Rockefeller,* 394 U.S. 526, 542 (1969).
2. *Reynolds* v. *Sims,* 377 U.S. 533, 580–581 (1964).
3. *Id.* at 578.

or natural or historical boundary lines, may be little more than an open invitation to partisan gerrymandering." [4]

GERRYMANDERING OF SINGLE-MEMBER DISTRICTS

Professor Dixon seems to believe that the Supreme Court will eventually have to confront the issue of partisan gerrymandering, even though "judicial policing of gerrymandering would be a herculean task bordering on the impossible." [5] The problem is one not only of policing gerrymandering but of setting standards. We know what perfect population equality is, and we can measure deviations from it in mathematical terms. But exactly what is a perfectly nongerrymandered district or combination of districts? There are risks in trying to judge the motivations of those who drafted the law or in interpreting the meaning of election returns. [6] When a majority party in a legislature engages in gerrymandering, it tries to waste the votes of the minority party. This can be done by creating districts in which the majority party can anticipate modest majorities and/or by creating a few districts which the state minority party will probably carry by lopsided majorities. But efforts at gerrymandering can backfire. Large-scale changes in voting patterns or long-term changes in population trends can have the effect of eroding the modest majorities anticipated for the state's majority party. When this occurs, the result may not be gerrymandering, whatever the intent. Moreover, it is difficult to pass judgment on a districting law in terms of possible gerrymandering until at least one election has been held and some of the damage done.

In one sense it is easier to measure racial gerrymandering, because it is easier to determine whether residents of a district are White or Black than whether they are likely to vote Democratic or Republican in legislative races. But it is more difficult to determine what is a perfectly nongerrymandered district, in racial terms. Black voters have the best chance of electing Black legislators in districts where they have a majority, but they are likely to have considerable influence over legislators in any district where they constitute a strong minority.

As an example of the problems in defining racial gerrymandering, consider a county with 600,000 White voters, 200,000 Black voters, and eight

4. *Id.* at 578–579.
5. Chapter 1, p. 32.
6. For an example of a judicial effort to determine whether partisan gerrymandering had occurred, see *Sincock* v. *Gately,* 262 F. Supp. 739 (D. Del. 1967).

seats in the state legislature. If the Black voters "deserve" two of the eight seats, this could be most certainly achieved by concentrating all 200,000 of them in two districts. Does this mean that racially segregated districts are the standard of nongerrymandering in racial terms? If two districts each contained 60,000 Black voters (out of 100,000) and two others each contained 40,000 Blacks (out of 100,000), Black voters would control two districts and have some influence in two others—a greater share of power than in the first example. If Black voters were evenly distributed among the districts—25,000 in each—their power would be minimized, but none of the legislators could (in theory) completely ignore their interests. The point is that there is no obvious standard of racial nongerrymandering, and in reality Black political leaders often disagree about the pattern of districting that will best serve Black interests.

The Supreme Court has never come to grips with the problem of defining racial gerrymandering. Justice Black, in the majority opinion in *Wright* v. *Rockefeller,* bypassed the issue, though he recognized the difficulty of defining criteria.[7] Justice William O. Douglas, dissenting, argued that "government has no business designing electoral districts along racial or religious lines" and that such "segregated" districts violated the Fourteenth Amendment.[8] On the other hand, Judge Leonard P. Moore, in one of the majority opinions being reviewed by the Supreme Court, argued that the concentration of a racial minority in one district might be desirable because it enabled such voters "to obtain representation in legislative bodies which otherwise would be denied to them." [9] The issue remains as judicially obscure as it was when the *Wright* case was decided in 1964.

REPRESENTATION IN MULTI-MEMBER DISTRICTS

While the effect of gerrymandering may be to reduce the representation of partisan or racial minorities, the effect of at-large elections in multi-member districts is to eliminate such representation. When most voters cast a straight party ballot, the majority party usually wins all of the seats in a multi-member district. Although members of a racial minority may be nominated and elected if party leaders want to run a balanced slate, the voters belonging to that racial minority cannot directly choose the legislators they want, if their votes are submerged in an at-large election in a multi-member district.

7. *Wright* v. *Rockefeller,* 376 U.S. 52 (1964).
8. *Id.* at 66.
9. *Wright* v. *Rockefeller,* 211 F. Supp. 460, 467 (S.D.N.Y. 1962).

It is important to distinguish between two different judicial criticisms of multi-member districts. Some courts have declared that the combination of single-member and multi-member districts in a state legislature discriminates against the voters in one or the other type of district. Others have questioned the use of multi-member districts because of the possibility of discrimination against minorities in such districts. It is noteworthy that, in exploring the effects of various districting methods, the courts are raising questions which ought to be answered by social scientists. Where such answers are available, the courts have sometimes utilized them; often, however, the courts have drawn their own conclusions.

One argument against combining the two types of districts is the mathematical one that the voters in multi-member districts have a larger number of legislators, each of whom may be able to cast the deciding vote on an issue.[10] It is possible that the courts will find this "higher math" argument to be persuasive, simply because it rests on mathematical proof rather than on theories about the representative process.[11] When the courts have tried to determine how the representative process differs in single- and multi-member districts, they have run into difficulties. Five members of the Iowa Supreme Court, for example, concluded that the voting power of a voter in a multi-member district was much greater because legislators from his district were members of a larger number of committees and he had greater likelihood of finding one or more legislators from his district who would be willing and able to advance his interests.[12] Four members of that court, however, argued that the voter in a multi-member district was handicapped by the long and cumbersome ballots and the lack of identifiable candidates and constituencies.[13] The five-judge majority recognized that both sets of voters might be discriminated against, but argued that this did not make such a mixture of districts unconstitutional; it stated that single-member districts "are as essential to the protection of an individual's rights under the Equal Protection Clause as are equally populated districts."[14] If the courts are going to make judgments about how well voters are represented in single- and multi-member districts, political scientists should be devoting more

10. J. F. Banzhaf III, "Multi-member Electoral Districts—Do They Violate the 'One Man, One Vote' Principle?" 75 *Yale Law Journal* 1309.

11. A federal district court that scrutinized the Indiana legislative districts was evidently impressed with this argument. *Chavis* v. *Whitcomb*, 305 F. Supp. 1364 (S.D. Ind. 1969).

12. *Kruidenier* v. *McCulloch*, 142 N.W. 2d 355, 370–371 (1966).

13. *Id.* at 368.

14. *Id.* at 375.

attention to this question, so that judicial decisions can be based on fact as well as theory.[15]

It is remarkable that, despite its invitation in *Fortson* v. *Dorsey*, the Supreme Court has not been directly presented with evidence that multi-member districts "operate to minimize or cancel out the voting strength of racial or political elements in the voting population." [16] While the effect of gerrymandering is very difficult to prove, the effect of multi-member districting is relatively easy to prove. The effect on a partisan minority is particularly obvious. In Marion County (Indianapolis), Indiana, for example, one party usually wins all the legislative seats, and relatively small changes in the partisan vote can lead to a complete change in legislators from one party to another. Until multi-member districts were abolished in Ohio in 1966, the minority party won few if any seats on the legislative delegations from metropolitan counties, although the party discriminated against varied from one county to another. The use of countywide districts in metropolitan areas has been declining in recent years. It is most frequently found in the South, where its discriminatory partisan effects have only recently become obvious, with the growth in the number of Republican legislative candidates.

In a number of states, North and South, the establishment of single-member districts (replacing multi-member districts) in metropolitan counties has led to the election of more Black legislators, usually from districts having a majority of Black voters.[17] Although some political leaders believe that Black voters have greater influence when they have some voice in the selection of all legislators from a metropolitan county, most Black political leaders strongly prefer a districting system that gives Black voters majority control over some districts. This not only increases the number of Black legislators, but guarantees that they will be chosen by Black voters rather than White politicians engaged in slate-making.

Because multi-member districting is particularly vulnerable to charges of racial discrimination, it is important to look closely at the opinion of the district court in the *Chavis* case, the first case in which this issue has been squarely faced. The court determined that a Black minority was discriminated against because, over a decade, only 5 percent of the Marion County senators and 6 percent of its representatives had come from an overwhelmingly Black ghetto area having 18 percent of the county's

15. See Malcolm E. Jewell, *Metropolitan Representation: State Legislative Districting in Urban Counties* (New York: National Municipal League, 1969).

16. *Fortson* v. *Dorsey*, 379 U.S. 433, 439 (1965).

17. Examples include Ohio, Tennessee, and Georgia. *Supra*, n. 15, pp. 15–17.

population. The court emphasized that suburban areas had been over-represented in terms of legislators.[18] (This suggests the possibility that multi-member districting might be shown to discriminate against other neighborhoods or parts of a county that were neither racial nor partisan minorities.)

It is noteworthy that the court in the *Chavis* case decided that the structure of the political party organizations contributed to discrimination against Blacks.[19] It found that the party organizations had considerable control over nominations of legislators and, consequently, considerable influence over their actions as members of the legislature. These factors made it difficult for even a Black legislator to represent the interests of the ghetto if they came into conflict with the wishes of party leaders. The court also suggested that multi-member districting contributed to the party organization's control over nominating—a conclusion that is supported in part by data from Indiana and other states.[20] The court's opinion is noteworthy for two reasons: it may portend more detailed judicial scrutiny of the partisan consequences of various methods of districting, and it demonstrates why it is important for political scientists to provide the courts with data and analysis concerning representative systems.

Professor Dixon's comments on the implications of the one man, one vote, doctrine for government in metropolitan areas are provocative, but I think he underestimates the potential impact on city councils. More than 60 percent of the cities (and one-third of the counties) in this country elect their legislative bodies at large rather than by districts, and the proportion of these has been growing. If the courts should decide that at-large multi-member-district elections for the state legislature discriminate against racial or partisan minorities, at least in some large counties, they are likely to discover that such discrimination is even more obvious in city councils which are elected at large. As I have pointed out elsewhere, in a single city or county "the discriminatory effect of at-large elections is absolute; there is no way of balancing out discriminations against various groups, and it is possible that voters who constitute some kind of minority (partisan or other) will be unable to elect a representative of their own over a period of many years. In other words, the use of at-large elections in a city or a county has the same effect on representation in that unit of government that statewide at-large elections would have on state

18. *Supra*, n. 11 at 1385–1386.
19. *Id.* at 1386.
20. *Supra*, n. 15, pp. 21–26, 37–44.

government."[21] In fact, it is difficult to see how any local legislative body—city, county, or metropolitan—can be perceived as giving adequate voice and vote to minorities if it is elected in at-large elections without any form of districting or proportional representation.

The courts have been remarkably slow in recognizing the Dixon doctrine that the quality as well as the equality of representation requires judicial scrutiny. There are increasing signs of such recognition in the lower courts—though it is difficult to predict whether the Burger Court will move in that direction. If it does, at-large elections in multi-member districts would seem to be the most obvious target for judicial review.

* * *

REJOINDER *by Robert G. Dixon, Jr.*

Professor Malcolm E. Jewell, whose previous writings on apportionment/districting are well known to political scientists and others, has graciously provided comments on my overview chapter to this volume—and the comments themselves are gracious, indeed. If a label were needed, it would seem that Professor Jewell and I belong to the emerging revisionist school of "one man, one vote." We are concerned with the qualitative as well as the quantitative aspects of the equal-population rule and of one man, one vote, theory generally. The fact that a girl is well apportioned does not tell you all you need to know about her; and the same applies to the forms of political representation.

I should like to add an observation of a semantic nature regarding our shared concern about the adverse effects of gerrymandering and multi-member districting. These evils are so closely related that it may contribute to clarity of thought to group them both under the single heading of gerrymandering. The central feature is distortion of the popular voting strength of any group. Starting with this premise, at least three sub-varieties of gerrymandering can be identified.

Form 1 of gerrymandering, which is the form traditionally thought of when the term is used, can be called ad hoc gerrymandering. It involves the placement of district lines, whether for single-member or multi-member districts, so as to spread one party's control over as many districts as possi-

21. Malcolm E. Jewell, "Local Systems of Representation: Political Consequences and Judicial Choices," 36 *George Washington Law Review* 800.

ble and to compact the opposition party's control in as few districts as possible. The first and best defense against this kind of gerrymandering is to block it at the outset by placing the function of reapportionment and redistricting in a bipartisan commission with tie-breaker. The second line of defense is judicial review; but I am not hopeful that judicial review will be very effective in this area, even though the attempt should be made.

Form 2 of gerrymandering is use of multi-member districts per se, even if all are the same size, for example—all three-man districts. This is a gerrymander because it inevitably submerges the voting strength of minorities —ethnic minorities or political-party minorities.

Form 3 of gerrymandering is use of different sizes of districts for the same legislative house—for example, some single-member districts and some multi-member districts of varying sizes. This is a gerrymander not only because of the already mentioned factor of submergence of minorities *within* the districts, but also because gross inequalities in political power are created automatically *among* the districts. The inequality in effective representation occurs because the voters in the larger districts with a larger number of legislators automatically have more chance that their legislators will be able to cast the deciding votes on an issue. This can be demonstrated with mathematical precision and can be called the "higher math" of one man, one vote.[1] It is true that voter influence goes down as district population goes up; but it does not go down in linear proportion. Rather it decreases inversely to the square root of the district population. Hence, if seats are added to the larger districts in linear fashion, which is our practice, there is an overcorrection. For example, a citizen in a four- or five-man multi-member district has more effective representation than a citizen in the single-member districts for the same house of the legislature in the ratio of 2:1 and 2.24:1, respectively. For thirteen- and fourteen-man districts, which have existed in Arkansas and Texas, the inequality ratios become 3.61:1 and 3.74:1. And yet under a simplistic one man, one vote, approach these districts, being proportional to gross population, look all right.

These last two forms of gerrymandering, the straight multi-member district plan (all of the same size) and the mixed district plan, may be called institutional gerrymandering. The inequality in representation is built into the basic structure of government. This form of gerrymandering can be abolished only in two ways. One is by modification of state constitutions to forbid such forms of districting (or by simply abandoning

1. Robert G. Dixon, Jr., *Democratic Representation: Reapportionment in Law and Politics* (New York: Oxford University Press, 1968), pp. 535–543.

the practice, if the constitution permits discretion). Since 1964 there has been a trend toward use of single-member districts. The other way is by court litigation to declare multi-member districting unconstitutional under the equal protection clause of the Fourteenth Amendment. This route was successful in the Iowa Supreme Court in 1966,[2] and a possibly important similar suit was pending in Arkansas in 1970.[3] Also pending in 1970 was Supreme Court review of the decision by a federal district court in Indiana invalidating, primarily on racial grounds, the multi-member districts in the state apportionment plan.[4]

The reshaping of our semantics concerning gerrymandering, suggested above, could have two distinct benefits, apart from general clarification of thought. Popular awareness that multi-member districting is merely the old gerrymander enemy in disguise may help to discourage the practice. And if courts realize that their actions against multi-member districting are really actions against gerrymandering, they may be more willing than they have been so far to exercise some judicial review also over traditional, or ad hoc, gerrymandering.

2. *Id.* at 476–484, 496–499, where the cases and the issues are intensively analyzed.

3. *Smith* v. *Rockefeller,* No. 5127, direct action in the Supreme Court of Arkansas, argument anticipated for fall 1970. For previous litigation on the same issue, see *Rockefeller* v. *Smith,* 440 S.W. 2d 580 (Ark. 1969).

4. *Chavis* v. *Whitcomb,* 305 F. Supp. 1364 (S.D. Ind. 1969), and see my explanatory Note 80, Chapter 1, p. 33. Technically the appeal allowed was only from the district court's replacement plan, but the state briefed all issues in the thought that the invalidation ruling and the replacement ruling were inseparable.

2

THE SUPREME COURT
AND REAPPORTIONMENT

Alexander M. Bickel

Passing the decade and a half of his tenure in review after he had announced his retirement, Chief Justice Earl Warren reflected that the most important achievement of the Court he had headed was the apportionment revolution. That is saying quite a bit, having regard to all else the Warren Court did. And it is a curious judgment.

There has been an apportionment revolution, in the sense that virtually all state legislatures have been reapportioned and most have redistricted their state congressional delegations. But Chief Justice Warren could not have meant that there has also been a consequent revolution in the nation's politics. Despite the most preposterously sanguine expectations with which the effort to engage the federal judiciary in the apportionment of legislatures has been invested ever since the 1940s, success has made little difference—a marginal one, if any, here and there—in the output of the political process.[1] Malapportionment, its foes had persuaded one another, was the source of most of our domestic ills. In it were the roots of the urban crisis and of the obsolescence of federalism. It was the essential reason why "wealth accumulates, and men decay." There are, it has turned out, other roots, less easily reached; other reasons, less easily understood. And if reapportionment has resulted in a redistribution of political power among various groups, the beneficiaries either don't know it yet, or don't know how to use their newly acquired power, or are not the ones who were expected to get it.

1. See Robert G. Dixon, Jr., *Democratic Representation* (New York: Oxford University Press, 1968), pp. 21–22, 574–581; J. T. White and N. C. Thomas, "Urban and Rural Representation in State Legislative Apportionment," 17 *Western Political Quarterly* 724.

Even if it were true that the apportionment revolution had enabled certain groups to get what they want out of the political process, that could scarcely have been Chief Justice Warren's reference when he spoke of the Court's most important achievement, as he saw it. The output of the political process—who gets what—is no business of the Court, and the Chief Justice would not have had, or avowed, any such concern. Most assuredly, he meant rather that the Court's apportionment decisions confirmed a fundamental principle of political organization which was valid regardless of the results it produced; he meant that the Court had secured a salutary observance of the principle of majoritarianism. That is what Chief Justice Warren was celebrating, for as Walter Lippmann wrote of earlier populists, the Chief Justice "is hypnotized by the belief that the great thing is to express the will of the people, first because expression is the highest interest of man, and second because the will is instinctively good." [2]

Actually, Chief Justice Warren is quite wrong. His court's apportionment decisions are no significant achievement. They gave us no new birth of majoritarianism, any more than they changed the substantive course of American politics. But the crucial point against them is that a rigorous majoritarianism is not what our institutions rest on, nor is it what the country needs. To quote Walter Lippmann again, the framers of the American Constitution "did not identify the power of the masses with democracy. They were able to see that the essential problem is to organize this power of the masses so that it may function as a democracy. That is why they made a lasting contribution to political thought. . . . The American founders saw that the problem was no longer what it had been under the Stuart kings against whom their ancestors had rebelled: to obtain protection for the common man as against his masters. In their time the common man already had the power of his former masters; the captains and the kings had departed. Their problem was how to organize the indubitable and inalienable power of the mass in order that it might achieve its own best interests. And since it was obvious that no mass of men can as a mass make more than the simplest decisions of yes and no, and is physically incapable of administering its affairs, the practical question was how a government could be made to represent the people." [3]

And so the American government—as Chief Justice Warren might have

2. Walter Lippmann, *Public Opinion* (New York: Harcourt, Brace, 1922), p. 312.

3. Walter Lippmann, *The Good Society* (New York: Grosset & Dunlap, 1943), pp. 252–253.

been expected to remember; nothing is stranger than a populist judge!—includes a Supreme Court which wields political power and is not only not majoritarian but is not elected at all. Our government includes a Senate, which, because its members are elected at large in each state, has often been more responsive in recent years to liberal and reforming trends than the House, but in which each state, regardless of population, has an equal vote that not even a duly enacted and ratified constitutional amendment can, without its own consent, deprive it of. Our government includes a House of Representatives in which each state has at least one vote, even though the whole state may be (as some are) considerably smaller in population than the average congressional district.

Aside from the fact that very few of our institutions of government (and none of them national) are out-and-out majoritarian, we don't choose to do everything by simple majority votes. It takes a two-thirds vote in the Senate to ratify a treaty and a two-thirds vote in the Senate and the House to propose a Constitutional amendment, which must then be ratified by the legislatures of three-quarters of the states. A Congress in which the entire House and one-third of the Senate are newly elected, and which is thus the authentic voice of a popular majority, if ever there is one in our national institutions, may pass a law, but a President, elected two years earlier and by now, quite possibly, altogether out of tune with the new majority, may veto the law. If he does, it takes a two-thirds vote in the Senate and in the House to override the veto and make a valid law.

One may view all these institutions and devices as outrageously undemocratic—as hardly less undemocratic than a malapportioned legislature—and be prepared to sweep them all away also, including conceivably the Supreme Court itself, the next time the majoritarian broom cleans out the stables. In truth, these institutions and devices tell us that throughout our history we have perceived other realities and other values in government beyond mere responsiveness to simple majorities of the moment, which are in any event not easy to find and as often imaginary as real. And we have defined democracy as the rather complex sum of these values, not just as uncompromising majoritarianism. We have, since Madison, realized that people tend to act politically not so much as individuals as in groups; that they have opinions, preferences, and interests which vary in intensity and thus call for varying degrees of respect and forebearance on the part of others, even if those others constitute a majority; that majorities sometimes act rashly and even mindlessly and may need to be given pause. We have realized, in short, that influence and even power should be distributed more widely than they would be in rigid adherence to the majoritarian principle, so that government may rest on widespread consent, rather than teetering on the knife-edge of a momentary majority. For we have wanted government to be stable and peaceable and to have the most limited need to resort to coercion. What we have evolved, therefore, is not majority rule, but a pluralist system, in Professor Robert Dahl's phrase, of minorities rule. We have striven, it may perhaps be said, not for a majoritarian, but for a participatory democracy, in which access to the process of government is continuously available to all groups. The sensible question to ask about any institution of government, therefore, is not whether it is purely majoritarian, but whether it tends to enhance minorities rule, whether it tends to include or to exclude various groups from influence, and whether, if it assigns disproportionate influence to some groups, they are the ones which are relatively shortchanged elsewhere, so that the total effect is the achievement of a balance of influence.[4]

From the beginning, the Warren Court's apportionment decisions have consistently asked the wrong questions about American political institutions. Not unnaturally, they have also come up with answers which, if they were right in the earliest cases, were accidentally so, and for the wrong reasons and in the end were plain wrong—and trivial, to boot.

The first of the Warren Court's apportionment cases was *Baker* v. *Carr,* decided in March 1962.[5] The position at the time, which had developed through the 1940s, was that apportionment cases raised a political question and were therefore not justiciable, or, as it might as well be put, that apportionment cases were not justiciable and therefore raised a political question. The position had the virtue of embodying a prophecy of the limitations of the judicial process as an instrument for solving the apportionment problem which the Warren Court was to validate in the 1960s. Nevertheless, the position was not altogether satisfactory, partly because apportionment cases do not all raise a single or the same question and the Court failed to discriminate among the various questions raised, and partly because the Court did not altogether adhere to its position. The result of one much-noted apportionment litigation was an inscrutable

4. I have expressed the views embodied in the last three paragraphs in a somewhat different context, but in similar form, in a short paper that appeared as an editorial in *The New Republic,* September 27, 1969, under the title, "Misreading Democracy." To the extent that I have borrowed from my earlier formulation, I do so with the kind permission of the editor-in-chief of *The New Republic,* Gilbert A. Harrison.

5. *Baker* v. *Carr,* 369 U.S. 186 (1962).

decision, saying nothing about nonjusticiability and the political-question doctrine, but suggesting instead that the particular apportionment did not violate any constitutional principles and was lawful.[6] Whatever may have been intended, this course of decision, characterizing the apportionment problem as political but sometimes omitting to say so, served to entrench the status quo. And the judiciary had no more call to do that than to undertake to solve apportionment problems, as the justices who had relegated those problems to the category of nonjusticiable political questions would have been the first to concede.

Baker v. *Carr* itself demonstrates how the apportionment problem parses out into a number of questions, not all of which carry the same aspect, from the point of view of their fitness for judicial settlement. Apportionment of the General Assembly of Tennessee, which was in issue, resulted in dramatic disparities among counties. Some as small as between two and three thousand in population had the same representation as counties of twenty-five to thirty-three thousand population. This feature of the case raised one sort of issue—equality of representation—which was the ultimate and most important one in the view of the litigants, and the one they emphasized. A different sort of issue was presented by the fact that the law under which the General Assembly of Tennessee was apportioned in 1962 dated back to 1901. In six decades—and what eventful decades in the demography of the country!—there had been no fresh apportionment in Tennessee. The Court could well have held that the question of whether there is a duty to apportion, a duty from time to time to apply mind and the resources of the political process to the apportionment problem, was not a political question but a justiciable one. And the Court could have held that the emanations of the census clause of Article I, Section 1, of the Constitution, combined with the republican-form-of-government clause of Article IV, Section 4, were sufficient to authorize the Court to enunciate a rule that each state has a federal constitutional obligation to apportion its legislative bodies or to reexamine its apportionment formula every ten years following the national census.

That was not what the Court held in *Baker* v. *Carr,* although its decision had the effect of causing Tennessee and virtually every other state to reapportion its legislature. What the Court held, rather, was that apportionment problems at wholesale, in all their aspects, were justiciable and no longer to be considered as raising political questions. The Court held secondly that the constitutionality of apportionments was to be adjudicated

6. Compare *Colegrove* v. *Green,* 328 U.S. 549 (1946) and *South* v. *Peters,* 339 U.S. 276 (1950), with *MacDougall* v. *Green,* 335 U.S. 281 (1948).

under the equal protection clause of the Fourteenth Amendment. Said Justice William J. Brennan, speaking for the Court:

> Nor need the appellants, in order to succeed in this action, ask the Court to enter upon policy determinations for which judicially manageable standards are lacking. Judicial standards under the Equal Protection Clause are well-developed and familiar, and it has been open to courts since the enactment of the Fourteenth Amendment to determine, if on the particular facts they must, that a discrimination reflects *no* policy, but simply arbitrary and capricious action.[7]

The passage just quoted was at best a shot in the dark, an arrow wafted skyward in the hope that some appropriate target might find it, and, at worst, an evasion of the problem. The problem in most of its aspects—the real problem, not some figment of wish and theory—was stated by Justice Felix Frankfurter, dissenting in *Baker* v. *Carr*:

> Apportionment, by its character, is a subject of extraordinary complexity, involving—even after the fundamental theoretical issues concerning what is to be represented in a representative legislature have been fought out or compromised—considerations of geography, demography, electoral convenience, economic and social cohesions or divergencies among particular local groups, communications, the practical effects of political institutions like the lobby and the city machine, ancient traditions and ties of settled usage, respect for proven incumbents of long experience and senior status, mathematical mechanics, censuses compiling relevant data, and a host of others.

The equal protection clause, Justice Frankfurter concluded, manifestly supplied no "guide for judicial examination of apportionment methods." [8]

As the close reader of Justice Brennan's opinion could divine, "it has been open to courts" under the Fourteenth Amendment to judge the rationality of legislation, or, more accurately, to hold the legislature to a duty of making policy that is not demonstrably irrational. Of course, to make policy is to choose, and to choose is sometimes to guess or simply to express a preference. A rational choice is far from an inevitable one; but some choices do fall, even if rarely, in an area where the state of human knowledge is such that they can be proved irrational. The difference between the irrational, capricious choice and one based on a permissible preference, which is yet arbitrary in the sense that it is not rationally compelled—that difference may be one of degree, merely. It may be that,

7. *Supra*, n. 5 at 226.
8. *Id*. at 323.

when we call a choice irrational, all we do is balk at an inference from fact or other admitted premises that is simply one degree more remote than other inferences which we accept; and that the fact or other admitted premise from which we proceed to an analytical assault on a legislative choice will in time be shown to be no fact at all, or no valid premise. The whole process is surely vulnerable. But it has done service in American constitutional law, providing the Court with a function that is at once grand enough for judges who are given supreme power, and inherently limited.

The function actually predates the Fourteenth Amendment, stemming as it does from John Marshall's opinion in *McCulloch* v. *Maryland*.[9] It was restated before the turn of the twentieth century by James Bradley Thayer in a paper of fundamental importance, "The Origin and Scope of the American Doctrine of Constitutional Law." [10] A statute was unconstitutional, Thayer said, "when those who have the right to make laws have not merely made a mistake, but have made a very clear one,—so clear that it is not open to rational question." The function of the Supreme Court was to be "the ultimate arbiter of what is rational and permissible." But, then, what is irrational about a legislative apportionment scheme which chooses to favor some groups or interests with disproportionate representation and to disfavor other ones, or which, looking ahead a decade, makes one or another demographic prophecy? Moreover, each district carved out by an apportionment measure represents a choice and a prophecy. There is no warrant for looking at all the choices in the aggregate and demanding that they be rational in the sense that they have an inner consistency, as Justice Tom C. Clark, concurring in *Baker* v. *Carr*, attempted to do. That would be willfully to ignore all the variables, cited by Justice Frankfurter, which infest the task of apportionment.

The equal protection clause, however, and its increasingly indistinguishable twin, the due process clause, have in our tradition authorized the Court to ask another question also: not only whether a legislative choice passes the rather special test of rationality that I have described, but also whether it is otherwise good, otherwise, in Thayer's word, "permissible." The legislature may also have made a very clear mistake, "not open to rational question," in that it went demonstrably beyond the power conferred upon it by the Constitution or demonstrably violated one of the constitutional prohibitions. "Let the end be legitimate," said Marshall in *McCulloch* v. *Maryland*, "let it be within the scope of the

9. *McCulloch* v. *Maryland*, 4 Wheat 316 (1819).
10. 7 *Harvard Law Review* 129.

Constitution, and all means which are appropriate, which are plainly adapted to that end, which are not prohibited, but consist with the letter and spirit of the Constitution, are constitutional." [11] The means chosen by the legislature must therefore not be irrational. But they must be constitutional in another sense, also. They may be rational and yet unconstitutional. And so "it has been open to courts since the enactment of the Fourteenth Amendment [and before] to determine, if on the particular facts they must, that a discrimination reflects" a perfectly rational policy which is unconstitutional.

But, in order to hold that a legislative policy, though rational, is yet unconstitutional, judges have had to find, avow, and formulate a principle which the legislative policy could be said to have violated, and they have had to declare their willingness, indeed their oath-bound determination, to live with that principle consistently. Otherwise, the judges would be in the position of substituting what was merely their own prudential, expedient judgment for that of the political institutions, of substituting their own not irrational preferences for those of the legislators; and it has never proved easy to explain, let alone to defend and justify, the authority of judges to do that. Legislative choices may not be irrational, but they need not be compelled by a process of reasoning from fact and principle, because they are responsive, or at least controllable. But choices made by judges may not be responsive—that is precisely what the idea of judicial independence forbids—and are in theory not controllable. We can scarcely be asked to accept them, therefore, unless we can perceive them as being compelled by a process of reasoning from premises which we do accept, or at least respect—or, if not even respect, then at any rate recognize. And, human reason being fallible, if we do not see a judicial judgment as being compelled by its premises, we must at least be persuaded that the judges themselves viewed it as being so compelled—and sincerely so viewed it.[12]

There was a period of floundering after the decision in *Baker* v. *Carr,* during which it was demonstrated that the apportionment problems had indeed the dimensions that Justice Frankfurter had ascribed to it, and that the arrow Justice Brennan had shot into the sky would remain targetless. The rationality test led nowhere; and within the year the Supreme Court had abandoned it.

Gray v. *Sanders,*[13] decided in 1963, concerned Georgia's notorious county-

11. *Supra,* n. 9 at 421.
12. See L. Jaffe, *English and American Judges as Lawmakers* (London: Clarendon Press Oxford, 1969), p. 38.
13. *Gray* v. *Sanders,* 372 U.S. 368 (1963).

unit system of electing governors. Each county in the state was assigned a unit vote that had little relation to how populous it was. The smallest county, with fewer than 2,000 persons had two unit votes, and the largest, with more than 500,000 persons, had six. The winner of the popular vote in each county got all the unit votes, and the governor was elected by a majority of unit votes. This is a rational system, federal and counterma-joritarian. The Court held it unconstitutional for this very reason. "The conception of political equality from the Declaration of Independence, to Lincoln's Gettysburg Address, to the Fifteenth, Seventeenth, and Nine-teenth Amendments," said Justice William O. Douglas for the Court, "can mean only one thing—one person, one vote." [14] The proposition was qualified only in that it was said to hold within any given constituency, such as the entire state over which the governor was elected to preside. "Once the geographical unit for which a representative is to be chosen is designated, all who participate in the election are to have an equal vote— whatever their race, whatever their sex, whatever their occupation, what-ever their income, and wherever their home may be in that geographical unit." [15] It was thus left somewhat uncertain whether the Court would consider that a whole state legislature or state delegation to Congress repre-sented a geographical unit in which votes must be equal, or whether dis-tricts might still in some measure be unequal so long as everyone within a given district had an equal vote. Here the Court skirted the real prob-lem, but it did skirt it. Here it approached the heart of the matter but instantly scurried off in another, more agreeable, direction. The question is, what is a proper constituency which may be viewed as a unit and federated with other ones? The answer is not easy to come by. But the Court had an easy answer, and it devoted itself to finding a question that could receive it.

The occasion might have been seized to introduce a limited guarantee of majoritarianism into the American constitutional scheme. Within the historic constituency which is a state, and to which a republican form of government is guaranteed by the Constitution, the Court might have held, at least one institution must be strictly majoritarian—must be capable, that is, of being called to account by a majority of voters in the entire constituency, each casting a vote equal in value to that of every other voter. The executive is not only the most suitable candidate for the role of the strictly majoritarian institution; he is also least suited to fulfill the function of reflecting each of a variety of groupings and interests, whereas

14. *Id*. at 381.
15. *Id*. at 378.

a multi-member institution can ideally be designed to do so, through un-equal districting. Hence, the Court might have concluded, the executive must be majoritarian unless it can be shown (as, under the modern electoral college arrangement in the federal system, it can be shown with respect to the President) that his constituency is weighted to balance the weighting of the legislature in favor of other groups. There was, how-ever, no trace of this approach in the Court's opinion.

Following its decision in *Gray* v. *Sanders,* the Court in fairly short order applied its easy answer—one person, one vote—to congressional districting (the House of Representatives, of course; the Senate, as I have noted, is out of reach, by the most explicit constitutional provision) and to the ap-portionment of both houses of state legislatures.[16] So far as Congress was concerned, the Fourteenth Amendment could not be invoked, but the Court, Mr. Justice Hugo L. Black writing, relied instead on Article I, Section 2, of the Constitution, which says that the House "shall be com-posed of Members chosen every second Year by the People of the several states." Justice Black brought to bear some questionable history and also propelled himself toward his result by stressing the word, "people," in the language just quoted. To the state legislatures the Court spoke through Chief Justice Warren, and for him the word "people," although it did not appear in the Fourteenth Amendment, which was now again in play, was also fraught with great and solemn significance.

In both decisions the Court took care to leave some opening for devia-tion. Only substantial equality of districts was required, said Justice Black, not mathematical precision. And only deviations from strict equality that were too egregious were unconstitutional, said Chief Justice Warren, not districts that had been rendered as nearly equal as was practicable. This was nothing but an arbitrary, expedient escape hatch, since perfect mathematical equality of districts is entirely practicable. It may rest on census figures that are dated, but so would an intentionally imperfect equality of districts; and there may be a question of who is to be counted —all residents, only those eligible to vote, or only those registered to vote —but once those questions are decided, perfect equality is fully practicable.

Because this escape hatch was a wholly arbitrary expedient, and be-cause of the altogether commendable tendency of the judicial process to seek a foundation in principle for its results and to eschew involvement in the making of arbitrary choices, the escape hatch was eventually shut, the practicable was recognized as practicable, and even very small devia-tions from mathematically precise equality of legislative districts were no

16. *Wesberry* v. *Sanders,* 376 U.S. 1 (1964); *Reynolds* v. *Sims,* 377 U.S. 533 (1964).

longer tolerated.[17] But the nagging misgivings about the absoluteness of the one person, one vote, rule, or, rather, about its essential rightness, which had caused the Court to open an escape hatch in the first place and which the Court eventually fought down in legislative apportionment cases, surfaced again when the Court came to apply its rule to school boards, among other local government bodies. Again the Court said that any voter had the "right to have his own vote given as much weight, *as far as is practicable,* as that of any other voter" (italics supplied); and again it suggested that "mathematical exactitude is not required," although—whatever this may mean—"a plan that does not automatically [as opposed to deliberately, or as opposed to sporadically?] discriminate in favor of certain districts" was required. And again, no doubt, the disingenuous escape hatch will eventually be closed.[18]

It was in *Reynolds* v. *Sims,* decided in 1964, two years after *Baker* v. *Carr,* which applied the one person, one vote, rule to state legislatures, that Chief Justice Warren gave voice to the full-blown populist majoritarianism whose triumph he celebrated in his postretirement reflections. To be sure, he spoke also of individual equality, the equal weight of one man's vote and another's. But he brought a great statistical apparatus to bear, to show that a malapportioned legislature enabled a minority to rule. He proclaimed:

> Legislators represent people, not trees or acres. Legislators are elected by voters, not farms or cities or economic interests. . . . Logically, in a society ostensibly grounded on representative government, it would seem reasonable that a majority of the people of a State could elect a majority of that State's legislators. To conclude differently, and to sanction minority control of State legislative bodies, would appear to deny majority rights in a way that far surpasses any possible denial of minority rights that might otherwise be thought to result. Since legislatures are responsible for enacting laws by which all citizens are to be governed, they should be bodies which are collectively responsive to the popular will.

It was unconstitutional, the chief justice also said, to take account of "economic or other sorts of group interests" in apportioning a legislature. "Citizens, not history or economic interests, cast votes." [19] In Colorado, from which one of the cases decided at that time came, a departure from

17. See, for example, *Swann* v. *Adams,* 385 U.S. 440 (1967); *Kirkpatrick* v. *Preisler,* 394 U.S. 526 (1969); Dixon, *Democratic Representation,* pp. 439–455.

18. *Hadley* v. *Junior College District,* 397 U.S. 50 (1960).

19. *Reynolds* v. *Sims,* 377 U.S. at 562, 565, 579–580.

the one person, one vote, standard had been approved overwhelmingly in a referendum. It was unconstitutional, the Court held, even for a popular majority to deny itself the right to rule as a majority.[20] And later, when closing the escape hatch of "practicability" in a congressional districting case, the Court said: "Missouri contends that [population] variances were necessary to avoid fragmenting areas with distinct economic and social interests and thereby diluting the effective representation of those interests in Congress. But to accept population variances, large or small, in order to create districts with specific interest orientations is antithetical to the basic premise of the constitutional command to provide equal representation for equal numbers of people." [21]

In 1966, in *Fortson* v. *Morris*,[22] the Court did deviate—quite arbitrarily and, within the terms of its prior and later decisions, quite indefensibly —from the basic premise of majoritarianism. In Georgia's general election of November 1966 (held as a popular election, the unit-vote system having been struck down three years earlier by *Gray* v. *Sanders*) Howard H. Callaway received 47.07 percent of the total vote cast for governor, and Lester G. Maddox, 46.88 percent. (Six percent of the vote went to a third candidate.) Under the Georgia constitution, if no candidate obtains an absolute majority, the decision is left to the legislature. The Supreme Court, in an opinion by Justice Black, held that the Georgia legislature could indeed make the decision and make it either way. The Georgia legislature was at this point still malapportioned, but that, held Justice Black, did not matter. In the event, the legislature gave the governorship to Maddox, the minority choice.

Justice Black did not really attempt to reconcile his conclusion with the basic premise of majoritarianism. Earlier decisions had not necessarily rested on that premise, he suggested. They concerned, rather and merely, the "equal right of 'all who participate in the election' to vote and have their votes counted without impairment or dilution." Dissenting, Justice Abe Fortas pointed out that his brother Black was reducing the earlier decisions to nothing but "much ado about form." Actually, he went on, the vote is "the basic instrument of democracy," and the earlier apportionment decisions protected "not merely the casting of the vote or its mechanical counting . . . [but] the function—the office—the effect given to the vote." The vote was "not an object of art. It is the sacred and most important instrument of democracy and of freedom. In simple terms, the

20. *Lucas* v. *Colorado General Assembly*, 377 U.S. 713 (1964).
21. *Kirkpatrick* v. *Preisler*, 394 U.S. at 533.
22. *Fortson* v. *Morris*, 385 U.S. 231, 233, 249, 250 (1966).

vote is meaningless—it no longer serves the purpose of the democratic society—unless it, taken in the aggregate with the votes of other citizens, results in effecting the will of those citizens provided that they are more numerous than those of differing views. That is the meaning and effect of the great constitutional decisions of this Court."

Fortson v. *Morris* was an aberration, the action of an umpire who momentarily thinks he may have made a wrong call against one team and evens the scales by making a wrong call against the other team, as well. That is, of course, not justice, and it is not law. The Court soon returned to a more faithful discharge of the function of adjudication. It not only reaffirmed the premise of majoritarianism in legislative apportionment cases following *Fortson* v. *Morris,* but, despite some initial hesitation, it reasoned consistently from the premise in cases involving local government bodies.[23]

Curiously enough, in the case in which it finally (and necessarily, from the point of view of inner consistency) made the wholehearted decision to apply the one person, one vote, rule to local government bodies, the Court drew a dissent from the same Justice Fortas whose paean to majoritarianism was the only redeeming feature of *Fortson* v. *Morris.* Now Justice Fortas complained that the one person, one vote, rule took no account of "a complex of values and factors" which complicated "the arithmetic simplicity of one equals one." Justice Fortas listed some of these values and factors in a fashion reminiscent of the Frankfurter dissent in *Baker* v. *Carr.*[24] They were, of course, values and factors that threw the rule of one person, one vote, altogether into doubt. Certainly they have application to statewide legislative bodies. Justice Fortas, who had objected in *Fortson* v. *Morris* to Justice Black's taking of an arbitrary distinction, chose to perpetrate one of his own. But the Court did not. This time, also, Justice Fortas was in dissent.

The one person, one vote, rule, I have suggested, gave us no new birth of majoritarianism. It is at best a triviality, the movement of mountains and the birth of mice. That is so because, even assuming the existence of a stable popular majority, any districted legislature is as likely to misrepresent as to register it. Obviously, the losing vote in narrowly divided districts, combined with the vote that prevails in other districts by a substantial margin may constitute the true majority, which may yet not

23. See, for example, *Kirkpatrick, supra,* n. 17; compare *Sailors* v. *Board of Education,* 387 U.S. 105 (1967), with *Avery* v. *Midland County, Texas,* 390 U.S. 474 (1968), and *Hadley, supra,* n. 18.
24. *Avery, supra,* n. 23 at 480, 496.

be represented in the legislature. The device for ensuring this result is called gerrymandering when it is used intentionally (although it is, of course, always a guess and cannot guarantee its own success); otherwise, it is simply called districting. But the result, whether fallibly intended or infallibly accidental, follows anyway. The Court has invented no means of rendering the intentional result more difficult to achieve, let alone of preventing it; and, in fact, the Court has made gerrymandering easier by requiring that the established boundaries of subdivisions of government, such as counties, be disregarded in the process of districting.[25] As to the same result unintentionally achieved—plain districting—the Court has also said nothing, and there is little it could say. To abolish districting would be not only to let the majority rule, but to let it rule quite alone without opposition, by entirely excluding the minority from representation.

Minorities, not unnaturally, are quite aware of the disadvantages that are imposed on them by at-large elections in undistricted constituencies, and they have sought judicial redress. Thus the at-large election of the Boston school committee, which goes back in that city's history to 1875, has been attacked (so far without success) in a suit brought by Black plaintiffs who claimed that their distinct community, constituting 13 percent of the city's population, was deprived of representation on the committee.[26] It is hard to see what sort of judicial remedy could be evolved in cases of this sort. Districting distorts majority rule. At-large elections deprive minorities even of a voice. Is the Court to entrench either evil in the Constitution?

The tendency of the one person, one vote, rule, which may appear to be neutral so far as this choice of evils is concerned, is naturally, and has in practice been, to encourage the enlargement of constituencies and thus to bring about the evil of at-large elections. Thus, the creation of multi-member legislative districts, in which all members are elected at large, has been a fairly common phenomenon as the states have striven to meet the requirements of the one person, one vote, principle. Not only have minority interests complained, but so have voters in other, smaller districts, on the theory that the majority in a large multi-member district enjoys disproportionate power because it elects more legislators than may a numerically almost equal majority in a smaller district having fewer assigned members.[27] The Supreme Court, so far, has indicated no general

25. See Dixon, *Democratic Representation,* p. 18.

26. *Owens v. School Committee of Boston,* 304 F. Supp. 1327 (D. Mass. 1969).

27. See J. F. Banzhaf III, "Multi-Member Electoral Districts—Do They Violate the 'One Man, One Vote' Principle?" 75 *Yale Law Journal* 1309.

disapproval of multi-member districts.[28] But a federal court in Indiana declared a large multi-member legislative district (with fifteen representatives and eight senators) covering Marion County, which includes Indianapolis and adjacent areas, unconstitutional on the ground that it deprived "Negroes and poor persons" living in well defined neighborhoods in Indianapolis of representation. Those groups, said the court, had distinct interests in certain legislative subjects which diverged from the interests of other voters in the county. The court seemed to accept the allegation of one of the Negro plaintiffs that he was a member "of a cognizable interest group which regularly engages in bloc voting but whose bloc voting is cancelled out by the voting of contrary interest groups in Marion County-wide elections." [29]

Indiana was ordered to break up the Marion County district. But how was Indiana to comply? The court estimated that the "Negro Center Township Ghetto" in Indianapolis was "sufficient in size" to elect approximately two representatives and one senator from single-member districts.[30] From any single-member districts? Certainly not. Yes, if the districts were gerrymandered or drawn, if you will, to contain a large Black majority.[31] Not otherwise. And suppose the existence of a Black community which has its special interests and is just as much in need of representation, but is too small to elect a legislator or a federal congressman? Do not all the considerations adduced by the court in the Marion County case counsel that a district should be malapportioned for such a smaller community? Why, to these ends, is gerrymandering a more acceptable means than malapportionment?

A solution can be found, to be sure, in proportional representation, but this is a device that has been known to have a powerful fragmenting effect on government, often paralyzing it by putting the entire burden of coalition-formation on the legislature itself, rather than encouraging the formation of initial coalitions in the electoral process. In any event, whether or not because it is aware of its disadvantages, the Court has not undertaken to impose the proportional representation method on multi-member units of American government.

And so we have been given an appearance of majoritarianism without

28. See *Fortson* v. *Dorsey*, 379 U.S. 433 (1965); *Burns* v. *Richardson*, 384 U.S. 73 (1966). See also *Smith* v. *Paris*, 257 F. Supp. 901 (M.D. Ala. 1966); but compare *Sims* v. *Baggett*, 247 F. Supp. 96, 109 (M.D. Ala. 1965).

29. *Chavis* v. *Whitcomb*, 305 F. Supp. 1364, 1367 (S.D. Ind. 1969).

30. *Id.* at 1385.

31. Compare *Wright* v. *Rockefeller*, 376 U.S. 52 (1964); *Wells* v. *Rockefeller*, 311 Fed. Supp. 48 (S.D.N.Y. 1970).

its substance. Appearances that are inconsistent with substance contain the seed of destruction because they are vulnerable to the charge of deception and cynicism. But one need not take such an apocalyptic view of the one person, one vote, rule and its consequences in order to deplore it. For the rule has very real present costs. It necessarily deprives discrete groupings and interests, regional, racial, and other, of direct representation. It makes impossible in state and local government the application in any degree of the method of federalism. At a time when division among groups and interests is as marked and deeply felt as ever; when unity is something to be striven for, to be painstakingly constructed and perhaps attained, but not to be taken for granted; when the call for functional decentralization in government is insistent; at a time, in sum, when the participatory aspect of our democracy needs the greatest emphasis and when, therefore, the device of federalism should be available for the freest and most imaginative use, the Court has virtually outlawed it.

It seems to be generally conceded that the structure of urban government is obsolete. The cities serve many more people, groups, and interests than they govern and can tax, given the present limits of their jurisdiction. Jurisdictional lines ought to be redrawn, therefore, as occasionally they have been in the past. This is conventional wisdom, but it seems nonetheless to be right. Yet, if the jurisdiction of central urban government is to be expanded to encompass outlying suburban areas, the one person, one vote, rule will surely be an insurmountable obstacle, one that must be removed. For metropolitan government organized on the one person, one vote, principle will necessarily mean either that the central city, increasingly Black and poor, governs the suburban middle class whose interests are distinct and in many respects adverse, or that the suburban middle class, combined with its remnants in the central city, governs the Black and the poor, whose interests are distinct and in many respects adverse. Neither result is possible politically; neither result is right. Again, Indianapolis provides an example. Its home-rule jurisdiction was enlarged on a one person, one vote, basis to take in all of Marion County under a system called, inelegantly enough, Uni-Gov. The Black community in Indianapolis promptly attacked Uni-Gov.[32] The solution, as the members of our own Philadelphia Convention discovered nearly two centuries ago and as subsequent consolidators of existing constituencies have discovered since, cannot be populist. It must be federal.

The federal solution is equally called for in the governance of public

32. *Supra,* n. 29 at 1359; see also, for example, *supra,* n. 24 at 486, 492–494 (Justice Harlan dissenting).

schools. For a variety of reasons, there has been a trend toward the consolidation of previously separate school districts in recent years. Where the units to be merged are pretty much alike in resources and in the ethnic, racial, and social composition of student bodies, there is no great problem. Where the units are not alike, however, their interests tend to diverge, and consolidation under a central authority on a one person, one vote, basis will be resisted, and is not right. Enlargement of administrative jurisdiction over schools offers the only practical possibility for any—if any—integration of the races in the public schools around urban centers throughout the nation. Enlargement of administrative jurisdiction in one fashion or another, and for this and perhaps some additional purposes, means consolidation of units, typically of a central-city school district with its suburban neighbors. The interests of urban and suburban districts do not altogether coincide, and the natures of their student populations and their resources differ; that is the whole point of the drive to integrate them. The federal method of consolidation is the fairest and most efficient, and it may be the only possible one. Yet the Court has set its face against it.[33]

There is a countertrend in the governance of public schools toward decentralization. The aim is to permit cohesive communities to control their own schools through locally elected boards. Schools in large measure may appropriately be viewed as extensions of coherent groups of families, but the education by any group of its children nevertheless has externalities which affect larger communities. The retention of some supervisory authority in a central board of education will, therefore, probably not be avoided. But if the central board is constituted on a one person, one vote, basis and elected at large, or if it must be elected from equal districts that are not coterminous with the local school communities (which are, in turn, very probably not going to be of equal size), then the authority of the central board may negate a good part of what decentralization seeks to attain. Hence, the federal solution is again appropriate.

The federal device was used naturally enough in the New York City decentralization statute. For the interim, the statute provided for a central New York City board of education consisting of five members, of which the president of each of the five boroughs constituting New York City would appoint one. The boroughs were unequal in population. As of February 1970, a permanent board was to be established, consisting of seven members, two to be appointed by the mayor and five to be elected, one from each borough. The scheme embodied a recognition that the

33. *Supra,* n. 18.

interests of the five boroughs in their schools did not coincide, since the racial and social composition of the student bodies varied from borough to borough. This scheme was a building block in constructing the decentralized school system; it was a feature of an elaborate adjustment of conflicting group interests. But it took no more than one individual to put it in question by suit in federal court, and the court inevitably struck it down, since its inconsistency with the one person, one vote, principle was beyond argument. (Ironically enough, the court held that, although the elected board was unconstitutional, the interim appointive one was not, as the one person, one vote, rule applied only to elections. That's democracy!)[34]

These problems, which arise at the level of local government, are not to be taken as proof merely that the one person, one vote, rule should not have been extended to local government. Rather they are, at the moment, the most salient illustrations of the inanities and deficiencies of the rule. The general verdict on the consequences of the rule at all levels of government is this: Nothing of importance was improved, much that was indifferent or acceptable was made worse, and a great deal that could be better was made more difficult.

*   *   *

COMMENTARY by Carl A. Auerbach

Writing in 1962, after *Baker* v. *Carr*[1] had been decided, Professor Bickel advised caution for those who thought that *Colegrove* v. *Green*[2] no longer had any applicability:

> The millennium has not arrived for urban voters. A crack in the judicial gate that should not have been closed in *Colegrove* v. *Green* has now been pried open, but the gate has not swung on its hinges. Urban voters will be snatching defeat from the jaws of victory if they now concentrate all their energies on law suits and focus their hopes of ultimate success on the judiciary.[3]

34. *Oliver* v. *Board of Education of City of New York*, 306 F. Supp. 1286 (S.D.N.Y. 1969).
1. *Baker* v. *Carr*, 369 U.S. 186 (1962).
2. *Colegrove* v. *Green*, 328 U.S. 549 (1946).
3. Alexander M. Bickel, *The Least Dangerous Branch: The Supreme Court at the Bar of Politics* (Indianapolis: Bobbs-Merrill, 1962), p. 195.

Bickel read *Baker* v. *Carr* as if it were intended only to prod state legislatures into action; once they acted to cure the situation in some degree, he thought, "there will be little more that the judicial process can or should do." [4]

I recall Bickel's failure to foresee the outcome of the reapportionment cases, not to make the point that even so close a student of the Court was wrong once and may be wrong again. That is our common fate. But I do so to warn of the hazards and inappropriateness of prediction when it is used to persuade others, particularly the Supreme Court of the United States, to take action that will make it come true. Prediction then merely expresses a policy preference and a hope that others will come to share it. Whether the reapportionment cases will give us a "new birth of majoritarianism" and change "the substantive course of American politics" will depend upon the result of struggles between the political parties and within each political party, which cannot now be foretold. In any case, the reapportionment cases are not, as Bickel claims, either "plainly wrong" or "trivial." [5]

ARE THE REAPPORTIONMENT CASES "PLAINLY WRONG"?

The Principled Nature of Supreme Court Adjudication in Area

Professor Bickel agrees that the Supreme Court had a legitimate and useful, but limited, role to play in reapportionment. It should merely have required that legislatures reapportion after each national census and that at least one institution of state government—the executive—be strictly majoritarian. Had the Court stopped there, it would indeed have been indulging "in merely empty rhetoric, sounding a word of promise to the ear, sure to be disappointing to the hope." [6]

Apparently, Bickel took this position because he did not—as Mr. Justice Frankfurter did not[7]—anticipate that the justices would formulate the "one vote, one value" principle and, to use Bickel's words, "declare their

---

4. *Id.* at 196–197.

5. My views on the reapportionment cases are elaborated in Carl A. Auerbach, "The Reapportionment Cases: One Person, One Vote—One Vote, One Value," 1964 *Supreme Court Review* 1. Elsewhere, too, Bickel has hedged his uncompromising verdict. "The future," he writes, "may yet belong to the Warren Court." Bickel, *The Supreme Court and the Idea of Progress* (New York: Harper & Row, 1970), p. 173.

6. Mr. Justice Frankfurter dissenting, *supra*, n. 1 at 270.

7. *Id.* at 268–269.

willingness . . . to live with that principle consistently." But this is precisely what the Court has done, thereby avoiding the "political thicket." *Fortson* v. *Morris*[8] is not the aberration from this principle that Bickel makes out. Mr. Justice Black held, correctly in my opinion, that if the U.S. Constitution does not prohibit a state legislature from selecting the governor initially, it follows that it does not prohibit a state legislature from selecting as governor one of the two men who received the highest number of votes in an election in which neither polled a majority. In this case, unlike *Gray* v. *Sanders,* the people of Georgia were entrusted with the final selection of the governor only if a candidate received a majority of the votes in the election; otherwise the people, in effect, nominated the two candidates between whom the legislature would choose. In *Gray* v. *Sanders,* the people were given the final choice, but their votes were counted in such a way that, as Mr. Justice Black explained, "the number of votes of persons living in large counties was given no more weight in electing state officers than was given to a far fewer number of votes of persons residing in small counties." [9]

Obviously, the system of selecting a governor upheld in *Fortson* v. *Morris* allows for more popular participation and is therefore more consistent with the spirit of the reapportionment cases, than initial selection of a governor by the legislature. It would have been anomalous to declare the former, but not the latter, system unconstitutional. Nor is it clear how the equal protection clause could be used to compel the popular election of state governors. Mr. Justice Fortas suggested the use for this purpose of Article IV, Section 4, which guarantees to states the republican form of government. But the implications of such use of this constitutional guarantee on the manner of selecting other state executive officials and the permissible functions of representative assemblies are far-reaching and troublesome.

Finally, it was difficult for the Court to hold that the Georgia legislature had no legitimate authority to select the governor because it was itself malapportioned. The Court had held that the Georgia assembly could nevertheless continue to function until May 1, 1968;[10] the election involved in *Fortson* v. *Morris* had been held November 8, 1966. Mr. Justice Fortas urged the Court to distinguish between ordinary legislative activities which a malapportioned legislature is permitted to carry on by virtue

8. *Fortson* v. *Morris,* 385 U.S. 231 (1966).
9. *Ibid.*
10. *Id.* at 235. See *Toombs* v. *Fortson,* 384 U.S. 210 (1966); *affirming, per curiam,* 241 F. Supp. 65 (N.D. Ga. 1965).

of judicial recognition of its de facto status as a legislature, and extraordinary activities which such a legislature should not be permitted to conduct.[11] Selection of a governor, like submission of a new constitution, should be deemed to be an extraordinary activity. While I am persuaded by Mr. Justice Fortas on this point, I do not think the Court's rejection of this argument and its final holding in the case tear at the principle of equal representation or merit Bickel's scorn.

Bickel acknowledges the principled nature of Supreme Court adjudication following *Fortson* v. *Morris,* but he thinks the principle enunciated is "plainly wrong."

Who Should Be Represented in a Democracy: Groups and Interests or Citizens?

Contrary to Bickel's contention, one who agrees with the reapportionment cases is not necessarily an advocate of a "full-blown populist majoritarianism." Of course, our institutions do not rest on an "uncompromising majoritarianism." Representation in Congress is not apportioned strictly according to population. Many congressional actions require more than a simple majority vote to become effective. The Constitution contains guarantees of individual and group rights which may not be invaded by the coalition of minorities constituting the temporary majority. These guarantees are enforced by an independent Supreme Court manned by appointed judges with life tenure. But all these facts of our political life may convince even one who is not a populist majoritarian that there is all the more need to strengthen majority rule by adhering to the one vote, one value, principle.

Professor Bickel's basic objection is that this principle "necessarily deprives discrete groupings and interests, regional, racial, and other, of direct representation." He would have a legislature apportioned so as to create, ideally, a "balance of influence" among the groups and interests in the society. This will require that a group or interest "shortchanged" somewhere in the system be favored elsewhere with representation disproportionate to its numbers. Bickel propounded this theme before the reapportionment cases were decided, and it is echoed in the dissenting opinions of Mr. Justice John M. Harlan and Mr. Justice Potter Stewart.

I have elsewhere affirmed that direct representation of group or interest is undesirable in a democracy.[12] The values sought by such representation are inconsistent with those promoted by geographic districting. While the

11. *Fortson, supra,* n. 8 at 245–246 (Justice Fortas dissenting).
12. *Supra,* n. 5, pp. 27–30, 36–57.

former exacerbates the clash of different groups and interests by politiciz-
ing them, the latter mutes the clash by emphasizing the role of the individual voter as citizen.

In any case, the systems of apportionment and geographic districting
that predated the reapportionment cases were hardly designed to insure
a "balance of influence" of all groups and interests. Furthermore, even if
an electoral district is relatively homogeneous in its composition, by
racial, religious, and social class, why should it be given representation
disproportionate to its population? Bickel's reply to this question, like
the dissents of Mr. Justice Harlan and Mr. Justice Stewart (but unlike
that of Mr. Justice Frankfurter in *Baker* v. *Carr*) has antimajoritarian
overtones reminiscent of Calhoun's theory of the concurrent majority.
With Professor Sidney Hook, I believe that the feared dictatorship of the
majority in a democratic state is a "bugaboo which haunts the books of
political theorists but has never been found in the flesh in modern history." [13]

It is strange that Bickel never once mentions political parties, to whom
we look to synthesize conflicting groups and interests and which function
as the principal instrument of political consensus in our democracy. Yet
Bickel does not advocate malapportionment as a means of weighting the
influence of the various regions, groups, or interests represented in each
political party.[14]

Is Malapportionment Consistent with Majority Rule?

Pressure groups achieve a degree of "functional representation" by their
direct and significant participation in the legislative and administrative
processes of lawmaking. Why should not the political party which suc-

13. Sidney Hook, *The Paradoxes of Freedom* (Berkeley; University of California
Press, 1962), p. 66.

14. See Alexander M. Bickel's Statement Before the Democratic National Committee's Rules Commission, Washington, D.C., May 17, 1969, and Alexander M.
Bickel, "Fair Representation of Minority Political Views," Memorandum Submitted
to Democratic National Committee's Commission on Party Structure and Delegate
Selection (undated). (The statement and memorandum have not been reprinted
but have been made public.) Bickel is willing to accept only two departures from
the principle of apportionment according to population of delegates to the Democratic National Convention. He would allow each state, regardless of population,
to have two delegates and a modest bonus for its Democratic voting strength. He
also recommends that each member of a convention committee and of the Democratic National Committee be accorded a vote weighted according to the national
convention vote his state is entitled to cast. The "minority" representation he would
assure would be only for minorities that grouped themselves about particular issues
or candidates.

ceeds in forming the coalition attracting the largest number of voters be able to govern? By and large, however, malapportionment has been used to give minorities either effective control of state legislatures or the power to veto any legislative action.

In 1960, for example, malapportionment in thirteen states gave a rural minority of the population a solid majority in both houses of the legislature; in six states, it gave a rural minority control over one house of the legislature and substantial overrepresentation in the other.[15] In eleven states in 1960, the majority of the population was rural, yet malapportionment was resorted to, not to protect the urban minority, but to seriously overrepresent the rural majority in both houses of the legislature.[16] In nineteen states, malapportionment attenuated the urban majority's control of both houses of the legislature.[17] In only these states could it be argued that malapportionment was a possible device for protecting the rural minority.

Is Malapportionment Necessary to Protect Minorities?

Bickel is particularly concerned about the political influence of racial and ethnic minorities and the poor. It is not very likely that malapportioned legislatures favoring those who live in small towns and the country will be eager to give the economically depressed racial and ethnic groups of our large urban areas more political influence than their numbers warrant. However, Bickel thinks there was a chance, somehow, to use malapportionment for this purpose and that the Supreme Court erred in killing it. He also claims that the one vote, one value, principle has stimulated resort to at-large elections in multi-member districts in order to quash minority interests. There is little evidence to date to support his charge. Moreover, there is no reason to suppose that a majority ready to impose at-large elections to this end would not also employ malapportionment for the same purpose.

For example, the governing majority of the Indiana legislature, seeking to weaken the influence of Negroes in Indianapolis, could have used malapportionment to this end, if that had been permissible. At the same time, it would also have had an incentive to create multi-member districts in order further to submerge the influence of Black voters.[18]

15. J. T. White and N. C. Thomas, "Urban and Rural Representation and State Legislative Apportionments," 17 *Western Political Quarterly* 724, 728.

16. *Id.* at 730.

17. *Ibid.* In the remaining state, Massachusetts, the urban majority of the population was slightly overrepresented in both houses. *Id.* at 726.

18. See *Chavis* v. *Whitcomb*, 305 F. Supp. 1364 (S.D. Ind. 1969).

While it is true, as Bickel writes, that the Supreme Court "so far, has indicated no general disapproval of multi-member districts," it has also indicated no general approval. In *Fortson* v. *Dorsey*,[19] the Court warned:

It might well be that, designedly or otherwise, a multi-member constituency apportionment scheme, under circumstances of a particular case, would operate to minimize or cancel out the voting strength of racial or political elements of the voting population. When this is demonstrated it will be time enough to consider whether the system still passes constitutional muster.[20]

In *Burns* v. *Richardson*,[21] the Court spelled out some of the circumstances under which multi-member districting might be subject to successful constitutional attack:

It may be that this invidious effect [of multi-member districts] can more easily be shown if, in contrast to the facts in *Fortson,* districts are large in relation to the total number of legislators, if districts are not appropriately subdistricted to assure distribution of legislators that are resident over the entire district, or if such districts characterize both houses of a bicameral legislature rather than one.[22]

The three-judge district court in *Chavis* v. *Whitcomb* found such an invidious effect and ordered statewide redistricting of both houses of Indiana's general assembly. It intimated that the districts would all have to be either single-member districts or multi-member districts of equal size and not so large "as to create the improper dilution of minority group voting strength found in the instant case."[23]

The district court in the Boston school committee case did not find such an invidious effect.[24] Because the at-large election of the school committee went back to 1875, the court concluded that it could not have been deliberately adopted for the purpose of minimizing the voting influence of Boston's Negroes. Nor was it shown, since the case arose on motion for a preliminary injunction, that prohibiting the at-large election was the only way to protect the voting effectiveness of the Negroes. The court raised the possibility—which Bickel ignores—that the Black minority,

19. *Fortson* v. *Dorsey*, 379 U.S. 433 (1965).
20. *Id.* at 439.
21. *Burns* v. *Richardson*, 384 U.S. 73 (1966).
22. *Id.* at 88, n. 14. The Court reiterated this caveat in *Kilgarlin* v. *Hill*, 386 U.S. 120, 122, 125, n. 3 (1967).
23. *Supra*, n. 18 at 1392.
24. *Owens* v. *School Committee of Boston*, 304 F. Supp. 1327 (D. Mass. 1969).

constituting 13 percent of the electorate, might, in some circumstances attending an at-large election, "in fact hold a balance of power position where it could effectively influence the election of all five members of the School Board." [25]

There are ways other than malapportionment to protect minorities, which have not been outlawed by the Supreme Court because they are consistent with majority rule. For example, even in multi-member districts, minority interests may be afforded a measure of protection by creating residential subdistricts and by requiring that at least one person to be elected come from each of the subdistricts. Indeed, the Supreme Court has stated that a multi-member district will be less subject to challenge if it is "appropriately subdistricted to assure distribution of legislators that are resident over the entire district." [26] In outlawing the multi-member district composed of Marion County, Indiana, the federal district court stressed the absence of residential subdistricts.[27] Furthermore, the Supreme Court has not required that residential subdistricts contain equal numbers of persons.[28]

Other, possibly more desirable, measures are also available to protect

25. *Id.* at 1329–1330. Bickel has justified ethnic-group constituencies under all circumstances. "I believe," he wrote, "the Silk Stockings should be represented by a man specially responsive and congenial to them, whoever he may be . . . I think the same of Negroes, Puerto Ricans, farmers, and other distinguishable groups of reasonable size." Alexander M. Bickel, Letter to Editor, 36 *Commentary* 344 (1963).

26. *Supra,* n. 21 at 88, n. 14.

27. *Supra,* n. 18 at 1387.

28. *Supra,* n. 19; *Dusch* v. *Davis,* 387 U.S. 112 (1967); *Sailors* v. *Board of Education,* 387 U.S. 105 (1967); *Board of Supervisors of Suffolk County* v. *Bianchi,* 387 U.S. 97 (1967); and *Moody* v. *Flowers,* 387 U.S. 105 (1967). None of these cases involved a state legislature. Professor Dixon doubts that the Supreme Court will tolerate unequal residential subdistricts for elections to state legislatures. Robert G. Dixon, Jr., *Democratic Representation* (New York: Oxford University Press, 1968), p. 513. Nor does he think it should do so, because if "it matters where within a large legislative district a given legislator lives . . . a single member district situation is being approximated; the equal representaton spirit of *Reynolds* v. *Sims* should apply and require equal population in the residence subdistricts" (p. 512).

I am inclined to disagree with Dixon because, as the Court stated in *Fortson* v. *Dorsey,* a legislator whose "tenure depends upon the county-wide [multi-member district] electorate . . . must be vigilant to serve the interests of all the people in the county, and not merely those of people in his home district; thus in fact he is the county's and not merely the district's" legislator. 379 U.S. at 438.

For this very reason, it is acknowledged, a legislator may not be as single-minded a representative of the people in his residential subdistrict as he would be if it were a single-member district. On the other hand, it is not obvious that the electorate as a whole would punish him for being such a representative, because his successor would also have to come from the same residential subdistrict.

minorities—"place" voting in multi-member districts, weighted and fractional voting, limited voting, cumulative voting, and proportional representation.[29] If we assume, as Bickel does, that a legislative majority is willing to use malapportionment to protect minorities, the same majority should be willing to use these other measures for the same purpose.

It is not always clear when Bickel accepts and when he rejects the principle of majority rule. He seems to argue that this principle, if based on one vote, one value, will make it impossible even to establish metropolitan government, which he thinks is necessary. If the majority of the metropolitan area's population is located in the central city, the middle-class people in the suburbs will not consent to such government. If the majority is located in the suburbs, the people of the central city—increasingly, the Black and poor—will not consent to such government. The "solution," Bickel insists, "cannot be populist, it must be federal." But why must it be so?

The Supreme Court has not said that a metropolitan government may not contain certain "federal" features—that is, a division of functions which will give the central city and each suburb the measure of home rule considered desirable under the circumstances. But obviously the metropolitan or regional government must have important powers over the area as a whole; otherwise, there is no point to its existence. Surely Bickel does not suggest that the Supreme Court should allow the "device of federalism" to be used to give the minority of people in the suburbs or the central city, as the case may be, control over the metropolitan or regional government. *Avery* v. *Midland County, Texas*[30] is an excellent example of how the "device of federalism" was used to defeat majority rule of the county government. Three districts with populations of 852, 414, and 828 could elect three county commissioners and control the county government; the fourth district, with a population of 67,906 (95 percent of the county's total population), could elect only one county commissioner.[31] The Supreme Court outlawed the device of federalism in this situation, and properly so.

Nor would the "federal method of consolidation" have been consistent with majority rule, or otherwise appropriate, in *Hadley* v. *Junior College District*,[32] as Mr. Justice Harlan, again in dissent, recognized.[33] The same

29. See generally, Dixon, *Democratic Representation*, pp. 503–527, and Ruth C. Silva, "Relation of Representation and the Party System to the Number of Seats Apportioned to a Legislative District," 17 *Western Political Quarterly* 742, 748–759.

30. *Avery* v. *Midland County, Texas*, 390 U.S. 474 (1968).

31. *Id.* at 476.

32. *Hadley* v. *Junior College District*, 397 U.S. 50 (1970).

conclusion is called for in *Oliver* v. *Board of Education of City of New York*.[34] Decentralization itself introduced an additional federal feature into the government of New York City's public schools. The division of functions between the local school board and the central board was intended to attain the basic objective of decentralization. There was no reason to assume that the discharge of the duties entrusted to the central board would adversely affect the overrepresented boroughs more than it did the underrepresented boroughs. The ratio of the non-White population to the total population in each of the boroughs does not warrant Bickel's assertion that the "racial and social composition of the student bodies" of the five boroughs vary so much as to create, on that ground alone, a conflict of interest among the boroughs, taken as entities. Furthermore, federalism in this situation was not a device expected to protect racial and ethnic minorities or the poor.[35] Under these circumstances, no

33. *Id.* at 67.

34. *Oliver* v. *Board of Education of City of New York*, 306 F. Supp. 1286 (S.D.N.Y. 1969).

35. The following figures are taken from the 1960 Census of Population, vol. 1, *Characteristics of the Population*, part 34, New York, pp. 174, 175, 177 (1963). Only the 1960 population figures were presented to the Court in *Oliver. Supra*, n. 34 at 1288. It should be noted, first, that the "federal solution" was inconsistent

Borough	Total Pop.	White Pop.	Non-White Pop.	Negro Pop.
Brooklyn	2,627,319	2,245,859	381,460 (14.5%)	371,405 (14.1%)
Queens	1,809,578	1,654,959	154,619 (8.5%)	145,855 (8%)
Manhattan	1,698,281	1,271,822	426,459 (25.1%)	397,101 (23.2%)
Bronx	1,424,815	1,256,284	168,531 (11.8%)	163,896 (11.5%)
Richmond	221,991	211,991	10,000 (4.5%)	9,674 (4.4%)
Total	7,781,984	6,640,915	1,141,069 (14.7%)	1,087,931 (14%)

with majority rule. The two appointed members of the school board, together with the elected members from Richmond and the Bronx, representing 1,646,806 persons (about 21 percent of the total population), could, theoretically, control a majority. If we assume the two appointed members of the school board split their votes, the elected members from Richmond, the Bronx, and Manhattan, representing 3,345,087 persons (about 43 percent of the total population) could, theoretically, control a majority. If the two appointed members voted together, any combination of elected members that could prevail against them would represent a majority of the population.

Furthermore, the above figures do not support Bickel's contention that a central board elected on the basis of one vote, one value, would be more likely to "negate a good part of what decentralization seeks to attain" than a central board composed of one member elected from each of the boroughs. A non-White person would

apportionment should be tolerated which prevents a majority of the people of New York City from electing a majority of the elected members of the central board.[36] The district court was quite correct in holding unconstitutional the apportionment of one elected member of the central board to each of the five boroughs.

The rejection of the "federal solution" does not dispose of the "rational compromise" argument suggested by Mr. Justice Harlan, dissenting in *Avery* v. *Midland County, Texas*:

> . . . the suburbanites will be reluctant to join the metropolitan government unless they receive a share in the government proportional to the benefits they bring with them and not merely to their numbers. The city dwellers may be ready to concede this much, in return for the ability to tax the suburbs.[37]

By itself, this argument called for giving control of Midland County to the 67,906 persons in the city of Midland who paid most of the taxes. Indeed, Mr. Justice Fortas, in his dissent in the same case, felt it necessary to argue that "the fact that city dwellers pay most taxes should not determine the composition of the county governing body." "We should not use tax impact as the sole or controlling basis for vote distribution." [38]

Neither Mr. Justice Harlan nor Mr. Justice Fortas, nor the Texas Supreme Court, sought to justify the "federal solution" in *Avery*, which they all agreed was constitutionally intolerable. They were willing to remedy the city's gross underrepresentation but wished to provide an

---

not have a much better chance to be elected on a boroughwide than on a citywide basis. See *supra*, n. 25 and accompanying text. Whatever "balance" the central board needs will probably have to be supplied by the mayoral appointees.

From the point of view of the non-White population, in whose interests decentralization is advocated, why does the "federal solution" make sense when Richmond, with the smallest total population and the smallest non-White population (4.5 percent), would have one of the five elected representatives on the central board?

36. Bickel thinks it is ironic for the district court to conclude that the method of electing the central board was unconstitutional, but the interim appointive board was not. The district court's conclusion is in accord with the Supreme Court's decision in *Sailors, supra*, n. 28. Every state must decide which of its state and local offices to make elective and which, appointive. It cannot be maintained as a general proposition that the decision to make an office appointive is necessarily less democratic than one to make it elective.

37. *Supra*, n. 30 at 493–494.

38. *Id*. at 508–509.

adequate, effective voice for the people in the county outside the city.[39] But how should we measure the "share" in metropolitan government that is "proportional" to the benefits suburb and central city, respectively, bring to the metropolitan area? The only practical answer to this question is to accept as proportional whatever shares are consciously and willingly conceded by a majority of the voters in each territorial constituency that will lose representation by departure from the one vote, one value, principle.[40] But in *Avery*, neither Mr. Justice Harlan nor Mr. Justice Fortas was willing to put the matter to the voters in the city of Midland.

Of all the reapportionment cases decided by the Supreme Court to date, only *Hadley* v. *Junior College District* might possibly have been upheld on the basis suggested, because a majority of the voters in the largest school district voted to become part of the joint junior college district, knowing that they would be disadvantaged by the apportionment of members of the governing board under the formula prescribed by the state legislature.[41] But since the Supreme Court has held that the constitutional rights guaranteed by the equal protection clause and vindicated in the reapportionment cases are "individual and personal in nature" [42] and therefore "can hardly be infringed simply because a majority of the people choose to do so," [43] it declared the apportionment in *Hadley* to be unconstitutional. Nevertheless, there is little evidence to date that a majority that would consciously and willingly underrepresent itself to protect minorities would not also resort to the other measures mentioned above to this same end.

39. Essentially, Mr. Justice Harlan and Mr. Justice Fortas maintained that the impact of county government was sufficiently greater upon the people living outside the city than upon the city-dwellers to justify giving the former control of the county government. The Court found otherwise. Speaking for the Court in *Hadley, supra,* n. 32 at 56, Mr. Justice Black said: "It is, of course, possible that there might be some case in which a state elects certain functionaries whose duties are so far removed from normal governmental activities and so disproportionately affect different groups that a popular election in compliance with [*Reynolds* v. *Sims*] might not be required . . ." Even this seeming concession to the thought of Mr. Justice Harlan and Mr. Justice Fortas would not cover *Avery* because the county commissioners are engaged in "normal governmental activities."

40. See generally *supra,* n. 5, pp. 73–87.

41. However, they may have accepted the underrepresentation unwillingly as the price to be paid for the joint junior college district under existing law. The case for the apportionment would have been stronger if it had not been prescribed by the state legislature but had been left to negotiation among the school districts involved and subsequent ratification by a majority in each district.

42. *Reynolds* v. *Sims*, 377 U.S. 533, 561 (1964).

43. *Lucas* v. *Colorado General Assembly*, 377 U.S. 713, 736–737 (1964).

ARE THE REAPPORTIONMENT CASES TRIVIAL?

Bickel advances a number of different arguments to support his charge that the one vote, one value, principle is trivial.

Because of the Inherent Nature of Geographic Districting?

Bickel affirms that "any districted legislature is as likely to misrepresent as to register" the popular majority. This expresses the criticism that advocates of proportional representation have always leveled at geographic districting[44] and that Mr. Justice Stewart adopted in his dissenting opinion in *Reynolds* v. *Sims*.[45] While it is possible, theoretically, even with legislative districts of exactly equal population, that 26 percent of the electorate could elect a majority of the legislature, the probability of this outcome is very small. Geographic districting has not often failed to register the popular majority. Furthermore, districts of unequal population enhance the theoretical possibility of minority rule. Prior to reapportionment, for example, 12 percent of the population, theoretically, could elect a majority of the Connecticut lower house.

Because of Gerrymandering?

Passing from theory to political practice, Bickel also asserts that gerrymandering may perpetuate minority rule even with legislative districts of exactly equal population and thereby render the reapportionment cases inconsequential. This may become a danger.[46] But Bickel's supposition that the Court will do nothing to prevent gerrymandering or to make it more difficult to achieve may be premature. The Court is willing to consider charges that multi-member districts are being used or single-member districts drawn,[47] to submerge the political influence of Negroes. It has also said that it will question the use of multi-member constituencies that "operate to minimize or cancel out the voting strength of racial *or political elements* of the voting population." [48] To date, however, the Supreme Court has not decided whether a charge of partisan gerrymandering of

44. *Supra*, n. 5, pp. 30–35.

45. *Supra*, n. 42 at 750, n. 12.

46. Professor Elliott suggests that the one vote, one value, principle may have stimulated gerrymandering. But the evidence he adduces does not support this hypothesis. Ward Elliott, "Prometheus, Proteus, Pandora, and Procrustes Unbound: The Political Consequences of Reapportionment" 37 *University of Chicago Law Review* 474, 483–488.

47. See *Wright* v. *Rockefeller*, 376 U.S. 52 (1964).

48. *Supra*, n. 19 at 433, 439 (emphasis added). See also, *supra*, n. 21 at 73, 88, n. 14, and *Kilgarlin, supra*, n. 22 at 120, 122.

single-member districts, which does not also involve race, is justiciable.[49]

Professor Dixon proposes that the Supreme Court should resolve the issue in favor of justiciability, but then impose a "stringent burden of proof" on those who allege partisan gerrymandering.[50] Because of the obvious difficulties the Court would encounter in trying to proscribe partisan districting, I do not think it would be wise for it to adopt Professor Dixon's proposal.

In any case, as Mr. Justice Brennan stated in *Kirkpatrick* v. *Preisler,* "opportunities for gerrymandering are greatest when there is freedom to construct unequally populated districts." [51] This is so even if political subdivisions, such as counties, are kept intact. Furthermore, why should inequities in apportionment be justified simply because inequities in districting cannot also be eliminated? I still hold to the view that the "great mobility of the American people, the accelerating pace of socioeconomic change and the increasing uncertainties in the futures of both major parties, may be expected to combine with constitutional apportionment to make partisan districting an increasingly risky enterprise." [52]

Because of Lack of Political Impact?

Bickel insists that the successful implementation of the reapportionment cases "has made little difference—a marginal one, if any, here and there

49. There are intimations that challenges to alleged gerrymandering of single-member districts are not justiciable. See *Bagley* v. *Hare,* 385 U.S. 114 (1966) and *WMCA* v. *Lomenzo,* 382 U.S. 4, 5–6 (1965) (concurring opinion of Mr. Justice Harlan). The district court in *Wells* v. *Rockefeller,* 311 F. Supp. 48 (S.D.N.Y. 1970), dismissed a charge of gerrymandering without resolving the issue of justiciability, about which it entertained "serious doubts" because it found no proof that the legislature had "wholly political motives in their creation of equal districts." *Id.* at 50. Judge Cannella, dissenting in part and concurring in part, said the court's opinion implied that the issue was justiciable. The Supreme Court affirmed the judgment summarily. 90 S.Ct. 1696 (1970).

50. Dixon, *Democratic Representation,* p. 498.

51. *Kirkpatrick* v. *Preisler,* 394 U.S. 526, 534 n. 4 (1969), citing Andrew Hacker, *Congressional Districting,* rev. ed. (Washington: The Brookings Institution, 1964), p. 59.

52. *Supra,* n. 5, p. 65. Professor Dixon chooses to interpret this passage as saying that "gerrymandering problems would evaporate or become inconsequential with 'one man—one vote.'" Dixon, *Democratic Representation,* p. 498, n. 7. Gus Tyler and David I. Wells have proposed "precise rules or guidelines" which they think would reduce discretion and make "geographic logic" the principal consideration in a "semi-automatic" districting process. Tyler and Wells, "The New Gerrymander Threat," 78 *American Federationist,* No. 2, February 1971, pp. 1, 7. If the principles guiding such a "semi-automatic" process could be elaborated with as much cogency as the one vote, one value, principle, the reluctance of the courts to entertain complaints about partisan gerrymandering might be overcome.

—in the output of the political process." This conclusion, too, is premature and not warranted by the evidence to date. The findings are not uniform, but contradictory, and the methodologies used in earlier studies have been attacked in later studies.[53] I hope this symposium will help to clarify the issues of methodology in question.

None of the published studies, in fact, attempts to measure the impact of the reapportionment cases. Practically all rely upon data gathered before June 1964, when the cases were decided. They commonly rank the states of the Union according to generally used criteria of malapportionment, from the best to the worst apportioned according to population. Then they determine the extent to which, if at all, this rank order correlates

53. The following studies support the proposition that malapportionment is unrelated to selected political and policy outcomes beneficial to urban groups: David R. Derge, "Metropolitan and Outstate Alignments in Illinois and Missouri Legislative Delegations," 52 *American Political Science Review* 1051; Richard T. Frost, "On Derge's Metropolitan and Outstate Legislative Delegations," 53 *American Political Science Review* 792 (criticizing Derge); Derge's reply to Frost, 53 *American Political Science Review* 1097; Thomas A. Flinn, "The Outline of Ohio Politics," 13 *Western Political Quarterly* 702; Herbert Jacob, "The Consequences of Malapportionment: A Note of Caution," 43 *Social Forces* 256; J. T. White and N. C. Thomas, "Urban and Rural Representation and State Legislative Apportionment," 17 *Western Political Quarterly* 724; Thomas R. Dye, "Malapportionment and Public Policy in the States," 27 *Journal of Politics* 586; Thomas R. Dye, *Politics, Economics and the Public: Policy Outcomes in the American States* (Chicago: Rand McNally, 1966), p. 280; and Richard I. Hofferbert, "The Relation Between Public Policy and Some Structural and Environmental Variables in the American States," 60 *American Political Science Review* 73; David Brady and Douglas Edmonds, "One Man-One Vote—So What?" 4 *Trans-action* (March 1967): 41.

The following studies support the proposition that reapportionment will affect selected policy outcomes: Ira Sharkansky, "Voting Behavior of Metropolitan Congressmen: Prospects for Changes with Reapportionment," 28 *Journal of Politics* 774 (criticizing Derge, Jacob, and Dye, but pointing out, as did Jacob, that policy changes that can be expected from increases in representation for the central cities may be thwarted by increases in representation for the suburbs); Allan G. Pulsipher and James L. Weatherby, Jr., "Malapportionment, Party Competition and the Functional Distribution of Governmental Expenditures," 62 *American Political Science Review* 1207 (criticizing Brady and Edmonds for the lack of discrimination in their statistical computations and all previous studies because they try to show that other variables may be more important than malapportionment in affecting expenditures, without appreciating that such a showing does not prove that malapportionment is not also important); and Robert E. Crew, Jr., and Roger A. Hanson, "Reapportionment's Impact upon Public Policy: A Comparative Analysis of Intra-State Variations in State Spending," unpublished manuscript, 1970 (criticizing prior studies because they did not demonstrate that socioeconomic conditions are highly related to levels of spending over time and pointing to some evidence that such conditions are becoming less related to state spending—for example, Richard I. Hofferbert, "Ecological Development and Policy Change in the American States," 10 *Midwest Journal of Political Science* 464).

with another rank order of certain outputs of the political process—commonly, amounts spent by the state for selected purposes beneficial to urban areas.

These studies are unsatisfactory for a number of reasons. All states before 1964 were malapportioned, according to the standards ultimately imposed by the Supreme Court. To correlate degrees of malapportionment with amounts spent proves little because it takes no account of the fact that reapportionment meeting the Court's standards may produce crucial changes by shifting potential control of a state legislature from one to another political party or from one coalition of groups to another within the same political party. For example, the fact that malapportioned New York or California, prior to 1964, spent more on social welfare than some other relatively better apportioned states or returned lesser amounts to the cities than some other relatively worse apportioned states, does not prove anything about the potential effect in either state of reapportionment strictly according to population.

A study of New York before and after reapportionment according to the Court's standards would be much more to the point. The only "before-and-after" study I have seen is an unpublished paper by Professors Robert Crew of the University of Minnesota and Roger Hanson of the University of Georgia.[54] They conclude that reapportionment did produce public policy changes, defined as significant increases in the level of spending by states on education (and even when calculated separately, on higher education, elementary schools, and high schools), highways, public welfare, hospitals, and natural resources and in the level of state aids to cities. They found that policy changes occurred in 21 of 49 possible instances in the reapportioned states but in only 17 of 96 possible instances in the non-reapportioned states in their control group. They submit that, for all of the reapportioned states, reapportionment is a sufficient, but not a necessary condition for significant increases in the levels of direct state spending and for most of them, a sufficient, and nearly a necessary, condition for significant increases in the levels at which they are allocating money to their cities.

Yet it may be too soon for such before-and-after studies. In most states, there have not been more than two sessions of the reapportioned legislature since 1964. This is an insufficient number for an adequate test of the impact of reapportionment. Among other things, it takes time for the new legislators produced by reapportionment to find their way and to exert their influence. It will be most instructive to ascertain the extent to

54. Robert E. Crew, Jr., and Roger A. Hanson, *supra,* n. 53.

which, if at all, the internal organization or control of state legislatures will change with reapportionment.

Moreover, even the reapportionments to date which have satisfied the Court's standards have been based upon the 1960 census. Apportionments following the 1970 census will effect more drastic changes in the composition of state legislatures, but it may not be until after 1975 that studies of the consequences can be undertaken fruitfully. Nor should the outcomes selected to determine the consequences be limited to categories of expenditure deemed beneficial to urban areas, particularly central cities. It would also be important, for example, to see whether reapportionment has any impact upon such issues as liberalizing the abortion laws or others having cultural, rather than economic, significance or upon popular views of the legitimacy of the state legislature.

As time goes by, all state legislatures will be reapportioned according to the principle of one vote, one value. It will then be impossible to constitute a control group of relatively malapportioned states. Singling out reapportionment as the cause of particular effects will become even more difficult.

CONCLUSION

My guess is that reapportionment will have its principal impact in shifting the balance of power within each political party. This shift will become more dramatic after the 1970 census, which will entitle the suburbs to even more representation, at the expense of both the rural areas and the central cities. What the policy impact will be is still an open question that depends upon the kind of appeal each party makes to win the allegiance of the suburbs and the success it encounters.

In any case, I share the view Bickel attributes to Mr. Chief Justice Warren that the Supreme Court was right to impose the one vote, one value, principle as a federal constitutional requirement, regardless of the results it produces. It is a fundamental principle of legitimacy in a representative democracy, a principle not for "the passing hour" but for "an expanding future." [55]

55. Benjamin N. Cardozo, *The Nature of the Judicial Process* (New Haven: Yale University Press, 1921), p. 83.

3

REAPPORTIONMENT AND
POLITICAL DEMOCRACY

Douglas W. Rae

Essentially equal apportionment of legislative districts by population will be a fact in late twentieth-century America. And, on any strictly formal criterion of fairness,[1] reapportionment is much to be admired. But, from the viewpoint of equalitarian democratic theory, one may ask whether the fact of reapportionment would be a major shift toward political democracy or a legal triviality. The answer lies between these extremes, and I propose to look for it in this essay.

The hypothesis connecting apportionment and equalitarian democracy is hardly new. In the Federal Convention of 1787, James Wilson proposed the essential idea of apportionment,[2] and in 1866 Walter Bagehot offered a scathing (though strikingly modern) account of democratic equality through apportioned representation. His account serves as a useful beginning for our analysis. The "ultra-democratic theory" of the English Constitution,[3] he suggests, has two elements: a condition to be accomplished

1. The equal protection clause, for example. Or, even more exactly, John Rawls's criterion of justice: "inequalities as defined by institutional structure or fostered by it are arbitrary unless it is reasonable to expect that they will work out to everyone's advantage and provided that the positions and offices to which they attach . . . are open to all." Hence, the inequality between legislator and voter is admissible and malapportionment, inadmissible. See "Distributive Justice," in Peter Laslett and W. G. Runciman, eds., *Philosophy, Politics and Society*, 3d series (Oxford: Basil Blackwell, 1967). Quote from p. 61.

2. ". . . equal numbers of people ought to have equal numbers of representatives, and different numbers of people different numbers of representatives." *Notes of Debates in the Federal Convention of 1787 Reported by James Madison,* reprinted (New York: Norton, 1966), p. 97.

3. Walter Bagehot, *The English Constitution,* London 1866, reprinted (New York: Doubleday, 1960). Quotes from p. 185. Walter Bagehot sees an intimate connection between apportionment and universal male suffrage itself, probably because working-class areas were underrepresented before (and after) the Reform Act of 1867. There is also, of course, a logical priority placing suffrage before apportionment.

(democracy) and an institutional method (equally apportioned legislative districts):

> DEMOCRACY: "Suppose that last year there were twelve million adult males in England. Upon this theory each man is to have one twelve-millionth share in electing parliament . . ."
> *To be accomplished by:*
> APPORTIONMENT: "The machinery for carrying out such a plan is very easy. At each census the country ought to be divided into 658 electoral districts, in each of which the number of adult males should be the same . . ."

Bagehot continues in horror, presuming uncritically that apportionment by population would lead straightaway to "ultra-democracy." But is equal apportionment of legislative districts so powerful as that? Suppose that reapportionment has reached its culmination in perfect mathematical symmetry. Districts which once varied by ratios of twenty to one are now identical, numerically indistinguishable. We may still wonder how much nearer we are to the ideal of equalitarian political democracy.

Any account of the problem based on the isolated value of individual votes is misleading. Votes are valuable in combinations, trivial in isolation. An alternative account, based on what I will call coincident coalitions, results from this argument. This leads, in turn, to what I believe is a natural index for the relative importance of reforms in relation to the (never fully realized) ideal of equalitarian democracy. This index is then applied to reapportionment in the American states, and the results are compared both with the hypothetical consequences of other more drastic reforms and with conditions before apportionment. These comparisons should help us to assess the democratic consequences of reapportionment as we have experienced it. Let me begin with the question of evaluating votes.

VOTES AND THEIR VALUE IN REPRESENTATIVE DEMOCRACY

What, if anything, makes votes valuable? The simplest answer is that elections are a way of protecting mass publics from exploitation by political elites: when a government takes actions violating the wishes of its public, votes are used as a substitute for revolution. But, as J. C. Calhoun rightly reminds us, this would be a sufficient account only "if the whole community had the same interests so that . . . the laws which oppressed or impoverished one portion would necessarily oppress and impoverish all others . . ." [4] Under these improbable circumstances, equality among the votes of ordinary citizens would be quite irrelevant. Any distribution of "weights" would have the same consequences as any other, and the question of apportionment would therefore evaporate.

This assumption of perfect mass cohesion defines one extreme view of voting and elections. The other extreme assumption is that every citizen is a potential enemy of every other citizen in a strictly distributive (constant-sum)competition. On this view, every voter (and thus every vote) is seen in alienation from every other. The object of voting is thus for each person to exact strategic advantage from his $(n-1)$ compatriots. I will reject this view—taking a view between the two extremes —but it is so influential that we must consider it in detail.

Alien Votes

In *Walden II*, B. F. Skinner has his Dr. Frazier suggest that the right to vote is merely the right to become a scapegoat for the actions of governments. This conclusion follows, he thinks, from the fact that the probability of deciding an election outcome with one's vote "is less than the chance that we will be killed on the way to the polls." [5] I will argue that the premise of his case (the improbability of single-handedly reversing an outcome) is roughly correct, but that the conclusion (that votes are trivial) does not follow. It does not follow because a further (and false) premise is required.

It is true that no single vote (even a fully equal vote) is apt to reverse an election outcome. Not even the outcome in one district, much less the aggregate partisan outcome of a legislative election, is likely to be controlled by any one citizen's vote. The probability of such an event is zero, if preferences are determinate (as with "party identification") and skewed toward one party or the other. Even on much more generous assumptions, the probability is very small in a large electorate. Suppose, for example, that preferences are fluid in a two-party contest and that every voter is equally likely to vote for either party's candidate. Suppose further that there is an odd number of voters. Now, for any voter, the chance of controlling the outcome is the chance that $(n-1)$ other voters would have produced an exact tie in the absence of his vote. Under our assumptions, the relevant probability (p) becomes:

4. C. G. Post, ed., *A Disquisition on Government*, 1853, reprinted (Indianapolis: Bobbs-Merrill, 1953), p. 13.

5. B. F. Skinner, *Walden II* (New York: Macmillan, 1948), p. 265.

$$p = \frac{(n-1)!}{2^{(n-1)}\left(\dfrac{n-1}{2}!\right)^2}.$$

The resulting values of p are modest, despite the very optimistic assumption of fluidity on which they are based. For district turnouts of the order encountered in American legislative elections, p is above the probability for a direct cranial hit by a meteorite, but nothing like a good bet. For example:

n	p^6
1,001	0.02523
10,001	0.00798
100,001	0.00252

Taking all districts into account, these figures decline still further. Moreover, the lucky citizen whose vote "paid off" in this sense, would (in the view of voting under discussion) have to face the fact that each of his copartisans could believe himself to have decided the outcome. Under the assumption of zero-sum or constant-sum competition among citizens, the expected payoff would, on average, thus be diluted by a factor of $\frac{1}{2}(n-1)$. If we set the value a given voter would place on single-handedly controlling the outcome in this sense at 1, then this must be discounted by the product of p and 1 over $\frac{1}{2}(n-1)$. The result for $n = 100,001$ would thus be about 5×10^{-8}, a very small number.

Calculations of this sort carry us toward the eventual extreme view of the alien vote. This is the view of electoral politics as an n-person game with a fixed sum of payoffs. Thus, if we consider Lloyd Shapley's value for an n-person game,[7] we are driven to the conclusion that the mean value of a vote must be one nth the value of the election. If we thought of politics as a purely competitive process, as this view suggests we should,

6. These calculations cannot be made directly and are based on an algorithm suggested by John Loosemore of Essex University, England. Using Sterling's approximation for large $n!$, Loosemore finds a logarithmic algorithm of the form: log $p = \frac{1}{2}$ log $m - 0.09806$. A comparison of this approximation with directly calculated values for smaller n suggests that it is very accurate.

7. See "A Value for N-person Games," 28 *Annals of Mathematical Study* 307–317. Also see Lloyd Shapley and Martin Shubik, "A Method of Evaluating the Distribution of Power in Committee System," 48 *American Political Science Review* 987–992. This line of analysis has also been prominent in the reapportionment literature. For example, John F. Banzhaf III, "Weighted Voting Doesn't Work: A Mathematical Analysis," 317 *Rutgers Law Review* (1965). Discussed in Robert G. Dixon, Jr., *Democratic Representation* (New York: Oxford University Press, 1968).

then it would be hard to argue that a resource as small as a single (equal) vote was worthwhile. But, this view is unrealistic: elections and politics are "variable-sum" processes in which one may satisfy more, rather than fewer, persons with no necessary diminution of their satisfactions.

It is, I believe, significant that the most rigorous analysis of the value assignable to a single vote leads its authors to emphasize considerations having *nothing to do with outcomes*. Thus, Professors William Riker and Peter Ordeshook propose that we consider the personal satisfactions attached to the act of voting—not to any control over outcomes which might (improbably) result *from* voting—the most important factor in individual decisions to vote or abstain.[8] One votes because he thinks it his duty as a citizen or because he feels social pressure to do so or because he finds a symbol of inclusion in the act.[9] All this is independent of the political consequences of voting (and of apportionment, as well).

I have suggested that the assumption of complete cohesion among ordinary citizens made apportionment seem irrelevant. Now it appears that the opposite assumption—that of an atomized and strictly competitive electorate—also makes the political aspect of voting, and therefore of apportionment,[10] seem unimportant and perhaps trivial. And, if this means that voting becomes a ritual act, then it also means that reapportionment cannot speak with any real force to the problems of equalitarian democracy. Elections themselves seem to lack such force, and reapportionment equalizes a trivial value—the miniscule chance to control the outcome with one's own vote for one's own benefit.

8. William Riker and Peter Ordeshook, "A Theory of the Calculus of Voting," 62 *American Political Science Review* 25–42. These authors offer an extended and detailed analysis of the value for p and the other factors in individual evaluation of individual votes. Theirs is easily the most sophisticated treatment of evaluation for isolated votes. The most influential work in this tradition is, of course, Anthony Downs, *An Economic Theory of Democracy* (New York: Harper & Row, 1957). See especially pp. 36–50 and 260–276. And William Riker, *The Theory of Political Coalitions* (New Haven: Yale University Press, 1962) presents an elegant analysis of many political processes, including elections, under the zero-sum assumption.

9. Or, as Dr. Frazier continued, "Do you think a man goes to the polls because of any effect which casting his vote has ever had? By no means. He goes to avoid being talked about by his neighbors or to 'knife' a candidate he dislikes, marking his X as he might defile a campaign poster—and with the same irrational spite." Skinner, *supra*, n. 5.

10. I am ignoring the pathologic extremes of malapportionment here. This holds I think, for malapportionment of the order being remedied in the United States at present, though not, perhaps, for the order found in eighteenth- or early nineteenth-century England. There, some districts were so small that individual votes were probably of real strategic importance by themselves.

But electorates are not collections of alien individuals, each in competition with every other. This is the fiction of game theory and the fable of Hobbes's state of nature. Electorates are always partitioned into groups whose members are related in either or both of two important ways: (1) they have the same stakes in an election, and therefore all seek similar outcomes; and (2) they define their interests sympathetically, so that the difference between *my* payoff and *our* payoff becomes blurred.[11] One may see this most clearly in the cases of groups like the American Blacks or the Belfast Catholics, groups living at a disadvantage. But it is no less characteristic of other groups, including, for example, the American farmers or the suburban middle class. This view, of an electorate partitioned (none too neatly) into groups identified by common interests and sympathy, leads, I believe, to a more sensible view of political democracy and of the part reapportionment can play in its fulfillment.

Pardon a necessary aside. One must think of two processes in talking about American legislative politics. First, there is partisan representation, relevant to issues where parties define their positions in an election and act cohesively in implementing them. But American legislative parties deviate often and importantly from this pattern.[12] One must therefore keep in mind a second process. In this one, each legislator decides his vote individually, ordinarily defining his district or a part of it as his reference group. This individual-district representation must also be considered. I will develop my argument for the first, partisan, process, but leave it general enough for a later look at the second process.

Grouped Votes

In an election, there are large groups of voters whose members want the same partisan outcome. They need not be conscious of their existence as a group in any strict sense, as with the blocs of party identities so

11. I am not proposing the so-called group theory of politics here. This observation belongs, rather, to the literature concerned with the more modest relationship between "cleavages" and political processes. For a survey of this literature, consult S. M. Lipset and Stein Rokkan, eds., *Party Systems and Voter Alignments* (New York: Free Press, 1967). For a more formal discussion of the problems entailed by this view, see D. Rae and M. Taylor, *The Analysis of Political Cleavages* (New Haven: Yale University Press, 1970). A most effective application of this general approach to electoral politics is William Keech's *The Impact of Negro Voting* (Chicago: Rand McNally, 1968).

12. See, for example, Malcolm E. Jewell and Samuel C. Patterson, *The Legislative Process in the United States* (New York: Random House, 1966), pp. 414–452, especially Table 17-1, pp. 420–421.

important in American electorates.[13] But, and this is the point, the members of these groups do *not* find themselves in competition with one another. Thus, a favorable outcome is a favorable outcome, whether an individual played a decisive strategic part in achieving it or not. A legislative party has won a majority; each of us prefers that to its alternative; we have together used our votes to good effect. These groups may bear a formal kinship to the elite parties of "like-minded men" Burke thought he knew, but there are real differences.

These groups have three important sociological deficiencies. First, they have very weak internal networks of communication. Few pairs of members know each other, and there is little or no conscious cooperation. The groups therefore depend for their effectiveness on the coincident responses of the members to the party and its candidates. They are thus termed "coincident coalitions."[14] Second, these groups are very large in the special sense that no single individual's contribution makes a perceptible difference"[15] to the outcome. This is the point which must be salvaged from the view of voting discussed above. And third, these are groups which produce public (in contrast to private) goods. As Mancur Olson writes, a public good is "such that, if any person X_i in a group X_1, ..., X_i, ..., X_n consumes it, it cannot feasibly be withheld from the other members in that group."[16] In our case, if any members of a coincident coalition attain a satisfying outcome, so must all the others, including those who did not even vote. We are dealing, then, with large coincident groups producing public goods.

Now, despite my earlier argument, there may be a special sort of competition within such groups. If, even considering the satisfactions Riker and Ordeshook discuss, an individual considers the act of voting a nuisance, he may be tempted to reason as follows: "I would rather have the party win, but rather not vote myself. If every other member of the "group" votes, then I will probably have my way without the bother of voting. If not, it probably wouldn't help for me to vote anyway. Therefore, I shall stay home."[17] This possibility makes such groups uniquely

13. These groups are often called categoric. The seminal analysis of party identification is A. Campbell *et al.*, *The American Voter* (New York: Wiley, 1960).

14. Later, we will consider another sort of coincident coalition—the class of persons believed by a legislator to favor or oppose a given policy.

15. Mancur Olson, *The Logic of Collective Action* (Cambridge, Mass.: Harvard University Press, 1965), p. 44.

16. *Id.*, p. 14.

17. This is derivative of Olson's larger thesis about suboptimal production of collective goods by large groups. *Ibid.*

vulnerable to collapse through sloth. And this is an important vulnerability which parties and candidates work hard to combat. But this is in any event a very different competition—a competition in sloth—from the one discussed earlier, and it in no way undercuts the position I am taking. We may still, that is, focus on competition between, not within, coincident coalitions.

If this much is accepted, then what counts is the value of a set of votes as opposed to the values of individual votes: the latter count only in and through their membership in the former—in coincident coalitions. As a citizen, I am thus interested in the value, not of my one vote *in itself,* but in combination with $m-1$ other votes for the same party, where that party receives m votes. Votes seen in these combinations are far from trivial, and reapportionment does not turn out to be irrelevant.

The value for a set of m votes is, in a two-party election, binary: win or lose. A coalition commands or does not command a partisan majority. And, this will be the starting point for our analysis of democratic reform: roughly speaking, numerically large coincident coalitions should win over small ones under a democratic regime. We should, however, recognize that party labels are often superficial in American legislative politics. Commanding a partisan majority may be quite meaningless.

Therefore, we must also keep in mind another pattern, in which party does not bind votes in the legislature. Here, we will define a coincident coalition as a group of persons sharing an interest or preference in a specific policy dispute, as seen by legislators. Here, we may imagine that each legislator has a look at his district—with a poll, by intuition, perhaps by listening to a small (probably biased) sample of constituents—and decides how to vote on a bill. Each legislator may or may not seek to follow a constituency majority. If apportionment is relevant, however, he will at least be sensitive to the apparent distribution of interest and opinion in his district.[18] (If, on the contrary, he follows polity-wide clusterings, apportionment seems irrelevant.) Looking across districts, we may imagine coincident coalitions of citizens who present like cues to their representatives and who are variously distributed across districts. Our interest will again center on the expected responsiveness of legislative majorities to coincident coalitions of various sizes.

We began by asking how important apportionment is to the realization of equalitarian democracy. Using grouped votes and voters (coincident

18. There is some, rather mixed, empirical evidence on this pattern of legislative behavior. See especially, Warren E. Miller and Donald Stokes, "Constituency Influence in Congress," 57 *American Political Science Review* 45–56.

coalitions), we are prepared to address this question. Let me begin by defining equalitarian democracy as it applies to coincident coalitions in legislative politics. I shall use the resulting definition as a means of comparing the potency of reforms, including various degrees of reapportionment, in approximating the ideal of perfect equalitarian democracy.

DEMOCRACY AND DEMOCRATIC REFORM

The single most important property of a democratic (or other) regime is the way it discriminates among coalitions. How small a coalition can be decisive? How large a coalition can fail to be decisive? If one could give the same answer to both questions—say $\dfrac{n+1}{2}$—he would be talking about a pure democracy. And, as the answers diverged, he would be talking about something less and less like pure democracy. I will try to define democracy accordingly.

A Formal Definition of Political Democracy

A regime is a pure equalitarian democracy if, and only if, the largest possible losing coalition is smaller by one person than the smallest possible decisive coalition:

$$(L_{max} + 1 < T_{min}) \rightarrow (\text{pure equalitarian democracy})$$

This is seldom quite the case. Only one regime, direct and unfettered majority rule, fully satisfies this constraint. Even a perfectly apportioned representative regime fails to meet this very stringent requirement. Even direct-decision rules other than simple majority rule fail this criterion. But it would be foolish to conclude from this that regimes simply are or are not democracies. We should like to make finer distinctions.

Therefore, let us define a continuous function for degrees of approximation to the ideal of pure equalitarian democracy. This function defines degrees of deviation from the ideal. It must, for that reason, assign a value of 1 to that regime (pure autocracy) which diverges furthest from the ideal. And, if it is to be an effective index, it must also assign a value of zero to direct majority rule. And it should order intermediate cases between these poles. The function (XD) may be defined thus:

$$XD = \frac{L_{max} - T_{min} + 1}{n + 1}$$

XD equals zero for direct majority rule. Consider the case of 1,000 and 1,001:

$$XD = \frac{500 - 501 + 1}{1,001} \qquad n = 1,000$$

$$= 0$$

$$XD = \frac{500 - 501 + 1}{1,002} \qquad n = 1,001$$

$$= 0$$

And XD displays the expected value, 1.0, for a pure autocracy. Imagine that 1,000 persons are ruled by an outside decision-maker. Thus:

$$XD = \frac{1,000 - 0 + 1}{1,001}$$

$$= \frac{1,001}{1,001}$$

$$= 1.0$$

These values are, respectively, the minima and maxima for our measure of deviations from pure equalitarian democracy. Intermediate cases, like the legislative systems of representation being reapportioned in the American states, fall between.

Our initial question may now be recast in terms of this function. "How substantially has reapportionment shifted our institutions toward the ideal of equalitarian democracy?" becomes "How substantially has reapportionment lowered the value of XD?" This may (for some purposes) be considered in absolute values of XD, but for other purposes we will want to normalize it with respect to the theoretical maximum attainable by reapportionment reform. I will therefore begin by establishing the theoretical limits for the changes attainable through reapportionment. These limits have two uses: (1) to indicate the "gross potential" of apportionment if it is carried to its extreme, and (2) to offer a reasonable base line for comparing improvements actually attained thus far in the reapportionment movement.

The Limits of Apportionment

Suppose we have a perfectly apportioned legislature; all districts have identical populations. And assume (unrealistically) that there is no interdistrict variation in turnout. Thus, if there are d districts, each has a population of n over d, and (with equal proportionate turnouts) votes cast are linear functions of this fraction. Hence, nothing relevant is hidden by considering populations (n), and not numbers of votes cast. Assume also that there are only two parties: a majority is thus required to win each district. Let the population of each district (n/d) be labeled D. These values are displayed in Figure 1.

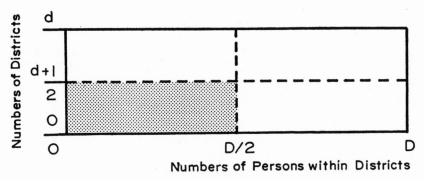

FIGURE I
Schema for a Perfectly Apportioned Legislature

We are interested in assigning values of XD to such a system of districts. We will use a trivial inference (D times d equals n) and the assumption of legislative majority rule in assigning these values.[19] Now, let us first consider the size of the smallest coincident coalition capable of commanding a legislative majority T_{min} in our equation for XD. Consider each horizontal strip in Figure 1 as a district: its spatial dimensions are 1 over d by D. If there is an odd number of districts, then T_{min} may be seen as the shaded lower-left quadrant of our diagram. Its dimensions are:

$$\frac{d+1}{2} \cdot \frac{D}{2}$$

Thus, for an odd number of districts, T_{min} may be calculated as:

$$T_{min} = \frac{d+1}{2} \cdot \frac{D}{2}$$

$$= \frac{D \cdot d + D}{4}$$

19. We also make the trivial (though incorrect) assumption that a majority of any district is D over 2. This produces an altogether negligible error factor in our limit equations.

And since $D \cdot d = n$, the term simplifies itself:

$$\frac{n + D}{4}$$

Thus, the smallest winning coincident coalition must contain D over 4 more than a fourth of the voter population. For an even number of districts, the value is slightly higher:[20]

$$T_{\min} = \frac{n + 2D}{4}$$

As a number of commentators have noticed, these values are, for d of the order found in American legislatures, about one-fourth.[21] This is true, but it is important to see that it depends on there being a large number of districts. It holds almost perfectly for the lower house in Connecticut, but not so for the upper house in Delaware.

The largest possible losing coalition is roughly but (due to breakage in d) not exactly the unshaded L in Figure 1. With an even number of districts, the largest coincident coalition not obtaining a legislative majority is calculated:

$$L_{\max} = \frac{d}{2} D + \frac{D}{2}$$

$$= \frac{Dd}{2} + \frac{Dd}{4}$$

$$= \frac{3n}{4}$$

If, however, d is an odd number, the figure is slightly lower, at:[22]

$$\frac{3n - D}{4}$$

---

20. $\dfrac{d}{2} + 1 \dfrac{D}{2} = \dfrac{dD}{4} + \dfrac{D}{2} = \dfrac{n + 2D}{4}$

21. The dependence of this limit ($0.25n$) on d is not generally recognized, and this will be an important element in any discussion of reform beyond apportionment. See Phillip B. Kurland, ed., *The Supreme Court Review* (Chicago: University of Chicago Press, 1964), p. 31. See also James Buchanan and Gordon Tullock, *The Calculus of Consent* (Ann Arbor: University of Michigan Press, 1962).

22. $\dfrac{d-1}{2} D + \dfrac{d+1}{2} \dfrac{D}{2} = \dfrac{dD - D}{2} + \dfrac{dD + D}{4} = \dfrac{3n - D}{4}$

A related analysis of considerable interest for these limits is found in Max Power, "The Electoral College and Proposed Reforms: A Theoretical Analysis," unpublished thesis, Yale University, 1970, Chapter 2.

These limiting values are summarized in Table 1.

TABLE 1

	$T_{\min}$	$L_{\max}$
d even	$\dfrac{n + 2D}{4}$	$\dfrac{3n}{4}$
d odd	$\dfrac{n + D}{4}$	$\dfrac{3n - D}{4}$

Interestingly, whether d is even or odd, the value for XD under perfect apportionment is the same. For an even d:

$$
\begin{aligned}
XD &= \frac{L_{\max} - T_{\min} + 1}{n + 1} \\[2mm]
&= \frac{\left(\dfrac{3n}{4}\right) - \left(\dfrac{n + 2D}{4}\right) + 1}{n + 1} \\[2mm]
&= \frac{2n - 2D + 4}{4(n + 1)}
\end{aligned}
$$

And for an odd d:

$$
\begin{aligned}
XD &= \frac{\dfrac{3n - D}{4} - \dfrac{n + D}{4} + 1}{n + 1} \\[2mm]
&= \frac{2n - 2D + 4}{4(n + 1)}
\end{aligned}
$$

Where n is a large number, we may safely simplify this limit to:

$$
= \frac{2n - 2D}{4n}
$$

This equation sets the limit on reapportionment's contribution to democratic reform. Where D (the population of each district) is very, very small, the limiting value for XD approaches one-half. But there it stops, no matter how well apportioned the districts. This means that reapportionment reform is confined almost entirely to the upper half of our function's range. And this, of course, is an important cautionary hint about what may be expected to follow from reapportionment in the way of democratization.

Expanding the potential domain of democratization thus requires a drastic reduction of the number of districts. The actual limit of XD for American legislatures at present varies from 0.472 in Delaware's eighteen-seat senate to 0.499 in the United States House of Representatives. In other words, perfect apportionment would in all cases leave a great deal undone unless the number of districts was greatly reduced. One could reduce the deviation from the ideal substantially below this range only by moving much closer to the sort of one-district (proportional representation) system found in the Israeli Knesset. Table 2 shows some sample values for the limiting minimum of XD:

TABLE 2

number of districts (n)	theoretical minimum for deviation from pure democracy (XD)	example
1	0.000	Israeli Knesset
2	0.250	—
3	0.333	—
5	0.400	—
18	0.472	Delaware Senate
25	0.480	Hawaii Senate
100	0.495	Indiana House
294	0.489	Conn. Assembly
435	0.499	U.S. House

Such drastic reductions are a practical impossibility and even on theoretical ground would be open to serious objection. I will therefore proceed on the assumption that the number of districts and therefore their mean populations are effectively fixed. In what follows, allowance has been made for variation among American legislatures, so that our theoretical minimum for XD is slightly lower for small bodies than for large ones.

Measuring Reforms

We will want to compare deviations from the ideal of pure democracy before and after reapportionment. This will be done in two ways. First, we will consider the absolute differences made by specific reapportionments in the value of XD:

$$\text{Absolute difference} = XD_{ante} - XD_{post}$$

Second, we will consider this difference relative to what might be accomplished:

$$\text{Relative difference} = \frac{XD_{\text{ante}} - XD_{\text{post}}}{XD_{\text{anti}} - XD_{\text{min}}}$$

REAPPORTIONMENT AND POLITICAL DEMOCRACY

Reapportionment is an important, though not revolutionary reform: it has made a drastic change within the narrow limits set by existing institutions. Indeed, we will see that the "first wave" of reapportionment came fairly close to exhausting the democratization possible under existing institutional constraints. But, and this is important, these limits are narrow, indeed.

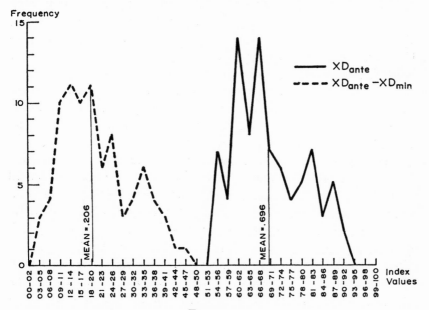

FIGURE 2
The Potential for Reform in January 1962
$(N = 85)$

The initial situation, in January 1962, is pictured in Figure 2. The mean deviation from pure democracy in the eighty-five state legislatures for which complete data were available[23] was about 0.7; the median slightly

23. Using approximations outlined in the Statistical Summary (p. 110), data were derived from the summary tables in R. G. Dixon, Jr., *Democratic Representation* (New York: Oxford University Press, 1968).

lower, at about 0.67. The legislatures were scattered over a very wide range, from a maximum of 0.92 in the Nevada senate down to a minimum of 0.54 in the Rhode Island house. And, as the frequency distribution shows, the other eighty-three legislatures were not tightly clustered at any given point between these extremes. It may also be worth mentioning that no systematic demographic or regional pattern seems to underlie the distribution.

Even within the constraints imposed by plurality election, this situation offered some opportunity for democratic reform. As the cross-hatched line in Figure 2 suggests, the state legislatures could be democratized substantially. On average, one-fifth (0.206) could be paired away from the deviation from pure democracy entirely on the basis of reapportionment. In only a few cases (the lower houses in Rhode Island, Massachusetts, and New Jersey) could one call the opportunity for reform through reapportionment trivial. In many others (the upper houses of Nevada, Arizona, California, and Florida are outstanding examples) malapportionment was extreme enough that a substantial democratization (in the sense defined above) was possible through reapportionment.

It is not, however, surprising that the absolute value of XD changed rather modestly with reapportionment. On average, about 17 percentage points were whittled away from the deviation from pure democracy by the first wave of reapportionment. A few legislatures with very high initial deviations and rigorous reapportionments (such as the upper houses in Arizona, Florida, and Maryland and the lower house in Utah) showed large absolute differences—in the vicinity of one-third. On the other hand, most state legislatures showed absolute changes in the vicinity of 0.1 to 0.2, and one would not on the face of it think that much had happened. The overall distribution is shown as a solid line in Figure 3.

But these data are, in a sense, misleading. They fail to take account of the limits within which reapportionment must operate. A more impressive distribution is generated by the relative change—the lowering of XD by reapportionment as a proportion of the possible decrease. Here, the mean value is about 0.78: on average, almost four-fifths of the possible democratization was indeed accomplished in the first wave of reapportionment. In one case, the Michigan senate, reapportionment came very near the theoretical minimum (0.996) and in at least twenty others, 90 percent of the possible democratization was in fact accomplished. The curve is shown (cross-hatched) in Figure 3.

There were, of course, legislatures where the relative change was unimpressive: seven failed to accomplish as much as half the possible democ-

ratization through reapportionment. But, in each case, the initial malapportionment was so gentle that no great deviation was implied. For
example, the Wisconsin assembly exhibited a relative change of only
0.49, leaving 0.51 of the space between the initial value and the theoretical minimum untouched. But, the space involved was quite small
$(0.605 - 0.495 = 0.11)$, so that no really great deviation remained (e.g.
0.056). With the partial exception of the Iowa senate (a space of 0.156
and a relative change of 0.314, leaving a gap of 0.107), all seven cases
exhibiting low relative changes fit this pattern.

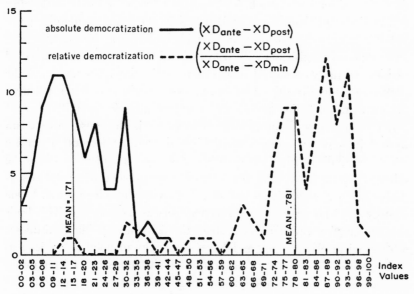

Frequency

$$\text{absolute democratization} \quad \rule[0.5ex]{1.2cm}{1pt} \quad \left(X D_{ante} - X D_{post}\right)$$

$$\text{relative democratization} \quad \text{-- -- --} \quad \left(\frac{X D_{ante} - X D_{post}}{X D_{ante} - X D_{min}}\right)$$

MEAN = .171

MEAN = .781

Index Values

FIGURE 3
Absolute and Relative Democratization

While innumerable asides would be required for full description of the
data,[24] a few simple conclusions are relevant to my analysis. First, reapportionment made a modest absolute contribution to the democratization
of state legislative elections in most cases. Second, however modest the
absolute change, it was a very substantial part of the change which might
have been achieved within the context of plurality elections. And, third,
it follows that the "lion's share" of the feasible democratization under
reapportionment per se is behind us, not in front of us. More broadly—

24. The legislature-by-legislature figures appear in the Statistical Summary, p.
110.

and the frequency lines give this a quantitative interpretation—reapportionment seems more than a legal triviality, but less than a democratizing revolution.

LOOKING FORWARD

What all this means is that reapportionment has narrowed the set of coincident coalition structures in which the few frustrate or dominate the many. There are fewer possible cases, and those cases have smaller numerical disparities, which lead to less arbitrary minority rule after reapportionment than before. It is now less likely that a minority party will win a legislative majority and less likely that in an inter-election dispute responsive legislators will form majorities contrary to the numerical division of the electorate. Reapportionment in the 1960s narrowed the prospect of minority rule in the present sense and left only a small margin for democratization by further reapportionment in the 1970s.

But if the reapportionment movement seems, in this sense, to have run most of its course, what must succeed it in the coming decades? There are several possibilities. First, the question of the gerrymander—in which the inherent openness of plurality election to undemocratic outcomes is deliberately exploited—is an important and very difficult prospect.[25] One strategy is ad hoc resistance to gerrymanders as they emerge. This leads to some genuine embarrassment about the domain of public institutions, as opposed to private ones, and forces the reality of political parties and their place in the operative Constitution on the courts or on legislatures, themselves. It also raises the question of proportional representation. The criterion of political democracy outlined here asks for much less than mirror-image representation, but it is apparent that not even a well ordered relationship between majorities and minorities can be guaranteed with plurality election in numerous districts. Indeed, not even proportional representation assumes this democratization unless the number of constituencies is very small.[26] To proscribe minority rule of this sort, one must (with big-district proportional representation, as in Israel or The Netherlands, or with large, nationally cohesive parties, as in Great Britain) abandon a major tacit premise in American political and constitutional thought. This is the premise that relevant political cleavages run

25. See Gordon E. Baker, "Gerrymandering," Chapter 4.
26. This argument is made in some detail in Rae, *Political Consequences of Electoral Laws* (New Haven: Yale University Press, 1967), pp. 74 ff.

along territorial lines. Sometimes they do; sometimes they don't.[27] When they do, the division of polities into small (presumably homogeneous) constituencies seems essential to democratic representation. When cleavages don't run territorially, such divisions are potential hindrances to democratic representation. I suspect that time runs with territorial randomization of cleavages and, therefore, against the territorial theory of representation. If this is so, and if it is acted on, reapportionment may eventually appear to have been a historical dead end. This is a guess, and a guess on which I should not like to bet money. But over the long-term future, it is quite a real possibility.

A second line of reform may concern itself with the bias of our legislatures toward the preservation of the status quo. These institutions, with their committee vetoes and restrictive decision rules, rest on the tacit logical premise that conservative coalitions deserve precedence over coalitions whose members seek change, that is, over liberal and radical groups. This premise seems less and less tenable in a society which makes rapid change an urgent necessity. Indeed, we probably are in a position to choose, not between legislative responsiveness and legislative resistance to change, but between changes made through representative institutions and changes made otherwise. I am thinking not just of race[28] and poverty, where a protective folklore has lost its credibility, but also of problems arising from the contamination of the environment, where an absorbent nature has lost its elasticity. These are cases in which small, blocking coalitions may protect the statutory status quo only at quite unacceptable costs. In this perspective, reapportionment will seem to have been a useful, though very inadequate, program of institutional reform.

But this must be understood for the statistical gamble which it is. Political democracy is a method, and, in Joseph Schumpeter's words, "incapable of being an end in itself, irrespective of what decisions it will produce under given historical circumstances." In a world whose future cleavages, whose future succession of coincident coalitions, is unpredictable, political democracy offers us the best bet for living with policies we like. But it offers nothing more than a bet, and the outcomes depend not just on the democratization of institutions, but on the sorts of circumstances and people who comprise the competing coalitions which are sorted out

27. It may be argued as well that territorial districts actually create (distributive) cleavages with territorial definitions.

28. I must confess that I have real doubts about the consequences of majoritarian decisions for the amelioration of racial hatred and exploitation. No regime assures that a society gets better policies than its members deserve.

STATISTICAL SUMMARY

DEMOCRATIZATION IN REAPPORTIONMENT
OF STATE LEGISLATURES

Legislature		Number of members	XD_{min}	XD_{ante}	XD_{post}	$XD_{ante} - XD_{post}$	$XD_{ante} - XD_{min}$	$\dfrac{XD_{ante} - XD_{post}}{XD_{ante} - XD_{min}}$
Ala.	L	106	.495	.747	.527	.220	.252	.873
Ala.	U	35	.486	.748	.522	.226	.262	.863
Alaska	U	20	.475	.675	.516	.159	.200	.795
Ariz.	U	28	.482	.890	.494	.396	.408	.971
Ark.	L	100	.495	.672	.523	.149	.177	.842
Ark.	U	35	.486	.576	.508	.068	.090	.756
Cal.	L	80	.494	.559	.520	.039	.065	.600
Cal.	U	40	.486	.905	.523	.382	.419	.912
Colo.	U	35	.486	.702	.499	.203	.218	.940
Conn.	L	294	.498	.882	.564	.318	.384	.828
Conn.	U	36	.486	.680	.534	.146	.194	.753
Del.	L	35	.486	.815	.510	.305	.329	.927
Del.	U	18	.472	.808	.502	.306	.336	.911
Fla.	L	112	.496	.857	.588	.269	.361	.745
Fla.	U	44	.489	.888	.547	.341	.399	.855
Ga.	L	205	.498	.778	.573	.205	.280	.732
Hawaii	L	51	.490	.615	.570	.045	.125	.360
Hawaii	U	25	.480	.790	.503	.287	.310	.926
Idaho	L	79	.494	.673	.533	.140	.179	.782
Idaho	U	44	.489	.834	.532	.302	.345	.875
Ill.	L	117	.496	.601	.509	.092	.105	.876
Ill.	U	58	.491	.721	.505	.216	.230	.939
Ind.	L	100	.495	.657	.537	.120	.162	.741
Ind.	U	50	.490	.606	.515	.101	.116	.871
Iowa	L	129	.496	.735	.519	.216	.239	.904
Iowa	U	59	.492	.648	.599	.049	.156	.314
Kans.	L	125	.496	.815	.512	.303	.319	.981
Ky.	L	100	.495	.664	.557	.107	.169	.633
Ky.	U	38	.487	.593	.547	.046	.106	.434
La.	L	105	.495	.659	.533	.126	.164	.768
La.	U	39	.487	.670	.517	.153	.183	.836
Me.	L	34	.485	.581	.505	.076	.096	.792
Md.	L	142	.496	.750	.524	.226	.254	.890
Md.	U	29	.483	.858	.526	.332	.375	.885
Mass.	L	240	.498	.549	.543	.006	.051	.118
Mich.	L	110	.495	.565	.499	.066	.070	.943
Mich.	U	38	.487	.723	.488	.235	.236	.996
Minn.	L	135	.496	.655	.528	.127	.159	.799
Minn.	U	67	.493	.599	.519	.080	.106	.755
Miss.	L	122	.496	.713	.519	.194	.217	.894
Miss.	U	52	.490	.694	.524	.170	.204	.833
Mo.	L	163	.497	.797	.514	.283	.300	.943
Mont.	L	94	.495	.639	.526	.113	.144	.785
Mont.	U	56	.491	.847	.541	.306	.356	.860
Nebr.		49	.490	.634	.507	.127	.144	.882
Nev.	L	37	.486	.650	.525	.125	.164	.762
Nev.	U	17	.471	.920	.496	.424	.449	.944
N.H.	L	400	.499	.562	.543	.019	.063	.302
N.H.	U	24	.479	.567	.503	.064	.088	.727
N.J.	L	60	.492	.543	.535	.008	.051	.157
N.J.	U	29	.483	.810	.498	.312	.327	.954

Legislature		Number of members	XD_{min}	XD_{ante}	XD_{post}	$XD_{ante} - XD_{post}$	$XD_{ante} - XD_{min}$	$\dfrac{XD_{ante} - XD_{post}}{XD_{ante} - XD_{min}}$
N.M.	U	32	.484	.811	.558	.253	.327	.774
N.Y.	L	165	.497	.618	.508	.110	.121	.909
N.Y.	U	65	.492	.631	.509	.122	.139	.878
N.C.	L	120	.496	.733	.529	.204	.237	.861
N.C.	U	50	.490	.641	.522	.119	.151	.788
N.D.	L	109	.495	.598	.532	.066	.103	.641
N.D.	U	49	.490	.681	.532	.149	.191	.780
Ohio	L	137	.496	.697	.527	.170	.201	.846
Ohio	U	32	.484	.606	.520	.086	.122	.705
Okla.	L	99	.495	.705	.514	.191	.210	.910
Okla.	U	48	.490	.765	.516	.249	.275	.905
Pa.	L	209	.498	.623	.530	.093	.125	.744
Pa.	U	50	.490	.679	.509	.170	.189	.899
R.I.	L	100	.495	.540	.511	.029	.045	.644
R.I.	U	46	.489	.829	.507	.322	.340	.947
S.C.	U	46	.489	.777	.535	.242	.288	.840
S.D.	L	75	.493	.615	.533	.082	.122	.672
S.D.	U	35	.486	.617	.529	.088	.131	.672
Tenn.	L	99	.495	.713	.530	.183	.218	.839
Tenn.	U	33	.485	.731	.512	.219	.246	.890
Tex.	L	150	.497	.617	.529	.088	.120	.733
Tex.	U	31	.484	.697	.506	.191	.213	.897
Utah	L	69	.493	.667	.524	.143	.174	.822
Utah	U	27	.481	.787	.519	.268	.306	.876
Vt.	L	150	.497	.884	.516	.368	.387	.951
Vt.	U	30	.483	.675	.532	.143	.192	.745
Va.	L	100	.495	.637	.535	.102	.142	.718
Va.	U	40	.488	.685	.531	.154	.197	.782
Wash.	L	99	.495	.647	.533	.114	.152	.750
Wash.	U	49	.490	.661	.524	.137	.171	.801
W. Va.	L	100	.495	.605	.545	.060	.110	.545
Wis.	L	100	.495	.605	.551	.054	.110	.491
Wis.	U	33	.485	.550	.516	.034	.065	.523
Wyo.	U	25	.480	.731	.526	.205	.251	.817
MEAN			.490	.696	.525	.171	.206	.781

NOTE ON COMPUTATIONS: These values were computed by the approximations explained below, using data for "electoral percentages" from Dixon.[29] His 1962 data were used for the "ante" columns, his latest figures for the "post" columns. The approximations are for T_{min} and L_{max}, and XD was computed as with exact data. With the exception noted in a moment, the approximations are apt to be very accurate.

T_{min} = electoral percentage/2, for even or odd numbers of districts. (e.g., the smallest number of persons able to elect a blocking coalition under majority rule in the legislature.)

L_{max} = 1 − (electoral percentage/2), for odd number of districts.

$$= \frac{2 - \text{electoral percentage} + \dfrac{n}{2}}{2}, \text{ for even number of districts.}$$

The last approximation is exact only in so far as the mean district and the median district have the same population. This should be expected to produce a small error, perhaps on the order of 0.005, which is negligible for present purposes.

29. *Supra*, n. 23.

by these institutions. Reapportionment occupies only a narrow band of the space filled by democratization; and democratization, in turn, fills only a part of what counts as the good society. In neither case can we hope to achieve certainty. We can only hope to improve our bets, and reapportionment offers one small hedge against the odds.

* * *

COMMENTARY *by David Braybrooke*

The chief point of Professor Rae's theoretical reasoning could, I think, be expressed differently and reached without considering the index XD: Given an electorate of n voters, there is a finite set of integers, each of which could be the number of a coalition of voters, ranging from a majority equal to n to a minority equal to 1. Under any unequal apportionment of n among a given number of constituencies (d), a subset of these integers will represent minority coalitions capable under the rules of electing a majority of the legislature if the voters belonging to such a coalition are distributed favorably to this end. Let us call such minorities "electorally possible" ones. In a given situation, the electorally possible minorities might number $n - \left(\dfrac{n}{2}+1\right)$ or $n - \left(\dfrac{n}{2}+2\right)$ or . . . or $n - \left(\dfrac{n}{2}+3{,}000\right)$ i.e., any of a subset so bounded of the original set of integers. Because of the unequal apportionment $n - \left(\dfrac{n}{2}+3{,}000\right)$, the number of the smallest minority electorally possible, is smaller than $\dfrac{n+\dfrac{n}{d}}{4}$, Rae's approximation for the smallest minority electorally possible under equal apportionment $\left(\dfrac{n}{d}=D\right)$. If reapportionment is carried through to equality for all constituencies, then $n - \left(\dfrac{n}{2}+3{,}000\right)$ and other minority numbers at the end of the subset will be cut away, and the smallest number in the remainder of the subset, the number representing the smallest minority electorally possible, will become $n - \left(\dfrac{n}{2}+x\right)$, which will equal $\dfrac{n+\dfrac{n}{d}}{4}$. Hence, although reapportionment does not eliminate the subset of electorally possible minorities, it excludes from the subset minorities smaller than $\dfrac{n + \dfrac{n}{d}}{4}$ and thus excludes the most scandalous cases electorally possible previously. Indeed it excludes all the cases that can be excluded compatibly with having d constituencies. Reapportionment also, as Rae says, makes it "less likely that a minority party will win a legislative majority," but it does so only on a purely a priori view, in which we assume that, because the subset representing electorally possible minorities diminishes, the probability of there being a victory for any of the minorities represented in the subset will diminish, too. (This assumption, despite its plausible face, is far from self-evident and in fact deserves to be regarded with grave misgivings.)

I say the chief theoretical point could be reached without considering the index XD (Rae's reasoning to $\dfrac{n + \dfrac{n}{d}}{4}$ does not invoke XD); indeed, I think the point itself is only a more exact formulation of what reapportionment has commonly been understood to promise. But I do not say these things to detract from Rae's argument. He does not claim any startling novelty for the point; and his approach to it, by way of considering XD, normalized to allow for the limits even of perfect reapportionment, enables him to connect the point with an ingenious and illuminating empirical assessment both of the actual efforts to date of reapportionment in the United States and of the scope for future advances there. I have no reason to suspect that any mathematical anomalies lurk in the index XD; and so far as I can see, Rae's treatment of the empirical data that he marshals is perfectly straightforward.

What does perplex me is the question of how far the index XD can be said to cover the whole body of advantages to be expected from reapportionment.

On the one hand, XD is apt to overstate the advantages of reapportionment. Not only does XD abstract, as Rae acknowledges, from the possibility that scandalously small minorities may triumph through a combination of plurality victories. The a priori argument, alluded to above, of there being less likelihood of a minority party's winning a majority in the legislature is not a safe guide to the genuine empirical probabilities of any particular case, even if majorities must be won in every constituency. Reapportionment may give greater weight than before to votes in constituencies where a minority party is well organized.

In general, given any apportionment, a number of specific practical alliances correspond to any one number in the subset of electorally possible minorities; and the number of practical alliances so corresponding is apt to change in either direction with reapportionment. An electorally possible minority such as $n - \left(\dfrac{n}{2} + 7\right)$, formed by allying butchers with bakers, may no longer be practical; but in compensation for this one lost possibility, two new possibilities may be gained: forming a minority of $n - \left(\dfrac{n}{2} + 7\right)$ by allying butchers with candlestickmakers or candlestickmakers with bakers. Reapportionment may thus increase the empirical probability of control by a minority, even if the subset of numbers representing electorally possible minorities diminishes. The same consideration operates against the contention (on a priori grounds) that a reapportionment reducing XD makes it "less likely that, in an inter-election dispute, responsive legislators will form majorities contrary to the numerical division of the electorate" (Rae, p. 108). No one can say, empirically less likely or empirically more likely, until he has looked at the effects in the particular case on the position of organizations within the constituencies and on the available forms of alliance.[1]

On the other hand, XD is likely to understate the advantages of reapportionment in various ways.

Persons in constituencies with reduced populations would find access to their representatives easier (if the proportion of constituents seeking access did not increase unduly). It would be easier for them to arrange appointments and more likely, one might expect, to get enough time and attention to accomplish their ends. These advantages, moreover, would extend, in the form of provisions in case of need (insurance provisions) to persons who did not themselves have occasions for seeking access. It is true that those in constituencies with enlarged populations would suffer corresponding adverse effects; but the value of the advantages that they would lose might be less than the value of the advantages gained in the reduced constituencies. They might hitherto have had more time and

---

1. In a characteristically counterfashionable article, Lewis A. Dexter has pointed out a number of disadvantages that may attend reapportionment. Some of these, like breaking up "natural" communications areas into different constituencies, might be long-lasting; others, like breaking up established organizations and traditions of participation, might be offset in time by new growths in the reapportioned constituencies. See "Standards for Representative Selection and Apportionment," in J. Roland Pennock and John W. Chapman, eds., *Representation* (*NOMOS X*) (New York: Atherton Press, 1968), pp. 155–166

attention than they really needed when they sought access and more in the way of insurance when they did not.

Another possible advantage of reapportionment, which demands similar treatment so far as it is real, lies in the greater impulse to take an active part in politics, beyond voting, that persons in reduced constituencies might feel. Persons in reduced constituencies might consider that they had a greater chance of being politically effective, of making a visible difference by their participation, to the success of a political campaign or to the weight thrown by their constituencies to one side or another of a given issue. Again, there would be corresponding adverse effects in the enlarged constituencies; but, again, these adverse effects might be more than offset by the gains in the reduced constituencies.[2]

Besides there being a favorable overall effect on the impulse to participate in politics, there might, as a result of reapportionment, be favorable effects both on the actual rates of participation and on the opportunities to make genuine visible differences by participation. More persons might wear campaign buttons and improve their candidates' chances by doing so. (The impulse to participate, of course, may vary independently of each of these two aspects of participation; and they, of each other. We would not think much of an impulse to participate that did not eventuate in actual participation, given favorable circumstances; but favorable circumstances may not be given: just as the impulse builds up, the opportunity may be taken away, for example, by a military coup. Furthermore, the impulse to participate may not lead to any increase in certain modes of participation.) [3]

2. Suppose there is a function connecting the mean personal impulse to participate with D (the population of a constituency); and that the function falls slowly in the range $0 < D \leq \frac{n}{d}$, but precipitously thereafter. Then if before reapportionment there were just as many constituencies substantially less than $\frac{n}{d}$ in population as there were substantially greater (without there being 0 of either sort), while all the remaining constituencies equaled $\frac{n}{d}$, the adverse effects for the whole country would be more than offset by the favorable effects on impulse, and likewise in many other cases. A similar function and a similar distribution of population before apportionment may be invoked to support the point about access.

3. Are any of these aspects of participation in fact connected with D by a function that (given certain distributions of n before reapportionment) would lead to a balance of favorable effects? Political scientists I have talked to are skeptical, and I am skeptical, too; other variables may well affect participation much more strongly than D, and if there is any function connecting D with participation, I suspect that it levels off for most people at a pretty low value of D—say, 5,000 or 10,000. I say

An important further advantage of reapportionment consists in the help that it gives to making the whole democratic process more intelligible. (Unfortunately, it is an advantage even harder to measure than those

---

"for most people" because I have the impression that professional people and academic people in Canada think and act on an assumption of much greater political efficacy vis-à-vis their national government than similar people in the States. Perhaps, given the size of most American constituencies, federal or state, very little empirical allowance has to be made for advantages from reapportionment which would link with participation. Nevertheless, I am astonished to find that students of participation seem to have neglected this topic almost entirely. There is no mention of any relation to size of constituency in either Flanigan's or Milbrath's synopses of work in the field (William H. Flanigan, *Political Behavior of the American Electorate* [Boston: Allyn & Bacon, 1968]; Lester W. Milbrath, *Political Participation* [Chicago: Rand McNally, 1965], which has a very comprehensive bibliography). The most recent sophisticated comparative study of participation that I have come across, Norman H. Nie, G. Bingham Powell, Jr., and Kenneth Prewitt, "Social Structure and Political Participation: Developmental Relationships" (in two parts) 63 *American Political Science Review*, no. 2, pp. 361–378, and no. 3, pp. 808–832 ignores the topic. The nearest thing to mentioning it that I have found is an assertion by Robert E. Lane, "A fairer system of apportionment . . . would create the political environment where participation would be nourished," which he supports with a quotation from Gosnell concerning increased participation in Switzerland (Robert E. Lane, *Political Life* [New York: Free Press, 1959], p. 353). But Gosnell, in the passage from which Lane draws the quotation, is talking (omitting statistics) about the effects of introducing proportional representation with the Swiss Federal Council elections of 1919 (Harold F. Gosnell, *Democracy: The Threshold of Freedom* [New York: Ronald Press, 1948], pp. 191–192); Lane himself, in the passage I have cited, does not distinguish between reapportionment and changing to proportional representation, which might well have special effects of its own. Maybe, to a sophisticated eye, the proposition that, given constituencies which will have large populations anyway, before or after reapportionment, no effects on participation will be observed is too truistic to be worth checking; but, in my view, it does not look any more so than many other propositions which social scientists have taken great pains to investigate. Some data even suggest that there may be evidence to the contrary. My colleague Dale H. Poel (whom I thank for discussing this comment with me) has examined the relationship between the number of persons enumerated as eligible to vote in the Ontario provincial election of 1967 and the mean voter turnout in each riding. (Let us suppose that voter turnout varies directly with other forms of participation.) There were 117 ridings (district or constituency), ranging in numbers of persons eligible to vote from 14,400 to 47,574, with a mean of 31,502. The mean voter turnout in the 55 ridings with fewer than the mean number of persons eligible to vote was 67.027, whereas the mean turnout in the 62 ridings with more than the mean number eligible was 64.659, a difference of 2.368, where $t \leq 1.967$ for significance at the 5 percent level. Poel points out that the 55 less populous ridings were predominantly rural; for this or other reasons, the effect of which cannot be disentangled without a good deal further work, the association between turnout and population may be apparent only; but does not the appearance deserve some attention?

Lane's hypothesis that "political activity increases with density of population" (*Political Life*, p. 267) moves me to point out that, if reapportionment increases

already mentioned—which is not to say, impossible.) Suppose it is accepted that representation must take the place of direct votes upon policies and also that representatives are to have some discretion about how far they are to press the desires of their constituents, in the light of discussion in the legislature and the need to bargain there with the representatives of other constituencies. Any citizen might well wonder how far the policies thus arrived at through representation will actually reflect popular desires in a reasonably democratic way. The most convincing approach to answering him is to set up an ideal model for representing the people in question, a model in which their desires about policies would be effective in choosing among candidates and in influencing the opinions of candidates during and after the process of choice. One would then calculate the results in adopted policies of operating such a model and finally compare those results with the actual ones eventuating in the real, non-ideal system. Such an ideal model would have equal apportionment as one of its features; otherwise (on grounds presupposed by Rae in setting up his index XD and quite generally shared by people with democratic beliefs) individual votes in the smaller constituencies would have indefensibly disproportionate weights. Scandalously small minorities would have a chance of pushing policies through against the desires of impressively large majorities. One might say, if the model is going to be ideal, then it will be ideal in this respect as well, or at least, for whatever it is worth. If the apportionment in fact is unequal, the ideal model can be applied to a given people and government only by correcting for the inequality, which would entail redrawing—in imagination—the boundaries of the actual constituencies or making imaginary transfers of population[4] or mentally introducing some other disconcerting novelty. But, if the apportionment in fact is equal already, the ideal model will in this prominent feature correspond directly to familiar reality; and the test into which it enters, requiring fewer departures from reality on the ideal side of the comparison, will be simpler. I do not suppose that many citizens will have just this point about a test involving an ideal model in mind; but, nevertheless, they can appreciate the fact that in evaluating the degree of democracy achieved by their government there

---

the number of constituencies situated in areas already high in participation, it will increase the proportion of constituencies high in this respect, and this effect might be reckoned an advantage. (Density of population might work the other way from size of population in a constituency without eliminating effects from the latter.)

4. As stipulated in the "indirect" test for collective preference given in Braybrooke, *Three Tests for Democracy* (New York: Random House, 1968), pp. 208–216.

will be one prominent feature that they do not have to correct for—one complication the less to confuse the issue.

The conclusion to be drawn from considering the various chances and mischances of advantage from reapportionment is, in part, the conclusion that, although the index XD gives us important information, that information is so limited in its implications that we cannot tell from it alone whether a net balance of advantages has been gained from reapportionment unless we consider that the achievement of a species of justice by the closest approximation possible to equality among voters in the effect of their votes is by itself a decisive advantage. But that achievement can be assessed without consulting XD; and what XD does peculiarly tell us—that a certain precaution has been taken against undue control by scandalously small minorities—loses a good deal of its force when we see that the precaution is imperfect.

The other part of the conclusion is happier: There are advantages, besides the advance toward justice, which XD leaves out of account, some of them only indirectly related to voting; and while we do not have any actual measurements of them, we may well think that fate would be very perverse indeed if they were entirely insubstantial.

*　　*　　*

REJOINDER *by Douglas W. Rae*

It is a pleasure to join issue with so distinguished a student of democratic institutions as David Braybrooke. And there are several points on which we fully agree. Nevertheless, his commentary contains a few mistaken and misleading suggestions which I shall note briefly.

First, Braybrooke seems unclear about the "chief point" of my essay. It is not a general assessment of reapportionment's consequences; rather, I have sought to relate this specific question to the broader problem of institutional democracy.[1]

Second, in developing his alternative to my numerical analysis, Braybrooke seems to confuse his definition of sets. Thus, in his opening paragraph, he seems to think that there is *one* "possible minority" of any

1. In a later paper, I apply a similar analysis to a variety of representational and decision-making institutions. See Rae, "The Democratic Guarantee: An Analytic Index and Its Theoretical Arguments," *American Political Science Review,* March 1971.

given size. This is, of course, false and renders his otherwise intelligent suggestion suspect.

Last, he offers four hypotheses about the consequences of reapportionment which seem groundless, trivial, or both:

"Reapportionment may give greater weight than before to votes in constituencies where a minority party is well organized." Quite so, but so too might reapportionment lead to a concentration of authority in the hands of the bicyclists. There is no reason at all to think that this will be true and some reason to suppose it improbable.

"Persons in constituencies with reduced populations would find access to their representatives easier if the proportion of constituents seeking access did not increase unduly." [2] This is trivial, except on the naïve supposition that the pertinent function is linear. It isn't. If a representative has a fixed quantity of time to be spent listening to his constituents (x), then a district of size D offers an average of x over D in access to each constituent. If D were being cut from 2 to 1, this would dramatically increase access time. If, more plausibly, it were being reduced from 20,000 to 10,000, the relative difference would be 0.00005 times x since the function is an inverse which is virtually flat over this relevant section of its range.[3] Voters could be forgiven if they noticed no appreciable change in ease of access.

"Besides there being a favorable overall effect on the impulse to participate in politics, there might, as a result of reapportionment, be favorable effects both on the actual rates of participation and on the opportunities to make genuine visible differences by participation. More persons might wear campaign buttons and improve their candidates' chances by doing so." This conjecture is pleasing, if groundless: People might also take to wearing mittens, but in neither instance do I see any good reason to make the prediction.

"An important further advantage of reapportionment consists in the help that it gives in making the whole democratic process more intelligible." Frankly, I doubt that our countrymen have noticed a marked change along these lines, and I cannot myself think up a single convincing reason to entertain Braybrooke's hunch.

If his purpose is to suggest that my essay leaves a good many stones unturned, Braybrooke succeeds admirably. But I cannot see why he began with such unpromising suggestions as these.

2. Note that this parenthetical assumption partly contradicts Braybrooke's further contention that reapportionment increases participation.

3. That is, $\dfrac{x}{10,000} - \dfrac{x}{20,000} = 0.0001x - 0.00005x = 0.00005$.

4

GERRYMANDERING: PRIVILEGED SANCTUARY OR NEXT JUDICIAL TARGET?

Gordon E. Baker

"[T]he achieving of fair and effective representation for all citizens is concededly the basic aim of legislative apportionment . . ."[1] With these words, Chief Justice Earl Warren, in *Reynolds* v. *Sims,* articulated the high hopes held by the Supreme Court majority in laying down the standard of one man, one vote. Since that landmark pronouncement in June 1964, the political maps of all states have undergone revamping—in most instances, of major dimensions. Most of the questions left open in the 1964 reapportionment cases have subsequently been answered, as state and lower federal courts, as well as the highest tribunal itself, have implemented those rulings. With the 1970 census certain to trigger a fresh round of redistricting throughout the nation, the political stakes were never higher.

The most troublesome question, however, not only remained unsettled, but loomed ever larger in significance. The gerrymander—the intentional manipulation of districts for partisan or factional advantage—comprised, in its various forms, the heart of the political thicket that the judiciary skirted most gingerly. Moreover, the Supreme Court had paradoxically encouraged the potential for widespread gerrymandering, while gradually developing a single-minded quest for mathematical equality. In particular, two decisions in the spring of 1969 laid the groundwork (no doubt, unintentionally) for proliferating the more advanced and subtle forms of discriminatory cartography. Inevitable legal challenges will pose a dilemma for the courts: whether to allow the ideal of representative

1. *Reynolds* v. *Sims,* 377 U.S. 533, 565-566 (1964).

equality to be undermined by pervasive gerrymanders, or whether to elaborate the standard beyond mere mathematical equality.

The term "gerrymander" customarily evokes images of contorted district lines, designed either to concentrate the voters of one party or faction in as few districts as possible, or to spread them among numerous constituencies, where their diluted voting strength will comprise a minority. This stereotype is understandable. Most schoolchildren learn about Governor Gerry's salamanderlike districting of Massachusetts in 1812. Yet over the years the term has become more inclusive. For example, long legislative failure to redistrict at all (the situation in *Baker* v. *Carr* that ended an era of judicial noninvolvement with malapportionment) was sometimes referred to as the "silent gerrymander," since discrimination in favor of the status quo stemmed from inaction rather than positive design. Or, even when a new reapportionment resulted in an overrepresentation of less populous counties or towns, the pattern obviously favored certain interests or parties at the expense of others just as effectively as a map with more tortured district lines. This point was forcefully noted by Andrew Hacker:

> It is sometimes argued that the creation of unequal districts is not actually gerrymandering. This, however, is mainly an aesthetic objection, and is based on the belief that cramming the opposition into a sardine tin is too heavy-handed an operation to be worthy of the mantle of Elbridge Gerry. The point is that gerrymandering is the maneuvering of district boundaries for partisan advantage.[2]

Finally, a point that has been neglected until recently is the fact that a genuine gerrymander can consist of compact and contiguous districts of equal population. As we shall note later, this type of gerrymander will pose the most serious challenge to courts, if they should ultimately take on the issue.

Furthermore, the use of multi-member districts can fall under the rubric of gerrymandering, even though this was not the original purpose of most such constituencies. Indeed, the opposite rationale is frequently advanced: electing a county's delegation at large eliminates the need for drawing district lines and consequently removes the temptation to do so in a partisan fashion. Many state constitutions forbid dividing any county internally into districts, so that before judicial intervention the only way

2. Andrew Hacker, *Congressional Districting* (Washington: The Brookings Institution, 1963), p. 52.

of adjusting representation to population was to devise multi-member districts for more populous, urban communities.

On the other hand, multi-member districts raise the objection that they do not adequately reflect the diversity of political views within such areas. The majority party in a given district frequently sweeps all, or nearly all, seats. It is no coincidence that major support for multi-member constituencies comes from cities and opposition to them, from rural areas.[3] Indeed, during the long era of rural overrepresentation, at-large elections in metropolitan centers were at times defended as allowing the Democratic party an opportunity to dominate city delegations as a means of counterbalancing their disadvantage in underpopulated rural districts.[4] However justified, the winner-take-all nature of the multi-member district seems to qualify it as a variety of gerrymander. And the judicial equalization of district populations has removed the "balancing" rationale just mentioned.

At this point, we may have approximated Robert G. Dixon, Jr.'s sardonic dictum that "all districting is gerrymandering."[5] If this is the case, then the courts have corrected only certain types of the art (the "silent" gerrymander and districts of disparate population), while so far avoiding others (multi-member, at-large districts and the partisan or factional manipulation of district boundaries). Before probing the prospects and desirability of judicial action regarding the latter category, we should first examine what the courts—in particular, the United States Supreme Court—have had to say on the subject.

MULTI-MEMBER DISTRICTS

In enunciating the principle of one man, one vote, in *Reynolds* v. *Sims,* Chief Justice Warren took pains to indicate the degree of discretion still left to state legislatures in devising districts of substantially equal populations. In doing so, the Court's opinion made specific reference to multi-member districts. For example, in discussing the impact of representative equality on bicameralism, the Court said: "One body could be composed

3. Maurice Klain, "A New Look at the Constituencies: The Need for a Recount and a Reappraisal," 49 *American Political Science Review* 1117.

4. See William P. Irwin, "Colorado: A Matter of Balance," in Malcolm E. Jewell, ed., *The Politics of Reapportionment* (New York: Atherton Press, 1962), pp. 64–80.

5. Robert G. Dixon, Jr., *Democratic Representation* (New York: Oxford University Press, 1968), p. 462. From the same work: "Gerrymandering is discriminatory districting. It equally covers squiggles, multi-member districting, or simple nonaction, when the result is racial or political malrepresentation," p. 460.

of single-member districts, while the other could have at least some multi-member districts"; and, again, "Single-member districts may be the rule in one State, while another State might desire to achieve some flexibility by creating multi-member or floterial districts." [6] Such statements may well have discouraged subsequent challenges to the validity of multi-member districts where population was proportionate. Nevertheless, a challenge to the at-large election of an area's multi-member delegation came to the Supreme Court during the term following the 1964 state apportionment cases.

In response to *Baker* v. *Carr* the State of Georgia had redrawn constituencies for one house—the senate—on a population basis, with the major urban counties each receiving from two to seven seats. Whereas district lines were drawn within the counties and candidates for election were required to live within their respective districts, the law provided that voting for all senators be countywide. A local court invalidated the at-large provision as being contrary to the then-existing state constitution, and the 1962 elections were held on a district basis. In that same election, however, voters ratified a constitutional amendment embodying provisions of the 1962 apportionment statute. This new constitutional proviso was invalidated by a federal district court, which held that the difference between electing senators in districts comprising a county or group of counties and at large in the multi-member counties, constituted invidious discrimination contrary to the Fourteenth Amendment to the United States Constitution.[7]

Hearing the case on appeal, the United States Supreme Court reversed the lower court decision on January 17, 1965, in *Fortson* v. *Dorsey*.[8] An opinion by Justice William Brennan referred to the flexibility allowed to states in *Reynolds,* but showed caution by disavowing any blanket endorsement of multi-member districts:

> [O]ur opinion is not to be understood to say that in all instances or under all circumstances such a system as Georgia has will comport with the dictates of the Equal Protection Clause. It might well be that, designedly or otherwise, a multi-member constituency apportionment scheme, under the circumstances of a particular case, would operate to minimize or cancel out the voting strength of racial or political elements of the voting population. When this is demonstrated it will be time

6. *Supra*, n. 1 at 577, 579.
7. *Dorsey* v. *Fortson*, 228 F. Supp. 259 (N.D. Ga., 1964).
8. 379 U.S. 433 (1965).

enough to consider whether the system still passes constitutional muster. This question, however, is not presented by the record before us.[9]

As the Court pointed out, the appellees had not seriously pressed the point of discrimination against racial or political minorities, except for a brief assertion not supported by evidence. Instead, those challenging the amendment stressed the theoretical possibility that a unanimous choice of voters in one of the residence districts could be defeated by the countywide vote. The Court rejected the mathematical argument as being highly hypothetical. Justice Douglas dissented, pointing to dicta in *Gray v. Sanders,* where the Court struck down Georgia's county unit system: "Once the geographical unit for which a representative is to be chosen is designated, all who participate in the election are to have an equal vote—whatever their race, whatever their sex, whatever their occupation, whatever their income, and wherever their home may be in that geographical unit." [10]

Fortson v. *Dorsey* is a perplexing case, in view of the fact that one ostensible purpose of Georgia's multi-member provision was to prevent the election of a Negro senator from Atlanta. The use of seven separate districts in 1962 resulted in the election of the first Negro legislator since the Reconstruction. When *Fortson* v. *Dorsey* restored the at-large provision, an all-White delegation emerged after the next election. This would seem to be one example of the kind of evidence that might still, in a case more skillfully argued and presented than *Fortson,* bring about judicial invalidation of the Georgia multi-member practice.

In another challenged apportionment involving several issues, the Supreme Court refused to invalidate multi-member districts in Hawaii.[11] The Court acknowledged that such a system might operate invidiously, but reiterated the point made in the Georgia case that any discriminatory effects asserted must be demonstrated in the record. Again, the door remained ajar for any future appeals which relied on proof rather than on hypothetical speculation.

In view of the Supreme Court's posture, it is not surprising that plaintiffs challenging multi-member districting as a form of gerrymandering began to take greater pains to document the discriminatory impact on political or racial minorities. The most significant development along this

9. *Id.* at 439.
10. *Gray* v. *Sanders,* 372 U.S. 368, 379 (1963).
11. *Burns* v. *Richardson,* 384 U.S. 73 (1966).

line arose in litigation contesting Indiana's use of a mixed system of single- and multi-member districts in both legislative houses. Joining in *Chavis* v. *Whitcomb* were members of several diverse minorities, including a Negro from central Indianapolis, a white Republican from that city's suburbs, and an independent voter who claimed that the long ballot in the state's most populous county frustrated his efforts to vote for the individual candidate rather than the political party. A three-judge federal district court on July 28, 1969, held against the state. The decision indicated that several assertions, including those of the suburban Republican and the independent voter, were not sufficiently proved. The same was true of charges by Negroes in some areas of the state. However, the court did find that the multi-member status of Marion County operated to minimize and cancel out the voting strength of Negroes residing in one section of Indianapolis. The record included elaborate and detailed documentation of the socio-economic and political characteristics of the area and demonstrated to the court's satisfaction a discriminatory impact on the minority group. While acknowledging that Negroes were not entitled to a certain number of legislators, that districts had to be drawn with an eye that was color-blind, the court also emphasized that "sophisticated gerrymandering has been soundly condemned." [12]

Even though these specific findings of proof in *Chavis* v. *Whitcomb* were confined to the state's most populous county, the district court concluded that it had to consider the challenged system as a whole and called for a redistricting for both houses throughout the state. This did not necessarily mean that only single-member districts would have been permitted; thus, if all districts were to have elected an identical number (such as two or three) of representatives, that would presumably have passed muster. The key to equal representation as viewed by the court was an application of the uniform district principle. But an apportionment scheme providing a mixed use of single- and multi-member districts was constitutionally suspect.

The federal district court in Indiana did not ignore the Supreme Court precedents in the Georgia and Hawaii appeals. Both were cited and quoted at length and then carefully distinguished. The situation in Indiana, the lower court insisted, presented circumstances which the high tribunal had carefully noted could invalidate a multi-member districting scheme.

12. *Chavis* v. *Whitcomb*, U.S. District Court, Southern District of Indiana, Indianapolis Division, No. 1P 69-C-23 (1969) in National Municipal League, *Court Decisions on Legislative Apportionment* vol. 32, p. 98. The reference is to *Gomillion* v. *Lightfoot*, 364 U.S. 339 (1960).

After the decision in *Chavis* v. *Whitcomb*, the Indiana legislature was unable to reach agreement on redistricting in the two months allowed by the court order. As a result, the district court issued its own plan of uniform, single-member districts for both houses, to go into effect in the 1970 election. In February of that year, however, the United States Supreme Court stayed the lower court order, granting Indiana until after the 1970 census to draft new districts. The high court did not rule on the constitutional validity of mixing multi-member and single-member districts in the same legislative house.

Further challenges to multi-member districts by politically disadvantaged groups are under way and seem bound to grow until the Supreme Court clarifies the matter. The political force of urban Negroes in the South has been blunted by at-large elections of county delegations. Indeed, documented records would be even more conclusive there than the persuasive evidence in Indiana, where at least some Negroes were elected. A recent instance is a suit filed in a federal district court in Alabama early in 1970 by the American Civil Liberties Union and the National Association for the Advancement of Colored People Legal Defense Fund. Plaintiffs challenged as discriminatory the state's countywide election of legislators. In the twentieth century, Blacks, constituting 30 percent of Alabama's population, had had no representative of their race in either house of the 141-seat legislature (though one was elected from a rural area in November 1970). Yet Negroes comprise 66 percent of metropolitan Birmingham's population and a substantial minority in other Alabama cities, usually in concentrated areas. The petitioner's brief called for dividing counties into house and senate wards along existing precinct lines, estimating that such a remapping would result in the election of approximately four senators and ten representatives from Black communities.[13]

While chances for success would appear strong in well documented cases involving racial minorities, the challenges to multi-member districts by disadvantaged political parties are more problematical. In the former category, there is by now a clear judicial sensitivity to various forms of racial discrimination and disfranchisement. However, vindicating the claims of an area's minority political party would seem to involve courts in the kind of "party contests" that the late Justice Felix Frankfurter warned of in *Colegrove* v. *Green*.[14] While Frankfurter's general doctrine of judicial noninvolvement has been set aside, a number of judges under-

13. See account in American Civil Liberties Union, *Civil Liberties*, March 1970, p. 2.
14. *Colegrove* v. *Green*, 328 U.S. 549 (1946).

standably continue to share his hesitancy when party disputes are at issue.

One example of this caution may be seen in a unanimous decision by the New Jersey Supreme Court in March 1970 upholding the state's legislative reapportionment, despite some admitted departures from the one man, one vote, standard. The legislature consists of a 40-member senate and an 80-member assembly. Senators were apportioned approximately on the basis of population among the state's twenty-one counties, with each county delegation being elected at large. For each senator, two assembly seats were allotted to a district within a county. Thus a county with five senators would elect them at large, and each of the five districts within the county would elect its own two assemblymen, as well. The New York *Times* account of the New Jersey court's decision indicated the stakes for political parties with this observation: "Today's decision was a blow to the Democrats in the state. Officials from both major parties contend that at-large elections increasingly tend to favor the Republicans as most of the state's population shifts from the decaying cities to the surrounding suburbs." [15] An example: In 1967 the long-time Democratic stronghold in Newark was unable to match Essex County's suburban vote, with Republicans electing all six senators and eight of twelve assemblymen. The New Jersey Supreme Court decision concluded that it would be "improper" for it to rule on the constitutionality of multi-member districts, since that question was then before the United States Supreme Court.

The election of legislative delegations at large poses two distinct kinds of problems. One involves the differences in influence between voters situated in districts of varying populations which elect proportionate numbers of legislators. The usual "common sense" assumption is that legislative strength should be proportionate: that a county five times as populous as an average single-member district should be assigned five times the number of seats in order to equalize representation. This is true *if* single-member district lines are drawn in the more populous county, but if the five legislators are elected at large, a different situation obtains. John F. Banzhaf III has demonstrated that a vote in the larger, multi-member districts has considerably more effective influence on elections and legislative outcomes than does a vote in a single-member or smaller multi-member district, assuming proportionate populations. Using a standard mathematical technique (related to the use of game theory in measuring power distributions in legislative bodies and other groups), Banzhaf showed that voter influence was in proportion to the square root of the

15. New York *Times,* March 7, 1970.

population of the district. Moreover, the ratios of effective representation are substantial—far more so than the variations in district populations that have concerned the judiciary.[16]

The second problem of multi-member districts is the impact of winner-take-all elections on minority groupings in a particular district. This issue would still exist if, for example, the objections just noted (by Banzhaf) were corrected by a system entirely composed of multi-member districts of approximately equal population, each electing an identical number of legislators. Of course, the inferior status of political minorities, while accentuated in at-large elections, is not exclusively confined to them. A district electing but one legislator obviously cannot expect him to represent all minority viewpoints. But single-member districts are more likely to do so *in toto,* because the creation of a large number of constituencies is more likely to accommodate the more significant minority groupings (such as Negroes, Puerto Ricans, Chicanos, suburban Republicans, or city Democrats, depending on the state and area involved). Such minorities frequently have sufficient geographic concentration in metropolitan areas to comprise their own districts.

Both problems posed by multi-member, at-large elections are extensively found in all sections of the United States. Court-ordered reapportionments have typically resulted in adding legislative representation to urban centers. These augmented delegations have, in turn, frequently been elected at large and usually have produced windfalls for political majorities in these areas. The result, though not always the intent, is a species of gerrymander. While some litigation has touched on the basic questions involving multi-member districts, only recently has the judiciary had an opportunity for serious consideration of well documented arguments.

The Indiana case mentioned earlier is indicative. The three-judge federal district court examined in elaborate detail the social, economic, and political status of the Negro minority in Indianapolis and found that at-large elections for Marion County put this minority at a demonstrable disadvantage. But the other aspect—the inferior power of single-member districts vis-à-vis Marion County's delegation—was also noted by the judges. Banzhaf's article (and his testimony before the court) received attention and cautious approval. Taking what it termed a simpler view

16. J. F. Banzhaf III, "Multi-Member Electoral Districts—Do They Violate the 'One Man, One Vote,' Principle?" 75 *Yale Law Journal* 1310–1338. Applying the mathematical technique to legislative houses in five states employing mixed single- and multi-member systems, Banzhaf computed effective representation variances ranging from 200 percent to 374 percent.

of the situation than the mathematically based article, the court agreed that each voter in Marion County had a greater theoretical opportunity to cast a critical or deciding vote. Moreover, the court found that the most populous county's delegations usually voted as blocs, concluding: "as each member of the bloc delegation is responsible to the voter majority who elected the whole, each Marion County voter has a greater voice in the legislature, having more legislators to speak for him than does a comparable voter in . . . [a] . . . single member senatorial district." [17]

The validity of multi-member districting appears to be the next most logical question on fairness of representation for the United States Supreme Court to resolve in the 1970s. While the Court has as yet given no encouragement to those challenging the election of delegations at large, it has nonetheless carefully left the door open to an examination of the issue, should it be properly presented. A well argued case involving a racial minority would seem to be the most likely prospect for a successful challenge, while an appeal by a partisan minority would be more problematical. This thornier issue could be sidestepped should the high tribunal be persuaded that, following Banzhaf's analysis, the at-large election of legislative delegations of differing size inherently violates the principle of one man, one vote. Such a holding by the Court would have far-reaching consequences, given the number of states using such district systems. At the same time, this ultimate ruling may be inescapable if the goal posited in the reapportionment cases of 1964 is to be realized—equal representation for equal numbers of persons.

BOUNDARY MANIPULATION

The most widely publicized type of gerrymander involves the drawing of district lines in a way that benefits the party or faction in charge of the map-making. The object here is to cause as many of the opposition's votes as possible to be "wasted," either by concentrating them in a few districts or spreading them as minority segments among many constituencies. Urban areas, where population is concentrated, have served as the primary target, since relatively minor shifts in boundaries can maximize differences in the electoral outcome. Before the reapportionment revolution of the 1960s, checks on periodically gerrymandered boundaries were few. One was political—the possibility of a partisan division in the control of state

17. *Chavis, supra*, n. 12, p. 99. The U.S. Supreme Court noted Banzhaf's article without comment in *Kilgarlin* v. *Hill*, 386 U.S. 120 (1967).

legislative houses or the governorship when redistricting was scheduled. Another was the frequent legal prohibition (and tradition) against breaking county or other local unit lines to form districts. Requirements in some state laws (as well as in several federal congressional apportionment acts before 1929) that districts be "compact and contiguous" could be ignored with impunity, since they were not enforced. They may have had some value as standards or models of what optimum districting should include. By contrast, the classic examples of gerrymandered districts were those that reminded the viewer of such objects as barbells, horseshoes, or strips of bacon.

When the United States Supreme Court in 1962 signaled its willingness to adjudicate apportionment controversies, the issue of boundary manipulation was certain to arise, as well. Indeed, a special kind of gerrymander case had already been adjudicated in the Court term immediately prior to the one that produced *Baker* v. *Carr*. That situation, of course, did not involve legislative districts. Rather, the Alabama legislature had redrawn the city boundaries of Tuskegee, where Negro voter registration was growing steadily enough to alarm the ruling white minority. Formerly a square area, the city was converted into what the Supreme Court later termed "an uncouth twenty-eight-sided figure," [18] which excluded all but four or five of Tuskegee's four hundred Negro voters, but no white voters. Lower courts had upheld the state's action on grounds of long-established precedent which permitted state governments to alter boundaries of political subdivisions without the consent of the inhabitants or judicial inquiry into motives.

On appeal in the fall of 1960, *Gomillion* v. *Lightfoot* posed a delicate question for several members of the Supreme Court. One of Alabama's arguments was the proposition that the judiciary traditionally had stayed out of controversies involving political districting. Justice Felix Frankfurter, in particular, was sensitive to any development that would undermine his slim prevailing opinion in the 1946 case of *Colegrove* v. *Green*,[19] a precedent that was already under challenge in some lower courts. At the same time, it was inconceivable that the highest tribunal would uphold such a transparent instance of racial discrimination. The Court, speaking through Justice Frankfurter, resolved the dilemma by unanimously reversing the lower court, thus invalidating the Tuskegee gerrymander, but basing the decision on Fifteenth rather than Fourteenth Amendment grounds. This strategy managed to avoid the broader ramifi-

18. *Gomillion, supra,* n. 12 at 340.
19. *Supra,* n. 14.

cations of the equal protection clause and to stress instead the prohibition against racial restrictions on the right to vote. Justice Frankfurter carefully attempted to distinguish *Gomillion* from the broader question of districting. The Tuskegee case, he asserted, did not involve "an ordinary geographic redistricting measure even within familiar abuses of gerrymandering." With typical magisterial eloquence, he added, "While in form this is merely an act redefining metes and bounds, if the allegations are established, the inescapable human effect of this essay in geometry and geography is to despoil colored citizens, and only colored citizens, of their theretofore enjoyed voting rights. That was not *Colegrove* v. *Green.*"[20]

The Tuskegee gerrymander was sufficiently distinct from legislative districting that it did not spur a rash of legal challenges to the manipulation of constituency boundaries. A precondition to such a bold step was judicial acceptance of justiciability in apportionment cases. As soon as *Baker* v. *Carr* articulated this in March 1962 the stage was set for testing a variety of electoral arrangements previously considered beyond constitutional adjudication. Of these, population inequalities among congressional and state legislative districts received the major attention.

In the fall of 1963 the Supreme Court heard nearly a week of oral argument on appeals from several states in cases that illustrated most of the significant varieties of districting controversies that had flooded state and lower federal courts following the decision in *Baker* v. *Carr*. The first two decisions were announced on February 17 of the following year, with the bulk of attention going to the Georgia case of *Wesberry* v. *Sanders,*[21] which declared that congressional districts must be as equal in population as is practicable.

The second case, overshadowed by the *Wesberry* decision, dealt with a different question. The range of population in New York's congressional districts, redrawn in 1961, was among the closest in the nation, with the outside limits falling about 15 percent above and below the state average —variations then considered within a reasonable standard of representative equality. But district boundaries in Manhattan brought a challenge from some Democratic county leaders. The Republicans, controlling both

20. *Supra,* n. 18 at 347. Justice Charles Whittaker wrote a concurring opinion, persuasively arguing that the Fifteenth Amendment was an inappropriate basis for the decision, since the right to vote had not actually been taken away. He regarded Alabama's action as a racial segregation contrary to the Fourteenth Amendment's equal protection clause; he added that this ground would not affect the *Colegrove* precedent.

21. *Wesberry* v. *Sanders,* 376 U.S. 1 (1964).

houses of the legislature, as well as the governorship, had carefully re-drawn the map to retain for their party one of the borough's four con-gressional seats, the Seventeenth District—a "silk stocking" constituency centering on the upper-income areas of the East Side.

The litigation, however, was cast in terms of a racial, not a partisan, gerrymander. The ethnic makeup of Manhattan's four districts yielded these statistics:

District	Percentage of Whites in District	Percentage of Negroes and Puerto Ricans in District
17th	94.9	5.1
18th	13.7	86.3
19th	71.5	28.5
20th	72.5	27.5

Armed with the above data, the plaintiffs relied on *Gomillion* v. *Lightfoot* as a precedent, and charged that Negroes and Puerto Ricans had been "fenced out" of the Seventeenth District. Support for the status quo, how-ever, came from several minority spokesmen, including the borough's single Negro congressman, Adam Clayton Powell, who filed as an inter-venor along with the state.

The Supreme Court upheld (by 7 to 2) the New York districting, hold-ing that there was no proof that the motive was racial discrimination. Speaking for the majority, Mr. Justice Hugo Black pointed out that the concentration of racial and ethnic voters in particular areas strongly con-ditioned the composition of the districts that could be formed. Justices William O. Douglas and Arthur Goldberg dissented, invoking various precedents regarding racial segregation. They insisted that the boundaries in question could be explained only in racial terms and that the facts constituted a prima facie case of segregated districts.

Nor did minority support for the prevailing system make a difference to Justice Douglas. He countered: "The fact that Negro political leaders find advantage in this nearly solid Negro and Puerto Rican district is irrelevant to our problem. Rotten boroughs were long a curse of demo-cratic processes. Racial boroughs are also at war with democratic stand-ards." [22] Douglas went on to compare the situation in the borough of Manhattan with the electoral register system, introduced by the British into India to give separate constituencies to religious and racial groupings.

22. *Wright* v. *Rockefeller,* 376 U.S. 52, 62 (1964).

Comparable arrangements in Cyprus and Lebanon were described, for good measure, in a lengthy footnote. Douglas concluded that such racial electoral registers had no place in the United States, where the important consideration should be the individual, not his race, creed, or color.

It is difficult to read the opinions (especially the dissenting ones) in *Wright* v. *Rockefeller* without a nagging sense of unreality. No one seemed to deal with the actual issue. Justice Douglas went into graphic detail regarding the way in which the new boundary zigzagged its course, acquiring territory for the Seventeenth District with virtually no minority voters, while yielding up to Representative Powell's Eighteenth District areas containing large numbers of Negroes and Puerto Ricans. The correlation of such shifts to partisan voting behavior went unmentioned by anyone. The state could hardly plead that the gerrymander was basically political, with racial implications being only incidental. A central fact of New York City political life is the heavy Democratic voting of Negroes and Puerto Ricans. Had these groups shown a Republican loyalty, the Seventeenth District would undoubtedly have been drawn to include far more Negroes and Puerto Ricans. Nor could the majority of the Supreme Court specifically recognize the obvious, for fear of lending judicial approval to the practice of gerrymandering.

The Court's reluctance early in 1964 to interfere with congressional districts in Manhattan is understandable enough. To have acted otherwise would have triggered appeals from other states, with incessant pressures for the judiciary to examine legislative motives in drawing boundaries. But, as events unfolded in the years following the 1964 reapportionment decisions, avoiding such pitfalls was to be no easy task.

As lower courts adjudicated the countless challenges to electoral districts following the Supreme Court's 1964 apportionment decisions, the major attention focused on population inequalities. *Wright* v. *Rockefeller* may have discouraged some from pressing complaints of gerrymandering. When the issue did arise, however, lower courts frequently questioned whether the problem was justiciable, and the Supreme Court did not take the few opportunities it had to clarify the matter (though the *Wright* decision seemed to assume the justiciability of at least asserted racial gerrymanders). In any event, plaintiffs challenging apportionment patterns were wise to state more than this single ground. Variations in district populations could always be faulted, since standards were evolving with no specific guidelines from above. As a result, lower courts at times commented disapprovingly on the evidence of gerrymandering, but would rest adverse decisions on population inequalities, even when these were quite modest.[23] This development indicated the possibility of indirect judicial undermining of partisan gerrymandering so long as any noticeable population deviations existed.

In April of 1969, however, the United States Supreme Court announced two decisions that struck most observers as an unintentional open invitation for state legislatures to gerrymander districts in the future. In *Kirkpatrick* v. *Preisler,* the high tribunal affirmed a lower court rejection of a Missouri congressional districting plan with deviations ranging from plus 3.13 percent to minus 2.84 percent, with an average variation of 1.6 percent. In the companion case of *Wells* v. *Rockefeller,* the Supreme Court reversed a federal district court which had upheld a New York congressional districting plan which had created constituencies with a maximum population range from plus 6.49 percent to minus 6.61 percent.

These decisions were widely interpreted in the press as indicating that no state could design districts that deviated as much as 3 percent from average population, a standard that a substantial majority of states did not meet. There had been, however, no such specific implication by the Court. Justice William Brennan's opinion, stripped to its actual holding, reiterated: (1) that the Court would spell out no fixed standards of equality, that the extent to which equality might practicably be achieved might differ from state to state and from district to district; and (2) that the burden of proof rested on the state to justify disparities from population equality. But the Brennan opinion also interpreted "as nearly as practicable" to mean that a state "must make a good-faith effort to achieve precise mathematical equality," that any disparities "no matter how small" had to be justified.[24] Justice Abe Fortas objected that the Court "then proceeds to reject, *seriatim,* every type of justification that has been—possibly every one that could be—advanced." [25]

The ominous implications for gerrymandering are found in the Court's contention that population inequalities of the "magnitude" found in the Missouri plan cannot be justified by the rationale of avoiding the fragmentation of political subdivisions. As a result, many have concluded that state legislatures now have a green light to gerrymander without regard to the former constraints of existing county lines. Brennan is ambivalent on this matter, pointing out that in Missouri closer numerical equality could have been achieved by transferring whole political subdivisions

23. See, for example, *Drum* v. *Seawell,* 250 F. Supp. 922 (N.D.N.C. 1966); *Sincock* v. *Gately,* 262 F. Supp. 739 (D. Del. 1967).

24. *Kirkpatrick* v. *Preisler,* 394 U.S. 526, 530–531 (1969).

25. *Id.* at 537.

from one district to another. But the majority opinion also expressed doubt that the temptation to gerrymander would be much inhibited by following subdivision lines, since the legislature would still be free to choose which of several such units would be included in various districts. The Court added that opportunities for gerrymandering were greatest when there was freedom to construct unequally populated districts, strangely citing as evidence of this point a book on congressional districting that dealt with population disparities existing before *Baker* v. *Carr*.[26] Such an example seems far from analogous to the issue in either case before the Court in 1969.

Concern over the Court's approach was thoughtfully expressed by Justice Byron White, in his first dissent in an apportionment case. He insisted that the new ruling was unduly rigid and would unnecessarily involve the courts in the "abrasive task" of drawing district lines. White also reminded his brethren of the Court's earlier statement in *Reynolds* v. *Sims* that "[i]ndiscriminate districting, without any regard for political subdivision or natural or historical boundary lines, may be little more than an open invitation to partisan gerrymandering."[27] White cogently summarized his concern in one of the most sophisticated critiques on the nature of apportionment yet to come from a member of the Court:

> In reality, of course, districting is itself a gerrymandering in the sense that it represents a complex blend of political, economic, regional, and historical considerations. In terms of the gerrymander, the situation will not be much different if equality means what it literally says—a zero variation—rather than only "substantial" equality which would countenance some variations among legislative districts. Either standard will prevent a minority of the population or a minority party from consistently controlling the state legislature or a congressional delegation and both are powerful forces toward equalizing voter influence on legislative performance. In terms of effective representation for all voters there are only miniscule differences between the two standards. But neither rule can alone prevent deliberate partisan gerrymandering if that is considered an evil which the Fourteenth Amendment should attempt to proscribe.

> Today's decision on the one hand requires precise adherence to admittedly inexact census figures, and on the other downgrades a restraint on a far greater potential threat to equality of representation, the gerrymander. Legislatures intent on minimizing the representation of selected

26. *Id.* at 534, citing Hacker, *supra,* n. 2.
27. *Supra,* n. 1 at 578–579.

political or racial groups are invited to ignore political boundaries and compact districts so long as they adhere to population equality among districts using standards which we know and they know are sometimes quite incorrect. I see little merit in such a confusion of priorities.[28]

While the *Wells* and *Kirkpatrick* decisions might have affected congressional districting in most states, few were likely to feel the possible impact until after the 1970 census. Not so Missouri and New York, however, which were ordered to redraw district lines prior to the 1970 election. The reliance on 1960 census figures, badly out of date a decade later, raised further questions about the logic of the decisions. In New York, state legislators from both parties denounced the Supreme Court for forcing the state into a second congressional redistricting within two years—and one valid for only a single election, at that. After the 1970 census, expected to result in a reduction of New York's congressional delegation from 41 to 39 seats, entirely new lines would have to be drawn. This context surrounding the districting bill passed by the New York legislature in January of 1970 won for it an informal sobriquet, "the Alice in Wonderland Memorial Plan."[29]

The newly enacted New York State congressional districting also served as a possible prototype of the "equal-population gerrymandering" feared by critics of the *Wells* and *Kirkpatrick* decisions. Republicans controlled both legislative houses, as well as the governorship. The new congressional plan was drawn, after several months of work, by only the Republican members of a joint legislative committee, with Democratic members of the committee learning about the plan from newspaper speculation. While the Republican leadership insisted that their concern was with population figures rather than politics, others were more candid. Donald Zimmerman, who had coordinated the districting as assistant counsel to the Senate majority leader, remarked: "The Supreme Court is just making gerrymandering easier than it used to be."[30] Observers estimated that the new district pattern could result in a shift of at least two, and possibly as many as six, seats from the Democrats, who comprised 26 of the 41 members of the delegation. (In the November 1970 election, Republicans made a net gain of two seats.)

28. *Wells* v. *Rockefeller*, 394 U.S. 542, 554–555 (1969).
29. Details in this and the following two paragraphs are based on lead articles in the New York *Times*, January 20–23, 1970.
30. Quoted in the New York *Times*, January 22, 1970. Information in this and the succeeding paragraph relies on accounts in the New York *Times*, January 20–25, 1970.

Democratic leaders initiated the inevitable legal challenge, but lost in a federal district court, after an impressive statistical showing by the state. Under the new plan, no district deviated by more than 490 persons (according to the 1960 census) from the state average—a miniscule variation of approximately 0.10 percent. Moreover, the configuration of district boundaries reveals generally compact and contiguous contours—indeed, more so than the 1968 districting. Maps 1 and 2 clearly reveal this. Com-

MAP 1   MAP 2

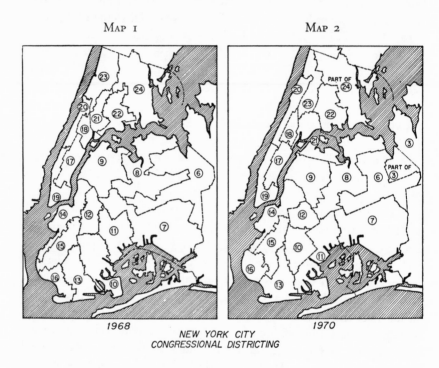

1968   1970

NEW YORK CITY
CONGRESSIONAL DISTRICTING

pare particularly districts 7, 12, 14 and 22, all of which appear much closer in the 1970 plan to models of compactness. Even the sixth and eighth districts are considerably less tortuous in outline, despite a last-minute amendment designed to help the Republican incumbent in the sixth. This should be a convincing example of how standards—both numerical and pictorial—of fair districting can conceal what every knowledgeable person realizes is a partisan gerrymander. Further, the skillful Republican cartography extended beyond New York City. Upstate cities were fragmented, with portions being joined to suburban and rural areas in an attempt to dilute concentrations of Democrats. Again, neither population equality nor standards of compactness posed an obstacle.

CONCLUSIONS

Developments during the 1960s indicate a clear need to reappraise the elements that encourage or deter gerrymandering. The traditional standards of approximate population equality, compactness, and contiguity, were not wrong, but merely incomplete and misleading. Equal population "as practicable as may be" is a necessary element of democratic representation. But the kind of precision suggested by the Supreme Court majority in 1969 does not yield more representative institutions, especially when the former minimal constraints on gerrymandering are discarded. At first blush, compactness seems to be an obvious check against boundary manipulation. Some attempts have even been made to define standards of compactness.[31] Yet here, too, it is questionable how productive such efforts can be in the face of modern realities. We have learned that compactness can readily cloak a genuine gerrymander, while districts that look untidy and suspect may merely reflect the irregular geography of natural political communities.

In the age of computers it is not surprising that this impersonal machine has received attention as an answer to partisan gerrymanders.[32] The computer does assume an increasingly important function in any redistricting, in view of its enormous capacity for information storage and processing. The variables most critical to the formation of new districts can include: population, population growth patterns, registered voters, governmental subdivisions, partisan strength, party loyalty, and a host of social and economic data. All of these can be accommodated by the computer in devising district lines.

While the computer is neutral, those who program it are not. During the redistrictings after the 1970 census, computers will be used extensively by legislative committees and party groups in all states of any size. As a result, far from being eliminated, gerrymanders will become rather more sophisticated, since those in charge of designing constituencies can draw on a wealth of data that would have been unavailable or unmanageable before the electronic age. Moreover, if local boundaries and communities of interest are completely ignored, the opportunities for ger-

31. Ernest C. Reock, Jr., "A Note: Measuring Compactness as a Requirement of Legislative Apportionment," 5 *Midwest Journal of Political Science* 70.

32. See, for example, James B. Weaver and Sidney W. Hess, "A Procedure for Nonpartisan Districting: Developments of Computer Techniques," 73 *Yale Law Journal* 288–308.

rymandering by computer are really maximized. The machine can be programmed to spew out any number of districts having equal populations that could serve a variety of purposes, but which would be remote from the goal of fair representation expressed in *Reynolds* v. *Sims*.[33] One can even envisage competing parties in apportionment suits presenting courts with alternative computerized redistricting proposals—and the judiciary employing its own technician to interpret the data.

The decade of the 1970s holds the potential for having the most extensive gerrymandering in the nation's history—an ironic capstone to the previous decade that accepted one man, one vote, as a constitutional principle. The potential exists for several reasons. One is the sheer magnitude of districting all state legislatures and congressional delegations to reflect new population patterns revealed by the 1970 census. Now, for the first time directly following a decennial census, positive remapping of legislative constituencies is to be enforced by courts. Population mobility has also extended two-party competition into more areas than in the past, with higher stakes resulting from reapportionment.

But perhaps the most important consideration is the Supreme Court's recent emphasis on only one variable—a precise notion of population equality—at the expense of others. While Justice Brennan professed in his *Wells* and *Kirkpatrick* opinions a sincere belief that gerrymandering would not be enhanced by the decisions, a reappraisal would surely reveal an error in his perception. Unless the Court modifies its 1969 decisions and encourages the practice of using political subdivisions as building blocks for districts, we can expect gerrymandering on a large scale in the coming decade. To keep such a prospect at least partly in check, the Court would not have to reverse any precedents, but would merely need to clarify the situation. Justice Brennan's obiter dicta in the Missouri and New York cases need not control the future, but state legislatures will act upon them unless the high tribunal explains what it means.

What is needed is a return to the spirit of *Reynolds* v. *Sims* and its concern with the goal of fair and effective representation of all citizens. This approach recognizes the importance of political subdivisions and community interests so long as "population is . . . the starting point for consideration and the controlling criterion for judgment in legislative apportionment controversies."[34] Such a reemphasis would not, of course,

---

33. Stephen Slingsby, "The Gerrymander," Ph.D. dissertation, Claremont Graduate School, Claremont, California, 1967, includes an experimental gerrymander of Los Angeles and Santa Clara counties, using four parameters.

34. *Supra,* n. 1 at 567.

eliminate the opportunities for gerrymandering, but it would at least condition them, to a degree.

Consequently, even if a partial reliance on political subdivision boundaries should be revived, the practice of manipulating districts for partisan or factional advantage will still exist and will apparently remain as the most significant unresolved fair-representation issue for the courts. As past decisions have shown, the judiciary undoubtedly would prefer to skirt this portion of the political thicket. Yet to do so would be to ignore a situation which erodes the principle of one man, one vote.

While the courts have so far avoided any direct examination of gerrymandering, the foundation for doing so indirectly can be traced to a 1967 Supreme Court decision in the Texas case of *Kilgarlin* v. *Hill*.[35] There the high tribunal noted that the lower court had failed to stipulate reasons for rejecting two alternative plans, one presented by the plaintiffs and the other by an *amicus curiae*. Doing so would have maximized opportunities for a number of interested parties to present the courts with diverse districting plans for judicial consideration. Such a procedure might build in some self-imposed restraints on state legislatures if they knew that their handiwork could be subject to scrutiny and to comparison with alternative plans. However, the success of this approach would require judicial acceptance of a modest range of permissible population deviation —perhaps something in the neighborhood of 5 percent above or 5 percent below the average. Otherwise, the courts would find it difficult to reject a computerized gerrymander with zero deviation. With a *de minimis* range, attention could then focus on which plan appeared to achieve the fairest balance among the various contending forces. It is, admittedly, a heavy responsibility to rest on the judiciary, but it seems preferable to abandoning the discretion entirely to the legislature.

If the Supreme Court should accept the challenge of gerrymandering, some helpful guidelines for them to formulate have been suggested. First, as to multi-member districts as a form of gerrymander, Robert G. Dixon, Jr., has made a convincing case that such constituencies be proclaimed unconstitutional unless specially justified by the state.[36] This would merely extend the principle, expressed by the Court in 1967,[37] that the burden of proof is on the state to justify any significant population disparities.

35. 386 U.S. 120 (1967).
36. Robert G. Dixon, Jr., "The Warren Court Crusade for The Holy Grail of 'One Man, One Vote,'" 1969 *The Supreme Court Review* 260.
37. See *Swann* v. *Adams,* 385 U.S. 440 (1967).

Boundary manipulation is a more complicated matter. In the case of multi-member districts, there is persuasive evidence that even mathematically proportionate votes do not place all voters on an effective, equal footing. But in the case of single-member district boundaries, there is the real possibility of gerrymandered districts whose populations are precisely or virtually equal. Though it might make a somewhat unsatisfactory constitutional case based on the Fourteenth Amendment's equal protection clause, it undoubtedly could be done. Might it not then be preferable for this one aspect of apportionment controversies to invoke the amendment's due process clause? [38] Gerrymandered boundaries seem peculiarly suited here, since they are partially the result of questionable procedures. Courts could even indicate procedural guidelines, such as requiring a redistricting act to have a substantial degree of bipartisan support in the legislature.

After the past few years of hyperactive reapportionment, in which some voters have been shifted with confusing frequency into a series of different districts, one is tempted to hope for a more stable and tranquil decade in the 1970s. This may eventually transpire, after the challenges that are bound to arise immediately following the census. But the short-run prospects suggest the need for the Supreme Court to complete the seamless web it began to weave in 1962. For, if widespread partisan gerrymandering replaces malapportionment as a major electoral problem, the reapportionment revolution will have won a hollow victory, indeed.

*   *   *

COMMENTARY by Charles Press

Professor Gordon Baker, quite properly I believe, uses a broad definition of gerrymandering, defining it as the intentional manipulation of districts for partisan or factional advantage. He thus includes a multitude of political actions that might be classed as gerrymandering, such as creating districts of unequal population or mixing single and at-large districts. He thus sets the stage for further judicial action beyond the population standard against what some reformers regard as major evils inherent in the American system of representative government.

38. Dixon, in *Democratic Representation,* pp. 135 ff., expresses a preference for using either the due process clause or the republican form of government (guaranty) clause in place of the equal protection clause for apportionment cases. I would confine due process to geographical boundaries for the reasons suggested above.

I have described his definition as covering political actions that "might be classed as gerrymandering" because he defines gerrymandering by the actor's motivation rather than by his overt behavior. The same behavior could be either gerrymandering or not depending on the *intentions* of the political actor. The same, of course, is true of the legal distinction between murder and manslaughter. The easiest practical way around this difficulty, I believe, is to expect that most actors most of the time will be motivated to act according to what the system pays off. They will, as Professor William Riker suggests, want to win, and the rules of the game tell them how they may. One should expect that their desire for partisan or factional advantage will lead most partisans to gerrymander where this is possible. One then asks what real difference this would make. If the answer is that the difference is significant enough to warrant control, one of three actions may be taken by government: (1) One is to outline detailed procedures and so to add costs of certain actions, which on the basis of higher than average probability, are motivated by the desire to gerrymander. The application of the standard of population equality is an example. (2) The government may seek to create a norm of professionalism among a special body created to carry out the apportioning so that they are encouraged to seek for neutrality, much as the courts and bureaucracy set up norms for their members or the Speaker of the House of Commons in Great Britain does for its members. The British boundary commission is such a body. (3) The government may create a system for carrying out the public duty in which opposing points of view have mutual vetoes much like the mother who allows one child to divide the dessert and the other first choice of the pieces. Bypartisan apportionment commissions or the requirement of bipartisan legislative majorities to adopt apportionment plans suggested by Professor Baker are examples.

The courts will possibly encourage all three approaches. The first is especially tempting, particularly if the judges continue to be guided by the crusader mentality so often found in the literature of civic reform.

The test that is most important to apply, I think, is how significant for the polity is the supposed gerrymandering practice? Reformers were, I believe, quite properly exercised over the great variation in population of state legislative districts a generation ago. It did seem to them and many others that the apportionment then in effect did make a great deal of political difference. Along with a number of others, early in the struggle, I signed the Twentieth Century Fund report *One Man One Vote,* and I note this lest my subsequent comments be misunderstood. State legislatures then came nowhere close to reflecting either partisan cleavages or the general division of opinion within their states. At one stroke in *Baker* v. *Carr* a major and long overdue democratic reform of considerable significance was begun.

One may, however, now question the political or partisan significance of the absolute population equality standard being applied by the Court. Like some detailed Civil Service regulations, it may well lead to hidden political costs less desirable than the evil they seek to correct. Professor Baker objects strongly to the recent decisions that sacrifice subunit district lines on the altar of absolute district equality because of the effect of these decisions in encouraging more gerrymandering. While I agree with his objection, it is not mainly for his reason. Such gerrymandering is to be regretted but is not a major cost for our polity to bear. Rather, I think the decision a bad one because of what such carving-up of subunits does to the costs of political participation.

The present difficulty is that the Supreme Court has only been able to field a hard-line majority for the population equality standard. This majority remains convinced that a real evil is being eliminated. A majority on a new standard has not yet come into being because of the difficulty in finding other real evils of the same magnitude to legislate against. Thus, population equality must be carried to its logical conclusion. Even the reformers implicitly accept this kind of pragmatic reasoning, that only great evils should be legislated against. This is suggested by the fact that no one as yet crusades against the unequal representation of population in the U.S. Senate or the requirement that the apportionment of House seats include at least one per state, regardless of population, or the constitutional rule against the crossing of state lines to bring about absolute equality in House seats. It is not alone because of the constitutional difficulties. It is because the reformers are not as yet convinced that any great evil results from these practices, though many minor ones do. In fact, those who control the Senate are generally viewed favorably by reformers. If the Senate turned into a body of rampant Joseph McCarthys or would turn into a body as conservative on foreign or domestic policy as the House has been, even since reapportionment, I predict that the arguments for population equality or for downgrading Senate prerogatives because of its lack of representativeness might well be trotted out for serious and extended discussion.

Professor Baker suggests that the creation of at-large seats is a gerrymander of sufficient importance to be regulated out of existence, particularly when at-large are mixed with single-member district seats. Some of the arguments he uses, however, could be used equally well against the single-member districts and would logically lead to a crusade for proportional representation. Certainly it takes no mathematical technique to demonstrate that a district that has been held by one party for generations cannot be said to represent equally the majority and minority party voters. The major distortions in representing opinion or partisan divisions now, in fact, are caused by the concentrations of voting groups. Only by throwing out compactness and contiguity could one set up district schemes that come closer to reflecting the division of partisan opinion in a state or of, say, Blacks and Whites. One would have to set up Illinois districts radiating out of Chicago, snaking just enough through the suburbs to get a balanced Republican and Democratic split or a balanced racial split. In this way one could correct the most important of all present distortions. Some reformers may in the future be attracted by this kind of gerrymandering to achieve what they see as good ends, just as some have embraced the Senate filibuster for the same reasons. To me it seems that gerrymandering for good ends is like the filibuster, it can be used against you as well as for you. One must, I think, accept individual district deviations and hope that distortions of opinion and partisan division are randomized, or at least are not of great significance. What is most important is a set of rules that are predictable over a period of time and understandable for the average voter. I thus again find myself in agreement with Professor Baker on what the Court should do about at-large districts, while rejecting part of his argument because I see more merit in other reasons for their action.

The important point, I believe, is that a system of representation serves other purposes than the precise mirroring of partisan factional or even opinion cleavage. It must also be designed so that the elected are able to fashion a governing coalition and carry out decisions, and I assume this is part of the reason for the unpopularity of proportional representation. Another is that the representative system be designed to keep the citizens' costs of participation as low as practicable. This is a major reason, I believe, that the Court should not encourage frequent shifting of district boundaries, the breaking up of subunits, or the creation of the long ballot by at-large election. What once seemed reasons of high principle when a real democratic pathology was present, now borders on crankiness. A representative system also should not complicate and add to the costs of political partisans, except for what are clearly important reasons. I am suggesting that the Court and reformers need to demonstrate evils before they make extensive changes. I am suggesting also that the nation can survive something less than perfection in districting—even, in fact, some intentional gerrymandering, if in the process other goals are served.

The anti-gerrymander crusade has become something of a cult. It is one of the pitfalls of turning political programs into religion. In my opinion the Court should seek out palpable evils rather than flitting after the will-o'-the-wisp of absolute principle. Where a clear and significant injustice, as was presented in *Gomillion*, occurs, the courts should strike it down without equivocation. Otherwise, the courts should maintain a position for districting that reasonably reflects major partisan and opinion cleavages without adding greatly to the costs of political participation for either the voter or the political activist. This means the addition of a new standard, that of changing districts as little as possible from the present district lines.

A rough equality of district populations, compactness, and contiguity seem to me to be essential for a workable system. Also desirable are a following of subunit lines, unless this results in clearly significant injustice, and the elimination of mixed at-large and single-member districting. For the rest, the anguish is not worth the trouble.

Political scientists and even justices of the Supreme Court now have other, more significant problems to explore.

* * *

REJOINDER *by Gordon E. Baker*

While concurring with the general thrust of my article, Professor Press has usefully supplemented it by calling our attention to certain dimensions I had not emphasized. It is indeed appropriate to ask what the significance of gerrymandering is for the polity and to understand what existing or potential harm it portends before prescribing the nature and extent of the remedy.

The problems posed by gerrymandering revolve, it seems to me, around the extent to which the practice undermines the theory of democratic representation. Three elements in particular are crucial here: the representative character of the legislative body, effective voter choice between policies and candidates, and the degree to which the system reflects changes in popular sentiment. It is not reasonable to expect (and probably not desirable to want) a legislative body which faithfully mirrors every significant feature of the general public. Moreover, in view of the complex network of overlapping and partially conflicting interests, such a result is literally impossible, in any event. At the same time, there should be some proximate correspondence between the actions of policy-makers and the interests of the voters who elected them. The whole rationale of the two-party system is that it should offer the electorate alternative choices of candidates and programs. In this way, the parties give meaning and purpose to public sentiment, while serving to strengthen the element of responsibility among governing officials. Ideally, parties should contest for public support in such a way that votes can be trans-lated into some sort of public policy. In a democracy there should be a reasonably direct relationship between predominant public opinion and the power to govern.

Extensive gerrymandering (including here the use of multi-member districts, as well as boundary manipulation) can obviously undermine these basic assumptions of a democratic electoral system. It can effec-tively dilute, indeed, even render impotent, the voting power of certain individuals and magnify the effective power of others—depending on their geographic locations. The party in power in the year of redistricting (and decennial or any periodic timing can be highly fortuitous and ca-pricious) is able to condition the fate of the opposition by diminishing its legislative voice. Finally, the reflection of future changes in public sentiment can be cushioned and even forestalled.

It is true, as Professor Press mentions, that no electoral arrangement short of proportional representation can guarantee an equitable ratio of votes to seats for the major parties. Even a district pattern with no hint of gerrymandering can produce great distortions, ordinarily in favor of the majority party. In practice, we count on diverse concentrations of party strength to balance out the overall results, at least roughly.

We might indeed ask whether gerrymandering is worth the worry or the struggle required to minimize it. After all, we have been accustomed to that practice for most of our history as a nation, and the polity has survived. Moreover, experience has shown that the best-laid plans of political cartographers are often only partially successful and at times, thwarted altogether. An answer to this logical query entails, first, an understanding of the kinds of restraints that have conditioned boundary manipulation in the past; and, second, some appreciation of why there is now reason to conclude that such constraints are less likely to be operative in the future

Prior to the reapportionment revolution of the 1960s, state constitu-tional provisions typically prohibited the breaking of county lines in forming districts. Consequently, gerrymanders were more common in urban than rural areas, and in a number of state legislatures urban delegations were elected at large. In others, a city or urban county was allotted only a single seat in one or both houses. This was, of course, a form of gerrymander written into the constitution, but one that obviated periodic line-drawing. Then, too, a large number of states simply failed periodically to redistrict. This resulted in status-quo gerrymanders, but disturbing them required extraordinary efforts. Finally, population mobility, especially after World War II, frustrated boundary manipulation in many areas in ways previously unanticipated.

Events during the 1960s completely changed these considerations. Reapportionments following the 1970 census will be the first in American history to witness revisions of legislative and congressional boundaries in *all* states. Prior constitutional restrictions regarding county or other boundary lines have already been undermined by the need to construct districts of approximately equal population. Not only will some of the former checks on boundary manipulation have disappeared, but the implications of the 1969 *Wells* and *Kirkpatrick* decisions, unless modified, will encourage legislators to believe that in forming new districts the only legal concern need be population equality, as precise as possible. Even the many legislative redistricting actions during the 1960s were conditioned by legislative uncertainty as to what the courts might say about alleged gerrymanders. If such hesitations are now removed by judicial preoccupation with numerical equality only, the prospects seem overwhelming for a vast increase in boundary manipulation or for at-large, winner-take-all constituencies. Finally, the use of computers to program gerrymanders has scarcely begun and will undoubtedly reach new heights of sophistication. The results are likely to be far more durable than the comparatively crude guesswork that formerly characterized even the more professional efforts at drawing constituencies for partisan advantage.

In worrying about the course of reapportionment during the 1970s, we cannot expect to attain perfection, even if we knew what that was. But a realistic recognition of our limitations should not rule out an attempt to avoid the more predictable pitfalls that loom ahead. The prospect that gerrymandering in its several forms will likely become the major fair-representation issue of the next decade justifies our concern and, particularly, the judiciary's scrutiny of its own role. This does not mean that we can eliminate partisan or factional advantage in the drawing of districts. In all likelihood, the best we can hope for is some measure of bipartisan compromise. This still falls short of the goal of "fair and effective representation" advanced by Chief Justice Warren in 1964. A typical product of bipartisan negotiation is an "incumbent gerrymander," emphasizing safe districts and reinforcing the political status quo. In spite of this, neutral, nonpartisan redistricting is largely a utopian vision. Regardless of motives or intent, the results of redistricting are never neutral toward parties, factions, and interests. Consequently, the most reasonable goal in the near future would be that of minimizing those practices that most obviously distort the general congruence of electoral behavior with patterns of representation.

We are faced with a continuing paradox in our thinking about representative bodies. On the one hand, we want them to reflect changes in public opinion so as to make elections meaningful. This necessitates at least a significant number of competitive districts, districts that can swing with shifts in popular sentiment. On the other hand, we typically want to represent communities of interest, to the extent that they can be geographically demarked. Yet, this more often than not yields noncompetitive districts in which one or the other party predominates, regardless of opinion shifts. An attachment to community representation is one reason why the use of political subunits as building blocks for districts is so entrenched in our thinking and practice. Even though the justification of gross malapportionments prior to *Baker* v. *Carr* invoked—often quite artificially—representation of communities that were hardly delineated by ancient subunit boundaries, the complete abandonment of such lines in the quest for precise population equality poses a potential hardly envisaged by either the one man, one vote, reformers or the Supreme Court between 1962 and 1964. The aim of representative equality did not rule out some retention of traditional ground rules, including local boundaries whenever possible, in forming districts. The view was best expressed by Chief Justice Warren in *Reynolds* v. *Sims*:

A state may legitimately desire to maintain the integrity of various political subdivisions, insofar as possible, and provide for compact districts of contiguous territory in designing a legislative apportionment scheme. Valid considerations may underlie such aims. Indiscriminate districting, without any regard for political subdivisions or natural or historical boundary lines, may be little more than an open invitation to partisan gerrymandering. . . .

. . . . So long as the divergences from a strict population standard are based on legitimate considerations incident to the effectuation of a rational state policy, some deviations from the equal-population principle are constitutionally permissible with respect to the apportionment of seats in either or both of the two houses of a bicameral State Legislature.[1]

The question now is whether the high tribunal will return to this general position. To do so would require a pulling back from the over-extended posture assumed by the Court's majority in the New York and Missouri congressional district decisions of 1969. A shift back to *Reynolds* would not require an overruling of these later decisions, but only distinguishing obiter dicta from the actual holdings. Taking this step, and resting the burden of proof on the states to show that an apportionment plan *in its totality* conforms to both equal protection and due process clauses of the Fourteenth Amendment, could furnish the best hope for checking the kinds of gerrymandering that otherwise seem likely to flourish as never before.

1. 377 U.S. 533, 578–579 (1964).

THE EFFECTS OF
MALAPPORTIONMENT IN THE
STATES—A MISTRIAL

William E. Bicker

Soon after the United States Supreme Court determined that the existence of wide disparities in the number of persons represented by a state's legislators was unconstitutional, several political scientists independently claimed to have established that this same phenomenon was inconsequential.

The Court based its decision on the grounds that such patterns of apportionment denied citizens the equal protection of the laws, as guaranteed under the Fourteenth Amendment. Specifically, it argued, in the electoral process, every man's vote for his representative should count equally.[1] Not concerned with "testing" the constitutional or philosophical bases of the Court's decisions, the political scientists based their claims on their failure to find evidence of the political and policy consequences which had been attributed to apportionment patterns in much of the literature on state government and legislative behavior.[2] Skeptical of the claims of

I would like to thank my colleagues Robert P. Biller and Eugene C. Lee and graduate students Jay Starling, Beverly Kearns and Dorothy Clayton for their helpful comments on the previous drafts of this article.

1. The most important court cases include *Baker* v. *Carr*, 396 U.S. 186 (1962), *Reynolds* v. *Sims*, 377 U.S. 533 (1964), and *Wesberry* v. *Sanders*, 376 U.S. 1 (1964). For the many other cases in this series and a comprehensive discussion of the development of the Court's reapportionment decisions, see Robert G. Dixon, Jr., *Democratic Representation: Reapportionment in Law and Politics* (New York: Oxford University Press, 1968).

2. There are five comparative state studies whose explicit objective is to test the effect of apportionment patterns on policy outcomes as those apportionment patterns existed prior to 1962: Herbert Jacob, "The Consequences of Malapportionment: A Note of Caution," 43 *Social Forces* 256–261; Thomas Dye, "Malapportionment and

those who argued that apportionment had an effect on policy outcomes and political life, because much of this literature was based on case studies of only one legislature or of only those legislatures in a particular region, these political scientists approached the question from a comparative perspective.

Either directly or indirectly, the skeptical analysts trace their intellectual heritage to Duane Lockard's consideration of malapportionment in his text *The Politics of State and Local Government,* published soon after the *Baker* v. *Carr* decision.[3] Lockard both states the critical question and presents the methodological approach for arriving at the answer:

> The final and crucial question on apportionment must be: what does it matter? What ultimate difference does it make that the rural-small town element is thus over-represented in most states . . . ?

> It is frequently said that the under-representation of urban areas results in neglect of urban problems by state government with the consequence that the city government must go perforce to Washington to get assistance in coping with its problems. . . .

> Turn the problem the other way and ask the question: Do states with fair apportionment systems respond to urban appeals more readily? If anyone has made a systematic study of this, I am unaware of it, but the limited evidence does not seem to indicate that the states with fair

Public Policy in the States," 27 *The Journal of Politics* 586–601; Richard Hofferbert, "The Relation Between Public Policy and Some Structural and Environmental Variables in the American States," 60 *American Political Science Review* 73–82; and David Brady and Douglas Edmonds, "The Effects of Malapportionment on Policy Output in the American States," The Laboratory for Political Research, Report No. 3, Department of Political Science, University of Iowa, a paper prepared for the annual meeting of the Midwest Conference of Political Scientists held in April 1966. [A revised version of this was later published under the title "One Man, One Vote—So What?" 4 *Trans-action* (March 1967): 41–46. Because the *Trans-action* version of their study does not provide many of the basic methodological and technical components of the study, discussion of Brady and Edmonds's study refers to the paper they delivered at the annual meeting of the Midwest Conference of Political Scientists.] These four studies rendered the verdict inconsequential and used basically the same analytical approach. The fifth article, Allen Pulsipher and James L. Weatherby, Jr., "Malapportionment, Party Competition, and the Functional Distribution of Governmental Expenditures," 62 *American Political Science Review* 1207–1219, has as its primary objective the determination of the impact of apportionment patterns on policy outcomes on a comparative state basis. But Pulsipher and Weatherby approach the subject from assumptions different from those of the authors of the previous four works and will be given separate consideration.

3. Duane Lockard, *The Politics of State and Local Government* (New York: Macmillan, 1963).

apportionment systems are more considerate of urban problems than are states with malapportionment.[4]

Lockard then compares the responsive and favorable treatment of cities by the "malapportioned" Connecticut legislature with the restrictive and almost hostile treatment accorded Boston by the "well apportioned" Massachusetts legislature.

Using rank-order correlation techniques (as well as cross-tabulation) Herbert Jacob and later Richard Hofferbert extend this to all states.[5] They both ask: Are states which are better apportioned than others more likely to be more "liberal" in their policy orientation, less likely to be restrictive regarding their cities, and less likely to have divided governments or noncompetitive political systems?

Using covariational statistical techniques, Thomas Dye and David Brady and Douglas Edmonds ask whether, to the extent that a state is malapportioned, it will be that much less likely to expend funds, to be responsive to urban needs, and to have a competitive political system.[6]

Even with these increasingly sophisticated techniques and varying policy and political "tests," the answers obtained by the skeptical analysts are quite clear and consistent, albeit differing somewhat in caution:

Our data demonstrate that malapportionment in and of itself is not associated with some of the major ailments of the states.[7]

On the whole, the policy differences of malapportioned legislatures are not noticeably different from the policy choices of well-apportioned legislatures. Most of the policy differences which do occur turn out to be a product of the socio-economic differences among the states rather than a direct product of apportionment practices.[8]

Structural characteristics and, if one prefers to give partisan variables a separate berth, the nature of the party system and its operation do not seem to go very far toward explaining the kind of policies produced in the states.[9]

[T]he whole Pandora's box of evil consequences which supposedly results from malapportionment—from right-to-work laws to not spend-

4. *Id.* at 318–319.
5. Jacob, *supra,* n. 2; Hofferbert, *supra,* n. 2.
6. Dye, *supra,* n. 2; Brady and Edmonds, *supra,* n. 2. Brady and Edmonds also employ cross-tabular analysis.
7. Jacob, *supra,* n. 2 at 260.
8. Dye, *supra,* n. 2 at 599.
9. Hofferbert, *supra,* n. 2 at 82.

ing enough money on school children—really has very little to do with malapportionment.[10]

Each study except the first, Jacob's, it should be noted, attempts to determine whether the attributed effects are more closely associated with the socioeconomic levels of the states than with their apportionment patterns.

SKEPTICS VERSUS REFORMERS

These articles, though varying in the particulars of statistical approach and measures employed, arrive at basically the same conclusion and incorporate the same general approach for testing this literature. Therefore, they will be referred to generically as the skeptics through the remainder of this essay. The authors of those publications the skeptics cite as providing the arguments for the recurrent theme—that apportionment patterns did have a demonstrable effect on the policies and political practices of states before *Baker* v. *Carr* will be referred to generically as the reformers.[11] Both of these labels are applied with the recognition that they do a disservice to individual authors in each group, but by this procedure I

10. Brady and Edmonds, *supra,* n. 2 (*Trans-action,* p. 46).

11. The reformers and their publications include: V. O. KEY, *American State Politics: An Introduction* (New York: Alfred A. Knopf, 1965), pp. 76 ff. MALCOLM E. JEWELL, *The State Legislature, Politics and Practice,* Studies in Political Science No. 37 (New York: Random House, 1962), pp. 30–33, cited by Jacob, Hofferbert, and Dye, *supra,* n. 2. GORDON E. BAKER, *Rural versus Urban Political Power,* Studies in Political Science No. 20 (Garden City: Doubleday, 1955), pp. 19–26, cited by Hofferbert and Jacob. CHARLES R. ADRIAN, *State and Local Governments* (New York: McGraw-Hill, 1960), pp. 306–307, cited by Jacob and Dye. CHARLES SHULL, "Malapportionment in the States," 17 *Law and Contemporary Problems* 417–421, cited by Brady and Edmonds, and Hofferbert. GORDON E. BAKER, *Reapportionment* (New York: National Municipal League, 1960), p. viii, cited by Brady and Edmonds. WILLIAM C. HAVARD and LOREN P. BETH, *The Politics of Mis-Representation* (Baton Rouge: Louisiana State University Press, 1962), p. 77, cited by Hofferbert. WILLIAM J. KEEFE and MORRIS S. OGUL, *The American Legislative Process* (Englewood Cliffs; Prentice-Hall, 1964), p. 86, cited by Hofferbert. DUANE LOCKARD, *New England State Politics* (Princeton, N.J.: Princeton University Press, 1959), p. 275, cited by Hofferbert. FRANK J. SORAUF, *Party and Representation* (New York: Atherton, 1962), pp. 22 ff, cited by Hofferbert. DANIEL GRANT and H. C. NIXON, *State and Local Government in America* (Boston: Allyn and Bacon, 1963), pp. 204–205, cited by Dye. Commission on Intergovernmental Relations, *A Report to the President for Transmittal to Congress* (Washington: U.S. Government Printing Office, 1955), p. 39, cited by Dye. I have not included Dye's reference to *U.S. News and World Report* or *Time* or Brady and Edmonds's references to the *New Statesman* or the *Reporter* under this definition of the reformers. Nor have the comments found therein been examined for inclusion in the following discussion of the reformers' arguments or positions.

hope to avoid unnecessary repetition while considering basically common arguments, procedures, and approach.

The thrust of the skeptics' argument is, first, that they have explicitly disproved the proposition of the reformers that malapportionment or apportionment patterns had an effect on policy choices and political characteristics of states prior to the Court's reapportionment decisions. Second, either implicitly or explicitly, the skeptics raise considerable doubt regarding the extent to which significant changes would result in state policies and political practices because of the states' reapportioning in compliance with the Court's decision. Third, the studies have added support to the general conclusion that political institutions, arrangements, and patterns have little, if any, effect on policy and politics. This is a recurrent theme in the whole genre of "input(socioeconomic)—political institution—output (policy consequences)" comparative state and local "systems" studies (many authored by the individuals quoted above) of which the reapportionment studies are just one part. Jacob and Michael Lipsky, for example, in concluding their thoughtful and generally critical review of this literature, state:

> Political scientists in attempting to divorce themselves from the prescriptiveness and formal-legalism of former generations, have succeeded in taking on, and destroying, a number of clichés about American politics and problems. . . . They have substantially discredited two highly regarded precepts of American political life—that malapportionment and low levels of party competition are substantially related to the level of outputs.[12]

Because they were carried out independently, appeared in rather quick succession, and employed a common overall analytic framework while varying in their use of statistical techniques and measures, and yet arrived at essentially the same conclusions, the four studies by Jacob, Hofferbert, Dye, and Brady and Edmonds, have had a substantial impact on much subsequent work and writing in this area.[13] My purpose here is to examine

12. P. 538, Herbert Jacob and Michael Lipsky, "Outputs, Structure, and Power: An Assessment of Changes in the Study of State and Local Government," 30 *Journal of Politics* 510–538.

13. Although an examination of some of the major texts in state government indicates that the effect may not have been as substantial as expected, it is particularly interesting to consider the "before and after" effect of these studies on the consideration of malapportionment given by the standard state government texts. Those which were quite skeptical of some of the broader claims of reformers such as Grant and Nixon and, of course, Lockard himself in their first editions remain as skeptical of the lack of effect of malapportionment these studies seem to demon-

these studies to determine whether the skeptics' assertions are well founded and therefore whether the wider impact which they have had in shaping current conceptions of American political systems—that political institutions have little real significance in determining public policy—is actually warranted.

Some people concerned with this area, including several of the skeptics, have argued that the critical assessment of the consequences of malapportionment will be found in "before and after" studies. In view of the many promised studies (several of which have appeared)[14] on the "before and after" effects of the reapportionment which took place immediately following the Court's 1962 and 1964 decisions, a brief explanation of the rationale for undertaking a critical assessment of this literature is in order at this time. These studies will undoubtedly make important contributions to our understanding of the problems involved in assessing the effects of malapportionment (as well as the particular effect of the apportionment process, itself). They may also constitute a partial test of many of the reformers' arguments. However, there are several reasons why it will be difficult to accept these as definitive tests of either the effect of pre-*Baker* v. *Carr* apportionment patterns or the general impact of reapportionment (and, therefore, the arguments of the reformers).

First, these studies will have difficulties in adequately controlling for the concurrent effects of the 1964 Johnson (or Goldwater) landslide, which may have substantially altered the composition of the legislative class of 1964 in many states. This is especially important because this group of legislators either made up the "after," or experimental, group elected to the legislatures redistricted according to Court order or were part of the "before," or control, group that also played some role in drawing new district boundaries in response to the Court's decisions.

Second, the upcoming round of reapportionment will be "more accurate"

---

strate. See Daniel R. Grant and H. C. Nixon, *State and Local Government in America* (Boston: Allyn and Bacon, 1963), pp. 202–209 (2d ed., 1968), pp. 281–296; Duane Lockard, *The Politics of State and Local Government* (New York: Macmillan 1963), pp. 309–321 (2d ed., 1969), pp. 289–293. However, the text which argues the case of the reformers most strongly, Charles Adrian, *State and Local Governments* (New York: McGraw-Hill, 1960), pp. 304–309, does almost a complete reversal on its consideration of the effect of malapportionment, citing Dye directly as the product of what can be seen to be his change in the text's position on the question. (2d ed., 1967), pp. 367–385.

14. See, for example, Frank M. Bryan, "The Metamorphosis of a Rural Legislature," 1 *Polity* 191–212; and William de Rubertis, "How Apportionment with Selected Demographic Variables Relates to Policy Orientation," 22 *The Western Political Quarterly* 904–920.

than those conducted in the midsixties, if only because they will be based on 1970 census data, while earlier redistricting was based on that of the outdated 1960 census. Moreover, in recognition of the fact that reapportionment must take place after 1970, there has been an intense awareness of the importance of the party or factional control of the 1971 state legislative class. With the lead time necessary for undertaking a sophisticated redrawing of district boundaries, many states have already begun the steps necessary for merging the 1970 census data with registration and voting data from recent elections. This more extensive and accurate data will be coupled with highly flexible computer-based manipulation capacities. Therefore, the redrawing of district boundaries which takes place during 1971 is likely to be far more indicative of what will occur in future apportionments at the onset of coming decades—given, of course, the absence of significant changes in Court policy in the area of partisan or other gerrymandering.

Third, there is an increasing recognition of the need to incorporate a longitudinal dimension in the analysis of public policy outcomes and political systems in comparative state studies. Because these studies are likely to extend back to the turn of the century, it is important to assess quite carefully this body of literature which argues that apportionment patterns as of 1962 were inconsequential and thereby implies that this variable need not be considered or incorporated in the design of such longitudinal analyses.

Fourth, and most important, is the possibility that some of the "before and after" studies that utilize the analytic power of the comparative state approach may, in attempting to confirm or refute the findings of the skeptics, succumb to the same errors and perpetuate the series of mistrials. By pointing out some of the basic conceptual and methodological problems in the skeptics' studies, perhaps these may be avoided in future efforts to ascertain the political and policy consequences of patterns of legislative districting both before and after the Court's entry into what political scientists seem to have found more of a briar patch than a thicket.

Here I will argue that the conclusions reached by the skeptics should not be accepted; that these studies do not constitute tests either of the arguments of the reformers or of the potential impact of the Court's reapportionment decisions on the policies and political practices among the states; that a mistrial must be declared. My primary reason for this judgment is the apparent confusion that testing the arguments of the reformers regarding the effects of malapportionment is equivalent to testing the effects of the Court's decision. This is not meant to imply that the problem is simply

one of projection from the past to the future. It is that the Court's definition of malapportionment and the reformers' definition of malapportionment are only partially related. For the Court, malapportionment is deviation from the principal of one man, one vote, in the electoral process, and
—with all due respect to the late Senator Everett Dirksen—little else. For
the reformers, malapportionment just begins where the Court stopped,
and in some instances would still exist within the Court's numerical
bounds.

The reformers have focused on the disproportionate legislative representation of particular popular interest and party. Their concern has been
not only with how many more persons live in some districts than in
others, but, more importantly, with who they are—what kind of persons,
with what type of partisan preferences, and with what kinds of needs—
in these "under-" and "over-represented" districts. Aside from the question
of race, the Court has judiciously, to say the least, avoided setting doctrine
which even touches on these points.

Second, there is a lack of sensitivity among the skeptics about the type
of political effects and policy outcomes which the reformers have attributed
to malapportionment and—particularly—about the limited and conditional
nature of their arguments. And, furthermore, there are serious methodological and conceptual problems in the skeptics' studies which are, in part,
a result of this confusion and lack of sensitivity.

Social scientists should, to use the vernacular of the Court, be strict
constructionists. But the burden of proof is quite the reverse of that in
court. Instead of laying the particular law alongside the Constitution to
see if it fits, and then discarding the law if it does not, the social scientist
sets the theory or propositions next to the data to see if the theory fits and
then, if it does not, discards the theory. In so doing, he must take care
both that the proper data are employed and that the test of the relationship implied by the propositions is convincingly applicable to the generalizations set forth. Therefore, before considering the problems of the
skeptics' arguments and definitions, I shall very briefly outline what they
claimed to be testing—the arguments and definitions of the reformers.

If one reads the skeptics, the reformers' arguments appear to be rather
common in their substance and direct in their claims. Reading the reformers, themselves, however, presents a quite different picture. For the
reformers malapportionment has no single, specific form. There are,
V. O. Key points out, many types of malapportionment. These have
been produced by many factors, some by conscious decision or indecision
and others as the result of historical accident (for example, the heavy con-

centration of Democrats in the Boston area of Massachusetts) or constitutional mandate.[15] In general, there seems to be agreement that malapportionment is a pattern of districting in which particular popular interests are not represented in the legislative chambers in proportion to their numbers in the population.[16] Because much of this disproportionate representation came into relief following the migration to urban centers during and after the Great Depression, and at the beginning of the "urban crisis," much of the concern about malapportionment came to be centered around the underrepresentation of urban interests, in comparison to rural interests.

The reformers also note that party ties can either ameliorate or exacerbate the effects of interest distortion. When party and interest coincide, as is frequently the case with urban and rural divisions, the result is likely to be particularly deleterious for the urban resident. If the underrepresented urban population is a majority in the state but is represented by a legislative minority, then a divided government is likely to result. When the executive and the majority in one or both legislative chambers are responding to different constituencies, there is likely to be a lack of action —particularly action desired by the executive's constituency—a Massachusetts standoff.[17]

Furthermore, while the urban/rural dichotomy, or confrontation of interests, is the focus of much of the reformers' work, it is not the only interest distortion considered in this literature. Murray Clark Havens' study, frequently cited in the reformers' literature, and the skeptics' studies argue that there is a disproportionate representation of areas in certain southern states, such as the Alabama black belt, where feelings against Negroes were particularly strong, which led to the adoption of discriminatory policies in the state which were probably unreflective of the attitude of the state as a whole regarding civil rights.[18] Hence, the argument need not be limited to urban/rural divisions, but can be extended to any areas in which interests are distorted through a pattern of

15. Key, *supra,* n. 11 at 64.

16. A reading of any or all of the references listed, *supra,* n. 11, will confirm the vital importance of interest distortion.

17. Key, *supra,* n. 11 at 65–66: "A part of the Democratic difficulty flows from one of the more or less inevitable frailties of geographical representation. Although Suffolk County (Boston) is not discriminated against in the allocation of legislative seats, the heavy concentration of Democratic voters in the county 'wastes' a good many votes in legislative races. Democrats there elect legislators by overwhelming majorities. The same number of popular votes distributed more widely over the state would yield a larger number of Democratic senators."

18. Murray Clark Havens, *City Versus Farm, Urban Rural Conflict in Alabama Legislature* (University of Alabama: Bureau of Public Administration, 1957)..

representation not based on population, particularly when a popular interest-majority is distorted to the degree that it becomes a legislative interest-minority.

Key and Malcolm Jewell, in particular, note that perhaps the most important effects may be on intra-party politics. In a state where interests and party coincide, a candidate of the minority party, which is at the same time the legislative majority party, who is running for statewide office will be forced to campaign with the party's legislative record, which may be abhorrent or at least negative to the popular majority.[19] If the party organization is strong in such a state, it is possible that the desire for control of the governor's chair and the fact that the bulk of votes are in underrepresented areas, can also lead the legislators of the rural areas to be more receptive to the interests of urban areas. This would be more likely in states where governors have some control over patronage and/or particularly long "coattails." Hence, in states in which governors can exert substantial control, the party organization, in turn, can have some impact on the selection of candidates at the local legislative level.[20]

In brief, centralization brought about by the power, or potential power, of a governor to grant patronage or electoral advantage, is likely to produce representatives from rural areas who tend to be less hostile, if not enthusiastically responsive, to the needs of urban areas.[21] The effect of malapportionment would therefore be greatest in states where party could not exert this type of influence, that is, in one-party states such as those in the Deep South.[22]

The policy areas most commonly cited by the reformers as being most likely to be affected by apportionment patterns come under the general heading of regulatory legislation—the exercise of the state's police power or powers of regulation. Rural insensitivity to urban interests in these regulatory and other policy areas affected both legislation which would apply to the whole state and that which would apply only to cities above a certain size.[23]

In summary, particularly when considering its political or policy consequences, the reformers define malapportionment in terms of the extent to which district boundaries are responsible for disproportionate

19. Key, *supra,* n. 11 at 64 ff; Jewell, *supra,* n. 11 at 31–33.
20. Keefe and Ogul; and Baker, *supra,* n. 11.
21. This is in fact the phenomenon which Lockard uses to explain malapportioned Connecticut's better treatment of its cities.
22. Jewell, *supra,* n. 11 at 31–33.
23. Baker, *supra,* n. 11 at 25; Havens, *supra,* n. 18.

representation of popular interests and partisan attachments. The modulating effects of political culture and institutional arrangements on the various forms of malapportionment, thus defined, are given due consideration.[24] The political consequences most often considered are those which result in divided governments and the results that divided governments, in turn, may produce at the intra-party level. Policy consequences are always tied to the particular pattern of interest distortion and are frequently seen as second-order results of the political effects (for example, the lack of action in a divided government). The types of policies most frequently cited by the reformers are regulatory or enabling legislation. Fiscal policy, when it is dealt with, is also tied to the particular pattern of interest distortion and hence usually concerns a disproportionate distribution of either tax burden or state funds that is the result of legislative adoption of a particular formula. These are not single-factor explanations. The generalizations are contextually rich. There are detailed paths in their explanatory chains. There is a series of "if, thens" which are critical to the final outcome proposed.

This very abbreviated discussion of the reformers' consideration of the consequences of apportionment patterns on public policy and political phenomena sets the context for an examination of the conceptual, theoretical, and methodological problems which lead to my declaration that the skeptics' studies are a mistrial. The problems or "errors" cluster around (1) the definition of malapportionment, (2) the choice of policies and political effects studied, and (3) the approach to and manner of testing how these may or may not be related.

TAKING THE MEASURE OF MALAPPORTIONMENT

Clearly, one of the most critical tasks in analyses which attempt to test the consequences of malapportionment is measurement of the phenomena. I have already noted the dilemma confronting those who would attempt to test both the reformers' arguments regarding the political and policy consequences of malapportionment and, at the same time, the potential significance of legislatures' reapportioning to conform to the Court's definition of proper apportionment. The attempt to satisfy both of these requirements presents an extraordinarily difficult task for the skeptics,

24. Loren P. Beth and William C. Havard, "Committee Stacking and Political Power in Florida," 23 *The Journal of Politics*, 57–83; and Beth and Havard, *supra*, n. 11.

particularly since they give no indication that they recognize the major differences separating the definitions of the reformers and the position of the Court.[25]

One or more of three separate measures have been used in the skeptics' studies. None, however, was developed by the skeptics specifically for the task at hand. The measures, as it were, are off the rack, rather than being custom-fitted to the particular individual or common objectives in the skeptics' studies. Of the three measures employed, the first was developed by Manning J. Dauer and Robert G. Kelsay. It measures the theoretical minimum percentage of a state's population which could elect the majority of the state's legislature.[26] This measure of representativeness was calculated by the following procedure:

> The districts of the legislative house being studied were arranged in order from smallest to largest population per representative. The total population with the smallest ratio were added until that number of representatives was reached which could give a majority. This subtotal was then divided by the total population of the state, thus giving the smallest percentage which could elect the majority.[27]

Jacob used two variations of the Dauer-Kelsay index. Dye recomputed its components for 1960 and employed the version summing the scores for both chambers into a single index for his study.

The second measure of malapportionment that has been employed is drawn from Paul T. David and Ralph Eisenberg's analysis of "The Devaluation of the Urban and Suburban Vote."[28] That study was under way as action was pending before the Supreme Court in *Baker* v. *Carr*. Their approach to the question partly reflects the rationale ultimately adopted by the Court, that is, the argument that malapportionment denies equal protection, as guaranteed by the Fourteenth Amendment. They focus on the relative right to vote:

> If one legislator, for example, represents a district with 10,000 inhabitants, and another a district with 40,000, it is often said that in the smaller district the right to vote is worth four times what it is in the larger district. The value of the vote, in other words, is recognized, as

25. Hofferbert's is the one skeptic study which does not argue that it is testing the potential impact of the Court's decision.

26. Manning J. Dauer and Robert G. Kelsay, "Unrepresentative States," 44 *National Municipal Review* 571–575, 587.

27. *Id*. at 572–573, note A.

28. Paul T. David and Ralph Eisenberg, *Devaluation of the Urban and Suburban Vote* (University of Virginia: Bureau of Public Administration, 1961).

varying inversely with the number of constituents who are accorded the same amount of representation.[29]

David and Eisenberg argue that this kind of measure must be employed for all the voters within a given jurisdiction.

To become useful as a statistical tool of measurement, however, the concept of variation and the relative value of both must be tied to some stable base to which the variations can be related. . . . For this purpose in dealing with state legislatures, the most useful value is the average value of the vote on a statewide basis. For convenience this value can be thought of as *one* . . . variations can be calculated as simple percentages of the statewide average. It can be said, for example, that in one locality the average vote is 50 percent of the statewide average, whereas in the other, it is 150 percent. In making such calculations, it can be further assumed that the average value of the vote for the members of one house is the same as the average value of the vote for members of the other; that the relative values for the two houses can be combined on an equal footing.[30]

With these basic assumptions, David and Eisenberg compute the relative value of the vote for representatives of persons living in counties of four different population categories (less than 25,000; 25,000 to 99,999; 100,000 to 499,999; and 500,000 and over). The actual computations to develop the average values of the right to vote were then done as follows:

Counties were categorized according to their population and the total representation accorded to each population group of counties was totaled. The population per representative for all counties in that category was determined by dividing the total population of each population category by the number of representatives that category possessed in the legislative chamber. Then the average value of the vote for that category was obtained by dividing the population per representative of that category into the state-wide average population per representative for the legislative chamber. The average value of the right to vote for members of the legislature as a whole was obtained by averaging the figures for the two legislative houses.[31]

The measure from the David and Eisenberg study used by Dye and by Brady and Edmonds (often called the David-Eisenberg index) is the relative values of the right to vote for representation in state legislatures in the largest categories of counties in 1960.[32]

29. *Id.* at 7.
30. *Ibid.*
31. *Id.* at 18.
32. *Id.* at 15.

Following the *Baker* v. *Carr* decision, published at approximately the same time as the major one man, one vote, decisions were being handed down by the Court, the Glendon Schubert and Charles Press index of malapportionment has been used in each of the skeptics' studies which were written after it was published.[33] It begins with the basic assumption that "what is to be measured is deviation from the ideal of equal representation for populations of equal size . . . The raw data for the measurement of malapportionment consist, therefore of the frequencies of general population and of representatives assigned to each legislative district for both houses of a legislature." [34] Specifically, it focuses on the extent to which districts for each of a state's legislative chambers vary in size from that which would be found by dividing the population of the state by the number of representatives in the particular chamber. The figure thus obtained, the theoretically ideal population size for districts according to the one man, one vote, principle, is then used as a base from which deviations are calculated.

For each chamber they find the mean population size for districts, then determine the deviation from it for each district, square this deviation in order, to arrive at positive numbers, and then sum these squared deviations, thus computing the standard deviation. To norm this for all states, they divide the standard deviation by the mean to produce the coefficient of variation. This, subtracted from 1 gives a standardized or comparable measure for each chamber in every legislature of the extent to which districts deviate from one man, one vote.

In addition, Schubert and Press calculate the extent to which the distribution of representational population units is skewed in one direction or another—that is, deviates excessively from being concentrated around the mean value by having many more districts whose populations fall above the mean (a negative factor) or many more districts whose populations fall below the mean value (a positive factor). The extent to which the distribution is peaked, that is, kurtotic, is also considered—the more peaked, the better. These two factors of skewness and kurtosis are given some weight in the calculation. Schubert and Press further argue that to be politically realistic the Senate must be weighted half again as much as the House. The formula is given below:[35]

33. Glendon Schubert and Charles Press, "Measuring Malapportionment," 58 *American Political Science Review* 302–327. Corrections in computational errors found here are given in the same review, pp. 966–970. It was employed by all except Jacob, whose article was published at approximately the same time.

34. *Id.* at 303.

35. This is a "spelled-out" version of the formula given by Schubert and Press, *supra,* n. 33 at 319.

Apportionment Score = 60 (Inverse Coefficient of variation for the Senate + a score indicating the skewness and kurtosis for the distribution of representational units of the Senate)
$$+$$
40 (Inverse Coefficient of variation for the House + a score indicating the skewness and kurtosis for the distribution of representational units of the House).

Dye, who employs each of the three indices, notes:

All three of these measures—the index of representativeness [Dauer-Kelsay], the index of urban under-representation [David-Eisenberg], and the apportionment score [Schubert-Press] . . . each measures . . . a slightly different aspect of malapportionment; each results in a slightly different ranking of the states. The simple correlation coefficients between these three measures are as follows: index of representativeness and index of urban under-representation: .45; index of representativeness and apportionment score: .50; index of urban under-representation and apportionment score: .70. The first focuses on the theoretical minimum proportion of the state's population which can control the legislature, the second focuses on urban under-representation, and the third measure focuses on the degree to which a state's apportionment scheme approaches the statistical concept of normality.[36]

But perhaps the most important statement in his article follows the above, for it applies equally to the other works which have used these measures, but is left unsaid or, in the case of Dye, forgotten when the time comes to draw some conclusions from the analyses: "In the analysis to follow we shall evaluate the political relevance of each of these measures." [37]

The political relevance of these indices, both because of what the skeptics selected from what the authors of the indices provided and because of what the indices did not provide, is open to serious challenge. Two of the problems in the measures of malapportionment employed by the skeptics in testing the arguments of the reformers are due to the failure of the skeptics to make full use of the information provided by the authors of the indices.

First, the skeptics' tests employ bicameral measures of malapportionment, with the exception of two variants of the Dauer-Kelsay index employed by Jacob.[38] However, the authors of each of the indices have pro-

36. Dye, *supra,* n. 2 at 590.
37. *Ibid.*
38. Jacob, *supra,* n. 2 at 257. His "Index of Rural Dominance . . . the proportion of the population which can control the least representative house of the legislature,"

vided apportionment scores (or all the necessary information to compute them) for each legislative chamber, as well as a combined index for each whole legislative body. And Dauer and Kelsay specifically warn the reader of the questionable validity of the measure arrived at by combining their scores for each chamber:

One house that is considered to be truly representative does not necessarily offset a most unrepresentative second house. A state with reasonably adequate representation in both houses might rank approximately the same. But legislation affecting urban areas, for example, might have a relatively easier chance of passage in the latter case than in the former, which raises some doubt as to the validity of such rankings. Nevertheless, this combined ranking does have some validity at least for the states at the top and bottom of the scale.[39]

David and Eisenberg seem to accept this position:

Obviously it cannot be argued that a general assumption of equality as between the two houses is valid for all states at all times, but it would seem to be more nearly valid than any other general assumption that could be made. It is the assumption that is generally made in the relevant studies of the mathematical distribution of voting power in a legislature. It would seem sufficiently valid for use in the present study.[40]

Schubert and Press object to equating the apportionment of the House and the Senate; so, to attain their objective of providing a common metric on which to array states and to achieve their criterion of bicameral unity, they combine the two chambers by weighting the Senate half again as much as the House.[41] This, in fact, was the second alternative approach to

---

and, "Index of Urban Underrepresentation" which is the "proportion of the population which can control the least representative house whose membership is based on population." Jacob's third measure, an index of equal apportionment, "[which is] computed for each state by dividing the most populous district into the least populous one for each house and adding the quotients" is, of course, bicameral.

39. *Supra,* n. 26 at 575.
40. *Supra,* n. 28 at 6.
41. *Supra,* n. 33 at 304. "We reject as utterly unrealistic the legalistic assumption that lower chambers in American legislatures are either equal to or greater in power than upper chambers, because they are 'closer to the people,' or because 'appropriation bills must originate in lower chambers,' or because they are 'larger' than upper chambers. Typically, upper chambers are more important, in part because they share (as lower chambers generally do not) in the gubernatorial appointment power, thus exerting considerable influence over policy-making and implementation in the other-than-legislative governmental—including frequently, if indirectly, judicial—decision-making processes. A recognition of differential status is found in the thirty-three state and federal constitutional provisions that specify a longer term for members of one

the question of bicameralism presented by Schubert and Press. They not only presented the apportionment scores (the inverted coefficient of variation plus the skewness and kurtosis of the distribution) for both chambers, but they also dealt with the question of bicameralism in another fashion. The first approach was to plot the positions of the states in accordance with the apportionment of their upper and lower chambers. This plot was then divided into segments which showed: A. the "well apportioned" states (those with both the upper and lower legislative houses in the upper halves of their respective distributions); B. the "unapportioned" states ("relatively well apportioned upper houses but poorly apportioned lower houses"); and C. the "misapportioned" states (those with both upper and lower legislative houses in the lower half of the distribution). In presenting these different categories of the relationship of apportionment between the chambers within the states, Schubert and Press discuss the differences in policy consequences which might result from each relationship—which further supports the argument that the authors of the indices should not be faulted because of the skeptics' failure to use the information provided on both chambers.[42]

Given the availability of modern computing techniques and technology and the substantial number of variables employed (particularly in the more recent of these studies), there is no reason for the skeptics not to have employed separate apportionment scores for each chamber. This might have been done, if for no other reason than to test some of the questions raised by the authors of all three indices, such as the extent to which one particularly poorly apportioned chamber can "drag down" a chamber which is better apportioned, or whether a more poorly apportioned senate than house would be more likely to hold up legislation.

Second, the skeptics' studies also fail to make use of the several time periods for the indices provided by both Dauer and Kelsay (1937 and 1958) and David and Eisenberg (1910, 1930, 1950, 1960). It would have been interesting if the skeptics had tested the effect of an increase or decrease in malapportionment as defined by these measures, and, as shall be seen below, they also could have made good use in some of their tests of apportionment scores based on periods prior to 1960.

---

house: in all such cases, the longer term is for the upper house. Moreover, precisely because upper chambers are without exception smaller than lower chambers in American legislatures, senators typically represent (within any state) larger constituencies than members of the lower house, and their broader power base tends to assure that senators generally will be more influential politicians than members of the lower house."

42. *Id.* at 316–319.

In addition to the skeptics' failure to take advantage of all the available information, there are two major problems which make these measures of malapportionment deficient at critical points for the skeptics' purposes. First, the extensive incidence of multi-member districts among the states is noted as a problem but not pursued in detail by the authors of the indices.[43] In the construction of the indices, multi-member districts were dealt with by apportioning their population proportionately to the number of district representatives. That is, a district was treated as if each of its representatives represented his proportion of its total population. The authors of the indices then proceeded to the next step in the calculation of their scores.

Failure to give special consideration or special weight to multi-member districts is a problem with two sparate aspects, with the importance of either depending upon the research objective. On the one hand, the winner-take-all aspect of the multi-member district makes it an instrument of malapportionment in the sense that it denies representation to significant but still nonmajority interests within the district. Hence, urban, countywide multi-member districts are not representative of the diversity of interests they contain, which run from the inner-city ghetto resident or the high-rise dweller, the middle- or upper-class suburban resident, and the blue-collar, home-owning resident of the central city.[44] On the other hand, in terms of actual voting power in the legislative body, the large multi-member district may be seen as a counterbalancing force to the over-represented downstate or rural areas represented by single-member districts.[45]

It has been argued in the reformers' literature that representatives from

43. The widespread occurrence of this type of districting was first brought to the attention of the discipline by Maurice Klain, "A New Look at the Constituencies: The Need for a Recount and a Reappraisal," 49 *American Political Science Review* 1105–1119. Klain showed that, as of 1954, 16 of the 48 state senates had some multi-member districts, while 36 state lower chambers employed the multi-member districts; in fact, in the latter 36 chambers, 2,616 members were elected from multi-member districts and 1,870 came from single member districts. At the time of *Baker* v. *Carr*, David and Eisenberg found that there had been an increase in the percentage of state senators elected from multi-member districts, but that the percentage of lower house members had dropped to 46 percent. *State Legislative Redistricting* (Chicago: Public Administration Service, 1962), p. 20.

44. See, for example, Manning J. Dauer, "Multi-member Districts in Dade County: Study of a Problem and A Delegation," 28 *The Journal of Politics* 617–638.

45. This and the following discussion of multi-member districts in terms of legislative voting power relies heavily on Robert G. Dixon, Jr.'s consideration of the "New Mathematics of Representation" in his *Democratic Representation, supra*, n. 1 at 537–543.

rural areas find it easy to join together in a coalition to block urban legislation, since rural representatives are likely to have similar constituencies
and similar personal backgrounds. Yet, in many of the states with both
large rural populations and major urban, industrial areas the large urban
counties are represented by a multi-member delegation, the membership
of which is generally of one party and has been "slated" in a "bedsheet
ballot" primary by the party organization.[46] Such delegations have even
more reason to act as a single, cohesive unit, particularly when the issues
involve the fortunes of their party or their local area, than delegates from
rural single-member districts. The large, urban multi-member delegation's
potential as a blocking force, it can be assumed, is both quite real and
quite visible to representatives from other parts of the states.[47]

Moreover, an understanding of the fluid nature of the coalitions on
which legislative votes are won or lost in the actual production of policy
outcomes gives these multi-member districts added significance. Robert
G. Dixon, Jr., has pointed out that (even assuming that multi-member
representatives do not vote as a block) it is demonstrable that:

> . . . citizens in larger multi-member districts have more influence on
> legislative outcomes than do citizens in either smaller multi-member
> districts or single-member districts, *even though* the district populations
> are proportionately equal. The larger the multi-member district, i.e.,
> the more legislators it elects, the greater the individual citizen's influ-
> ence on legislative outcomes. The total or overall influence on legislative
> outcomes of the voter in a multi-member district (or his "effective
> representation") can be shown to be *proportional to the square root of
> the population of the district,* and thus varies with district size.[48]

This consideration of the multi-member district by Dixon would seem
to discount to some extent the counterargument that, particularly in some
strong party states, the members of delegations from multi-member districts vote together no more often than do representatives from the same
party from single-member districts.[49]

46. Here, for example, Cuyahoga County (Cleveland), Ohio; Dade County
(Miami), Florida; Marion County (Indianapolis), Indiana.

47. See, for example, Charles S. Hyneman's discussion of the feelings of "downstate" Illinois legislators regarding their block-like vision of metropolitan Chicago
delegations; "The Illinois Constitution and Democratic Government, 46 *Illinois Law
Review,* 511–575 (September–October, 1951).

48. Dixon, *supra,* n. 1 at 541.

49. See, for example, Howard Hamilton, "Legislative Constituencies: Single-Member Districts, Multi-Member Districts, and Floterial Districts," 20 *Western Political
Quarterly* 321–340.

Hence, if the focus is on the relationship between policy outcomes and apportionment patterns, and therefore ultimately on citizen impact on, or effective power in relation to, legislative decision-making—lacking consideration of the extent to which particular states have multi-member districts, how large these are and which people they represent and don't represent—the kind of indices which have been employed in these studies are totally inappropriate. Residents of urban multi-member districts may *in the electoral sense have had their votes devalued* to an extraordinary degree, but nevertheless *in the legislature* they may have been capable of overpowering the downstate areas with fewer persons per single-member district, whose votes *in the electoral sense are overvalued.*

The second, and, given the definitions of malapportionment and the thrust of the arguments in the reformer literature, perhaps the most important, deficiency in the indices is their highly limited consideration of whether the apportionment patterns distort the relative strength of the "interests." The Dauer-Kelsay and Schubert-Press indices are strictly mathematical formulations showing the deviation from a numeric ideal of, respectively, a percentage of the population electing representatives and the size of individual legislative districts.[50] The David-Eisenberg index shows the extent to which residents from counties having populations of different sizes are obtaining their proportionate share of the vote for representation. This gives the index a distant relationship to the dimension of urban/rural interest, that is, some content which could be expected to be related to certain types of policy outcomes. Therefore, it should not be surprising that among the skeptics' studies this index provides the few instances where the apportionment of legislatures has been found to have an impact.[51]

However, the David-Eisenberg index does not consider *the extent* to which the interests have been distorted. As John P. White and Norman C. Thomas have demonstrated, it is only in a few states that an urban popular majority has been turned into a legislative minority. The more frequent case is for the proportion of the legislative representation ac-

50. It is interesting to observe that in their writing Schubert and Press fault Dauer and Kelsay for not having any interest component in their index, therefore lacking political realism, while, at the same time, they rule out any consideration of gerrymandering: "We shall not be concerned in this article with gerrymandering, which is a question related to but quite independent of malapportionment. Gerrymandering consists of establishing district boundaries in relation to existing demographic patterns in such a way as to discriminate on the basis of some special parameter of the general population, such as political party, racial, or ethnic affiliation." *Supra,* n. 33 at 303.

51. Dye gives explicit recognition to this point, *supra,* n. 2 at 599.

corded to the urban population to be reduced to a lesser majority in states in which it was a majority in the first place.[52] Furthermore, one of the central arguments of the reformers has been concerned with the distortion of the numerical strength of *partisan* interests brought about by districting patterns. The skeptics make several "tests" of the political consequences of malapportionment, yet none of the indices considers the extent to which particular parties are under- or overrepresented in legislative bodies because of classic gerrymandering of district boundaries. On this basis alone, it would appear that the tests on which the skeptics base the claim that they have disproved the reformers' arguments regarding the effect of apportionment patterns on political systems are invalid.

A disconcerting point is the implication, or the possible interpretation, that the articles of the skeptics which have employed more than one of these indices somehow cover the spectrum of what malapportionment means and that the use of two or three indices will somehow compensate for their individual inadequacies. But to use more than one of these indices in such studies is simply to use more than one inappropriate index. If the elements or considerations incorporated in each of the indices were used to develop a new composite index, it would represent a start in the right direction. But, before considering what an appropriate independent variable should incorporate and how it might be developed, I will examine the dependent variables used in the skeptics' tests.

POLICY OUTCOMES AND POLITICAL EFFECTS USED TO ASSESS THE EFFECT OF MALAPPORTIONMENT

"Measuring state policy choices is an even more difficult task than measuring malapportionment. In the 1960–61 legislative sessions, more than 104,000 bills were introduced in the state legislatures throughout the nation. Each bill rejected or enacted represents a separate policy choice. What policies are to be selected in order to assess the impact of malapportionment?" [53]

The truth of Dye's statement here regarding the difficulty of this problem is borne out by the policies as well as the political phenomena he and the other skeptics selected for testing. Unfortunately, the dependent variables used in these studies—the policies and political effects that have been measured—are such that, even without the problems of the manner

52. John P. White and Norman C. Thomas, "Urban and Rural Representation and State Legislative Apportionment," 17 *Western Political Quarterly* 724–741.

53. Dye, *supra*, n. 2 at 590.

in which malapportionment has been measured, the tests would still have to be declared a mistrial.

Policy Consequences

Dye answers his own question without reference to the reformers. His selection is based on the "importance" of the policy. Specifically, Dye selects "thirty measures of state policy in three of the most important subject matters of state politics—education, welfare, and taxation. Education is the largest category of state spending . . . Welfare expenditures are the second largest category of state expenditures." [54] He naturally also considers how the state is to pay for its programs, by measuring revenue and taxation policies.

It is difficult to see how some of his variables, such as "Male School Teachers as a Percent of Total, 1961–62" or "Percent of Selective Service Examinees Disqualified for Failing Mental Test, 1962" represent one of or even a simple aspect of one of the 104,000 separate policy choices made in the several state legislatures in the 1960/1961 biennium. [55] Beyond the question of whether these variables really are measures of policy decisions, Dye's choice of primarily broad expenditure and revenue variables as measures to use in assessing the effect of apportionment patterns on policy choices is open to serious question, as is Hofferbert's choice of "welfare orientation," which in his study is "the sum of the individual ranks of the mean expenditures for ten years" on five variables. [56] Similar variables are used by Jacob and by Brady and Edmonds. [57]

Gross expenditure and revenue items are, in fact, the measures of state policy most commonly used in testing the effects of apportionment patterns. For several reasons this type of variable is, in general, inappropriate for comparative state tests of the political impact of particular institutional arrangements for a particular slice of time (in this case, a given legislative session). First, Dye notes in his own state and local text, that "over 50 percent of state finances come from special 'earmarked' funds. What is left, 'general fund expenditures,' are also largely committed to existing state

54. *Ibid.*, p. 591.
55. *Id.* at 590–591.
56. Hofferbert, *supra*, n. 2 at 75.
57. The list of variables is far too long to give here. The three such variables employed by Jacob are found *supra*, n. 2 at 258. The thirty employed by Dye are listed *supra*, n. 2 at 590–591. Hofferbert uses five such variables to develop his index of welfare orientations; *supra*, n. 2 at 74, note 6. Brady and Edmonds use seventeen such measures; they are listed *supra*, n. 2 (Iowa version) at 3–A. Pulsipher and Weatherby's variables test of fourteen expenditures is found *supra*, n. 2 at 1210.

programs, particularly welfare and education." [58] Second, fiscal policy is perhaps the most difficult for either individual legislators or for the legislature as a whole to deal with or manipulate directly. Budgetary decisions are, as Aaron Wildavsky, Ira Sharkansky, and others have pointed out, dominated by the weight of inertia. Hence, fiscal policy reflects cumulative decisions that started many sessions before a particular year's level of expenditures was determined. [59]

Third, budgeting is also a policy arena in which legislators, particularly in the nonprofessional chambers found in the majority of states prior to *Baker* v. *Carr,* are least equipped to cope with the expertise and resources of the bureaucracy. Fourth, in many states, this type of policy is one in which the governor plays a particularly crucial and dominant role; both by the detailed preparation of revenue and budget measures and by using his "blue-pencil power," he may actually determine the budget's final form. [60]

Finally, many states are constitutionally prohibited from enacting deficit budgets; their levels of revenue are limited by the aggregate wealth of the state itself. To "demonstrate" therefore, as Dye, Hofferbert, and Brady and Edmonds do, that the expenditure per capita for a given program area is more closely correlated with the socioecenomic development of the state than with its political characteristics, is not too surprising.

Another major problem with the gross fiscal variable is that it is analyzed in a manner which assumes an almost universal political liberalness, and that willingness to spend is equally distributed throughout the country in all states. The extent to which, for example, the majority of the citizens of Utah or Wyoming or Indiana and Ohio had the same desires, as were attributed to them by Allen Pulsipher and James Weatherby, to "spend more on the governmental function in question" when the governmental function in question is welfare does not seem to me to stand up in the clear light of day. And to assume that just because the state has a low welfare payment or fails to support its schools in relation to its wealth—that is, drops below the limit "demanded" by the investiga-

58. Thomas R. Dye, *Politics in State and Local Communities* (Englewood Cliffs: Prentice-Hall, 1969), p. 163.

59. See, for example, Aaron Wildavsky, *The Politics of the Budgetary Process* (Boston: Little, Brown, 1964) and Ira Sharkansky, *Spending in the American States* (Chicago: Rand McNally, 1968).

60. For confirmation of the latter two points, see Ira Sharkansky "Agency Requests, Gubernatorial Support and Budget Success in State Legislatures," 62 *The American Political Science Review* 1220–1231.

tor's regression line—does not indicate that it is the legislature itself that is not reflective of a great majority of citizen views.[61]

Each of the above objections might apply to the use of this variable in all cross-sectional comparative state tests of the effects of legislative institutional attributes. But with regard to malapportionment the problems are even more critical. When they considered policy, the reformers focused not so much on how badly the districts were out of alignment with the one man, one vote, doctrine in terms of population, as they did on who was being under- or overrepresented. When they dealt with the dependent variable (the particular policy question they had in mind), their focus was not so much on how much, in gross terms, was being spent, but on who, particularly, was benefiting and who was paying. The great majority of the variables used in these studies don't include policies which are clearly redistributional in nature. Unfortunately, those which do so, as we shall see, suffer from the problem of "fitting" the effect with the appropriate independent variable or measure of malapportionment.

One further problem of a primarily technical nature is that most of the measures of fiscal policy used in this area of study have included both state and local expenditures in their calculation of fiscal policy outcomes. As a consequence, this class of dependent variables which is already open to a great deal of challenge has been even further confounded. It makes little sense, for example, to test the extent to which the apportionment pattern of a state legislature is related to the expenditures per student or per capita for elementary and secondary education when those expenditures depend, in a degree which varies from state to state, on decisions by local taxpayers and local governmental units. Certainly, none of the reformers gave any indication that he expected that, just because a given state's legislature was malapportioned, the citizens of that state would be less likely to vote for local bond issues and tax overrides to support their schools.[62]

However, several policies are used as tests that do appear to be of a type which might be indicative of attitudes and opinions of legislators, and therefore reflective of any distortion in their representativeness.

Jacob, Hofferbert, and Brady and Edmonds, in contrast to Dye, indicate that they selected their policy tests on bases at least suggested by the reformers. Examining the material they cite, it is difficult to see how some measures were selected, unless there were serious misinterpretations of

---

61. *Supra*, n. 2.
62. The significance of this aggregation of both state and local expenditures for the results obtained is demonstrated in Sharkansky, *supra*, n. 59.

just what the reformers were arguing or reporting—particularly of the extent to which the reformers claimed the effects of malapportionment were universal. The most striking example of the misinterpretation of a reformer occurs where Brady and Edmonds note:

> Thus, given enough time, the investigator could find a number of major effects of malapportionment that could be handled in an efficient manner. [But] Fortunately one reformer has summarized the consequences of malapportionment in a brief form, and thus the researchers were spared this task.
>
> Charles Shull interviewed 204 prominent figures in various states and compiled a list of eight major consequences of malapportionment. Because this list was obtained through interviews with persons concerned with state government in general and legislative apportionment in particular, it is of double value for our purposes. The list compiled by Shull follows: 1) Labor and Management; 2) Support of public education; 3) Highway fund distribution; 4) Local government subsidies and support (liquor laws); 5) Social welfare programs; 6) Taxation and public finance; 7) Legislative organization; 8) Imbalance of party strength. We propose to examine all of the above points except for three and seven.[63]

Since Shull's article, "Political and Partisan Implications of State Legislative Apportionment" [64] is cited by Hofferbert, as well as by Brady and Edmonds, as one which presents arguments which they are testing, it's worth examining specifically what Shull stated:

> [Shull mailed] certain questions to informed individuals in the various American states. A questionnaire with 6 principal questions was devised and sent out to some 204 persons within these various political units of the United States. The response has been quite heartening, representing over 50 per cent return from the individuals and covering at least 45 of the states.[65]

The question that seems to have drawn most of the attention was:

> In your opinion does your state legislative apportionment figure as an issue in the following situations . . .
>
> | | | |
> |---|---|---|
> | 1. Labor and management | yes | no |
> | 2. Support of public education | yes | no |
> | 3. Highway fund distribution | yes | no |

63. Brady and Edmonds, *supra*, n. 2 (Iowa version) at 3.
64. Shull, *supra*, n. 11 at 417–439.
65. *Id.* at 430.

4. Local government subsidies and support	yes	no
5. Social welfare programs	yes	no
6. Taxation and public finance	yes	no
7. Legislative organization itself	yes	no
8. Imbalance of party strength	yes	no[66]

In short, the list was part of a questionnaire mailed by Shull to his 204 "experts," just more than half of whom responded by checking either a *yes* or a *no* for their particular states. It was not a listing or grouping of responses to what Brady and Edmonds seem to have thought an "open-ended" question.

Shull presents his results both in terms of the number of individuals who checked *yes* or *no* for each question and of how these responses group in terms of the state in which his experts resided. Shull's presentation is in a discursive format which is reduced to a more concise form in Table 1.[67]

As this table shows, among Shull's respondents, as individuals, the highest percentage of agreement was negative; that is, 74 percent indicated that "labor and management" issues were not related to apportionment. The next highest agreement Shull obtained was among the 70 percent who agreed that legislative apportionment did figure as an issue with regard to "legislative organization itself"—an area left unexamined in all of the skeptics' studies. This was followed closely by the 69 percent who agreed that "highway fund distribution" was related to legislative apportionment. But after that Shull's "experts" are far from consensus, with agreement ranging from 61 to 46 percent. It is interesting to note that the 46 percent was for "social welfare programs," one of the prime areas of policy studied in the work of the skeptics.

The second column of figures in Table 1 summarizes Shull's report of the extent to which his respondents agreed that malapportionment was related to these situations, according to the states in which they resided. There is no way of determining from Shull's report the extent to which states were likely to be listed as agreeing either with a *yes* or *no* answer, rather than being listed as *divided,* simply because the number of respondents varied from state to state. However, employing the information he does provide, we see that, once again, the highest percentage of agreement by state (59 percent) is that "Labor and management" is not related to legislative apportionment and, following the pattern previously seen in the individual responses, the next highest percentage of agreement by

66. *Id.* at 433.
67. These results were derived from *id.* at 433–435.

TABLE 1
The "Experts" Divided

Distribution of Responses by Shull's Correspondents to the question, "In your opinion, does your state legislative apportionment figure as an issue in the following situations?"

	Individual Respondents Yes (n)	By States*			
		Yes	Divided	No	
Labor and management	26% (93)	37%	4%	59%	100%
Support of public education	55% (94)	24%	59%	17%	
Highway fund distribution	69% (96)	39%	41%	20%	
Local government subsidies and support	58% (94)	30%	48%	22%	
Social welfare programs	46% (93)	17%	48%	35%	
Taxation and public finance	61% (94)	35%	41%	24%	
Legislative organization itself	70% (97)	46%	33%	22%	
Imbalance of party strength	56% (98)	37%	24%	39%	

* The percentages under "By States" are based on a total of 46 states. This was the common sum obtained when Shull gave either the number of states or listed by name states for each of the *Yes*, *Divided*, or *No* categories. For four of his "situations" (labor and management, support of public education, highway fund distribution, and social welfare programs) he either gave the number or listed the states for but two of the three categories. Hence, the percentages given above for those four "situations" for which information was incomplete may be based on fewer than 46 states, given his comment that the return covered at least 45 states.

state is in the *yes* category, on the question of whether apportionment does figure as an issue with regard to "legislative organization itself."

Viewing this table, one can find very little support for the argument that Shull's research should or could be used as a basis for hypothesizing that apportionment patterns have a consistent impact across all states on any of the particular programs, or situations, as he calls them, with the possible exception of "legislative organization." [68] This, of course, is a rather extreme example of how quite limited, tentative statements or findings seem

68. It should be noted that, in commenting upon his results, Shull generally argued that "divided" states provided evidence of the possibility that there was some sort of effect of apportionment in these areas in those states.

to have been turned into hard universal propositions. But it should serve to alert the reader to some of the problems that occurred as the reformer literature was transformed into propositions in the comparative state tests.

Beyond the question of whether these measures represent a "true" test of the reformers' arguments or propositions, there are other problems with many of the nonfiscal measures of policy. This is particularly true if they are considered in terms of the extent to which as policy choices they can be expected to reflect the apportionment patterns as measured in 1962, or, for that matter, of how much they can be the primary responsibility of the legislative body, as such.

Jacob, for example, argues that if the reformers are correct and apportionment does make a difference in how well states treat their cities, states with well apportioned legislatures are likely to grant home rule to cities, whereas states with malapportioned legislatures are not. Jacob tests this proposition by comparing the proportion of home-rule states among those with the ten best apportioned legislatures, with that in states with the ten worst apportioned legislatures (as defined by his three measures of malapportionment). He finds little difference.[69]

The extent to which the granting of home rule is indicative of a legislature's being responsive to urban needs is itself debatable; but more problematic, of the thirty-two states which provide for home rule, twenty-seven do so in their constitutions. Constitutional amendments in all but seven of the fifty states (Arizona, Arkansas, Minnesota, Missouri, North Dakota, South Dakota, and Virginia) require, first, an extraordinary majority in both chambers of the legislature and/or approval by the legislature in two consecutive sessions. This is followed in all states, with the exception of Delaware, by approval of the majority of the electorate.[70] In these twenty-seven states, at least, home rule seems a doubtful test of the extent to which apportionment patterns may or may not produce a legislative distortion of the public's will. The argument that allowing home rule would require positive legislative action in those states where it was included in the constitution is valid. However, of the twenty-seven constitutional home-rule states, twelve had this provision in their constitutions prior to 1920 and six more added it between 1920 and 1940. Only eight adopted it within the two decades before *Baker* v. *Carr*. These included Alaska and Hawaii which had home rule in their constitutions when they entered the Union.

69. Jacob, *supra*, n. 2 at 256, 259.

70. See "Constitutional Amendment Procedure: By the Legislature," *Book of the States 1962–63*, vol. XIV (Chicago: The Council of State Governments, 1962), p. 13.

Of the five states which adopted home rule by legislation instead of including it in their constitutions, three did so before 1920. The other two, Georgia and Connecticut, adopted it in 1947 and 1951, respectively. In brief, it is difficult to accept the absence or presence of home-rule provisions as a test of the effect of apportionment patterns in 1962.[71]

In another test, Brady and Edmonds argue that if the reformers are correct, state income-tax plans, since they are "liberal," should be found more commonly in well apportioned than in poorly apportioned states. Using this as a test, they trichotomized states into "well," "medium," and "poorly" apportioned groups, using first the 1960 David-Eisenberg and then the Schubert-Press index scores.[72] Looking at the extent to which there is a difference in the adoption of state income-tax plans among the three different apportionment groups, according to either the David-Eisenberg or Schubert-Press score, Brady and Edmonds find no significant difference.[73] But this should be no surprise. Of the thirty-nine states described as having some kind of income-tax plan, fourteen adopted them before 1929 (Wisconsin being the first, in 1911), and nineteen more followed during the Depression years between 1929 and 1937. This leaves only eight—once again including Alaska and Hawaii—that adopted income-tax plans during the period from 1938 to the time of the *Baker* v. *Carr* decision. Thus, as a test of whether apportionment patterns between 1960 and 1962 are related to policy outcomes, the validity of this variable is subject to many of the same caveats as is that of home rule.[74]

Arguing that alcoholic beverage control systems are another significant

71. Dates and source of home rule provisions given in Russell Maddox and Robert F. Fuquay, *State and Local Government,* 2d ed. (Princeton: Van Nostrand, 1966), p. 456.

72. As noted above, both the Dauer-Kelsay and David-Eisenberg indices present scores for several periods of time. The five studies examined here, however, make use only of the last time period given by the authors, i.e., 1960 index for David and Eisenberg, while Dye recalculates the Dauer-Kelsay index for 1960.

73. See Brady and Edmonds, *supra,* n. 2 at 15–16.

74. For dates on which states adopted components of an income tax plan, see "State Net Income Taxes in Effect July 1, 1958, by Type and Date of Adoption," in Clara Penniman and Walter M. Heller, *State Income Tax Administration* (Chicago: Public Administration Service, 1959), p. 7 (Table 1). The two states which adopted income tax plans between 1958 and 1962 (South Dakota and West Virginia) were located by comparing the information provided by Penniman and Heller with the source cited by Brady and Edmonds for their variable, Bureau of the Census, *Compendium of State Governmental Finances in 1962* (Washington, D.C.: Department of Commerce, U.S. Gov't Printing Office, 1963). (I assume Brady and Edmonds's source to be "Table 5—Tax Revenue, by Type of Tax and by States: 1962," p. 11). It is likely that a constitutional amendment allowing for the adoption of an income tax was required in some states.

area of policy decision likely to be affected by the malapportionment of legislatures and that state monopoly systems are "conservative" means of controlling the sale of alcoholic beverages, Brady and Edmonds examine the extent to which there is variation in this practice in relation to the two groups of states trichotomized according to the David-Eisenberg and Schubert-Press apportionment scores.[75] They find no "significant" differences.

Without discussing the validity of the argument that "socializing liquor" is conservative, state liquor monopolies and other issues taken to be conservative present a major conceptual and methodological problem in these studies of malapportionment. Such legislation requires the governor's signature to become law. Since he is elected by the majority of the people, it is difficult to lay the responsibility upon a malapportioned legislature for a "conservatively oriented" policy's becoming law. The legislature might, of course, be able to muster the extraordinary majorities that most states require of both houses to override the popularly elected governor's veto, but this factor has not been considered in the studies.

Here too, the question of the relationship of the time of the enactment of the policy and that of the measurement of malapportionment is important. Of the seventeen states which had liquor monopolies in 1962, fifteen had adopted this system by 1936—that is, within three years after they turned "wet" following repeal of the Eighteenth Amendment in 1933. Again one must question whether, if legislative apportionment as of 1962 does make a difference, it can be tested by policy decisions made in part by a legislature elected in 1930.[76]

"Right-to-work" laws represent one nonfiscal policy that is not quite so problematic in regard to time. The laws had to be adopted following the 1946 enactment of the Taft-Hartley Act; hence, the legislative action took place at least within the two decades prior to the measurement of malapportionment. Both the Jacob and the Brady and Edmonds studies employ right-to-work legislation as a test of the extent to which apportionment has an effect. Both assume the adoption of such legislation as an example of a "conservative or non-liberal policy" and therefore one more likely to

75. Brady and Edmonds, *supra*, n. 2 at 15–16.

76. This was determined by comparing the states listed as having state monopoly systems in Leonard V. Harrison and Elizabeth Laine, *After Repeal: A Study of Liquor Control Administration* (New York: Harper and Bros., 1936), p. 43, with the reports of the method of control for each state presented in *Public Revenues from Alcoholic Beverages*, 1962 (Washington, D.C.: Distilled Spirits Institute, 1963). It is likely that this decision involved at one time a majority vote of the population and perhaps a constitutional amendment in several states.

be adopted by a malapportioned legislature, if apportionment patterns do have an effect. Jacob finds no difference among his ten best and ten worst apportioned states. Brady and Edmonds find a "significant" difference between the adoption of right-to-work laws in the states trichotomized according to the David-Eisenberg index, but no significant difference in states trichotomized according to the Schubert-Press index.[77] Again, the interpretation of these findings is difficult, for in the nineteen states which had right-to-work laws as of 1962, seven had adopted them following the adoption of enabling constitutional amendments. Of the remaining twelve, eight were southern. Five of these had less than a majority of their populations in areas considered urban by the rather loose definition of the Bureau of the Census. One of the four nonsouthern states, Indiana—with a legislature brought in by the Johnson landslide—repealed its right-to-work law in 1965, following reapportionment. None of the three non-southern states (Nevada, Iowa, and Utah) has the type of major industrial area which would indicate that the law was enacted over the angered cries of an underrepresented majority of union or potential union members and their families.[78]

In addition, the same question must be raised here regarding the consideration given in the studies to the governor's veto power; for the purposes of these analyses, it is appropriate to assume that if an official elected by the majority of the population felt that the people did not want a policy, he would in fact veto it.

Another policy used by Brady and Edmonds to determine the effect of apportionment illustrates yet one more problem with the selection of variables in this research. Specifically, Brady and Edmonds use participation by states in the federal Kerr-Mills program for medical aid to the aged as a test of the conservativeness of the legislature, arguing that malapportioned legislatures would be more conservative and hence less likely to adopt this program.[79] Using the same basic approach that they employed with liquor control and income tax, they examine the extent to which states have participated by actually providing funds for the program. Here there is neither the problem of constitutional amendment nor that of time, since the Kerr-Mills plan was adopted in 1960 and required action within the two years preceding the measurement of malapportionment employed by Brady and Edmonds.

77. Jacob, at 258–259, and Brady and Edmonds, at 14–15, *Supra,* n. 2.

78. For time and manner of adoption of state right-to-work laws, see *Congress and Nation, 1954–64* (Washington, D.C.: Congressional Quarterly Inc., 1965), p. 600.

79. Brady and Edmonds, *supra,* n. 2 at 13–14.

But even the most hidebound conservative rural legislator might find it difficult to vote against a program which would provide aid to his constituents who were becoming increasingly elderly. Aside from the validity of medical aid to the aged as a test of liberalism there is another difficulty, a major source of problems for those selecting policies to use in assessing the effects of political institutions in comparative state studies; specifically, this difficulty is the federal formulas concerning state and federal contributions. As the *Congressional Quarterly* pointed out at the time the bill was enacted, "quick state action (was) expected under the new medical plan." [80] Because of the manner in which the benefit payments were to be calculated, in twenty-five states there would be no necessity for allocating any funds. Those states would, in fact, receive an overall federal bonus for participation in the Kerr-Mills program. Brady and Edmonds's failure to consider this leads once again to doubt concerning the extent to which their analysis of Kerr-Mills adoptions provides any significant or substantial test of the importance of apportionment patterns to the responsiveness of the legislature to social needs.[81]

Thus, even beyond gross revenue and expenditure items, the great majority of variables which have been used to test the effects of malapportionment or apportionment patterns are inappropriate because of: (1) the lack of relationship between the time of the adoption of a program and that of the measure of apportionment; (2) the variation in both the requirement of constitutional coverage and the procedures among the states for the adoption of particular programs; (3) the failure in these studies to consider the veto power of the governor, particularly in connection with policies which are held to have a conservative bias; or (4) contamination of variables by federal requirements and regulations.

There is, moreover, the further problem of the conceptual fit between what might otherwise be appropriate variables and the index of malapportionment chosen. Here, in particular, these studies demonstrate a lack of theoretical sensitivity to the relationship between the independent and dependent variables.

Hofferbert, for example, tests the effect of apportionment patterns in relation to state aid to cities—specifically, what portion of each state's budget goes to its two largest cities. He finds no relationship. But rather

80. See, "Fact Sheet on New Medical Program," *Congressional Quarterly Weekly,* September 16, 1960, pp. 1588–1590.
81. More likely, adoption of the Kerr-Mills promise was more a test of the shrewdness of the administrators of some states to quickly take advantage of an increased coverage for their citizens while reducing the overall state health and welfare budget requirements than a test of legislative responsiveness.

than using the David-Eisenberg index, which specifically measures the extent to which there is a devaluation of the urban and suburban vote, he employs (as he does throughout his article) the Schubert-Press index, which gives no indication of the extent to which the apportionment pattern in urban or rural areas could be expected specifically to deny state aid to cities. As noted above, the extent to which any particular area of the state deviates from the mean has an impact on the Schubert-Press index of malapportionment; there is no reason to believe that the under- or overrepresentation of a specific set of farmers would be related to the distribution of aid to cities.[82]

Political Consequences

Attempts to test the political effects of apportionment provide further evidence of the conceptual and theoretical problems of these studies. As noted above, none of the indices employed actually incorporated any consideration of the extent to which partisan forces in a state were being under- and overrepresented, and hence there was no particular reason that any of the indices would be related to political phenomena, particularly those discussed by the reformers. This, however, did not deter the skeptics. Hofferbert states that "malapportionment has been accused of being a major hindrance to responsible party government. It is maintained that this legislative inequity weakens the two-party system in a variety of ways. One of the most frequently suggested is that malapportionment denies legislative control to an occasionally successful aspirant for the governorship from a state's normal minority party. V. O. Key has stated, 'By far the most important element producing [divided control] is the malapportionment of representation . . . .' "[83] Hofferbert then tests the extent to which there is an association between divided governments and malapportionment, as measured by the Schubert-Press index. He finds none. It is difficult to accept this as a refutation of Key, however. If the quotation from Key cited by Hofferbert is continued, it reads, ". . . in the legislature, but other institutions and procedural factors also contribute. The *varieties of legislative malapportionment reflect the range of human ingenuity in adapting political geography to partisan advantage* [emphasis added]."[84] Key then goes on to cite what he calls the old-

82. Hofferbert, *supra*, n. 2 at 76–77. Note also that the same criticism can be applied to Jacob's attempt to relate differential distribution to gasoline tax revenues among urban and rural roads with his "interest-free" measures of malapportionment, which he naturally finds are not associated. Jacob, *supra*, n. 2 at 258.

83. Hofferbert, *id*. at 77.

84. Key, *supra*, n. 11 at 64–65.

fashioned gerrymander and the silent gerrymander. Both focus on the distortion of partisan strength through the apportionment of the legislature—phenomena that the Schubert-Press index explicitly ignores.[85]

Hofferbert also tests whether apportionment affects party competition. This test, of course, suffers from the same lack of consideration of partisan distortion as his measure of malapportionment. In addition, however, his measure of party competition does not include any consideration of the votes for the state legislative seats, but combines the votes for President, governor, and U.S. senator.[86] He makes reference to the argument of Key, which was expanded by Jewell, that malapportionment is likely to have adverse effects on the statewide candidates of that party which is a popular minority but a legislative majority.[87] It is not clear that this effect on intra-party politics is really what he is testing. In any event, it can be assumed that the President and, in most instances, candidates for the U.S. Senate are not forced to run on the records of the state legislatures, no matter how they may be apportioned. Hence, the index, of which two-thirds is made up of the vote in the presidential and U.S. senatorial elections, would not be likely to reflect the phenomena with which Key and Jewell are concerned.

Dye also measures the impact of malapportionment on party competition by examining the relationship between malapportionment and party competition in the state legislatures, which he measures as "the percentage of total seats in each house of the legislature between 1954 and 1964 which were held by the majority party. Percentages are then inverted so that the competition scores in the House and Senate [where the minority party did not hold a single seat during those years] are set at 0 and all other scores range upward." [88] Dye argues that "if it is true that malapportionment affects party competition, then malapportioned legislatures should be less competitive than well-apportioned legislatures, and the differences in competition should be attributable to malapportionment rather than to some other socio-economic condition." [89] Dye then presents the simple and partial correlation coefficients between this measure of party competition and the Dauer-Kelsay, David-Eisenberg, and Schubert-Press apportionment scores. He separates upper and lower chambers in calculating his party-competition score but, following the standard

85. *Ibid.*
86. Hofferbert, *supra,* n. 2 at 77–78.
87. Key, *supra,* n. 11 and Jewell at 24.
88. Dye, *supra,* n. 2 at 593.
89. *Ibid.*

mode of procedure in each of the skeptics' articles, he fails to do the same for his apportionment scores.

By not using the separate indices provided by each of the index authors for the individual chambers, Dye avoids the opportunity for testing the extent to which the apportionment of a particular chamber is associated with competition for that chamber. Even though none of the indices incorporates a party component, Dye does obtain a "significant" partial correlation, after controlling for the effects of economic development, with the David-Eisenberg index and party competition in both upper and lower chambers. The particular meaning of that, however, given his failure to separate the apportionment scores for the individual chambers, is certainly far from clear.

ASSESSING THE RELATIONSHIPS

After pointing out the major difficulties with the measures of malapportionment and the policy outcomes and political effects that have been used, it may be that an examination of the techniques of analyses employed by the skeptics is unnecessary.[90] But, with the ultimate objective of actually having an adequate test of the consequences of apportionment patterns for policy outcomes and political life among the states, a few points should be noted. This is particularly important, for it will allow for a discussion of the one nonskeptic attempt to study the pre-*Baker* v. *Carr* effects of malapportionment on a comparative state basis—Pulsipher and Weatherby's "Malapportionment, Party Competition, and the Functional Distribution of Governmental Expenditures."[91]

This study has not been classed among the skeptics, for it does not approach the subject from the perspectives of testing the reformers or of questioning the probable impact of the Court's reapportionment decisions.

90. I will only note the shortcomings associated with the use of rank-order correlations employed by both Jacob and Hofferbert, *supra*, n. 2. They ask the questions statistically, at least, in the following words: "Are states which have better apportionment scores likely to produce 'better' policies than states which have lower apportionment scores?" In using rank-order analyses, Jacob and Hofferbert "lost" the size of the intervals separating the states on the malapportionment scores. The same weight, for example, is given to the 9.7 difference between the Kansas score of 11.5 and the Minnesota score of 1.8 as is given to the difference of 0.1 between Mississippi's score of 42.4 and Rhode Island's score of 42.3 on the Schubert-Press index used in Hofferbert's analysis. While their data are not displayed in a similar fashion for the policy variables, it is likely that interval differences among the states are just as great if not greater in, for example, welfare support or distribution of highway funds.

91. Pulsipher and Weatherby, *supra*, n. 2.

Instead, the authors set out two major hypotheses and the premises upon which each is based. Only the first is of concern here:

Hypothesis I.—The greater the degree of [mal]apportionment in a state, the *lower* the level of per capita expenditure will tend to be *for the governmental function in question.*

We interpret this hypothesis to be consistent with the following two premises:

Premise I.1.—The greater the degree of malapportionment in a state, the greater will tend to be the divergence between the actual results of the political decision-making process and the "true" preferences of the electorate for the category of governmental expenditures in question.

Premise I.2.—The "true" preferences of the electorate call for a higher level of expenditure on the function in question than the actual level produced by the political decision-making process.[92]

The premises, as noted above, are not by any means beyond question. Too many politicians are elected by campaigning on the platform that they will reduce expenditures for anyone to assume that the true preferences of the electorate are that more should be spent on "the governmental function in question." Their admittedly reluctant choice of the Schubert-Press index and their choice of variables, which include local as well as state expenditures, make them at least partial though unwilling victims of the problems discussed above.

Be that as it may, they do point out by example that the use and interpretation of partial correlation techniques both by Dye and by Brady and Edmonds leaves something to be desired. Dye, for example, demands that, after controlling for socioeconomic level, the resulting partial correlation with his three indices of malapportionment be statistically significant. If malapportionment had no effect after socioeconomic factors were accounted for, the partial correlation should be very low, if not zero. It would therefore seem theoretically significant that the correlations between the David-Eisenberg Index and many of Dye's policy variables in some cases actually increased, in many others were only reduced slightly, while in only a few instances were reduced to zero after the socioeconomic level was partialled out.[93]

The test of significance used by Dye and by Brady and Edmonds does not require that the difference made by malapportionment be in a particular direction. That is, they employ a "two-tailed" test of statistical signifi-

92. *Id.* at 1208.
93. Dye, *supra,* n. 2 at 596–597.

cance. Pulsipher and Weatherby approach the same basic task with more rigorous and direct tests. They compare the coefficients of mutiple determination (R^2) obtained from two regression models—one including only the socioeconomic variables to predict the expenditures level, and the second including the socioeconomic variables and the Schubert-Press index to predict the expenditures level. They then use a one-tailed t test to determine whether the difference between the coefficients of multiple determination (R^2) *is greater in the predicted direction* than one would expect on the basis of chance (and, of course, the effect of an addition of another variable to the equation).

In short, they are looking to see whether there is an effect in the expected direction—not an effect which is of dominating importance, but some effect that cannot be attributed merely to chance. Therefore, even while they are not claiming to be testing the reformers, their statistical approach is much closer in terms of the demands it places on the importance of malapportionment than those techniques used by the skeptics. Unfortunately, both the independent and dependent variables used in these tests still render their findings subject to the serious questions raised above.

MALAPPORTIONMENT IN OTHER COMPARATIVE STATE STUDIES

In addition to the studies we have considered, measures of malapportionment have been used frequently in comparative state studies whose primary objectives did not include testing the impact of malapportionment. Because, there too, the same measures of malapportionment were used generally with the same or similar measures of policy outcomes and socioeconomic controls, the same results have been obtained. And the same objections apply.[94]

94. See, for example, M. Kent Jennings and Harmon Zeigler, "The Salience of American State Politics," 64 *American Political Science Review*, 523–535; Sharkansky, *supra*, n. 59; Brian R. Fry and Richard Winters, "The Politics of Redistribution," 64 *American Political Science Review* 508–522. The Jennings and Zeigler study is a rather strange example of the use of malapportionment indices. They argue that the "good government types" would be apt to assume that in the better apportioned state people would find state government more salient. Salience, i.e., paying attention to, should not be equated with "liking." That would be to equate paying attention to the war in Southeast Asia with approval of it. Moreover, if one were willing to make this rather dubious assumption, the results would seem to indicate that those who have been particularly well represented are most likely to find state government salient—older people, living in small southern towns. Sharkansky's study, which demonstrated the importance of longitudinal analysis, did not, un-

One study, however, approaches the question of policy outcomes from a very different perspective, and, while its concern with the effects of malapportionment are secondary, it is worth considering both because it arrives at quite different conclusions than previous studies and because it is suggestive of how adequate tests might be conducted in the future. Perhaps the most convincing evidence about the policy effects of pre-*Baker* v. *Carr* apportionment patterns and about many of the arguments of the reformers is found in Jack Walker's "The Diffusion of Innovations Among American States." [95] Walker measures policy in terms of its "adoption" rather than its "level." His data span the years from 1870 to 1966 and include eighty-eight separate policies. He defines innovation as:

> a program or policy which is new to the states adopting it, no matter how old the program may be or how many other states have adopted it. Even though bureaucratic innovations or new departures by regulatory commissions or courts may be mentioned in the course of the discussion, *the data used to measure the relative speed of adoption of innovations consist exclusively of legislative actions, simply because the data was readily available only in that form* [emphasis added].[96]

Walker's first and basic objective is to "explain why some states adopt innovations more readily than others." He bases his study on the analysis of the eighty-eight programs which he tried to "make . . . as comprehensive and representative as possible," by examining ". . . six to eight different pieces of legislation in each of these areas: welfare, health, education, conservation, planning, administrative organization, highways, civil rights, corrections and police, labor, taxes, and professional regulation." [97]

His scores for the states are based on the relative speed with which they adopted each program after it had been adopted in one state.[98] Rather

---

fortunately, make use of the longitudinal data provided by the Schubert-Press or Dauer-Kelsay indices of malapportionment. Nor did he consider the extent to which changes in apportionment might be related to, or in some way responsible for, some of the changes in spending which his analysis uncovered. Unfortunately, while Fry and Winter focused on redistribution of state income by employing the explicitly interest-free Schubert-Press index of malapportionment, they did not allow for any consideration of the extent to which under- or overrepresentation of particular interests might be related to varying patterns of redistribution of wealth within the states.

95. Jack Walker, "The Diffusion of Innovations Among American States," 63 *American Political Science Review* 880–899.

96. *Id.* at 881.

97. *Id.* at 882.

98. The innovation score for each state is calculated by the following procedure: "The first step was to count the number of years which elapsed between the first

than being the problem it was for Jacob and for Brady and Edmonds, the variation from state to state in the time of adoption of legislation is employed by Walker as a major component of his study. In addition to using it in calculating his innovation scores, he further considers the time dimension by dividing his analyses into three basic segments of time (1870–1899, 1900–1929, and 1930–1966), scoring states within each, as well as calculating an overall, or composite, innovation score. This procedure allows him to analyze policy output in relation to socioeconomic and political characteristics for comparable periods of time. Independent and dependent variables are temporally matched as he compares innovation scores for the period between 1870 and 1899 with the socioeconomic and political data for that same period, as he does for the other two periods. This provides the necessary conditions for a test both within and across time periods of the relationships of socioeconomic variables, political and institutional variables, and policy outcomes or responses.[99]

For political variables Walker employs measures of party competition and malapportionment. He correlates the innovation scores separately for each of the three time periods and correlates the composite score with party competition for the governorship (percentage of total vote going to a gubernatorial candidate coming in second, times 2, which yields a scale from 0 to 100) during that period. Walker also correlates the David-Eisenberg index of urban underrepresentation with his innovative scores for the

---

and last recorded legislative enactment of a program. Each state then received a number for each list which corresponded to the percentage of time which elapsed between the first adoption and its own acceptance of the program. For example, if the total time elapsing between the first and last adoption of a program was 20 years, and Massachusetts enacted the program ten years after the first adoption, then Massachusetts received a score of .500 on the particular issue. The first state to adopt the program received a score of .00 and the last state received a score of 1.00. In cases in which all states have not yet adopted a program, the states without the program are placed last and given a score of 1.00." *Ibid*. Walker does note several precautions which he took which the reader should be aware of: The first was that if a program began its diffusion before a state came into existence, the issue was not included in figuring the innovation score for that state. He also notes that the diffusion process is highly complex and may be related to highly idiosyncratic influences, for example, ". . . an official with an unusually keen interest in a particular program, a chance reading of an article or a book by a governor's aid, or any number of other circumstances peculiar to any one issue might lead to rapid adoption of a piece of legislation by a state which is usually reluctant to accept new programs." *Id*. at 883.

99. Perhaps the most comparable study in that it measured policy in terms of adoption over time and correlated this with measures of political institutions attributes and socioeconomic development is Phillips Cutwright's, "Political Structure, Economic Development, and National Security Programs," 52 *The American Journal of Sociology* 537–550. This was carried out on a cross-national scale.

latter two time segments (1900–1929 and 1930–1966) and the composite score.[100] He finds:

> Legislative apportionment is not correlated with the innovation score in the 1900–1929 period, but is related in the 1930–1966 period. Since legislatures steadily became less representative of urban populations after 1930, it may be that we have here some empirical evidence of the impact of malapportionment on policy making in the states.[101]

Employing essentially the same multiple and partial correlation approach used by Dye, Walker controls for economic development, but his analysis of the correlates of the composite innovation index shows:

> [T]he consistent strength of the correlation between innovation and the David and Eisenberg index of urban representation. Earlier studies, using expenditures as a measure of policy outcomes, have consistently found that apportionment has little importance as an explanatory variable. Our findings indicated that apportionment does make a difference where innovation is concerned. Although the other political factors do not have great independent impact on innovation, the clear implication . . . *is that those states which grant their urban areas full representation in the legislature seem to adopt new ideas more rapidly, on the average, than states which discriminate against their cities* [emphasis added].[102]

Walker argues that this finding is due to the greater receptiveness of urban representatives to new ideas; this hypothesis is not inconsistent with some of the reformer literature.[103]

I have already noted the problems of determining exactly which one or which combinations of the four David and Eisenberg urban underrepre-

100. David and Eisenberg calculated their index for four discrete points in time— 1910, 1930, 1950 and 1960. Unfortunately, Walker does not indicate whether he used the 1910 or 1930 David-Eisenberg index score or the average of the two for his correlation with his 1900–1929 innovation score. Nor is it clear which of the scores or the average of which he used for 1930–1966 or, for that matter, which apportionment score or scores he used to correlate with his composite innovativeness score.

101. *Supra,* n. 95 at 886.

102. *Id.* at 887.

103. Havens, for example, notes that "further antagonism developed over the bill providing for the employment of depositions in judicial proceedings. This measure was patterned after the rules of the Federal Court system. Many rural lawyers, having less experience with the new system than most of their urban colleagues, oppose the new method. This measure is not the first instance of opposition by some rural legislators to change, largely because it is change." *Supra,* n. 18 at 29–30.

sentation scores Walker employed for each of the temporal innovation scores or for the composite. There are problems with Walker's dependent variable, as well. Walker avoided the trap that Jacob, and Brady and Edmonds fell into when they correlated legislation adopted in the 1930s and before with apportionment scores based on the 1960s, but he appears to have joined them in forgetting about governors and—more important—constitutional amendments. He states that his focus is on legislative adoption. I assume that adoption means more than just the legislative passage of a bill, but also that, in fact, the bill becomes law, which takes the governor's signature. Given that the thrust of his concern is with the acceptance of "new" legislation, this is not as important a question as it would be, for example, in the case of the right-to-work laws, where the majority of a state was presumed to be against the particular piece of legislation. It is also unclear how Walker treats or scores adoptions which require constitutional amendments in some states, for he includes among his eighty-eight programs right-to-work laws and home rule, which, as noted above, were incorporated into many state constitutions.

Not knowing whether, in fact, Walker calculated the innovation score after final approval was obtained from the voters or after the legislature had passed, with the appropriate majorities and/or consecutive sessions, the legislation necessary to put the items on the ballot for voter approval, one is at a loss to know how much reliance should be placed on Walker's findings. In the absence of his consideration of the extent to which these policies required constitutional—that is, majority vote—approval, this uncertainty is particularly crucial. State constitutions vary in comprehensiveness from the approximately 217,000 words of Louisiana's, which, for example, includes even the official state road map, to the tight-lipped Vermont document of fewer than 5,000 words.[104] Thus, in some states all of Walker's policies could have been adopted without constitutional amendment, while in others the majority might have required constitutional approval.

There is, of course, the further question of whether the innovations were accepted via initiative and referendum. If legislative action is the key, such nonlegislative innovation would be inappropriate to his study, but if having a law on the books is the key, then it is not. In any event, the matter is left unclear. Hence, the reader, once again, is left with a malaise; the extent to which the legislature can act independently is not clearly delineated or even made a part of a consideration of the author. It should, however, be noted that with these exceptions Walker's study at

104. *Supra,* n. 70 at 14. See Article VI, Section 22, Louisiana Constitution.

least moves us in the right direction if we are to actually test the effects of apportionment patterns and other components of the political system on policy and political outcomes.

If Walker's data were reanalyzed with consideration of the "constitutional coverage" variable, it would be interesting to make differentiations among policies in order to test arguments other than the "greater urban receptivity to new ideas" found in the reformers' literature. Specifically, if Walker's data were reanalyzed with innovation scores being calculated on the basis of the adoption of several different types of policies, such as those that specifically benefited rural areas (like the adoption of farming extension programs), those that specifically benefited urban areas (like enabling legislation for creating city parking areas), and those for general interests (like the adoption of legislation prohibiting discrimination on account of age or the establishment of a school for the deaf). As the data are scored in Walker's article, there is no such differentiation, and the adoption of any one of the eighty-eight policies "counts" just as much toward the innovation score as any one of the others.[105]

With this kind of differentiation, the relationship of these scores to the David-Eisenberg urban underrepresentation index, or some modification of it, could be reanalyzed. For example, a critical test could be made of whether (and to what extent) it is the urbanism of the representatives which is responsible for their being more receptive to innovations, or whether in fact they are being more receptive to innovations which are directly related to the interests which they represent disproportionately. The latter conclusion would be reached if innovation scores which excluded farm-oriented or rural policies would be more highly correlated with the David-Eisenberg index, while scores based on acceptance of innovations more beneficial to rural areas would have a lower correlation, or even one which was reversed in sign.

Of course it would also be quite reasonable to argue that the frequency of reapportionment according to population criteria might be considered an innovation which itself could properly be included in the innovation index; hence, willingness to reapportion might be just one more indication of a state's "innovativeness," rather than the acceptance of innovation's being dependent upon the apportionment pattern.

---

105. Walker, however, promises to report in later work: ". . . the results of comparisons of diffusion patterns of issues from different subject matters. Preliminary efforts at such comparisons, however, have not revealed significant variations. There does not seem to be much difference in the diffusion pattern of issues of different types." *Supra,* n. 95 at 882n.

Even with the problems noted above, however, Walker's study offers some guidelines and some potentially useful dependent variables for those who might wish to make a new attempt at testing the effects of apportionment patterns on public policy.

SUGGESTIONS FOR
ASSESSING THE IMPACT OF STATE
APPORTIONMENT PATTERNS ON POLICY AND POLITICS

In the concluding section of his study, Dye warns that "Quantification necessitates a simplification of what may be a very complex question. The consequences of reapportionment may be so subtle and diverse that they defy quantitative measurement. Perhaps the consequences in each state will vary so much that inter-state comparisons are inappropriate." [106] There is some truth to this. Yet, once the conceptual stumbling blocks are removed and the position of the Court and the arguments of the reformers distinguished, the task of assessing the effects of apportionment patterns on policy and political life becomes feasible, if costly.

How can adequate tests of the kind of arguments posed by reformers be carried out? First, there is no reason why the basic considerations or even the starting points employed in the reformers' literature cannot be employed in comparative state tests. Analysts might approach the question from the perspective of what results are likely to be produced by a given pattern of interest and party distortion, or what types of policy are thought likely to be produced by a given pattern of party or interest distortion. In either case, any comparative state tests of the arguments of the reformers regarding the effects on policy and political behavior of apportionment patterns either before or after the reapportionment decisions cannot be carried out without a considerable effort of costly, tedious data collection, coupled with extensive theoretical development directed toward the linkage of interest, institutions, and policy.

The point of departure may be either the given pattern of apportionment or a question of policy. Both, of course, will have to be considered. The most difficult part of the enterprise will be in the development of adequate measurements of the kind of malapportionment described by the reformers. The measures of apportionment patterns should begin from the kind of variance approach employed by Schubert and Press. In fact, one could begin by employing the data provided by Schubert and Press on the

106. *Supra*, n. 2 at 600.

population sizes of each state's legislative districts as of 1962, which they have made available in the archives of the Inter-University Consortium of Political Research.

The next, and perhaps the most costly, step is the addition of basic socioeconomic census data for each district. All available voting and registration data should also be added. Once such a merged file is obtained, calculations can be made to determine the extent to which deviations from the mean, as found by Schubert and Press, are associated in one direction or another; that is, above or below the mean, with different types of persons, in terms of, for example, occupation, income, housing, and party affiliation or voting history.

Different dimensions should be established for each chamber as to the extent to which the apportionment patterns "discriminate" against various interests by either disproportionately representing one end of the dimension (underrepresentation of renters, in contrast to owners) or by "interest" gerrymandering (concentration of blue-collar workers in a few districts). The next step should be to determine the particular clustering of attributes of those who are proportionately under- and overrepresented.

This accomplished, one could then determine the extent to which party affiliation would be likely to act either as an extenuating or an attenuating influence on these divisions, by determining the extent to which the party affiliations were coterminous with interest divisions. Once this was established for each chamber, comparison of the two chambers could be made to determine the extent to which they both discriminated against similar interests, or whether, in fact, their disproportionate representation of interests was such that one chamber canceled out the other.

Interest distortion and the modulating effects of either bicameralism or partisanship having thus been established, the question of relative deprivation of representation would remain. Have particular interests been discriminated against by districting, to the point where they are completely wiped out of the political spectrum, for example, as when the pattern of districting so totally diffuses the representation of this interest, or cluster of interests, within the districts that it is a minority in any district, or where the extent to which representation of an effective interest majority (above 60 percent) has been changed into a minimal majority (51 percent) or even turned into a minority?

In short, in studying the effects of legislative districting practices, it is not the gross parameter values used in previous studies that are important; it is, instead, the internal distributional characteristics. It is not a question of how many Democrats or Republicans live in a state if one wishes to determine how many Democratic and Republican legislators are likely to be elected to the legislature, but a question of how these Democrats and Republicans are concentrated or dispersed in legislative districts according to the apportionment pattern. It is not a question of the mean per-capita income of the state; it is a question of where the income is located and how it is distributed that is relevant to apportionment patterns and income-tax programs, for example. It is not a question of the number of needy aged in a state, but of the distribution of the needy aged in relation to the distribution of effective legislative power that must be tested, if we are to examine the question of apportionment patterns. It is not a question of industrialization or the percentage of union members that should be measured if we are to examine the relationship between gross apportionment patterns and right-to-work laws, but of the distribution of union and potential union members and their families in relation to the effective legislative power, determined in part by the apportionment pattern, that must be considered.

In addition, consideration must be given to the extent to which there are attenuating or counterbalancing election arrangements, such as multi-member districts, which might alter the effective power of given population interests such that, at least as they enter the system, they have the capability for action which would be comparable to their popular strength.

Institutions, as well as states, have internal complexities in addition to distributional attributes which require investigation at the "gut," rather than the gross parameter, level. Therefore, the next step is to consider, for each legislative body, the manner in which the institutional arrangements of each chamber are likely to mute or amplify the interest distortion produced by the apportionment pattern. Here, for example, consideration should be given to the manner of assignment to committees, to rules, to practices, to the manner of selection of speakers, to the power of speakers, and to the extent to which the compensation of legislators is such that it would allow particular interests to send individuals to that body who were "representative" of them. Here, too, there is the question of whether or not legislators have sufficient staff capabilities to keep themselves aware of the needs of their districts, or at least rationally to evaluate the programs presented to them by the governor. Do the representatives have enough time during the session to consider thoughtfully the legislation the executive presents, not to mention enough time to generate and consider bills of their own? The list of questions that should be asked about the institutional structure only begins here, but these are some of the factors which should be considered in comparative studies.[107]

A truly adequate test would be longitudinal and, ideally, would go back to the turn of the century. In as much as many state legislatures relied on counties for their district boundaries prior to *Baker* v. *Carr,* data compilation might not be as difficult as it might appear. This data base would allow the examination of the extent to which interest distortion has changed in either kind or degree through the decades.

The longitudinal approach is particularly important when we consider that the kinds of policies which apportionment patterns, or most other institutional arrangements, are likely to have affected, are nonbudgetary in nature. Their annual or biannual appearance and their apparent precision make revenue and taxation measures tempting dependent variables, yet, as noted above, they are among the most difficult factors for legislators to change. Hence, policies which are malleable—or even considered to be malleable by legislators themselves—should be the major source of dependent variables. Financial policy or variables should not be totally eliminated as a class, but those which are employed should provide fairly clear, redistributive decisions, such as the allocation of highway funds, the amount of school tax aid given as a minimal foundation, or other areas where differential allocation is a clear choice. Primarily, however, the focus of policy analysis should turn from finance to areas encompassed by the police and regulatory powers of the states. The type of variables Walker analyzed are appropriate, if care is given to the degree to which each legislature can constitutionally exert its power in a certain area.[108]

Given knowledge of the variation from state to state in the kind and extent of facilities, staff, and other accoutrements which are available to the legislators, consideration could be given to the types of policies about which the legislators in different states can gain information which exceeds the personal knowledge of day-to-day life they gain through their own occupational pursuits or through their experience in their districts.

An additional question would be the extent to which the policy involved was a "zero-sum" type, in which one interest would definitely lose while

107. The influence of staff, pay, and other factors which contribute to the professional capability of legislators have been shown to be related to policy outcomes by John Grumm, "Structural Determinants of Legislative Output," a paper presented to the Conference on the Measurement of Public Policies in the American State, Ann Arbor, Michigan (July–August 1968).

Walker also points out the probable significance of the associations and conferences which are attempting to upgrade and provide assistance to legislative bodies and other branches of the state governments. *Supra,* n. 95.

108. *Supra,* n. 95 at 880–899.

another one gained (gasoline taxes, reapportionment). In the enactment of such zero-sum or redistributive policies, the distortion of both chambers ought to be considered, since the enactment requires an affirmative action, whereas, when we are speaking about inaction or the nonacceptance of innovations, it only takes one chamber to protect an interest which it disproportionately represents. Hence, again, unless they both conform in interest representation, it is important to keep the consideration of the two chambers apart to insure the capability to understand the extent to which both positive and negative action was taking place regarding various types of legislation.

Above all, the choice of policy to be studied should be determined by what previous analysis has shown to be a distinct pattern of under- and overrepresentation of particular interests in several states, with other states where this pattern does not hold providing the comparative base for the test. One of the major problems in this type of study is that little attention is paid by the public to its legislators, and vice versa. The "role studies" indicate that many legislators do not see themselves as being responsible to their districts alone. Legislators frequently conceive of themselves as representing a wider constituency of a particular occupational or an educational or ethnic group, or perhaps even the state as a whole.[109] Much of this mutual disinterest can be attributed to ignorance both by the representative of his constituency and by the constituency of its representative. Given the developments in professionalization and technological capabilities which are likely to occur in the coming decades in our legislative bodies, this ignorance may be greatly reduced. And questions raised in earlier years concerning interest distortion and political power may come to be of paramount importance in understanding the legislatures of the future.

POLICY OUTCOMES, APPORTIONMENT PATTERNS, AND THE IMPACT OF THE REAPPORTIONMENT DECISIONS ON THE FUTURE

The capacity of the state legislatures in the 1971 round of apportionments to arrange their districts to conform to particular interests and political

109. The low visibility of congressmen to their constituencies is shown in Donald Stokes and Warren E. Miller, "Party Government and the Saliency of Congress," 26 *Public Opinion Quarterly* 531–546. State legislators can be expected to be even less visible. The varying "areal" orientations of legislators themselves, is shown off by John Wahlke, Heinz Eulau, William Buchanan, and Leroy C. Ferguson, *The Legislative System, Explorations in Legislative Behavior* (New York: Wiley 1962).

configurations with unprecedented precision and accuracy must be considered to be a major question for the future. At the beginning of this essay, the 1971 round of apportionments was noted as the first for which all the state legislatures have known they must be prepared. To this end, they have access to data provided by the Bureau of the Census, basic socioeconomic data which they will be able to merge with voting and registration data collected by the legislatures or their agents (computer software is available to aggregate and display the varying configurations of this data down to and including precinct or even block-sized units).

Therefore, within the bounds set by the one man, one vote, doctrine, state legislatures will be free to design districts which will conform to the socioeconomic and political configurations they desire. The composition of the legislative districts in the coming decades can be almost as heterogeneous or homogeneous as the "marginals," or degree of heterogeneity, of the state allow and the legislators could desire. They will, of course, be subject to the powerful constraint of maintaining districts for incumbents of the majority party (or those of both parties, given a divided government). But with the availability of technical resources and with the necessary lead time to prepare for their use, at a minimum, legislators can have a very precise and detailed knowledge of the socioeconomic and political attributes of the constituencies of each district.

Therefore, the questions raised by the reformers of the fifties regarding the effect of apportionment patterns on policy outcomes and political practices remain among the most critical confronting the policy-makers and academics and citizens who are concerned with the 1970s and 1980s. Legislative districts can—and we must assume to some degree will—be configured in a manner which will under- or overrepresent certain interests and political parties with a precision and to an extent undreamed of by the reformers in their writings of the 1940s and 1950s.

Coupled with a concurrent growing emphasis on upgrading the efficiency and capacity and on generally professionalizing state legislative bodies, the conditions are present for the development of a new set of theories (if there ever has been an old set) of legislative behavior and representative government.[110] In at least one legislature (California) a committee preparing for the 1970/1971 apportionment wishes to continually

110. The relative weakness of the state legislative bodies, in terms of both their professionalism and their institutional strength, makes them more likely than the United States Congress to make use of, or at least try out, the kind of capability described. The state chambers are being pushed to change and have both fewer procedural traditions and, in general, fewer senior members who could be expected to have a stake in the continuation of existing traditions.

be able to update the political-socio-economic data file being developed for the apportionment (recognizing, no doubt, the problems of population migration in the state). It is, of course, within the power of the legislature to require state departments to report according to legislative districts both the types and the extent of state services rendered (as is already done, when state departments report by county, where county and district boundaries are contiguous), as well as the types and extent of tax revenue or other costs (some nonfiscal, like arrests and convictions for marijuana possession) withdrawn from each district.[111]

Given these resources, legislators, in a body or as individuals, will soon have the capacity to engage in a kind of legislative program budgeting or cost-benefit analysis before casting their votes. That is, each legislator will be able to determine from his district's particular tax base and population attributes whether it is likely to incur an overall loss or gain from a particular bill or amendment, and cast his vote accordingly. In the growing number of state legislatures which are equipped with on-line computer terminals situated on the chamber floor and now used for displaying the current status of bills and for retrieval of existing statutes, this would require merely the addition of another configuration of software, plus a continued updating of the data being assembled for redistricting which the legislature could require from the various state departments.

Whether such developments will have policy and political consequences, or even force a reexamination of some of our basic institutions, is open to question. According to much of the budgetary literature, these new capabilities may not have any significant effects, and those that may are likely to be unanticipated.[112] On one hand, since this type of precise additional information could greatly constrict the maneuvering room now enjoyed by legislators with the basically incremental budgetary process, the legislators may themselves abstain from employing them. On the other hand, if legislators do use this capacity, they may be more willing, on the basis of its apparent precision, to make cost-benefit or program budget choices that would entail far larger risks than the current muddling-through process, with its attendant "inefficiencies" and "redundancies" in many programs. Rather than deciding to continue to give moderate support to several mental-health programs, for example, legislators might decide to

111. Even without requiring state departments to report according to legislative districts, the type of procedures employed by Fry and Winter, *supra,* n. 94, together with the knowledge regarding the types of people in their district that will be visible as a by-product of the reapportionment process in 1970, scholars, not to mention lobbyists, will be able to make in-depth estimates for the same kind of cost-benefit analyses.

112. Cf. Wildavsky, *supra,* n. 59.

put all of a state's resources behind one approach or program. If the favored program failed, of course, the results could be catastrophic. While continuing several overlapping programs that are not exceptionally successful or efficient, policy-makers at least avoid the problems of having "all their eggs in one basket." In short, if the availability of such information does have policy consequences, much of the budgetary literature would agree that these would include an increase in the extent and scope of error, as well as the possibility of unanticipated effects or outcomes of the policy process.

Academic budgeteers, however, have always conceived of the legislator as responding to particular budgetary requests, or as being the man-in-the-middle between the executive and the agency's bureaucracy. But, armed with the type of informational capability described above, it is possible to conceive of legislators' developing their own programs, calculating the particular effects of their own alternatives, and thereby breaking out of their traditional role as arbitrators and respondents. Recognizing legislators to be the highly political animals they are, it should not be assumed that, in order to make use of the new informational capability, they cannot provide themselves with the room required for their personal maneuvering and bartering and at the same time preserve some of the slack or redundancy required to reduce the possibility of the devastating ultimate failure predicted by the budgetary literature.

Therefore, even if the Court moves into the areas of interest and partisan gerrymandering or if it attempts to consider apportionment in terms of impact on policy outcomes, our conception of representative government may undergo a profound series of changes in the coming years. Legislators will gain, for the first time, at least the capability of actually knowing quite explicitly and with apparent precision the extent to which they are representing their districts' interests.[113]

113. The potential of the interaction effect of reapportionment plus professionalization is brought out clearly by two articles which appeared in the Florida *Times-Union* and Jacksonville *Journal*. Allen Morris, the Assembly clerk in the feature, "It's a New Kind of Ball Game in Tallahassee" (Florida *Times-Union* and Jacksonville *Journal*, March 29, 1970, pp. 8–9), begins, "Law-making by committee, computer, and the twelve-month calendar finally has lifted the Legislature of Florida boldly and bodily into the 20th Century, ready for the 21st" and then continues to extol the new professionalism that will allow the representatives to better perform their role in the state's system. But two months later, the same paper editorialized that the new system had killed a plan proposed "to minimize the enormous differences in per pupil expenditures between the counties" (*Times-Union* and *Journal*, May 31, 1970, p. A-20). The plan was not different in kind from that which had passed before professionalization and reapportionment. The paper asks, "What happened to it? It died in committee, impaled on bickering to the effect that 'my county won't get its share.'"

And citizens may gain a far better picture of how they are being represented; the impact could easily pervade the whole legislative process, beginning with campaigns for election. Legislators will have to consider the specter of reelection campaigns in which their opponents are able to present the voters with a balance sheet which is likely to be—or seem—far more meaningful than those currently provided by Americans for Democratic Action, the AFL-CIO, or Americans for Conservative Action concerning the representative's performance for his particular set of constituents.

The effect of pre-*Baker* v. *Carr* apportionment patterns on the policies and political practices of the states has yet to be tested. Until the Supreme Court leaps even further into the thicket and considers partisan and interest distortion in districting, as well as disproportionate legislative power, to be within its purview, the Court's reapportionment decisions do not speak to the crucial questions in this matter, so many of the questions of the policy and political effects of apportionment patterns are still to be answered. However, the catalytic effect of the reapportionment decisions, coming as they did at this point in our technological development, may prove to have quite profound consequences on the representational system of government in the states.

* * *

COMMENTARY *by Russell D. Murphy*

Who shall decide when doctors disagree,
And soundest casuists doubt, like you and me?
ALEXANDER POPE

One of the striking features of American political history has been the enduring preoccupation among political activists with the formal arrangements of government institutions. Evidence of this preoccupation can be found, for example, in the recurring efforts to modify these institutions and in the bewildering array of governmental forms and procedures that have resulted from these efforts. Behind these efforts has been a belief that the structures of government make a significant difference in the behavior of men and in the policies that governments pursue—a belief, that is to say, that the very institutions and procedures that facilitate the orderly and organized conduct of public affairs at the same time work to the advantage of some and to the disadvantage of others.

The belief that government structures have policy implications, once a major tenet in the depository of orthodox American political faith, has been challenged in recent years with increasing frequency and confidence. The focal point of this challenge has been the field of comparative state and local politics. Among those who have labored in this field, there appears to be considerable doubt about the accuracy of the traditional belief that institutional arrangements, alone, have an important bearing on the shape of public policy. Admittedly, there is no unanimity in this regard, and there are studies that dispute this challenge.[1] But the weight of professional opinion today, in contrast with that in years past, is that the effects of political institutions on policy are inconsequential. How government is organized matters less, it seems, than how a state (or locality) ranks with respect to industrialization, urbanization, or wealth.

Whatever the specific finding, few of these studies are concerned with fundamental questions of analysis. One major exception is William Bicker's thoughtful essay "The Effects of Malapportionment in the States —a Mistrial." In his essay Bicker examines the comparative literature on state apportionment and concludes that the existing studies share common conceptual and methodological difficulties that render them inconclusive. Virtually all the studies disregard, for example, those policy areas where the effects of malapportionment are most likely to be felt and, in particular, ignore that broad policy area that might be called state regulation and control of municipal affairs.[2] Equally important, the studies employ empirical indicators that fail, according to Bicker, to measure significant political dimensions of the phenomenon. Apportionment indicators typi-

1. Two notable exceptions are: Brian R. Fry and Richard F. Winters, "The Politics of Redistribution," 64 *The American Political Science Review* 508–522; and Robert L. Lineberry and Edmund P. Fowler, "Reformism and Public Policies in American Cities," 61 *The American Political Science Review* 701–716.

2. In a formal legal sense, cities are creatures of the states, and their powers are strictly limited to those explicitly granted by state governments. Historically, this "creature theory" served as the legal basis for what early reformers like Charles Beard and Frank Goodnow condemned as the unwarranted and unconscionable interference by states in local affairs. Home rule provisions have not changed this legal relationship. While cities are given some option on the form of local government, for them to act even with respect to such minor matters as changing the date of budget submissions, waiving the reading of ordinances, establishing departments, or leasing municipal lands still requires state authorization. This aspect of intergovernmental relations must be examined systematically and in different historical contexts before any definitive conclusions will be possible about the influence of malapportionment. Such an examination might begin with a study of special local acts and enabling legislation: how these measures are initiated; the types of measures introduced or not introduced; the ways in which they are processed, particularly in the pre-enactment stage; and the significance of state action or inaction for various classes of cities.

cally combine in a single score both houses of the legislature, a practice that would lead to the anomalous situation where a state with two moderately well apportioned houses would be ranked the same as a state with one poorly and one fairly apportioned house. And indicators of policy output are constructed from combined state and local figures, even in those analyses that concern the functioning of state government, alone.

Much of Bicker's general criticism of the apportionment literature is applicable to the literature on other government institutions, as well. The comparative study of state and local politics has proceeded at a rapid pace, but it has proceeded with little apparent regard for methodological and conceptual considerations other than those, perhaps, that relate to computer and programming techniques. Yet, as Bicker's essay demonstrates, there are major issues yet to be resolved, and these issues warrant far more serious and extended treatment than they have received thus far in the comparative literature. Three such issues are summarized briefly below, by way of further elaboration of Bicker's basic theme that it is time to pause to take stock of the premises underlying existing approaches to the comparative study of state and local politics and policies.

1. Among these issues, reliability of data is surely one that must rank high in any evaluation, or reevaluation, of this literature.[3] As a general rule, these studies rely on official data series published by government agencies or private associations. One can sympathize with this common practice of exploiting the material that is available. Working with these data series is an exacting chore and one that requires considerable patience and good humor. To require, in addition, that analysts generate their own data series for fifty states and/or thousands of municipalities would seem an unreasonable demand on their limited emotional—to say nothing of their financial—resources. Besides, as two authors recently

3. Two closely related points deserve brief mention here. First, despite the considerable data available to contemporary social scientists, these data do not always bear directly on important social and social science questions. To my knowledge, there are no national series, for example, on local or primary elections. Nor are there data on population mobility that would permit analysis of such questions as whether cities are attempting to redistribute income and whether this policy has a bearing on the reported drift in the country toward a dual society. Second, establishing reliable data series will require the active cooperation of government agencies and private associations. Short of this, analysts could considerably facilitate efforts to understand and evaluate their work by making explicit the content of the data categories they now employ. At present it is often difficult to determine what is included in these categories—whether, for example, expenditure items include capital outlays, or whether intergovernmental transfers include aid to special districts (including school districts) that are coterminous with, but not under the jurisdiction of, particular city governments.

observed by way of justification, the published data "enjoy widespread use among social scientists."[4] Repeated use, it would seem, has bestowed upon these data an aura of respectability and reliability.

Yet, how reliable are published data series and what are the grounds for assuming, as some do, that "the recorded information is a reasonably accurate reflection of the fact"?[5] These questions are seldom examined in the literature, and one is often left with the unsettling impression, doubtless unwarranted, that data series are chosen more on the basis of their availability than on the basis of their reliability. This impression is strengthened when one examines the data sources themselves. An admittedly casual comparison of entries in one frequently cited source, the United States Bureau of the Census *Compendium of City Government Finances,* with entries in the *Quadrennial Report of Indebtedness, Receipts and Expenditures of Municipalities* published by the Connecticut state tax commissioner, reveals substantial discrepencies in the amounts reported for some items (most frequently intergovernmental transfers and expenditures for education) for some cities.[6] Results of a similar comparison between the *Compendium* and the *Special Report on Municipal Affairs* issued by the New York state comptroller were much the same.[7]

These discrepencies may be special cases. As I noted, the comparison was unsystematic and, though exhausting, by no means exhaustive. Whatever the case, the existence of different entries in different sources need not invalidate the published findings. It may be that the variations in the amounts recorded for state aid or for education expenditures result from the use of different classification schemes or that generally the differences are random within and between states. Unfortunately, neither of these possibilities was immediately apparent in the documents cited. As a result,

4. Ira Sharkansky and Richard I. Hofferbert, "Dimensions of State Politics, Economics and Public Policy," 63 *The American Political Science Review* 873, n. 20.

5. *Id.* at 873, n. 20.

6. State of Connecticut, Office of the Tax Commissioner, *Quadrennial Report of Indebtedness, Expenditures and Receipts of Municipalities, 1960,* Public Document No. 22, Tax Document No. 344 (Hartford: May, 1963); *Quadrennial Report, 1964,* Public Document No. 22, Tax Document No. 351 (Hartford: April, 1967). U.S. Bureau of the Census, *Compendium of City Government Finances* (Washington: U.S. Government Printing Office, 1959, 1960, 1963, and 1964). Different fiscal years were examined for different cities, depending on the availability of comparable fiscal year entries in the *Compendium* and the *Quadrennial Reports.* In one city, New Haven, the ratio of *Compendium* figures to those reported by the state ranged from 2.6 (state aid) to 1.002 (property tax).

7. State of New York, Office of the Comptroller, *Special Report on Municipal Affairs* (Albany: March 18, 1969). U.S. Bureau of the Census, *City Government Finances in 1968-1969* (Washington: U.S. Government Printing Office, 1970).

the comparison, limited though it was, did little to inspire confidence in findings based on data series in the *Compendium,* and the less so since the literature gives no indication of how, if at all, these and similar discrepencies[8] bear on the outcome of analysis.

2. Reliable data, quite obviously, are merely a necessary and not a sufficient condition for analysis, and refining data series is but one of the tasks confronting persons in the field of comparative state and local politics. Raw data need to be processed and transformed into theoretically relevant empirical indicators. There was a time when this processing and the critical examination of its products were of major concern to students of politics. This stage of political analysis is apparently over, or so it would seem from a reading of the comparative state and local literature, which by its silence implies that problems of measurement and index construction are all but settled.

As Bicker demonstrates, these issues are far from settled in the area of apportionment; and what is true of apportionment is true of other areas, as well. To cite but one example, existing analyses of the relationship between party competition and social welfare policies are inconclusive inasmuch as they do not measure adequately the central concepts in the traditional formulation of this hypothesis.

Measures of party competition, for example, like those of apportionment, often merely "display some particular aspect or dimension of [competition] rather than provide an independent variable" for analysis. Theoretically, party competition is significant, in the sense that it occasions uncertainty about the outcome of elections. The legislator or executive, constrained by this uncertainty, would cast about for electoral support and, in particular, would adopt liberal social welfare policies in a bid for the support of the numerically superior but politically less active have-nots.

Any test of this hypothesis clearly must deal with a number of intricate and complex problems, among them, establishing the identity of the have-nots and specifying their preferences. These problems aside, available indicators of party competition are, at best, only imperfect measures of the political phenomenon. Such commonly used indicators as turnover in office, closeness of vote, or some variation or combination of these, merely suggest the uncertainty experienced by elected officials. Moreover, competition and uncertainty are most salient in terms of politics and policy

8. Among them, the differences in state income data reported by the census and by the Office of Business Economics. See: U.S. Bureau of the Census, *Income Distribution in the United States,* by Herman Miller, A 1960 Census Monograph, (Washington: U.S. Government Printing Office, 1966), pp. 169–211.

outcomes to those elected incumbents who plan to run again. Existing indicators of competition ignore this facet of the hypothesis, despite the substantial turnover of legislative personnel in the states—the very political systems where the hypothesis is usually tested. To these must be added the problems often associated with measurement of social welfare policy, and in particular the frequent reliance on averages such as per pupil expenditures for education.[9] Such averages may well conceal the redistributive effects of public policies. Per-pupil expenditures, for example, tell us little about variations within states, within localities, or within individual schools. And on the basis of per pupil expenditures, alone, it is difficult to know whether states that rank high on this scale are more redistributive than those that rank low; logically, at least, the reverse could be true.

However reliable the data or valid the indicators, there remain a number of problems associated with the inferences based on the evidence presented in the comparative studies of state and local politics and policies. One of these problems is the common assumption in the literature that policy preferences and the policy categories of published sources are uniform across state lines, that the preferences of particular groups, be they city-dwellers, racial minorities, or feminists, transcend political boundaries, and that the same broad policy labels such as education, welfare, or law-enforcement, mean the same thing in different political contexts. These assumptions are not explicit in the literature; nor, to my knowledge, have they been systematically explored. As a result, inferences about the effects on policy of institutional or any other factors must be adjudged to be quite tentative. If states with varying degrees of malapportionment or party competition differ not at all, or only slightly, with respect to some aggregate indicator of policy, one might conclude that these particular institutional factors had little or no bearing on the outcome of public policy. But aggregate figures, alone, do not rule out the possibility that the same overall (or per-capita) amount is being allocated in different states for different program activities. In one group of states the expenditures of welfare departments might be devoted to improving the well being of the disadvantaged and disinherited through income maintenance and through such supportive services as day-care centers, family counseling, homemaking programs, and career guidance. In another group of states having the same aggregate expenditures the emphasis might be on the surveillance of welfare recipients and the minimization of welfare cheating. Somewhat analogous conditions might prevail in different states

9. An exception to this is the article cited *supra,* n. 1 by Fry and Winters.

with respect to state aid to localities. The purpose of this aid and the degree to which it is earmarked for programs preferred by the recipients must be specified before any firm conclusions can be reached on the basis of aggregate data alone. One of the complaints voiced by early champions of home rule was that state legislators often dictated expenditures for programs which the elected local officials themselves opposed.[10] Today this practice is not as blatant as it was in the past, but it is not known whether it continues in more subtle and indirect ways. Clearly, more information is needed on this question, as well as on the preferences of local political leaders[11] (and other political groups) in different political contexts and on whether these contexts affect the probabilities that these preferences will be realized.

Yet another assumption common to the literature on state and local politics and policies is the insignificance of history and, by implication at least, a denial that tradition and inertia have any bearing on the shape of the policies in effect at any given time.[12] Policy indicators are based on overall revenue and expenditure figures for particular years, and no allowance is made for annual increments of change. Yet these annual increments are the very ones with which legislators, executives and administrators are most likely to be concerned, so these should be a major focal point in comparative studies. This is especially the case for comparative

10. Early studies of municipal government and administration report numerous colorful and dramatic illustrations of this interference. Whether or not rural domination of state legislatures was *one* of the important factors in this, as these early studies claimed it was, it is easy to appreciate the indignation often expressed in this literature regarding this practice. Among others, see: Frank J. Goodnow, *Municipal Home Rule: A Study in Administration* (New York: Columbia University Press, 1903); Charles Beard, *American City Government: A Survey of Newer Tendencies* (New York: The Century Co., 1912).

11. Data on the preferences of local leaders should include information about the relationships among these leaders and whether disagreements at home among party officials, mayors, and state legislators might not quite possibly harm a city's case at the state capitol to an even greater extent than malapportionment.

12. As Bicker notes, apportionment studies do not allow for the fact that different states may have adopted a given policy at different times. This is a common failing, both in studies that purport to explain policy outputs and in those that attempt to explain variations in political institutions. This weakens the explanatory power of these studies. Descriptively it may be accurate to report that in a given year cities with particular social or demographic characteristics are likely to have a particular form of government. Data for a single year is of little value, however, if one is interested in the characteristics of cities that are likely to adopt a given form of government, as most studies indicate they are. To do this, information is needed about the characteristics of cities at the time they adopted (or rejected) a particular form. No study that I know of has done this.

analyses of the effects of reapportionment in the post-*Baker* v. *Carr* era, since it is highly probable that reapportioned legislatures will engage in incremental, not zero-base, budgeting.

As I noted at the outset, comparative studies of state and local politics have challenged traditional beliefs about the interactions between government institutions and policies with increasing frequency, and confidence. The confidence is premature, and the answers to the ancient and honorable questions who gets what, when, how, which are promoted in these studies are largely inconclusive. And they will remain inconclusive until they are subjected to more informed analysis, analysis that includes a resolution of such problems as the reliability of data series, the validity of empirical indicators, and the ability of these data and indicators to reflect the rich contextual variety that is the mark of state and local politics and policy in the United States.

6

REAPPORTIONMENT IN THE 1970s:
ITS EFFECTS ON CONGRESS

Milton C. Cummings, Jr.

Many of the procedures, norms, and practices of the United States House of Representatives and Senate tend to reduce the rate of change in the operations of the Congress. Yet, even so, the potential effects of reapportionment and congressional redistricting for the new Congress that will be elected in November 1972 are substantial. And over the decade they may well be greater than the consequences of the reapportionment and redistricting process following any other census in this century.

These consequences are likely to be extensive because of the combination of two factors. First is the enormous population changes of the 1960s that have been measured and reflected in the 1970 census. And second, for the first time extensive redistricting for the House of Representatives is to take place under the restraints of the federal courts' one man, one vote, decisions within two years after a new census. (In the 1960s, the bulk of the redistricting in compliance with the 1962–1964 court rulings on equal districting was not completed until 1966. By then the redistricting was based on census figures that were already six years out of date.) As a result, the electoral base of the new House is likely to reflect the actual makeup of the United States population with greater accuracy than in recent previous decades; and the major trends that are likely to emerge from the new census are therefore of special interest and importance for the Congress.

The author would like to thank Jack Fischer for his help as a research assistant during the preparation of this chapter.

MAJOR POPULATION TRENDS, 1960–1970

The detailed analyses of the 1970 census will undoubtedly reveal a wide variety of data of import for the new Congress that will convene in January 1973. But at least five broad trends of special importance are virtually certain to emerge from the new census figures:

1. Between 1960 and 1970, the rate of population growth varied considerably from state to state and from region to region. Consequently, as after earlier censuses, there will be some changes (though smaller than earlier estimates suggested) in the size of the delegations that some states send to the House.
2. As expected, the bulk of the population growth between 1960 and 1970 occurred in the nation's metropolitan areas. Residents of metropolitan areas increased both in absolute numbers and as a percentage of the total American population.
3. Within the nation's metropolitan areas, the total population of the central cities has grown hardly at all; and the population of a substantial number of central cities actually declined between 1960 and 1970.
4. Nearly all of the enormous metropolitan growth during the decade— probably more than 15 million persons—occurred in the suburban areas that ringed the central cities.
5. The number of Blacks living in the central cities increased sharply during the 1960s. Although there is some uncertainty about whether the number of Blacks living in central cities will continue to grow as rapidly in the 1970s, the number of Black residents of the center city is almost certain to increase. The population in three American cities now is more than 50 percent Black. During the 1970s several other cities may have Black majorities.

Between 1960 and 1970, the total population of the United States (including Armed Forces overseas) increased by about 25 million—from 180 to 205 million.[1] The average rate of growth through the decade was about 1.3 percent a year. This rate of population increase, however, was by no means evenly reflected in the different states. According to census estimates, three states (North and South Dakota and West Virginia) actually lost some of their population during the 1960s. At the other extreme, there were eight states where the average rate of population growth probably exceeded 2 percent a year—for gains of more than 20 percent over the

---

1. U.S. Bureau of the Census, "Estimates of the Population of the United States to May 1, 1970," Series P-25, No. 446, June 22, 1970, of *Population Estimates and Projections* (Washington: U.S. Government Printing Office, 1970).

decade. The states with the big population increases included California and Florida, which will gain the most new House seats in the Ninety-third Congress. A list of the fifty states, grouped according to their probable growth rate during the past decade, appears in Table 1.

TABLE 1
ESTIMATES OF AVERAGE ANNUAL VARIATION OF
U.S. POPULATION, BY STATE, 1960–1968
(NATIONAL AVERAGE = 1.3%)

Lost	Gained 0.1–0.5%	Gained 0.6–1%	Gained 1.1–1.5%	Gained 1.6–2%	Gained Over 2%
N.D.	Iowa	Ala.	Ark.	Colo.	Alaska
S.D.	Maine	Idaho	Ga.	Conn.	Ariz.
W. Va.	Mont.	Ind.	Ill.	N.J.	Cal.
	Nebr.	Kans.	La.	N.H.	Del.
	Pa.	Ky.	Mich.	Tex.	Fla.
	Wyo.	Mass.	N.C.	Utah	Hawaii
		Minn.	Ohio	Va.	Md.
		Miss.	Oreg.	Wash.	Nev.
		Mo.	S.C.		
		N. Mex.	Tenn.		
		N.Y.			
		Okla.			
		R.I.			
		Vt.			
		Wis.			

Source: Supporting data accompanying the "Statement by Conrad Taeuber, Associate Director, Bureau of the Census, before the House Committee on Banking and Currency, June 3, 1969" (U.S. Bureau of the Census, mimeographed copy), Table 29. One additional state that was expected to lose population between 1960 and 1970, Wyoming, actually registered a very small gain in population in 1970. Wyoming, therefore, has been placed in the "Gained 0.1–0.5%" column, *Congressional Quarterly Weekly Report*, December 4, 1970, p. 2920.

It is, however, the changes in patterns of residence within states, rather than the net shifts in total population from state to state, that provide the most striking indications of change in the residential composition of the American electorate. For, during the 1960s, close to three-fourths of the nation's entire population growth occurred in metropolitan areas located in all but four of the fifty states. Between 1960 and early 1969, the Bureau of the Census estimates that the United States population (excluding many members of the Armed Forces) made a net gain of about 21.3 million. Of this net growth, 15.9 million occurred in the nation's metropolitan areas—the 212 Standard Metropolitan Statistical Areas, as defined by the census in 1960.

But within these metropolitan areas, practically all of the growth took place within the suburban rings, not the central cities. The central cities as a whole grew only about 1 percent; the suburban rings, by 25 percent. And many central cities, particularly older cities in the northeastern quarter of the country, actually lost population between 1960 and 1970. Taken as a whole, the central cities gained between half and three-quarters of a million persons between 1960 and 1970. In the suburban rings outside those central cities, the net population growth was more than 15 million.

This suburban population explosion is, of course, the result of trends that have been visible for many years. The suburbs ringing the nation's central cities have been growing faster than the central cities since 1920. By 1960, the suburban areas had only slightly fewer people than the central cities. During the 1960s the balance shifted; and today, for the first time, more than half of the Americans who live in metropolitan areas live outside the central cities. This concentration of the nation's largest population bloc in the suburbs is likely to continue to grow.[2] And it is, for the future of American politics, probably the most important single trend to be confirmed by the 1970 census. (Census estimates comparing the 1969 United States population with that of 1960, according to place of residence, appear in Table 2.)

Within the central cities, one other population trend of major importance took place during the 1960s: the population of many American cities became increasingly Black. Between 1960 and 1969 the census bureau estimates that the Negro population in the central cities increased by 2.6 million persons. (There was a decline of 2.1 million in the central cities' White population.)[3] As a result, the population of the central cities, which was 16 percent Negro in 1960, was 21 percent Negro in 1969. In central cities in metropolitan areas of one million or larger, Negroes made up 25 percent of the population. The percentage of suburbanites who were Black remained at 5 percent through most of the decade. (Data comparing the patterns of residence of Whites and Negroes in 1960 and 1969 appear in Tables 3 and 4.)

It is not certain, however, that this concentration of Negroes in the

2. Statement by Conrad Taeuber, Associate Director, Bureau of the Census, before the House Committee on Banking and Currency, June 3, 1969 (U.S. Bureau of the Census, Mimeographed), p. 2.

3. Statement by Conrad Taeuber, Associate Director, Bureau of the Census, before the House Committee on Banking and Currency, October 14, 1969 (U.S. Bureau of the Census, Mimeographed), p. 1.

TABLE 2
RESIDENCE OF U.S. POPULATION IN THE SIXTIES

	1960[a]		1969[b]	
	No. (in thousands)	%	No. (in thousands)	%
Total	178,458		199,754	
Metropolitan areas[c]	112,901	63.3	128,801	64.5
In central cities	57,790	32.4	58,492	29.3
Outside central cities	55,111	30.9	70,310	35.2
Nonmetropolitan areas	65,557	36.7	70,953	35.5

a. For comparability with data from the 1969 Current Population Survey, figures from the 1960 census have been adjusted to exclude members of the Armed Forces living in barracks and similar types of quarters.

b. Five-quarter average centered on January 1969.

c. Population of the 212 Standard Metropolitan Statistical Areas, as defined in 1960.

Source: Supporting data accompanying the "Statement by Conrad Taeuber, Associate Director, Bureau of the Census, before the House Committee on Banking and Currency, October 14, 1969" (U.S. Bureau of the Census, mimeographed copy), Table 1.

TABLE 3
DISTRIBUTION OF U.S. POPULATION, BY RACE, IN THE SIXTIES
(in thousands)

	Whites		Negroes	
	1960[a]	1969[b]	1960[a]	1969[b]
Total	158,051	175,311	18,793	22,331
Metropolitan areas[c]	99,740	111,736	12,168	15,594
In central cities	47,463	45,348	9,687	12,317
Outside central cities	52,277	66,387	2,481	3,278
Nonmetropolitan areas	58,311	63,577	6,625	6,736

a. For comparability with data from the 1969 Current Population Survey, figures from the 1960 census have been adjusted to exclude members of the Armed Forces living in barracks and similar types of quarters.

b. Five-quarter average centered on January 1969.

c. Population of the 212 Standard Metropolitan Statistical Areas as defined in 1960.

Source: Supporting data accompanying the "Statement by Conrad Taeuber, Associate Director, Bureau of the Census, before the House Committee on Banking and Currency, October 14, 1969" (U.S. Bureau of the Census, mimeographed copy), Table 1.

TABLE 4
PERCENTAGES OF NEGROES IN U.S. POPULATION IN THE SIXTIES

	% Negro 1960	% Negro 1969
All metropolitan areas		
Total	11	12
Central cities	16	21
Suburban rings	5	5
Metropolitan areas of 1,000,000 or more		
Total	11	14
Central cities	18	26
Suburban rings	4	5
Metropolitan areas of less than 1,000,000		
Total	10	10
Central cities	14	16
Suburban rings	5	5
Outside metropolitan areas	10	9

Source: Supporting data accompanying the "Statement by Conrad Taeuber, Associate Director, Bureau of the Census, before the House Committee on Banking and Currency, October 14, 1969" (U.S. Bureau of the Census, mimeographed copy), Table 3. The definition of metropolitan areas and the data bases used for computing the percentage Negro in 1960 and 1969 are the same as those used in *supra*, Tables 2 and 3.

central cities—and their exclusion from many suburbs—will continue at this rapid a rate in the 1970s. The authors of the report of the National Advisory Commission on Civil Disorders, which was completed early in 1968, spoke of the "accelerating segregation of low-income, disadvantaged Negroes within the ghettos of the largest American cities." [4] They foresaw an increase in the Negro population in all central cities from around 12 million in the late 1960s to 20.8 million by 1985, if existing trends continued. They also noted that populations in Washington, D.C., and Newark, New Jersey, were already more than half Negro. And they estimated that a continuation of recent trends would cause the following major cities to become more than 50 percent Black by the indicated dates: New Orleans and Richmond, in 1971; Baltimore and Jacksonville, in 1972; Cleveland, in 1975; St. Louis, in 1978; Detroit, in 1979; Philadelphia, in 1981; Oakland, in 1983; and Chicago, in 1984. [5]

On the other hand, at least two more recent studies have suggested that the rate of increase in the Negro population of the central city may

4. *Report of the National Advisory Commission on Civil Disorders* (New York: Bantam Books, 1968), p. 389.

5. *Id.,* p. 391.

have begun to decline in the second half of the 1960s, and that Negroes are beginning to move into the suburbs in increasing and significant numbers. One study, by David L. Birch, found that in the early 1960s central cities gained in Black population at the rate of 400,000 a year, while suburbs gained at the rate of 52,000. Then, late in the decade, central-city gains dropped to 262,000 a year, and suburban gains of Negroes rose to 85,000, reflecting a "continuous and sharply increasing black migration into suburban towns." [6] Another student of Negro migration to the suburbs, Reynolds Farley, has concluded that "Negroes, similar to European ethnic groups, are becoming more decentralized throughout the metropolitan area after they have been in the city for some time and improved their economic status." [7]

Nevertheless, it is the rate of Negro population growth in the central cities in the 1970s that is in doubt. No one questions that there will be some increase and that it will be substantial. And the extensive concentration of Negroes that occurred in the nation's central cities between 1960 and 1970 is certain to be reflected in congressional politics, as well as in municipal and state politics, throughout the decade.

POPULATION TRENDS AND THE SENATE

As the preceding discussion makes clear, the decade of the 1960s was a period of dynamic growth and change in the American population. But neither reapportionment nor redistricting will change the formal electoral base of the United States Senate. Each state will continue to have two senators, regardless of the size of its population; and the Senate will remain as unrepresentative as ever in terms of the one man, one vote, criterion. If anything, it will be slightly more unrepresentative in terms of population. As Professor Gordon E. Baker has pointed out, after the 1960 census, a Senate majority made up of the 26 least populous states represented only about 17 percent of the nation's population.[8] After 1970, the

6. New York *Times,* July 12, 1970, p. 22.
7. *Ibid.*
8. Gordon E. Baker, *The Reapportionment Revolution* (New York: Random House, 1966), p. 68. Professor Baker went on to note that this was only a "theoretical control" percentage—many "real life" issues do not cause a sharp political cleavage between the states with large and small populations. One important issue that did, however, was the 1959 battle in the Senate over filibuster reform. A bipartisan proposal to allow a simple majority of the entire Senate to invoke cloture after fifteen days of debate was defeated decisively by a vote of 67 to 28. "Yet this large Senate majority (with its core of strength in the Solid South and sparsely populated Great Plains and Rocky Mountain regions) actually represented a minority of the nation's voters." *Ibid*

26 states with the smallest population are likely to contain about 16 percent of the national total.[9]

Many issues do not pit the least populous against the most populous states, however; and, despite its unrepresentative base, on many issues the Senate was probably more responsive to urban interests than the House during the 1950s and 1960s.[10] Moreover, the broad trend of the population movements of the 1960s is likely only to make the Senate more responsive to metropolitan voters. In 1960, in 23 of the 50 states half or more of the total state population resided in major metropolitan areas, as defined by the census bureau; and in 30 states metropolitan areas contained 40 percent or more of the total state population. In 1970 three more states had populations that were more than 40 percent metropolitan.[11] And it is now only a small number of senators who do not have significant metropolitan areas in their constituencies.

When the detailed census figures are available, a good deal of analysis will be possible, tracing out the population changes in individual states and speculating on the changes in these electoral constituencies that are likely to be reflected in the behavior of members of the Senate. But the greatest changes for Congress stemming from the new population figures will be caused by House redistricting; and so it is to the House of Representatives that we now turn our attention.

REAPPORTIONMENT FOR THE HOUSE:
STATE AND REGIONAL PATTERNS

If the advance census estimates of the probable state population totals as of April 1970 are correct, there will be only a moderate amount of change in the size of the House delegations allocated to each state by reapportionment for 1972. And these changes will be smaller than was anticipated in the mid-1960s. The biggest gainer will be California, which will supplant New York as the state with the largest House delegation, with an increase of five seats. Florida will gain three. At the other extreme, Pennsylvania and New York are likely to lose two House seats each.

9. Based on supporting data for the statement of June 3, 1969, by Conrad Taeuber, Table 29.

10. See, for example, Michael N. Danielson, *Federal-Metropolitan Politics and the Commuter Crisis* (New York: Columbia University Press, 1965), pp. 193–194. For a related discussion, see also Chapter 6, "Why the Senate Is More Liberal Than the House," in Lewis A. Froman, Jr., ed., *Congressmen and Their Constituencies* (Chicago: Rand McNally, 1963), pp. 69–84.

11. Based on supporting data for the statement of June 3, 1969, by Conrad Taeuber, Table 30.

Among regions, the Mid-Atlantic states are expected to lose four House seats, and the Midwestern and Plains states, two seats each. Border state congressmen will probably be cut by one. The South is likely to record a net gain of three seats, all in Florida or Texas; Rocky Mountain states will gain two, and the Pacific Coast area will gain four, all in California.[12] These changes represent a net shift of nine House seats from the northeast and north central portions of the country to the South and West. Yet overall, the net change, which affects about 2 percent of all House seats, is not large. California's five-seat increase is smaller than the California gains both in 1962, when the state's delegation grew from 30 to 38, and in 1952, when the delegation increased from 23 to 30. And of the 50 states, 36 will have no change at all in the size of their House delegations.

Nor is it clear whether one party or the other stands definitely to be the prime beneficiary of such changes as are caused by reapportionment. Of the states losing House strength, Ohio, North Dakota, and Iowa normally elect a predominantly Republican House delegation, and West Virginia has been predominantly Democratic. New York, Pennsylvania, and Wisconsin have been closely balanced in their voting for the House during the 1960s. Of the five states gaining House strength, all but Arizona now have Democratic congressional majorities. Both in Texas and Florida, however, there has been a clear trend toward increased voting strength for Republican House candidates; and in California, also, the Republicans are now stronger than they were in 1962. Moreover, in all of these states, the most important question that will affect the parties' prospects for House contests in 1972 and thereafter is which party will be in control of the new congressional redistricting following the elections for governor and state legislature in November 1970. And that question will be explored shortly.

REDISTRICTING FOR THE HOUSE:
CHANGES WITHIN THE STATES

It is from redistricting changes within the states, rather than from net changes in House strength among the states, that the greatest change in response to the 1970 census is likely to come. As has been noted, the first major wave of court-enforced redistricting to reflect population equally

12. *Congressional Quarterly Weekly Report,* September 4, 1970, p. 2193. Estimates have been updated after release of the final census figures for each state on November 30, 1970. *Congressional Quarterly Weekly Report,* December 4, 1970, p. 2918.

TABLE 5
REAPPORTIONMENT OF U.S. HOUSE SEATS AFTER 1970 CENSUS

State and Region		Number of Seats 1962–1970	Probable Number of Seats 1972	Probable Net Change
NEW ENGLAND				
Conn.		6	6	0
Maine		2	2	0
Mass.		12	12	0
N.H.		2	2	0
R.I.		2	2	0
Vt.		1	1	0
	Total	25	25	0
MID-ATLANTIC				
Del.		1	1	0
N.J.		15	15	0
N.Y.		41	39	−2
Pa.		27	25	−2
	Total	84	80	−4
BORDER STATES				
Ky.		7	7	0
Md.		8	8	0
Mo.		10	10	0
Okla.		6	6	0
W. Va.		5	4	−1
	Total	36	35	−1
SOUTH				
Ala.		8	7	−1
Ark.		4	4	0
Fla.		12	15	+3
Ga.		10	10	0
La.		8	8	0
Miss.		5	5	0
N.C.		11	11	0
S.C.		6	6	0
Tenn.		9	8	−1
Tex.		23	24	+1
Va.		10	10	0
	Total	106	108	+2

TABLE 5 (*continued*)

State and Region	Number of Seats 1962–1970	Probable Number of Seats 1972	Probable Net Change
MIDWEST			
Ill.	24	24	0
Ind.	11	11	0
Mich.	19	19	0
Ohio	24	23	−1
Wis.	10	9	−1
Total	88	86	−2
PLAINS STATES			
Iowa	7	6	−1
Kans.	5	5	0
Minn.	8	8	0
Nebr.	3	3	0
N.D.	2	1	−1
S.D.	2	2	0
Total	27	25	−2
ROCKY MOUNTAIN			
Ariz.	3	4	+1
Colo.	4	5	+1
Idaho	2	2	0
Mont.	2	2	0
Nev.	1	1	0
N. Mex.	2	2	0
Utah	2	2	0
Wyo.	1	1	0
Total	17	19	+2
PACIFIC COAST			
Alaska	1	1	0
Cal.	38	43	+5
Hawaii	2	2	0
Oreg.	4	4	0
Wash.	7	7	0
Total	52	57	+5

Source: U.S. Census estimates released February 1970. The New York *Times*, February 17, 1970, p. 25. Updated after release of the final census figures for each state on November 30, 1970. *Congressional Quarterly Weekly Report*, December 4, 1970, p. 2918.

occurred between 1962 and 1966, although in a number of states redistricting continued between 1967 and 1970. Yet by the time this redistricting was completed, the census figures on which it was based were at least six years out of date. In the 1970s the response to the dynamic population changes will come much faster.

In a meticulous and revealing analysis, Professor Richard Lehne has underscored some of the broad consequences of three different waves of congressional redistricting: the redistricting for the 1962 elections, following the 1960 census, that took place before the federal courts began to enforce the one man, one vote, principle; the new redistricting between 1962 and 1966 to reflect population more equally in compliance with the new court standards; and estimates of the probable consequences of the new redistricting to take place in 1971 and 1972 for the 1972 congressional elections. Lehne classified the House districts by location, according to whether in 1962 and 1966 they were predominantly metropolitan (central city, suburban, or mixed) or nonmetropolitan.[13] Then, using the estimated state populations for 1970, districts were apportioned to the states for 1972. Finally, using various assumptions that are likely to be approximated reasonably closely in the real world of politics during the 1971/1972 redistricting period, boundaries were drawn within each state to create districts roughly equal in population for 1972.[14] The results of his analysis are set forth in Table 6.

Several key findings emerge from the data. First, the net shift in House strength from nonmetropolitan to metropolitan areas in 1971 and 1972 is likely to be two to three times as extensive as the shift toward urban areas that accompanied the 1962 to 1966 wave of redistricting. Between 1962 and 1966, metropolitan areas gained about ten House seats. In 1972 the metropolitan areas are likely to pick up an additional 27 seats. Through the remainder of the 1970s, therefore, the House of Representatives, long noted for giving special weight to rural and small-town America, will have an electoral base in which congressional districts in metropolitan areas outnumber the nonmetropolitan districts by about two to one.

13. The precise criteria used for these classifications are explained in Table 6. For a fuller discussion of the method of classification, see Richard Lehne, "Shape of the Future," 58 *National Civic Review*, No. 8: 351–352.

14. In defining the probable shape of the districts to be drawn for 1972 under the one man, one vote guidelines, Professor Lehne followed these general criteria. Counties were not divided unless previous state practice permitted it. The "most minimal standards of compactness and contiguity were honored," and traditional districts were maintained wherever possible. "Every effort was made to maximize the nonmetropolitan representation, even at the expense of other standards." *Id.* at 352.

TABLE 6
METROPOLITAN AND NONMETROPOLITAN U.S. HOUSE DISTRICTS, 1962, 1966, AND 1972 (ESTIMATED)

	Number of Districts		
Type of District[a]	1962	1966	1972 (estimated)
Central city	106	110	100
Suburban	92	98	129
Mixed	56	56	62
Total Metropolitan	254	264	291
Total Nonmetropolitan	181	171	144

a. The criteria for classification were as follows: If a majority of a district's residents did not live in a metropolitan area, as defined by the census bureau, the district was labeled nonmetropolitan. If the majority of a district's population lived in a metropolitan area, the district was first classified as metropolitan, and also as either "central city" or "outside central city," as defined by the Bureau of the Census, if 50 percent of its total population lived in either of those areas. It was also classified as a "central city" or "outside central city" district if 45 percent of the total population lived in the central city or outside central city regions and no more than 30 percent lived in either the central city, outside central city, or nonmetropolitan areas. In some cases, neither of these criteria was met, yet the district still had a majority of its population in metropolitan areas. In these cases, the district was labeled "mixed metropolitan."

Source: Richard Lehne, "Shape of the Future," 58 National Civic Review, No. 8: 351–352.

The 1971/1972 redistricting will differ from the redistricting of 1962 to 1966 in other respects as well. The shifts between 1962 and 1966 enabled both the central cities and their suburban fringes to gain House strength at the expense of the nonmetropolitan areas. But in 1972, as a reflection of the population trends traced earlier in this chapter, virtually all of the new gains should be made by the suburbs. The central cities, it appears, should actually lose about ten House seats, compared with 1966. The suburban areas should gain thirty-one.

In the past, state legislatures have resorted to a variety of tactics to dilute the influence of urban voters on the House. In some states, urban and especially suburban voters were concentrated into a small number of populous House districts. In other states, urban residents were dispersed among several districts, each with a nonmetropolitan majority.[15] But these evasive tactics will be much harder now. The court standards enjoining substantial equality of population are stringent. In many of the

15. Id. at 353.

bigger states only a minority of the population lives outside the metropolitan areas. And the 1971/1972 redistricting will be carried out by state legislatures that were themselves redistricted to comply with the courts' one man, one vote, doctrine during the 1960s.

The resulting changes in the electoral base of the House will be extensive. Not only will the central cities lose representation in the House, but for the first time suburban representatives will outnumber those from the core cities. Moreover, the odds are that during the 1970s a number of those districts that are classified as "mixed, central city-suburban" will become increasingly suburban in their makeup. Even in 1972, if one assumes that half of the districts with mixtures of suburban and central city populations are more suburban than urban, it is clear that the suburbs are likely to have the biggest block of House districts in the new Congress. And it is the suburban areas, of course, that are currently experiencing the most dynamic population growth. During the 1970s an increasing number of the representatives from these mixed districts are likely to find that suburban dwellers form the majority of their constituents.

In all this there is a very considerable irony. The battle for greater urban representation in the House in the 1950s and 1960s was often accompanied by rhetoric stressing the need to help the central cities, who, it was asserted, were penalized by rural overrepresentation. Now that the one man, one vote, doctrine is being implemented, however, it is the suburbs, not the central cities, that stand to gain the most.

REDISTRICTING AND THE HOUSE:
POSSIBLE CONSEQUENCES FOR THE POLITICAL PARTIES

The drift of the argument thus far has been that shifts in the electoral base of the House among states and regions will be perceptible, but not strikingly large. On the other hand, the shifts in congressional district boundary lines within many states, to reflect the growing metropolitan and especially suburban populations there, are likely to be substantial. But which political party is likely to gain by this redistricting process? The experience of redistricting during the late 1960s suggests that state legislatures will comply quite closely with the one man, one vote, doctrine in drawing congressional districts that are, in fact, substantially equal in population. Nevertheless, within this context, gerrymandering to benefit the party in control of the redistricting process may be quite extensive.

The great majority of states will have to redistrict in 1971 and 1972 as a result of the changes being reflected in the 1970 census. The crucial point, then, is which political party is likely to be in charge of drawing the new district boundary lines. In most cases, of course, the process of enacting redistricting legislation formally involves the governor and two houses of the state legislature. In states where one party controls both houses of the legislature and the governorship, that party tends to fare well when redistricting becomes necessary. If there is a split in partisan control of the state, by contrast, a complex inter-party bargaining process is usually required to obtain redistricting legislation. In most of these cases, neither party is heavily favored by the redistricting legislation. By looking at which party is in control of the various state governments and the number of House seats that are likely to be allocated to those states for 1972, one can get some idea of how many House districts will be redrawn under the control of one or the other of the major parties.

If Republican strength in governorships and state houses had remained as strong after the 1970 elections as it was in 1969 and 1970, the GOP would have been in a markedly better position than the Democrats to draw congressional district boundary lines to their advantage in 1971 and 1972. In the South, Democratic congressmen still would have had a reasonably good chance of seeing the redistricting in friendly hands. As of 1970, Democrats control both the state house of representatives and the governorship in southern states where 71 House seats may be redistricted after reapportionment based on the 1970 census returns. In southern states where another 37 districts may require redistricting, the partisan control of the state legislature and the governorship was split, and Republicans controlled at least one house of the state legislature or the governorship.

Outside the South, however, the potential redistricting situation going into the 1970 fall elections heavily favored the Republicans. Only 28 seats were likely to be in northern states where the Democrats were in firm control of the governorship and both houses of the state legislature in 1969 and 1970, compared with 188 seats in states that were under full Republican control. There will also be a large block of 100 seats in nonsouthern states where partisan control was split in 1970. In the country as a whole, the seats to be allocated to states fully controlled by the Republicans outnumbered those to be allocated to states under Democratic control in 1969 and 1970 by nearly two to one. These findings are underpinned by the data presented in Table 7.

The Republicans enjoyed this marked advantage going into the 1970 elections in considerable measure because of their strong control of the state governorships. In 1970, Republicans occupied the governors' man-

TABLE 7

PATTERNS OF PARTY CONTROL IN THE STATES BEFORE THE 1970 ELECTIONS AND HOUSE SEATS TO BE REDISTRICTED IN 1971/1972

Control of State Legislature and Governorship before 1970 Elections	Probable House Seats for 1972
SOUTHERN STATES	
All Democratic	71
All Republican	0
Split	37
NONSOUTHERN STATES	
All Democratic	28
All Republican	188
Split	100
ENTIRE COUNTRY	
All Democratic	99
All Republican	188
Split	137

NOTE: State governments listed as "All Democratic" or "All Republican" are states where one party controlled the governorship and both houses of the state legislature in the spring of 1970. State governments were listed as "Split" if the second major party controlled any one of the three governmental organs in the state—the governorship or one house in the state legislature. In some of these states the partisan control of the two houses of the state legislature was split. In others, both houses of the state legislature were controlled by the same party, but the other party controlled the governorship. Nebraska and Minnesota, which technically have nonpartisan state legislatures and will have a total of 11 House seats in 1972, are excluded from the analysis.

Source: *Congressional Quarterly Weekly Report*, "Election 1970: A Pre-Primary Supplement," February 20, 1970. Figures updated after release of the final census totals for each state on November 30, 1970. *Congressional Quarterly Weekly Report*, December 4, 1970, p. 2918.

sions in about two-thirds of all the states, and in six of the largest seven (New York, Pennsylvania, Michigan, Ohio, Illinois, and California). In Table 8, a new arrangement of our state legislative and gubernatorial data is set forth. As these figures make clear, the Democrats were not too far behind the Republicans in terms of the number of seats that are potentially to be redistricted in state legislatures where the Democrats are in control (159 D, 198 R). But 60 of the 159 seats under the jurisdiction of Democratic-controlled legislatures were in states where there was a Republican governor. By contrast, only 10 of the 198 seats with a currently Republican-controlled legislature were in states where the Republican legislature could expect to bargain with a Democratic governor. Republican gubernatorial strength in the South also made 29 out of 100 southern House seats under a Democratic legislature subject to inter-party bargaining.

TABLE 8

PATTERNS OF PARTY CONTROL OF STATE LEGISLATURES AND GOVERNORSHIPS BEFORE THE 1970 ELECTIONS AND HOUSE SEATS TO BE REDISTRICTED IN 1971/1972

Control of State Legislature Preceding 1970 Elections	Probable House Seats for 1972	House Seats Under Dem. Governor	House Seats Under Rep. Governor
SOUTHERN STATES			
Democratic	100	71	29
Republican	0	0	0
Split	8	8	0
NONSOUTHERN STATES			
Democratic	59	28	31
Republican	198	10	188
Split	59	2	57
ENTIRE COUNTRY			
Democratic	159	99	60
Republican	198	10	188
Split	67	10	57

NOTE: In states where party control of the legislature was listed as Democratic or Republican, one party controlled both houses of the state legislature in the spring of 1970. In states where party control was listed as Split, Republicans controlled one house and Democrats controlled the other house of the state legislature. As in Table 7, Nebraska and Minnesota are excluded from the analysis.

Source: Congressional Quarterly Weekly Report, "Election 1970: A Pre-Primary Supplement," February 20, 1970. Figures updated after release of final census totals for each state on November 30, 1970. Congressional Quarterly Weekly Report, December 4, 1970, p. 2918.

POSSIBLE CONSEQUENCES OF REDISTRICTING
FOR THE PARTIES: THE SPECIAL
IMPORTANCE OF THE 1970 ELECTION

The partisan control of the states as of 1969 and 1970 may not be a good guide to the partisan control of the states during the crucial 1971/1972 redistricting period, however. In the November 1970 elections the Democrats made a net gain of eleven governorships and also increased their strength in a number of state legislatures. As a result, the patterns of party control of the states that will be redistricting for 1972 were altered substantially.

The new situation is underscored by the data in Table 9. In 1972 the largest number of House seats will be in states where partisan control of the statehouse and the governor's mansion is split during 1971/1972. But it is also clear that the Republicans' prospects of benefiting from the new redistricting received a setback in the November 1970 elections. Before the 1970 voting, the Republicans were in full control of the state governments in states that will have 188 House seats in 1972. After the 1970 elections, the Republicans were in full control of the redistricting process in states with 85 House seats for 1972.

TABLE 9

PATTERNS OF PARTY CONTROL IN THE STATES AFTER 1970
AND HOUSE SEATS TO BE REDISTRICTED IN 1971/1972

Party Control of State Governments after 1970 Elections[a]	Probable House Seats for 1972			Probable House Seats, Related to Patterns of Party Control before 1970 Elections
	Southern States	Nonsouthern States	Entire Country	
All Democratic	90	56	146	(99)
All Republican	0	85	85	(188)
Split	18	175	193	(137)

a. Nebraska and Minnesota are excluded from the analysis.
Source: *Congressional Quarterly Weekly Report*, December 4, 1970, pp. 2918–2921.

COMPETITIVE AND NONCOMPETITIVE HOUSE DISTRICTS: THE PROSPECTS AFTER REDISTRICTING

The marked increase in suburban House districts that is in the offing raises another question about the probable future behavior of suburban congressional electorates. Are the new suburban districts likely to be less competitive or more competitive than other types of House constituencies? To this no definite answer can be given, because suburban, as well as urban and rural, congressional voting patterns may be different in the 1970s than they have been in the recent past. Nevertheless, the voting trends in these different types of districts are of considerable interest and may, particularly those in the late 1960s, provide some indication of the probable trends after 1971.

In Tables 10 and 11, the closeness of the House vote from 1962 to 1968 in four types of House districts outside the South (suburban, urban, rural, and mixed) is examined. The criteria used to classify these districts probably overstate the number of districts that are designated as rural, as well as understating the number of suburban districts. Nevertheless, the restrictiveness of the definitions used does mean that every district that was labeled suburban or urban deserved to be put in those categories. (An explanation of the method of classification employed appears in the footnotes to Tables 10 and 11.)

As the data indicate, in the North during the 1960s the districts classified as rural or mixed were generally more closely fought in the general election than either suburban or urban House districts. At the same time, suburban districts appear to have become more competitive over the decade. By the late 1960s, suburban House seats were substantially more likely to be hotly contested than were the big-city districts, which by 1968 were the least competitive of the four broad types of districts.

A similar analysis of southern House districts was hampered by the fact that in the 1960s there were very few suburban districts in the South. By 1968, however, contests in the suburban districts that had been created in the South were tending to be more closely fought than those in other southern districts, and rural southern districts remained the most likely to be dominated by one party. The figures for 1968 in southern House districts were as follows:[16]

	Suburban Districts (N = 5)	Urban Districts (N = 14)	Mixed Districts (N = 32)	Rural Districts (N = 45)
45–55% of vote went to Democrats	20%	7.1%	9.3%	2.2%
40–60% of vote went to Democrats	80%	14.2%	28.0%	13.3%

Another measure of the actual competitiveness of House districts is the actual number of House seats in the different types of constituencies that switch from the control of one party to that of the other. In making an

16. The criteria used to classify southern House districts for 1968 are identical to those used in Table 11.

TABLE 10
CLOSENESS OF HOUSE CONTESTS OUTSIDE THE SOUTH, 1962 AND 1964

	Percentage of House Districts with Close and Less Close House Contests			
	1962 ELECTION[a]			
Democratic Percentage of House Vote 1962	*Suburban Districts* (N = 48)	*Urban Districts* (N = 89)	*Mixed Districts* (N = 64)	*Rural Districts* (N = 128)
45–54.9	6.3	14.6	22.0	26.4
40–44.9 or 55–59.9	31.2	15.8	28.2	33.6
30–39.9 or 60–69.9	48.9	33.6	39.1	30.5
0–29.9 or 70–100	14.6	35.9	11.0	9.3
	1964 ELECTION[b]			
1964	*Suburban Districts* (N = 45)	*Urban Districts* (N = 82)	*Mixed Districts* (N = 53)	*Rural Districts* (N = 112)
45–54.9	17.6	10.9	30.1	44.6
40–44.9 or 55–59.9	33.4	12.2	22.6	18.8
30–39.9 or 60–69.9	33.2	29.2	33.9	27.7
0–29.9 or 70–100	15.5	47.6	13.2	9.0

a. The classification of House districts for 1962 is based upon the *Congressional Quarterly (CQ)* analysis of August 21, 1964. The *CQ* definition of urban generally followed the census bureau's definition of central cities of over 50,000 population in some 213 urbanized areas. *CQ*'s definition of suburban generally corresponded to what the census bureau defined as urban fringe—the closely settled areas contiguous to central cities. All areas not classified as urban or suburban were classified as rural, and it should be noted that the residents of many medium-size cities were classified as rural because their populations were less than 50,000.

In the *CQ* classification, districts where the population was at least 50 percent urban were classified as urban. Districts with a population that was at least 50 percent suburban were classified as suburban. The mixed label was applied where a predominant urban or suburban population group did not constitute at least 50 percent of the total population within the district. The mixed category was also extended to include those predominantly rural districts where the rural population did not equal 60 percent of all residents.

In its practical effect, the *CQ* classification scheme yielded suburban and urban districts which were rather pure examples of their type, but probably overstated the number of districts that should have been called rural. For a more detailed explanation of the *CQ* classification scheme, see *Congressional Quarterly*, "CQ Census Analysis: Congressional Districts of the United States," August 21, 1964, pp. 1786 and 1792.

b. The classification of House districts for 1964 follows the *CQ* analysis used for 1962, except that those districts which were redistricted between 1962 and 1964 are excluded from the analysis.

TABLE 11

CLOSENESS OF HOUSE CONTESTS OUTSIDE THE SOUTH,
1966 AND 1968

	Percentage of House Districts with Close and Less Close House Contests			
	1966 ELECTION[a]			
Democratic Percentage of House Vote *1966*	*Suburban Districts* *(N = 51)*	*Urban Districts* *(N = 89)*	*Mixed Districts* *(N = 91)*	*Rural Districts* *(N = 70)*
45–54.9	17.6	10.0	26.4	24.3
40–44.9 or 55–59.9	9.8	21.3	24.2	14.3
30–39.9 or 60–69.9	46.9	26.9	36.3	50.0
0–29.9 or 70–100	25.4	41.5	13.2	11.4
	1968 ELECTION[b]			
1968	*Suburban Districts* *(N = 51)*	*Urban Districts* *(N = 89)*	*Mixed Districts* *(N = 91)*	*Rural Districts* *(N = 70)*
45–54.9	17.7	8.9	14.3	27.1
40–44.9 or 55–59.9	11.7	13.5	15.4	24.3
30–39.9 or 60–69.9	45.1	33.8	53.9	40.0
0–29.9 or 70–100	25.5	43.7	16.5	8.7

a. Districts classified as suburban for 1966 include all districts classified as suburban in the 1964 *CQ* analysis that were not substantially changed before the 1966 election. They also include newly created districts in the suburban fringe of central cities having populations over 75 percent urban, as conventionally defined by the census bureau. Districts classified as urban for 1966 include all those so categorized in the 1964 *CQ* analysis, plus newly created districts located primarily in central cities with populations 90 percent or more urban. Districts classified as rural are those districts having populations 55 percent or less urban as conventionally defined by the census bureau. Districts classified as mixed are all districts not fitting into one of the above categories. *Sources:* U.S. Bureau of the Census, *Congressional District Data Book (Districts of the 88th Congress)* (Washington: U.S. Government Printing Office, 1963), and the *Supplement to Congressional District Data Book: Redistricted States*, published by the Census Bureau for each state that redistricted between 1962 and 1966.

b. All districts not redistricted between 1966 and 1968 retain the same classification for 1968 as they had for 1966. Districts that were changed between 1966 and 1968 are classified according to the criteria specified in Note a.

analysis of this type, the number of districts examined had to be reduced somewhat because of extensive changing of district boundary lines between 1962 and 1968. Nevertheless, the following figures give some indication of the number of House seats that switched partisan control in the

| Election Year | Suburban Districts | House Seats Switching Party Control (figures in parentheses = number of districts analyzed) | | |
		Urban Districts	Mixed Districts	Rural Districts
1964	13.3% (45)	6.1% (82)	13.2% (53)	20.5% (112)
1966	4 % (50)	3.4% (89)	18.2% (88)	17.6% (68)
1968	5.9% (51)	1.1% (89)	4.4% (91)	4.3% (70)

different types of House districts outside the South in 1964, 1966, and 1968:[17]

In terms of switches in party control during the 1960s, suburban House seats were more volatile than the urban seats, but they were less likely to turn over than were seats in mixed and rural districts.

But, granted that some districts may be more closely fought than others, the crucial questions affecting control of the House of Representatives are which party predominates in winning the different types of House districts, and how great is the relative advantage which the dominant party enjoys? In Table 12, figures are presented which indicate the percentage of seats won by the Democrats in suburban House districts during the 1960s and give similar indications of Democratic House strength or weakness in the other three types of districts.[18]

The data underscore several points that are exactly as would be expected. In the North, the urban districts are the most solidly Democratic; the rural districts are the most Republican. In the South, the rural districts remain a bastion of Democratic strength. But the suburban districts in the North, which in 1962 were fairly heavily Republican, were by the end of the decade more closely balanced between the parties. And the small number of suburban House districts in the South were, by the late 1960s, showing a pronounced Republican trend.

The result is that considerable uncertainty surrounds the electoral patterns that the new suburban districts are likely to foster in the 1970s. If

17. The criteria used to classify House districts for each election are identical to those used in Tables 10 and 11. Districts which were redistricted during the two years immediately before a given election year are excluded from the analysis for that election year.

18. Caution should be used in comparing the percentage of seats won by the Democrats in mixed and rural districts in 1966 and 1968 with the Democratic percentages in those two types of districts in 1962 and 1964. The basis for classifying districts in those categories changed somewhat between 1964 and 1966. The practical effect of the change was to increase the number of mixed districts and reduce the number of rural districts. See the notes to Tables 10 and 11 for an explanation of the methods of classification used.

TABLE 12
Percentage of House Seats Won by the Democrats
in South and Non-South, 1962–1968
(By type of district)

Type of House District[a]	Non-South							
	1962		1964		1966[b]		1968[b]	
	%	N	%	N	%	N	%	N
Suburban	39.6	(48)	46.5	(45)	43.0	(51)	47.0	(51)
Urban	79.8	(89)	81.7	(82)	80.8	(89)	80.3	(89)
Mixed	42.3	(64)	52.7	(53)	42.9	(91)	39.6	(91)
Rural	36.7	(128)	57.2	(112)	31.5	(70)	31.4	(70)

	South							
	1962		1964		1966[b]		1968[b]	
	%	N	%	N	%	N	%	N
Suburban	50.0	(2)	50.0	(2)	40.0	(5)	20.0	(5)
Urban	85.7	(14)	100.0	(13)	78.5	(14)	71.6	(14)
Mixed	66.6	(15)	64.3	(13)	75.2	(32)	75.2	(32)
Rural	95.5	(67)	93.2	(58)	86.8	(45)	84.6	(45)

a. The criteria used for classifying House districts are identical to those used in Tables 10 and 11.

b. Caution should be used in comparing the percentage of seats won by Democrats in mixed and rural districts in 1966 and 1968 with the percentage of Democratic seats won in those two types of districts in 1962 and 1964. The basis for classifying districts in those two categories changed somewhat between 1964 and 1966. The practical effect of the change was to increase the number of mixed districts, and reduce the number of rural districts after 1964.

the voting trends of the late 1960s are a partial guide to the future, party control of the House seats of suburban districts in the North may be fairly closely balanced. Those contests will also probably be more potentially competitive than those for House seats in the big-city districts, though not necessarily more competitive than those in mixed districts or even rural districts in the North. In the South, the creation of a significant number of new suburban constituencies may be one more factor fueling the Republican challenge to the traditional Democratic hegemony in the region's congressional elections.

The net impact of the new redistricting on the fortunes of the two parties in the House is far from clear. To the extent that potentially close suburban constituencies displace normally solidly Democratic urban House seats, the GOP stands to record some gains. But the other type of district in the North whose representation will be reduced most sharply is rural, and, as we have seen, in 1966 and 1968 two of every three of these seats were Republican.

On balance, the Republicans will probably gain from redistricting in the South. But, throughout the country, the new redistricting will add one more general cause for uncertainty. The odds are that about thirty new suburban House constituencies will be created in 1971 and 1972. In quite a number of these districts, there will be no established incumbent standing for reelection. In the new districts, therefore, another element of uncertainty will be introduced, and, to the extent that the new congressmen elected in 1972 can then establish themselves in those districts, the House contests fought in 1972 may be of greater than average importance.

REAPPORTIONMENT, THE HOUSE,
AND THE PROBLEM OF POLICY OUTCOMES

Of all the questions relating to the probable effects of reapportionment and redistricting on the House, perhaps the most intriguing and important, as well as the most difficult, is what consequence redistricting is likely to have for the kinds of public policy decisions that emerge from the House. In the early 1960s, when redistricting for equal population under court sanctions was first implemented, there was considerable speculation that the new redistricting might make the House more "liberal" on domestic policy issues. Perhaps the most striking example of redistricting's working to the disadvantage of an established conservative leader in the House occurred in Virginia in 1966. There the Eighth Congressional District of Representative Howard W. Smith, the chairman of the powerful House Committee on Rules, was redistricted to include a sizable portion of Fairfax County, a suburb of Washington, D.C., where relatively liberal voters were numerous in the active Democratic primary electorate. In the July 12 primary Smith lost Fairfax County decisively. He failed to make up the difference in the more conservative rural areas he had been accustomed to representing. And in the district as a whole, he lost to his opponent, state delegate George C. Rawlings, Jr., a relatively liberal Virginia Democrat, by 645 votes. (The effect on the political complexion of the House was lessened, however, when the district elected a relatively conservative Republican to the House in the November general election.)

The broader question of the overall policy consequences of redistricting prompted several scholarly analyses in the 1960s which attempted to determine whether new districting would in fact make the House more liberal. These studies, however, produced little evidence to indicate that the establishment of equal district populations would automatically liberalize the House. Professor Andrew Hacker, for example, employed a weighted-vote analysis, which adjusted the value of each member's vote on important roll calls to reflect the actual population of his district. He concluded that, in the Eighty-seventh Congress (1961/1962), a number of important items of liberal legislation would not have fared markedly better under an equal population apportionment. Listed below are three examples:[19]

		Actual Vote	Weighted Vote
1961 Expansion of the House Committee on Rules			
	For	219	211
	Against	214	222
1962 Proposal to Create a Department of Urban Affairs			
	For	156	145
	Against	271	282
1962 Farm Bill			
	For	212	183
	Against	222	251

In a similar weighted-vote analysis of roll call votes in the Eighty-eighth Congress (1963/1964), William L. Goss also concluded that the change stemming from equal population redistricting would not be great. The pattern of two important votes, when subjected to the weighted-vote analysis, was as follows:[20]

		Actual Vote	Weighted Vote
1964 Civil Rights Act			
	For	290	289
	Against	130	131
1964 Economic Opportunity Act			
	For	226	226
	Against	185	185

19. Andrew Hacker, *Congressional Redistricting* (Washington: the Brookings Institution, 1963), p. 90.

20. William L. Goss, "Measuring the Impact of Congressional Reapportionment," University of Indiana, unpublished manuscript.

It is possible, of course, that analyses of this type may understate the actual change that such redistricting would make over time. For one thing, to assess the impact of redistricting, considerably finer breakdowns of the policy dimensions of specific issues than "liberal" or "conservative" may be required. The forthcoming redistricting of 1971 and 1972 is going to bring about a substantial increase in suburban representation in Congress. Even the "liberal-conservative" analyses that were undertaken in the 1960s suggest that the effects of redistricting may be greater with respect to some types of legislation than to others. Note that one of the pronounced changes reflected in Professor Hacker's analysis of the Eighty-seventh Congress occurred on the 1962 Farm Bill vote. On this issue, where a pronounced urban-rural cleavage was manifested in the vote, districts that were redrawn to reflect population equally might have made a substantial difference.

The consequences of the new redistricting also may vary according to whether an issue fosters unity or division within the suburbs. Over the nation as a whole, there are enormous internal divisions in what are loosely called the suburbs. As Michael N. Danielson has pointed out in his study of commuter legislation, the most pronounced characteristic of suburban representatives often has been the fragmentation of their interests and objectives.[21]

Yet rural areas, which in the past often collaborated in Congress for their mutual advantage, were diverse also. In addition to the fact that they were rural, most shared a fundamental role as producers of primary goods, especially foodstuffs. And for many years they sent to Washington representatives who were able to work together to secure a wide range and variety of benefits for their constituents.

One common strand that loosely unites many suburbanites today is that they are the consumers, or the potential consumers, of an extensive range of services. In education, transportation, recreational facilities, pollution control, and other areas, the suburban role as a consumer is clear.[22] And in time it should prove worthwhile to trace the response of the new Congress in the 1970s to proposed federal programs in these areas.

As has been pointed out, representatives from the central city areas and the suburbs, combined, will account for about two-thirds of the

21. Michael N. Danielson, *Federal-Metropolitan Politics and the Commuter Crisis* (New York: Columbia University Press, 1965), pp. 195–198.

22. This discussion of the producer role of rural districts and the consumer role of suburban districts is drawn from Richard Lehne, *supra,* n. 12, p. 354.

membership of the House after 1972. One very important question affecting policy outcomes, therefore, will be whether an issue is one on which urban and suburban representatives share a common interest, or whether the issue is one where the basic objectives of urban and suburban constituencies conflict.

Issues that promote urban-suburban cleavage are not difficult to imagine and appeared frequently in the 1960s. Should there be more money for public welfare expenses (a special concern of the cities), or should there be more funds for education (of special interest in the suburbs)? And what of school busing, housing policies, crime control, or funds for urban renewal? On a wide range of issues, the potential for urban-suburban conflict is very clear. Frequently, the rural representatives that remain may also be aligned against the cities.

On certain other types of issues, however, suburbanites and urbanites may share a common interest. The building of mass transit systems in large metropolitan areas is one possible example. In 1970 new subways were being built in San Francisco and Washington, D.C., and were being planned in Atlanta, Baltimore, Los Angeles, Miami, Minneapolis/St. Paul, Pittsburgh, and Seattle. Extensions of existing rail transit systems were being built or planned in five other cities; and subway construction was being considered in Buffalo, St. Louis, Dallas, Houston, and Detroit. In all, transportation experts estimated that between twenty and thirty-six metropolitan areas in the United States could support urban rail transit.[23] If both suburban and urban voters wanted mass transit in the 1970s, the combined weight of urban and suburban representation in the new Congress would be likely to produce increasing federal funds for such projects over the decade.

Perhaps the greatest impact of redistricting on public policy depends upon how the newly drawn boundary lines affect the fortunes of the two major parties. And the consequences of that, in turn, depend upon how the parties perceive and choose to exploit major potential issues. As we have seen, the probable effects of redistricting on the parties are by no means certain, especially since the new suburban seats themselves are likely to be less solidly dominated by one party than either northern urban seats or southern and northern rural seats (the three blocks of House seats that have been won disproportionately by Democrats or Republicans in the recent past). In any event, it is clear that both parties, in congressional elections as in presidential contests, will have to bid

23. *U.S. News and World Report*, May 25, 1970, pp. 48–49.

effectively for the votes in the suburbs or else lose control of the House of Representatives.

NEGRO CONGRESSMEN AND THE
HOUSE IN THE 1970S

During the 1960s the House of Representatives became somewhat more representative of the United States population as a whole in one important respect. An increasing number of Black congressmen were elected to the House. In the 1970s, this trend is certain to continue. As recently as 1960, only four United States congressmen were Black. Between 1962 and 1970, eight more Negroes were elected to the House (Table 13).

TABLE 13
NEGRO CONGRESSMEN, 1970

	Year First Elected	District
William L. Dawson[a]	1942	Ill. 1st (Chicago)
Adam Clayton Powell[b]	1944	N.Y. 18th (Harlem)
Charles C. Diggs, Jr.	1954	Mich. 13th (Detroit)
Robert N. C. Nix	1958	Pa. 2nd (Philadelphia)
Augustus F. Hawkins	1962	Cal. 21st (Los Angeles)
John Conyers	1964	Mich. 1st (Detroit)
Shirley Chisholm	1968	N.Y. 12th (Brooklyn)
William Clay	1968	Mo. 1st (St. Louis)
Louis Stokes	1968	Ohio 21st (Cleveland)
George Collins	1970	Ill. 6th (Chicago)
Ronald V. Dellums	1970	Cal. 7th (Oakland, Berkeley)
Parren J. Mitchell	1970	Md. 7th (Baltimore)

Source: Congressional Quarterly Weekly Reports; and various issues of the Congressional Directory (Washington: U.S. Government Printing Office).
a. Replaced by Ralph Metcalf in January 1971.
b. Replaced by Charles B. Rangel in January 1971.

All of the current Negro members of the House come from northern big-city districts, and all are Democrats. They have usually first been elected when a new predominantly Negro district has been created or when the population in an old racially mixed district approaches or exceeds being 50 percent Negro. As has been shown, in 1970 there were more than 12 million Negroes living in the nation's central cities—about 2.6 million more than in 1960. As a result, the number of congressional districts with Black majorities is almost certain to be larger in 1972 [24] and will grow further as the number of Negroes living in the cities increases. The odds are, therefore, that during the 1970s the number of Black congressmen will rise from the current twelve to close to twenty or more.

REDISTRICTING AND THE CURRENT
COMMITTEE CHAIRMEN IN THE HOUSE

One factor that often contributes to continuity rather than change in the House is not likely to be greatly affected by redistricting and reapportionment, however. Most of the present committee chairmen are not likely to be endangered by redistricting, if they choose to run again. About half (eleven of twenty-one) come from states where their party is currently in control of the state government. The others might face a hostile state legislature and governor at redistricting time, but several of them are from areas of their states which are strongholds for their parties. In the last general election in 1968, six of the incumbent committee chairmen were unopposed, and all but three won with more than 60 percent of the vote. Although the Republicans do not have a sizable block of unopposed House seats, the ranking Republican members of the House committees also generally come from districts that are safe for their party.

One or two Democratic committee chairmen might have to worry after the new redistricting, however. Congressman Samuel N. Friedel of Baltimore, the chairman of the Committee on House Administration, currently finds himself under increasingly sharp challenge from a Black Democratic primary opponent in a district where the Black portion of the population has been increasing. If he wins in the September 1970 primary, he will need sympathetic treatment in the new redistricting in Maryland if he is to stay in Congress much longer. Congressman Wayne N. Aspinall of Colorado, the chairman of the House Committee on Interior and Insular Affairs, always seems to win; but he has encountered several close general election contests in his district in the past. His margin in 1968 (54.7 percent) was not large, and the Colorado state government currently is in Republican hands. He also could be affected adversely by redistricting.[25]

24. In some cities, the number of House districts with Black majorities may be reduced somewhat if a conscious redistricting policy is to divide the predominantly Black areas of the city among several congressional districts having White majorities, rather than to create districts which are predominantly Black.

25. The other committee chairmen to poll less than 60 percent of the vote in their districts in 1968 were: John L. McMillan, of the District of Columbia Com-

REAPPORTIONMENT AND REDISTRICTING:
OTHER POSSIBLE EFFECTS

Most of the possible changes in Congress discussed thus far bear a fairly direct relationship to recent electoral and population trends. In any event, to the extent that the forecasts are in error, it should be reasonably easy to ascertain and measure the error. Yet other, more subtle changes may occur in Congress during the 1970s, and these changes, also, may take place at least in part because of reapportionment and redistricting. Any discussion of these possible changes must be frankly speculative, but, to the extent that they actually do materialize, they could well be some of the most interesting changes to be reflected in the Congress in the 1970s. They also could provide some intriguing avenues for congressional research after 1972.

Compared with the central-city and rural small-town electorates which they replace, the electorates in the new suburban districts are likely to be somewhat younger and better educated and to have a higher proportion of the work force in professional, managerial, and other white-collar employment. They are also likely to be more affluent and (compared with the rural small-town districts) less Protestant. The new constituencies will, in short, be more metropolitan; over time, these differences will probably be reflected in the characteristics of the congressmen which these districts send to Washington.

Several years ago Samuel Huntington commented on the relative absence of an exchange of leaders between Congress and the administration. He also stressed the lack of movement of leaders between Congress and what, in that earlier day, could still nonpejoratively be called establishment institutions—great national corporations, foundations, universities, large law firms. In addition, congressmen "were much more likely to come from rural and small-town backgrounds than (were) administration and establishment leaders." [26]

There were also striking differences in geographical mobility between congressmen and private and public executives. In 1963, "seventy-seven percent of the congressional leaders were living in their states of birth,

mittee, who received 58.3 percent of the vote in the Sixth District in South Carolina; and Richard H. Ichord, of the House Committee on Internal Security, who was reelected in the Eighth District in Missouri with 58.5 percent of the vote.

26. Samuel P. Huntington, "Congressional Responses to the Twentieth Century," in David B. Truman, ed., *The Congress and America's Future* (Englewood Cliffs, N.J.: Prentice-Hall, 1965), pp. 11–12.

while 70 percent of the administration leaders had moved out of their states of birth." [27] As a result, he suggested, administration and establishment leaders were more likely to be metropolitan in their policy attitudes, while congressmen were more likely to be "oriented toward local needs and small-town ways of thought." [28] "The country at large has become urban, suburban, and metropolitan. Its economic, social, educational, and technological activities are increasingly performed by huge national bureaucratic organizations. But on Capitol Hill the nineteenth-century ethos of the small-town, the independent farmer, and the small businessman is still entrenched behind the institutional defenses which have developed in this century to insulate Congress from the new America." [29]

As long as congressmen are elected in local constituencies, they are likely to be strongly attuned to local needs and local concerns. But the shape of the new census and the prospects for redistricting immediately ahead suggest that some of the characteristics of the Congress which Huntington emphasized in 1964 will be reduced in the 1970s.

Other changes also may flow from the forthcoming change in the electoral base of the House of Representatives. Party organization—and the nature of the congressman's relationships with his local party—may be different in many of the new suburban constituencies, especially in comparison with central-city House districts. In describing three suburban districts in metropolitan Chicago, Leo Snowiss has stressed that there is a "widely shared political ethic which is antagonistic to, if not incompatible with, organization politics." [30] "Republican township leaders have had to make extensive use of issue-oriented volunteer workers as the fundamental basis of party organization in the suburbs. The result in each of the three districts has been an organization which is non-materially oriented, undermanned, undisciplined if not disunited, decentralized, and easily penetrated by external elites from the primary electorates." [31] Candidates in these constituencies, he noted, often relied on nonpatronage volunteer workers in election campaigns and tended to be issue-oriented.[32]

By no means will all of the suburban districts be like the Chicago suburban constituencies described by Snowiss. There is certain to be enormous diversity among them. Yet, to the extent that the new suburban congress-

27. *Id.*, p. 13.
28. *Id.*, p. 15.
29. *Id.*, p. 16.
30. Leo M. Snowiss, "Congressional Recruitment and Representation," 60 *American Political Science Review* 631.
31. *Id.*, p. 631.
32. *Id.*, p. 634.

men come from districts with less cohesive local partisan organizations, the consequences for the patterns of congressional leadership recruitment, the campaign strategy, the choice of issues, and the actual behavior of congressmen in the House could be substantial. Compared with their big-city brethren, the new suburban legislators may be more independent of their party—at home and in Congress, itself.

These changes in the organizational base back home may, in turn, be reflected in changes in the patterns of selection and recruitment, and in the mode of operation of congressional staffs, especially the members' personal staffs. The number of congressional offices where House staff positions represent a few additional jobs at the disposal of a local political organization may be fewer. And staff selection criteria and the orientation of congressional staff members toward their jobs may be modified accordingly.

The consequences for the career patterns of congressmen themselves also may warrant study during the 1970s. A substantial number of suburban representatives are likely to be near the center of ideological and political gravity in their states. They will also come from areas which, in many cases, will cast the biggest block of votes in their states. For decades, big-city political leaders have been prominent potential contenders for statewide office. For example, Joseph Clark was elected to the Senate from Pennsylvania in 1956, after serving four years as mayor of Philadelphia. In the 1970s, suburban congressmen may increasingly be found presenting themselves as candidates for statewide office in their states. In his 1968 bid for reelection to the Senate, Clark was defeated by Richard Schweiker, the Republican congressman from Montgomery County in suburban Philadelphia. And in the 1970s there may be an increasing number of suburban senatorial or gubernatorial candidates such as Congressman Richard Ottinger, the Democratic senatorial nominee from suburban Westchester County, New York, in 1970.

In their broadest consequences, the forthcoming changes could have at least a marginal impact on the nature of the political relationships between the House and the Senate and between Congress and the executive branch. Scholars have long stressed the differences in the constituencies of the House, the Senate, and the executive branch, and the differing aggregations of interests to which these three institutions appeal and respond. In terms of a broad range of domestic political concerns that might loosely be labeled metropolitan, the Senate has often been more responsive than the House, and the executive branch, more responsive than the Congress.

The differing constituencies and institutional loyalties of the three bodies are still likely to lead to pronounced differences in their responses to many questions of public policy. But the net effect of the forthcoming redistricting and reapportionment for the House will probably be to lessen somewhat the gulf between the Senate and the House on questions of policy affecting metropolitan areas. It could also reduce very slightly the cleavage between the Congress and the presidency on such issues.

The new census and the court-enforced redistricting is going to alter the electoral base of the Congress substantially by 1972. It should be a fascinating topic for observation and for scholarly research, to determine how the Congress responds to these changes during the 1970s.

*   *   *

COMMENTARY by Charles O. Jones

If Milton Cummings had not gone into political science, I am sure he would have been a clock-maker. When he puts together a piece of research, every bit and piece is carefully set and meshed with every other piece. The only question is how long it will run—i.e., how much it will explain. Given the limits of the symposium format, Cummings could only do so much, so I judge this to be about an "eight-day-clock" essay. As usual, I hope he is working on perpetual motion, so that I can have all my questions answered.

The central purpose of this research is to analyze the probable trends and to speculate about the possible effects of congressional reapportionment and redistricting in the 1970s. This is obviously an enormous task—which is why I refer to Cummings's piece as an eight-day-clock essay. One must pick and choose among vast quantities of data and various types of analysis. After all, the real question is: What do reapportionment and one man, one vote, redistricting mean for political representation in a legislature? Cummings lays a foundation for answering that question by examining some of the variables that may possibly predict and explain changes in the policy behavior of legislators. He analyzes population trends, reapportionment among the states, redistricting within the states, consequences for the political parties, and competitiveness of districts. How do these affect the policy behavior of representatives in Congress? Though he discusses some possibilities, Cummings admittedly is less confident in his analysis of that question.

Complicating the analysis of the effects of reapportionment on behavior and policy is the institutionalization of Congress. It would not be quite so complex if representatives were meeting in some temporary convocation. But Congress has developed the most elaborate set of lawmaking mechanisms of any legislature in history. And as Cummings says, "many of the procedures, norms, and practices of the United States House and Senate tend to reduce the rate of change in the operations of Congress."[1] Thus, the fresh-faced urban or suburban California representative, replacing a tired old face from a declining coal region in Pennsylvania, finds an elaborate internal order in the House of Representatives that has developed over time to cope with the public business. So it is, then, that despite the growth in population and the consequent addition of fifteen representatives since 1950, California still had only one House chairmanship in 1970—held by George Miller, of the Committee on Science and Astronautics. Texas and Maryland led the states with four and three chairmen, respectively.

In general, House standing committee chairmen seemed to survive quite well during the decade of redistricting. Cummings takes note of the fact that Howard W. Smith of Virginia, chairman of the House Committee on Rules, lost his seat in the House as a result of redistricting changes. But the only other chairman who seemed to be so clearly affected by redistricting was Brent Spence of Kentucky, who found himself in Frank Chelf's district in 1962. Spence, who was 88 at the time, retired. Surely as remarkable as the Smith and Spence cases, however, is the fact that eight chairmen served their committees in that capacity throughout the 1960s. Further, of the fourteen chairmen who stepped down in that period, only four had been defeated in primary elections and one, in the general election. Of these, only Smith of Virginia seemed to have lost primarily because of redistricting.[2]

This is not to say that, because Congress is an institution, reapportionment can have no effect on the House or on the policy behavior of its members. It is rather to suggest that the effects are extremely difficult to discern in the short run. And, though he doesn't say it in so many words, I think that is the thrust of what Cummings has to say, as he discusses the complications of various issues dividing or uniting suburban and core-city representatives.

1. Nelson W. Polsby has examined how certain of these practices have developed in the House of Representatives. See "The Institutionalization of the U.S. House of Representatives," 62 *American Political Science Review* 144–168.

2. Redistricting was certainly a factor, however, in other defeats—notably, that of Tom Murray in Tennessee in 1966.

Therefore, searching for immediate effects of reapportionment and re-districting on major policies is a questionable endeavor, since most of those discovered are likely either to be spurious or trivial. Nor, as Cummings rightly warns, should we reduce everything to that simpleminded liberal-conservative continuum, when most of what Congress deals with doesn't fit it. I would think we would want to concentrate our attention on the extent to which reapportionment and one man, one vote, redistricting affect institutional procedures and specific legislation. That means developing some measures of whether (and, if so, how) reapportionment and redistricting result in (or are major explanatory variables for) leadership change, procedural reform, party reorganization, or turning the corner in some major policy area.

The starting point for such analysis would logically seem to be those members who came to the House in the redistricting of the 1960s. With these members we have a basis for studying the longer-term effects of redistricting on the institution. What, for example, had happened to the "California Eight" and the "Florida Four"—the representatives picked up by those states as a result of the 1960 census? Have they been successful in getting reelected (a first order of business, if they are to have any influence)? What committee assignments have they had? Have they risen to positions of influence? Have they led attacks on the establishment? What legislation have they introduced, and with what success? How do they vote? What reforms have they proposed, and with what success?

Two of these questions can be answered quickly. They were highly successful in getting reelected—a tribute, perhaps, to the redistricting skills of their respective state legislatures. Eleven of the twelve were still in the House in 1970.[3] The one exception, Edward J. Gurney of Florida, voluntarily left the House to wage a successful senatorial campaign in 1968. Of the remaining eleven, ten were Democrats.

Their committee assignments are also easily compiled. As indicated in the accompanying chart, those members who made no shifts ranked in the middle of their committees (though Van Deerlin had risen to eighth on the important commerce committee). Those who shifted to the more important committees (armed services, appropriations, rules, ways and means), remained low-ranking. Others dealt in some of the cheaper properties (Post Office and Civil Service, District of Columbia, veterans' affairs) and moved up rather quickly. It appears that by 1970 these eleven members were working their way into the decision-making apparatus in the House, but it is also apparent that the process is ever so slow.

3. George E. Brown of California would not return in 1971, however. He gave up his seat to run unsuccessfully in the California senatorial primary in 1970.

COMMITTEE POSITIONS OF BONUS REPRESENTATIVES
FROM CALIFORNIA AND FLORIDA

	Shifts Among Committees	Additions of Committees	Recent Assignments and Rank
California			
Leggett (D)	1	1	Armed Services (16/23)* Merchant Marine & Fisheries (17/21)
Edwards (D)	1	1	Judiciary (10/20) Veterans' Affairs (11/14)
Talcott (R)**	1	—	Appropriations (16/21)
Hawkins (D)	—	1	Education & Labor (10/20) House Administration (11/14)
Brown (D)	1	—	Science & Astronautics (10/18) Veterans' Affairs (7/14)***
Wilson (D)	2	—	Armed Services (15/23) Post Office & Civil Service (8/15)***
Hanna (D)	—	1	Banking & Currency (11/21) Merchant Marine & Fisheries (16/21)
Van Deerlin (D)	—	—	Interstate & Foreign Commerce (8/21)
Florida			
Pepper (D)	1	1	Rules (8/10) Internal Security (2/5)
Fuqua (D)	—	1	Science & Astronautics (9/18) District of Columbia (7/14)***
Gibbons (D)	1	—	Ways & Means (15/15)

* Indicates rank in party (e.g., 16th of 23).
** Serves as a regional minority whip.
*** A subcommittee chairman on this committee.

Now we are prepared to examine precisely what these members have done and whom they represent. Then we can extend the analysis to include other members whom we can identify as bonus representatives or redistricting beneficiaries. Obviously that analysis goes beyond the scope of

these comments but does illustrate what must be done if we are to discover long-term effects of reapportionment and redistricting on institutions
and policy. Even with this type of study at hand, however, one should
proceed cautiously unless some means can be found to determine what
might have happened if there had been no reapportionment (as there was
not in 1920—a case never examined carefully, to my knowledge) or no one
man, one vote, decision by the Supreme Court.

And that brings me to one minor disagreement with Cummings's
analysis. He makes the point, as have many others, that the Senate has
been more responsive to urban or metropolitan interests than the House
of Representatives. Redistricting to follow population trends in the 1970s
will probably "somewhat lessen the gulf between the Senate and the
House on policy questions affecting metropolitan areas."

I am bothered by that statement for several reasons related either to the
question mentioned above of "what might have happened if . . ." or to
the problem of determining just what responsiveness means. First, if it is
true that the Senate is more responsive (a proposition yet to be demonstrated, in my opinion), surely that casts some doubt on the importance of
redistricting as a determinant of responsiveness to metropolitan interests.
The Senate has not been redistricted since 1787. One man, one vote, resulting in "responsiveness" to our needs has been an article of faith with
some democrats despite—perhaps because of—the lack of evidence on the
matter. Second, if the House does accurately reflect population trends, one
would expect more representation from suburban areas. Cummings's
estimates confirm these expectations. Most people believe that the most
severe problems requiring federal action are in the core cities, however.
Based on Cummings's data on population trends and districting probabilities in 1972, one could as easily make the case that the House will be less
responsive to core-city problems, but perhaps more responsive to metrop-
olis-wide interests and opinions.

Finally, and most fundamentally, I think that the whole question of
House versus Senate responsiveness to urban or metropolitan interests
remains to be studied. Like representation, responsiveness is a very complicated concept. It frequently is interpreted in terms of a liberal-conservative continuum that hides as much as it reveals. Being responsive to public
problems in metropolitan areas today may mean no action at all because
those involved simply cannot find a basis for compromise. For example,
the House was criticized for failing to pass a bill giving federal aid to
education during the 1950s. But the issue had religious, racial, economic,

and strong political dimensions—all of which were well represented in the House Committee on Education and Labor. Should the committee be criticized for not being responsive? Or for being too responsive to the many groups involved? In 1964 the House passed the Economic Opportunity Act with little or no criticism and virtually no amendments. Was the House being responsive? Or should it have been criticized for failing to study the issue more carefully in order to avoid the administrative and political horrors that later occurred in trying to implement that legislation? I remain optimistic about our ability to develop some measures for comparing House and Senate action that will provide a basis for generalizing about responsiveness to public needs. But, unless I am reading the wrong literature, no such measures are being employed at present.

One final bit of tinkering with this timepiece. Congress, particularly the House of Representatives, appears to be on the verge of some important changes in leadership and procedures. Most of these appear to be the result of responsiveness by political parties to new demands. Speaker John W. McCormack is stepping down, and Carl Albert has become the first speaker born in this century. His new floor leader faces a party a majority of whom have been elected since 1960 and a large percentage of whom belong to the Democratic Study Group. Both parties in the House have study groups evaluating possible changes in the seniority system (including setting age limits for members). And the House passed a reorganization bill in 1970—accepting an amendment to allow recorded teller votes in the Committee of the Whole.

These changes may have an important impact on legislation during the 1970s. To what extent can they be traced to reapportionment and redistricting? Are these changes sponsored by members who reflect the population trends of the 1960s? And what is the likely effect of such changes in coping with the problems of a properly apportioned America? If it can be demonstrated that redistricting in particular has influenced these changes, then perhaps, as some have asserted, the one man, one vote, decisions of the Supreme Court will have been of tremendous significance for American public policy.

Professor Cummings has provided us with an excellent review and analysis of what changes we may expect in our one man, one vote, congressional districts in the 1970s. He also has offered some guidelines for studying the political effects of this reordering of districts. He has set the charge for scholars in the 1970s. With data already available from the 1960s, it should be possible in the next decade thoroughly to examine the impact of apportionment and redistricting on public policy and therefore to contribute significantly to a theory of political representation. Indeed, by the end of the decade we may even be able to measure the effects of one version of "all the power to the people."

7

CONGRESSIONAL REPRESENTATION: THEORY AND PRACTICE IN DRAWING THE DISTRICTS

David R. Mayhew

For that small public audience concerned with congressional districting, the 1960s was a decade of permanent revolution. The first series of changes was brought about by the decennial reapportionment of 1960, in which twenty-five states gained or lost congressional representation. Twenty-one states (including North Dakota, which did not have to do so) responded to the census returns by drawing new lines for use in 1962; five others added at-large seats. Then came *Wesberry* v. *Sanders*[1] in 1964. Two years later twenty-nine states—including twelve that had redistricted in 1961 or 1962—had anticipated or followed the court decision by preparing new lines in time for use in the election of 1966.[2] Seventeen states, including thirteen that had redistricted at least once before in the decade, drew fresh districts for use in 1968. The states remapped for 1968 included seven of the ten largest in the country; the districts affected numbered more than two hundred.[3]

There was more to come. On April 7, 1969, the Supreme Court struck down districting statutes in New York[4] and Missouri,[5] the latter be-

Because relevant new information is coming in fast, it should be said that this article was completed before the 1970 elections and before digestible 1970 census returns became available.

1. 376 U.S. 1 (1964).

2. The foregoing figures were gathered from "Special Report: Congressional Redistricting," *Congressional Quarterly Weekly,* September 16, 1966, pp. 2003–2139.

3. The figures for 1967 and 1968 were gathered from *Congressional Quarterly Weekly* reports on the separate states during those years.

4. *Wells* v. *Rockefeller,* 89 S.Ct. 1234 (1969).

5. *Kirkpatrick* v. *Preisler,* 89 S.Ct. 1239 (1969).

cause it had produced districts with an unjustified maximum population variance from mathematical equality of 3.1 percent. Further line-drawing ensued, most notably in New York.[6] One estimate is that the 1970 decennial reapportionment will alter the size of congressional delegations in sixteen states;[7] the new census returns will provoke further boundary changes within states almost everywhere. By 1974 there may exist congressmen who have served five consecutive terms and represented five "different" districts. There are congressmen who do not find that prospect an inviting one. In the words of an Illinois Republican, "[T]hese decisions have resulted in chaos in this country. . . . Surely local counties ought to have some idea of wherein they lie and who represents them in the Congress. . . . Somewhere this has to stop." [8]

Yet, surely one important phase of the revolution is now over. That is, the *Wesberry* decision is now irreversible; argument will continue about its precise mathematical charge, but not about its essential validity. The districts drawn for the 1970s will be, by some rigorous definition, equal in population size. This much is clear. But to require only numerical equality is to leave unmasked and unanswered a good many other questions. It may be in order for both scholars and public servants to engage in some hard thinking about the whole subject of congressional representation before district lines are frozen into law for the 1970s. The subject is a timely one; probably the most salient feature of American politics today is, as Herbert Kaufman writes, a widespread "quest for representativeness." [9]

The analysis below, a treatment of theory and practice in congressional districting, will be divided into three parts: a formal statement, for the record, of constraints that will bind state legislatures as they draw congressional lines in the foreseeable future; a discussion of different theoretical ends that can be sought by legislatures working within the specified set of constraints; and a discussion of the actual districting practices of legislatures and the consequences of those practices. The focus will be solely on the delineation of congressional districts; that is, no attention will be

6. One early estimate was that invocation of the *Kirkpatrick* standard would induce as many as thirty-two states to redraw before 1970. *Congressional Quarterly Weekly,* April 11, 1969, p. 503. In fact, only a few took action during this latest round.

7. *Congressional Quarterly Weekly,* October 31, 1969, pp. 2154–2156.

8. The comments were made by Congressman William L. Springer. *Congressional Record* (daily ed.), 91st Cong., 1st Sess., 1969, CXV, H3346.

9. "Administrative Decentralization and Political Power," 29 *Public Administration Review* 5.

given to the somewhat different political processes and theoretical problems involved in the drawing of state legislative districts.

CONSTRAINTS

The following rules—the products of constitutional law, statute, or custom—will guide legislators as they ply their trade in coming years.

ALL DISTRICTS WITHIN A STATE MUST BE EQUAL IN POPULATION. Just how equal we do not yet know. The odds are that all deviations from absolute equality not stemming from respect for local political boundaries will be treated by the courts as intrinsically suspect.[10] And it is not likely that the following of local boundaries will allow much leeway, either. In judging permissible deviations, the courts are armed with a remarkably flexible standard. The legislatures are in something like the unenviable plight of Zeno's athlete who could never cross the finish line because there was always a theoretical distance between himself and his goal. Litigation will therefore continue. If states are held to the mathematics of *Kirkpatrick* v. *Preisler* (the Missouri case) the equality criterion will be stringent indeed—far more stringent, in fact, than the criteria applied in either Canada[11] or Great Britain,[12] both of whose parliamentary elections produce governments, as well as assembly majorities.

ALL CONGRESSMEN MUST BE ELECTED FROM THEIR OWN SEPARATE DISTRICTS. That is, in the future there will be no multi-member or at-large districts. Back in the early 1840s there was still a possibility that House elections would go the way of the electoral college; a number of states, for reasons of partisan advantage, insisted upon electing their congressmen on statewide slates rather than from districts. Congress imposed a single-district

10. This was the reasoning applied to state legislative redistricting in *Reynolds* v. *Sims,* 377 U.S. 533 (1964). *Drum* v. *Seawell,* 250 F. Supp. 924 (1966), supplies an example of unjustified deviation in the drawing of congressional lines: "The conceded rationale of the legislature to protect incumbent congressmen by placing them in different districts and by changing the existing districts as little as necessary to bring the plan within presumed minimum acceptable percentages causes us to conclude that the plan does not come 'as nearly as practicable to equal population.'"

11. Canadian constituencies may vary in population up to 25 percent above or below the average district size in each province. Norman Ward, "A Century of Constituencies," 10 *Canadian Public Administration* 117. "It is still true that urban seats are larger than rural, a fact clearly acceptable to Parliament" (p. 121).

12. British boundary commissions give considerable weight to local political boundaries, community ties, historical continuity, and communications difficulties. The largest British constituencies include over three times as many voters as the smallest. Scotland and Wales are persistently overrepresented. Vincent E. Starzinger, "The British Pattern of Apportionment," 41 *Virginia Quarterly Review* 321–341.

requirement in 1842. In succeeding decades House members were occasionally chosen at large, and with impunity, but statewide election came to be looked upon as a deviation from the norm rather than a possible norm itself. Congress discontinued its statutory ban in 1929 but reinstated it in 1968.[13] The new law is simply a codification of custom. The Supreme Court, for its part, has raised no objection to the principle of single-district elections. The one man, one vote, pronouncement, could quite reasonably have provoked a rehashing of old arguments about proportional representation, but, in its rhetoric as well as its rulings, the Court has followed Anglo-American tradition rather than Continental logic.

EACH STATE MUST DRAW NO MORE AND NO FEWER DISTRICTS THAN THE NUMBER AWARDED IT UNDER THE FEDERAL APPORTIONMENT FORMULA. Here the important point is that state quotas are geared to the size of the House. Since 1913 each district has contained, in theory, 1/435 of the population of the total roster of states. (In the small states, of course, districts have commonly been a good deal smaller or larger than the principle would suggest.) The House survived Alaskan and Hawaiian statehood without increasing its membership, and there are no signs that the level will be raised in the near future. The 1960 census produced districts with an average population of about 410,000; after 1970 the figure will go to about 471,000.[14] How one congressman can serve nearly half-a-million constituents is a question for which there is no ready answer. Nine countries belonging to the United Nations have smaller populations.

EACH DISTRICT MUST BE CONTIGUOUS. "A contiguous district is one in which a person can go from any point within the district to any other point without leaving the district."[15] The constraint here is one of custom, reinforced in some cases by state law. It is true that bodies of water have occasionally stirred controversy. Current districts straddle San Francisco Bay and the Straits of Mackinac, and there has been spirited debate over the problem of which section of Brooklyn should be joined with Staten Island. But as a general matter the contiguity rule is inviolable; in recent decades, at least, there have been no congressional districts shaped like Pakistan or Prussia, and there are not likely to be any in the future.

NO DISTRICT MAY CROSS STATE LINES. This rule, an obvious if not a trivial one, completes the set. There are places where state lines could sensibly be crossed; for example, the Delmarva Peninsula, which includes parts

13. U.S., *Statutes at Large,* 81, 581. The earlier statutes and practices are discussed in Joel F. Paschal, "The House of Representatives: 'Grand Depository of the Democratic Principle'?" 17 *Law and Contemporary Problems* 281–282.

14. *Congressional Quarterly Weekly,* October 31, 1969, p. 2154.

15. "Reapportionment," 79 *Harvard Law Review* 1284.

of Delaware, Maryland, and Virginia, is of about district size and is geographically and demographically a discrete unit. But the subject is closed.

It is safe to predict, then, that the districts of the 1970s will be: equal in population, intrastate, and contiguous. Each will harbor nearly half-a-million constituents, and each will be the preserve of a lone congressman. These guidelines may appear restrictive, but in fact they leave legislatures considerable room to maneuver. As long as the legislatures maintain control over district *shape,* they will still be able to draw lines to achieve any of a number of alternative ends. The Court's equality standard does not offer deterministic solutions,[16] and, from the standpoint of representative theory, it is fortunate that it does not. For the Supreme Court, like the legendary hedgehog, "knows one big thing": namely, that citizens' votes should be counted equally. But there are a number of other things to know about representation, many of them having to do with systemic consequences rather than with citizen equality.[17] There is, for example, the question of the relation between districting and the workings of the political parties.[18] The following section of this paper will deal with three theoretical goals that still can be sought, after *Wesberry,* in the drawing of congressional lines. The first of these, *compactness,* has probably been given as much thought and emphasis as it deserves; the others, *competition* and *community,* have been given rather less than they deserve.

THEORIES

COMPACTNESS. How, indeed, should districts be shaped? It has become an almost reflexive American response that they should be compact. The

16. As Robert G. Dixon, Jr., has argued, "For courts to limit their concern to bare population equality would be to build a reapportionment edifice of judicial bricks without straw." *Democratic Representation* (New York: Oxford University Press, 1968), p. 458.

17. Justice Felix Frankfurter drew attention to the many facets of the problem: "Apportionment, by its character, is a subject of extraordinary complexity, involving —even after the fundamental theoretical issues concerning what is to be represented in a representative legislature have been fought out or compromised—considerations of geography, demography, electoral convenience, economic and social cohesions or divergencies among particular local groups, communications, the practical effects of political institutions like the lobby and the city machine, ancient traditions and ties of settled usage, respect for proven incumbents of long experience and senior status, mathematical mechanics, censuses compiling relevant data, and a host of others." *Baker* v. *Carr,* 369 U.S. 323 (1962).

18. As Donald E. Stokes has pointed out, the vast body of literature on parties is "rarely connected to the concept of representation." "Political Parties in the Normative Theory of Representation," in J. Roland Pennock and John W. Chapman, eds., *Representation* (New York: Atherton Press, 1968), p. 150.

term may be found on the statute books of a large number of states. For a brief period the requirement was given recognition in Washington; Congress added a compactness standard to federal law governing congressional districting in 1901,[19] then excised it in 1929. (No one ever enforced it.) In recent decades Congressman Emanuel Celler has invested considerable time and energy in an unsuccessful effort to have it reinstated.[20] The compactness principle has attracted vocal support. A special committee of the American Political Science Association gave an endorsement in 1951.[21] It is widely believed in newspaper editorial rooms that the adequacy of a districting plan can be tested by gauging the regularity or irregularity of lines on a map.[22]

Until recently compactness had not been very precisely defined. Celler, dealing with the concept in 1952, wandered off into nonspatial considerations: "As to the requirement of compactness, such elements as economic and social interests of an area, its topography, means of transportation, the desires of the inhabitants as well as of their elected representatives and finally the political factors should all be considered."[23] But in the 1960s, with the quickening of interest in districting, there came a brisk traffic in exact operational definitions. One compactness index hinges on "the relationship between the area of the district and the area of the smallest possible circumscribed circle."[24] Another is based on the ratio of the perim-

19. One account of why it was added was given at the time by Congressman William H. Ryan (D-N.Y.): "[T]hat word was put in in order to give the Democrats of the North a fair opportunity to be returned. The legislatures in the Northern States are all Republican, and if they were permitted to shoestring the districts, it would be impossible for the few Democrats from the Northern States you have to get here. It was put in by the Democrats on the committee, with the consent of the chairman of the committee, to show that he intended to be fair with the Northern Democrats." *Congressional Record,* 56th Cong., 2d Sess., 1901, vol. 34, pt. 1, 606.

20. The congressman has fought for other districting criteria as well, his last important legislative effort being a prolonged but ultimately fruitless one in the Ninetieth Congress. There is a discussion of districting standards in Emanuel Celler, "Congressional Apportionment—Past, Present, and Future," 17 *Law and Contemporary Problems* 268–275.

21. Report of a special American Political Science Association committee, "The Reapportionment of Congress," 45 *American Political Science Review* 153–157.

22. See, for example, the New York *Times* editorial "Gerrymander Forever!"— a reaction to New York's congressional district statute of 1968, February 27, 1968, p. 42.

23. *Supra,* n. 20 at 274.

24. Ernest C. Reock, Jr., "Measuring Compactness as a Requirement of Legislative Reapportionment," 5 *Midwest Journal of Political Science* 71.

eter of a district to the perimeter of a circle of equal area.[25] Another is built on the minimization of the sum of the differences between length and width of all districts in a state.[26] Still others invoke the non-geometric variable of population density, producing compact districts nestled around centers of settlement.[27] The general objective of these ventures is to supply equitable districting formulas that can be automatically implemented, that reduce or eliminate "the element of human discretion." [28]

Compactness, as a districting end, has seldom been bolstered by elaborate theoretical rationales. The reason is doubtless that in the American context it has not needed any. It has drawn strength from the same assumption about representation that has animated the Court in its one man, one vote, rulings: namely, the assumption of atomistic individualism. Representation, by this test, is a simple and direct relation between individuals and government. Accordingly, proper districting consists in the removal of impediments in the way of a mechanical counting of discrete noses. Compactness, the virtues of which are customarily stated in negative terms,[29] is an efficient remover of one set of impediments—it prevents politicians from drawing odd-shaped districts to serve other and less hallowed ends. To be sure, compactness may itself, by accident, serve an attendant cause. It may often produce districts that are socially and economically homogeneous. But the connection is usually not made. Instead, considerations of district homogeneity or heterogeneity, of the stability of lines over time, and of party competition are normally written off as irrelevant. The compactness quest has great appeal; in the long run, if married to the American propensity to solve theoretical problems by converting them into technical puzzles, it may well prove irresistible.

COMPETITION. The compactness rule is, in fact, a simple answer to a question that demands a complex answer. To build compact districts is to ignore, among other things, the role of intermediary groups between citizen and government and the consequences of the operations of these groups. In American theory and practice the political party has been and

25. Joseph E. Schwartzberg, "Reapportionment, Gerrymanders, and the Notion of 'Compactness,'" 50 *Minnesota Law Review* 444.

26. Curtis C. Harris, Jr., "A Scientific Method of Districting," 9 *Behavioral Science* 221.

27. James B. Weaver and Sidney W. Hess, "A Procedure for Nonpartisan Districting: Development of Computer Techniques," 73 *Yale Law Journal* 292.

28. *Supra,* n. 26 at 219.

29. For example, "The principal purpose of requiring that districts be compact is as a check upon gerrymandering." *Supra,* n. 24 at 71.

remains the most important of these intermediary groups. And, as any politician knows, districting—after *Wesberry* no less than before—affects political parties. In particular, districts can be drawn either to inhibit or to facilitate party competition. Whether any given congressional district is "competitive" or not may be of interest only to ambitious local politicians; but whether cumulative line-drawing decisions produce a generally competitive or generally noncompetitive array of congressional districts is of great importance to the working of American national institutions.

Assume for a moment that party competition can be maximized or minimized (the point will be elaborated later). Why is competition important at the congressional level? There are at least four arguments that speak to the question:

1. *Party competition is good because it gives voters a "real choice" among candidates.* Here, as in the Court decisions, the emphasis is on citizen equality. All voters, the argument goes, ought equally to be given a "real choice" or an "effective choice" among congressional candidates. Voter choice can be meaningful only when candidates articulate opposing viewpoints and when electoral outcomes are not foreordained. Hence the very existence of districts that are "safe" for one party or another renders impossible the exercise of a right of citizenship. Accordingly, districts ought to be structured—to the greatest possible extent—so that Republicans and Democrats can compete evenly within them. It is even conceivable, albeit surpassingly unlikely, that the Supreme Court will be led by its own logic to prescribe such a requirement.[30]

How persuasive is the argument? Not very. It has the familiar deficiency of addressing itself entirely to the question of citizen equality and not at all to the problem of systemic consequences. But the validity of the equality argument itself is not intuitively obvious. We may come to agree, if we can cross unharmed the formidable theoretical minefield along the way, that voters ought to have an "effective choice" in the election of *governments;* theories of voter choice normally tie together governments and the entire constituencies that they serve. Thus we may expect to find —and applaud when we find it—close party competition in the election of American mayors, governors, and Presidents. But when governments are rooted exclusively (as in Britain) or partly (as in America) in assemblies

30. "If the principle behind the reapportionment cases is that every individual has a right to an equally effective vote, subject to the limitations imposed by retention of geographically based constituencies, the courts may be required to restrain abuses of districting as well as of apportionment. The tendency for gerrymandering to produce 'safe' districts diminishes the number of voters whose vote can affect the electoral outcome." "Reapportionment," 79 *Harvard Law Review* 1283.

whose members are chosen by district, the argument becomes blurred. In either the British or American case, the notion that elections of individual members of assemblies should necessarily be close strikes an odd chord. Why, indeed, should voters want them to be close? What is wrong, on the face of it, with having at least some congressmen like John Conyers, Jr. (Detroit) or H. Allen Smith (Los Angeles County) who apparently "speak for" overwhelming majorities of their constituents? No congressman, after all, governs by himself; each is merely a component member of a large assembly. It should be added that to abolish safe legislative districts would be to cast aside several centuries of Anglo-American electoral tradition; there may be other and better reasons for considering such a course, but the goal of equalizing voter choice hardly supplies by itself a sufficient reason.

2. *Congressmen from "competitive" districts behave differently than congressmen from "safe" districts.* Here the focus shifts to the consequences of electoral arrangements—consequences that can to some extent be empirically measured. If safe and competitive congressmen do behave differently, then it is relevant to consider in what proportions the electoral system should produce them.

What kinds of differences are there? First of all, the popular myth that electoral insecurity in and of itself induces congressmen to be "liberal," and that, conversely, electoral security induces or allows them to be "conservative," can be dismissed as no better than a popular myth. There is neither evidence to support it nor any obvious reason why it should be true.[31] District demography is a good predictor of congressional ideological hue; district electoral margin is not. Nor is there any conclusive evidence that electoral margin size is related (with other variables controlled) to congressmen's party loyalty in roll-call voting.[32] Again, district demography is the important consideration. Indiana Republicans and New Jersey Democrats vote regularly with their parties; most Massachusetts Republicans and Alabama Democrats do not.

31. Hence the subject has not attracted scholarly attention. Examples cannot prove the negative case but they can illustrate it. Safe congressmen of recent years have included men like William Colmer (D-Miss.), L. Mendel Rivers (D-S.C.), and Otto Passman (D-La.)—but also men like James Scheuer (D-Bronx), Emanuel Celler (D-Brooklyn), and Ogden Reid (R-Westchester County). Congressmen serving chronically marginal seats in the 1960s have included men like John Brademas (D-Ind.), William St. Onge (D-Conn.), and George Brown (D-Los Angeles County)—but also men like Joel Broyhill (R-Va.), Roy Taylor (D-N.C.), and W. R. Hull (D-Mo.).

32. The literature on the point is reviewed in Wayne Shannon, "Electoral Margins and Voting Behavior in the House of Representatives: The Case of the Eighty-Sixth and Eighty-Seventh Congresses," 30 *Journal of Politics* 1028–1045.

But there are other significant ways in which congressmen can differ. In a study of role cognitions, for example, Roger Davidson has found that marginal congressmen are much more likely than their safe colleagues to look upon themselves as delegates rather than trustees, and as district-oriented rather than nation-oriented. That is, in both style and focus, the orientations of the insecure are less "Burkean" than those of the secure.[33] Davidson does not go on to gauge the behavioral consequences of differences in role cognition. As good a guess as any would be that insecure non-Burkeans devote disproportionately more time and energy to "tending their districts" and less to the drudgery of legislation and oversight. Hence, as Davidson suggests, "In fact, the complicated division of labor that has evolved in the House would most likely be impossible if all the districts were poised at the electoral tipping-point." [34]

Most of the scholarship on competitive and safe congressmen is speculative rather than conclusive.[35] And, of course, no one can say with precision what a House teeming with marginal congressmen would be like because no one has ever seen one. But even in dealing with the House as it is, the effort to measure the effects of safeness and marginality raises theoretical as well as empirical problems. After a certain point it becomes necessary to challenge the assumption that the safe and the unsafe are comparably isolable and autonomous servants of their districts. The fact that a marginal congressman is more likely to be affected by the fortunes of parties and Presidential candidates arguably makes him a "representative" of a different kind. There will be more on this point later.

3. *Party competition produces turnover in House membership.* Here again the focus is on the effects of electoral arrangements. The discussion in this section will deal with the consequences of membership turnover in general, rather than with the special consequences deriving from changes in party balance.

The proposition that party competition produces turnover has an ob-

33. Roger H. Davidson, *The Role of the Congressman* (New York: Pegasus, 1969), chapter 4. The study is based on interviews with members of the Eighty-eighth Congress.

34. *Id.,* p. 142.

35. There is fragmentary evidence, for example, that, on civil rights and social welfare issues, safe congressmen surpass their competitive colleagues in the accuracy with which they perceive and register the attitudes of members of the district majorities that sustain them. The evidence, drawn from Survey Research Center data, is reported in Malcolm E. Jewell and Samuel C. Patterson, *The Legislative Process in the United States* (New York: Random House, 1966), pp. 441–444.

vious validity; some incumbents lose their seats to the opposition. It is no less obvious that turnover can occur for other reasons. Members can die, retire, or lose their nominations in primary elections. But, in fact, congressmen rarely lose their seats in primaries.[36] And in recent decades they have manifested an increasing reluctance to retire. The nineteenth-century tradition of Jacksonian turnover has given way to the twentieth-century congressional career.[37] The seeking of House careers has produced, probably in combination with other variables, a remarkable change in the nature of the House membership. In every Congress before 1900 more than 30 percent of the members were freshmen; in no Congress since 1938 have as many as 25 percent been freshmen. The trend line has continued irregularly downward, registering for the Ninety-first Congress, elected in 1968, a freshman membership percentage of 9.2—the lowest in American history.[38]

The decline in voluntary retirements (except those for reasons of age) sets party competition in sharp relief as an agent of congressional turnover. Hence in considering the virtues of competition it is necessary to consider the virtues of turnover. There are points on both sides.[39] The argument against turnover is essentially an argument for expertise. Congress needs experienced personnel, it is said, in order to hold its own in an era of complex issues, proliferating bureaucracy, and growing Presidential power. The shift in institutional emphasis from legislation to oversight in itself requires the presence of members who can watch over the executive establishment year after year.

The argument on the other side is that there is a trade-off between expertise and representativeness, that a man who stays too long in Washington loses touch with what is going on in the rest of the country.

36. The point is documented in Julius Turner, "Primary Competition as the Alternative to Party Competition in 'Safe' Districts," 15 *Journal of Politics* 197–210. Turner concluded that "the primary is not a successful alternative to two-party competition in most parts of the United States," p. 210. Only four congressmen lost their primaries in 1968; three were advanced in age, and one had suffered the misfortune, through redistricting, of being thrown into a district with another incumbent. *Congressional Quarterly Weekly,* October 4, 1968, p. 2668.

37. The case is made in H. Douglas Price, "The Congressional Career: Risks and Rewards" in Nelson W. Polsby, ed., *Congressional Behavior* (New York: Random House, in press) and in Nelson W. Polsby, "The Institutionalization of the U.S. House of Representatives," 72 *American Political Science Review* 144–168.

38. All the figures except the one for the Ninety-first Congress were taken from Polsby, "The Institutionalization," p. 146.

39. None of which hinges on a supposition that the House membership is getting older. Rather surprisingly, it is not. The average age in 1901 was 54; in 1931, 49; in 1969, 52.

President Eisenhower, himself a Cincinnatus figure, decried the very principle of careers in public office: "When a man makes a lifetime career of politics, too often he comes to think largely in political terms, with his actions geared primarily to the next election. To an extent, he goes apart from the everyday world, loses his sense of reality. . . . To be truly representative, our national legislative body needs a constant infusion of new blood from business, the professions, and from the workaday world where most of us live." Eisenhower would have barred congressmen and senators from serving for more than twelve years.[40] Along the same line, Samuel P. Huntington argues that the old kind of Jacksonian turnover now occurs only in a change of Presidential administrations: "A thousand new officials descend on Washington, coming fresh from the people, representing the diverse forces behind the new President, and bringing with them new demands, new ideas, and new power. Here truly is representative government along classical lines and of a sort which Congress has not known for decades. One key to the 'decline' of Congress lies in the defects of Congress as a representative body." [41]

4. *Party competition produces fluctuations in party balance in the House.* Here the focus is on turnover of a special kind. To assess the importance of party fluctuations is a difficult undertaking, and it will be advisable to begin by spending some time on the more basic question of what we mean when we speak of congressional representation. Of great use in this effort is the subtle analysis supplied by Hanna Pitkin in her recent book, *The Concept of Representation.*[42] Pitkin, while insisting that the term "representation" does have coherence, explores the many shadings of meaning that we assign to it. To abstract from her analysis is probably to do violence to it, but nonetheless, some of her categories and arguments will be put to use below. The case will be made that, when we think of congressional representation, we may be thinking of two rather different things.

Let us call the first of these "representation by reflection." The term may be used to capture the ways in which individual members of assemblies continuously "stand for" and "act for" [43] the public between elec-

40. Dwight D. Eisenhower, "Let's Make Government Work Better!" *Reader's Digest,* January 1967, pp. 63–64.

41. Samuel P. Huntington, "Congressional Responses to the Twentieth Century," in David B. Truman, ed., *The Congress and America's Future* (Englewood Cliffs, N.J.: Prentice-Hall, 1965), p. 17.

42. Hanna Pitkin, *The Concept of Representation* (Berkeley: University of California Press, 1967).

43. The terms are discussed and distinguished. *Id.* in chapters 4, 6.

tions. That is, the emphasis is on the inter-election period, rather than on anything that happens in elections or as a direct consequence of the electoral process itself. Assembly members are said to represent the public because of both what they are and what they do. Thus, in the first case ("standing for"), an assembly may be referred to as a mirror of the public, or, in John Adams's idealized version, "an exact portrait, in miniature, of the people at large. . . ." [44] An assembly is expected to record popular diversity. Thus the term "represent" may be used meaningfully in the following fashion: "Congress does not represent the country very well because it does not have enough Negroes or young people as members." But assembly members are expected to act as well as to exist; they are said to speak for or act for their constituencies, or even for the nation as a whole. For John Stuart Mill, a representative assembly was a place "where every person in the country may count upon finding somebody who speaks his mind, as well or better than he could speak it himself." [45] Relations between members and constituents are expected or assumed to be intimate and immediate. Thus we might say, using the Eisenhower argument: "Congressman Smith is not representing his people well; he's been in Washington altogether too long." Or we might say, "we won't know how the nation feels about the tax cut until Congress comes back from its Easter recess."

The idea of representation as a linkage supplied by individual assembly members is, of course, an old one. It held sway before the rise of mass parties and elective executives—or, more broadly, before the rise of elective governments. In America it was inscribed in eighteenth-century federal and state constitutions and consequently has more force today here than in any other Western nation. A premodern doctrine, not surprisingly it assigns no necessary role to political parties. The criteria it sets down for appraising quality of representation are irreducibly vague, but nevertheless meaningful. The general requirement is that a public should be, in some sense, "re-presented" in an assembly. Hence an appraiser may wish to examine turnover rates, or assembly demographic composition, or district size, or communications between members and constituents, or the positions of members on the Burkean delegate-trustee and local-national dimensions. [46] All these considerations and more are

44. Quoted *supra,* n. 42, p. 60.
45. J. S. Mill, *Considerations on Representative Government* (Chicago: Regnery, 1962), p. 111.
46. The Burkean categories have been employed in recent empirical studies: John C. Wahlke, et al., *The Legislative System* (New York: Wiley, 1962), Chapters 12, 13; Warren E. Miller and Donald E. Stokes, "Constituency Influence in Congress,"

important in the study of American legislatures. But representation by reflection is undeniably a rather weak form of linkage. Any modern nation that tried to channel its representation through eighteenth-century assemblies alone—that is, without elective executives or political parties— would probably collapse. The twentieth century looks to Caesar, not to the Senate.

Let us call the second of the categories "representation by authorization." Here the emphasis is on the election of governments rather than assemblies, and on what happens in elections rather than between them. A formal consequence of elections is that governments are empowered to rule, and we sometimes speak of the electoral transaction as one authorizing representation. Thus we might say: "Yes, of course. The Democrats will represent us for the next four years. They won the election." The time limit is important, for it adds accountability as a formal qualification to the original authorization.[47] So far nothing has been said here about the content of governmental policies. But we normally think of an election as an occasion not just for the production of a government but for the sending of messages. Thus we refer to "platforms," "instructions," and "mandates." It is not meaningless to say: "The Nixon Administration will represent us as long as it sticks to the Republican platform of 1968."

It is possible, in short, to build theories of representation that hinge on what happens in elections rather than what happens between them. The critical linking mechanism is usually the political party, which gains power, displays its abilities, and then is judged on its performance.[48] In such theories the independent actions of legislators doing their own continuous "reflecting" are something of an embarrassment.[49]

What has all this to do with the House of Representatives? The im-

---

in Angus Campbell, et al., eds., Elections and the Political Order (New York: Wiley, 1966), chapter 16; Davidson, The Role of the Congressman. Today, of course, Burke's categories are a good deal more relevant in America than in Britain.

47. "Authorization" and "accountability" conceptions of representation are discussed in Pitkin, supra, n. 42, chapters 2, 3.

48. See, for example, Committee on Political Parties of the American Political Science Association, Toward a More Responsible Two-Party System (New York: Rinehart, 1950), and Anthony Downs, An Economic Theory of Democracy (New York: Harper & Row, 1957). Or the spotlight may be more directly on presidential administrations, as in V. O. Key, Jr., The Responsible Electorate (Cambridge, Mass.: Harvard University Press, Belknap Press, 1966).

49. In parliamentary regimes, whether based on single-district or proportional representation, reflection becomes a quite secondary mode of representation. In Communist regimes both reflection and accountability disappear, leaving only the initial revolutionary authorization as a representative link.

portant point is that the House helps to supply both kinds of service—not just representation by reflection but also representation by authorization. The House began as an autonomous eighteenth-century body, but was quickly caught up in partisan and presidential electoral tides. We have become accustomed to viewing changes in congressional party balance as voter judgments. Even in midterm elections, which often come close to being no more than recordings of party identification,[50] "messages" can be imparted; thus, Gerald H. Kramer, in a study of House elections in midterm as well as presidential years, has found a strong relation between changes in real income and ups and downs in party fortunes.[51] Politicians and analysts find a good deal of meaning in midterm outcomes like those of 1874, 1894, 1910, and 1946.

But electoral tides clearly have more effect on Congress in the presidential years.[52] Over the decades there has been an impressive relation between party percentages registered for congressional and presidential candidates running on the same ticket.[53] Few things are more important to the conduct of national politics; the award of an increment of congressional seats to the party of an incoming President may properly be considered a component of a party's "authorization" to govern. In the words of V. O. Key, Jr., "By the partisan linkage of candidates, Democratic and Republican, from California to Massachusetts, from North Carolina to Montana, great decisions on the general direction of governmental action can be made by the voters."[54] After an election, the electoral tie "helps to account for the fact that the House is often more responsive than the Senate to presidential leadership."[55] The policy consequences are clear; the Congresses swept in with Woodrow Wilson,

50. Thus "from 1892 to 1960 the standard deviation of the two-party division of the mid-term congressional vote was 3.9 per cent; of the presidential-year congressional vote, 5.5 per cent; of the presidential vote, 8.2 per cent." Donald E. Stokes and Warren E. Miller, "Party Government and the Saliency of Congress," in Angus Campbell, *supra,* n. 46, p. 202. See also Barbara Hinckley, "Interpreting House Midterm Elections: Toward a Measurement of the In-Party's 'Expected' Loss of Seats," 61 *American Political Science Review* 694–700.

51. Gerald H. Kramer, "Short-term Fluctuations in U.S. Voting Behavior, 1896–1964" (paper presented at the 1968 meeting of the American Political Science Association).

52. Popular presidential majorities were, in Willmoore Kendall's words, "engrafted on" the earlier Madisonian system. "The Two Majorities," 4 *Midwest Journal of Political Science* 336.

53. Milton C. Cummings, Jr., *Congressmen and the Electorate* (New York: Free Press, 1966), chapter 1.

54. V. O. Key, Jr., *Politics, Parties, and Pressure Groups* (New York: Crowell, 1964), p. 545.

55. *Id.,* p. 558.

Franklin Roosevelt, and Lyndon Johnson are remembered for their important and irreversible legislative decisions.

Now, for the party pendulum to swing effectively, there must be marginal districts through which it can cut its swath. To be sure, safe congressmen often fall, and marginal ones heroically survive, but it is the close districts that account for a disproportionate share of party turnover. Table 1 shows, as an example, the relationship between Republican marginality in 1962 and Democratic congressional victories in 1964. Over the years some districts have remained chronically close; of the 105 districts Malcolm Moos listed as marginal (40–60) in 1950, about half (many with altered boundaries) were still competitive in the middle 1960s.[56]

TABLE 1
PARTY TURNOVER IN THE HOUSE AS A FUNCTION OF MARGINALITY

Republican percentage of two-party vote in districts carried in 1962	No. of districts	No. of districts switching to Democrats in 1964[a]	Percentage of districts switching to Democrats in 1964
50–54.9	37	18	48.7
55–59.9	56	20	35.7
60–64.9	50	9	18.0
65–69.9	24	0	0.0
70–74.9	10	1[b]	10.0
uncontested	1	0	0.0
Total	178	48	27.0

Source: "Complete Returns of the 1962 Elections by Congressional District," *Congressional Quarterly Weekly*, April 5, 1963, pp. 473–517; and "Complete Returns of the 1964 Elections by Congressional District," *Congressional Quarterly Weekly*, March 26, 1965, pp. 465–524. Connecticut, Michigan, and Wisconsin redrew their congressional lines between 1962 and 1964; the 1962 figures used here for these states are *Congressional Quarterly* estimates of 1962 Republican strength within the 1964 boundaries. *Congressional Quarterly Weekly*, Oct. 2, 1964, p. 2271, and Oct. 23, 1964, pp. 2496, 2511. In the few cases where Republicans won by-elections between 1962 and 1964 the by-election percentages are treated here as 1962 outcomes.

a. It should be noted that ten districts shifted in the other direction in 1964. The Republicans won seven seats in the Deep South, one each in California and Idaho, and one as a consequence of redistricting in Wisconsin.

b. The victim here was Congressman Thor C. Tollefson (6th, Washington), whose electoral percentage plummeted from 71.1 to 47.9.

56. Malcolm C. Moos, *Politics, Presidents and Coattails* (Baltimore: Johns Hopkins Press, 1952), pp. 25–26.

Congressmen with small margins lead precarious lives and build little seniority; their districts are doubtless shortchanged in the distributive decision-making in which the House engages. But it can be said, though it will be of little comfort to them, that the insecurity of the insecure serves a latent function; it makes national swings possible. And it is not obviously proper to judge marginals by the standards of representation by reflection. Especially when partisan turnover is heavy, we expect a fair number of congressmen to go to Washington, vote the party line for two years,[57] and then vanish forthwith into private life. Thus the Republican leaders of the Eightieth Congress, in passing the Taft-Hartley Act and the Twenty-second Amendment, could call upon the votes of a solid bloc of six Republicans from Philadelphia. In 1965 the Democrats, in launching Medicare, aid to education, and the Department of Housing and Urban Development, could count on the votes of a solid bloc of six Democrats from Iowa. Both the Philadelphians and the Iowans justly earned historical footnotes, but by some constituency tests their actions could be characterized as distortion rather than reflection. The country probably needs sporadic distortion of this sort in order to break legislative logjams and reach hard national decisions.

Partisan swings depend, then, upon the existence of marginal districts. Generally speaking, (a) the more marginal districts there are, the more partisan turnover there will be, and (b) the more partisan turnover there is, the more weight is assigned to representation by authorization rather than by reflection. And, as every politician knows, it is possible to draw districts so as to make them competitive. Given the existence of data on party registration, party identification, or past election returns, it is, in fact, almost as easy to draw a set of districts maximizing competition as it is to draw a set maximizing compactness. There is even a computer program that could be used to achieve this end. The Hale-Whitney program carves metropolitan areas into wedges; each district is "designed to be heterogeneous in nature—with the small tip end in center city and the remainder fanning out toward or into the suburbs."[58] (The State of New York would pose problems; there would have to be about thirty districts strung through Westchester County like cables through a

57. For accounts of the behavior of freshmen Democratic congressmen in the Eighty-first and Eighty-ninth Congresses, respectively, see David B. Truman, *The Congressional Party* (New York: Wiley, 1959), pp. 210–227; and Thomas P. Murphy, "The Extraordinary Power of Freshmen in Congress," *Trans-action*, March 1968, pp. 33–39.

58. "Computer Districting Programs Pose Policy Problems," *Congressional Quarterly Weekly*, November 5, 1965, p. 2242.

conduit.) It is possible, in short, to create a national districting system that would be very sensitive to the slightest changes in attitudes toward parties or presidential administrations. In landslide years the opposition party would be reduced to a parliamentary remnant.[59]

Before this image of district sensitivity is dismissed as fantasy, it will be useful to emphasize that the party linkage is a reasonably strong one and that the direct linkage between public and congressmen is rather weak. In the Stokes and Miller study of the 1958 congressional elections, 84 percent of all voters were Republicans or Democrats voting according to their party identifications.[60] But in districts where there was competition, only 54 percent of the voters claimed to have read or heard anything about either candidate. In districts where there were incumbents running, 39 percent of respondents knew something about the incumbents and 20 percent something about their opponents.[61] Even so, a representative assembly built on a maximization of competition would be rather an odd assembly. And, in fact, there is little likelihood that anyone will ever build one. It is in the interest of all the principals in congressional districting —states, parties, and politicians—to minimize competition rather than to maximize it. Hence, competitive districts are almost always the by-products of other decisions rather than the products of conscious choice.

But it may be time to inject into the matter an element of conscious choice. The reason is that congressional party turnover seems to be declining.[62] More specifically, national net partisan swings—the instruments of authorization[63]—seem to be declining in amplitude. Since the freezing of the House membership at 435, the average net partisan swing for the set of congressional elections in each decade has been as follows: 1914–1920, 43; 1922–1930, 38; 1932–1940, 40; 1942–1950, 45; 1952–1960, 22; and 1962–1968, 23. To extend the comparison back farther in time, it is necessary to abandon absolute values and switch to percentages. In the data prepared for Table 2 (data designed to get around the problems of chang-

59. Something like this happened in Connecticut in the 1950s. The state senate elected with Eisenhower in 1956 was 31–5 Republican; the senate elected with Governor Abraham Ribicoff in 1958 was 29–7 Democratic. Connecticut cataclysms are probably caused more by ballot form than by district marginality.

60. Stokes and Miller, "Party Government and the Saliency of Congress," in Campbell, *supra*, n. 46, p. 197.

61. Figures on knowledge of candidates, *Id.*, p. 204.

62. The point is made in Charles O. Jones, "Inter-Party Competition for Congressional Seats," 17 *Western Political Quarterly* 461–476.

63. Although the net swings catch almost everyone's attention, it should be said that district switches in the "wrong" direction sometimes help to define a mandate; thus, in 1964, Democratic congressional losses in Alabama added an important election footnote.

ing House size and third-party congressmen) "net partisan swing" for
any election is defined as the difference between (a) the percentage of total
House seats won in the election by the major party showing the greater
(or normally the only) improvement in membership percentage over the
previous election, and (b) the percentage of total House seats won by the
same party in the previous election. The value for each decade is the
average of values for all the biennial elections therein.

TABLE 2

HOUSE NET PARTISAN ELECTORAL SWINGS BY DECADE, 1872–1968[a]

	Average net partisan swing	Greatest single net partisan swing
1872–1880	12.9%	32.0%
1882–1890	11.0	22.1
1892–1900	12.6	33.4
1902–1910	7.5	14.4
1912–1920	9.7	15.5
1922–1930	8.8	17.1
1932–1940	9.3	22.2
1942–1950	10.5	17.2
1952–1960	5.1	11.1
1962–1968	5.2	10.8

a. Net partisan swing, for any election, is defined as the difference between the
percentage of total House seats won in the election by the major party showing
the greater (or only) improvement in membership percentage over the previous
election, and the percentage of total House seats won by the same party in the
previous election.

In Table 2, as in the earlier absolute figures, the 1950s and 1960s stand
as monuments of electoral placidity. Despite the Eisenhower and Johnson
landslides, and despite the opening of the South to partisan combat, average net turnover in these recent decades has been about half as high as
in previous decades. And the great sweeps of recent years hardly match
even those of the 1930s and 1940s. The 1966 net Republican gain of forty-
seven seats (a quarter to a third of them products of redistricting) and
the 1958 Democratic gain of forty-nine stand against the 1948 Democratic
total of seventy-five and the 1938 Republican total of eighty. Two recent
Presidents, Kennedy and Nixon, have entered office without causing
visible ripples in the congressional electorate.[64]

64. When Woodrow Wilson took office in 1912 with about the same percentage
as Nixon, the Democratic percentage of House membership shot up from 58.4 to
66.7.

The time series may be too short to permit the drawing of any significant conclusions. It could be that a combination of Keynesian economic techniques and an avoidance of large wars has produced a twenty-year interlude of relative political satisfaction and that a return to extreme economic or foreign adversity would quickly awaken dormant electoral furies. (One does rather wonder what kind of foreign adversity would be required.)

Yet it is possible that something else has been at work besides voter satisfaction; it is possible, namely, that congressmen have somehow become more insulated from presidential and partisan electoral currents. There is evidence to suggest that they have. Below, figures are presented on split election results in congressional districts in presidential years from 1920 through 1968.[65] The value for each election records the proportion of districts carried by a presidential nominee of one party and a House nominee of another:

1920	3.2%	1948	21.3%
1924	11.8%	1952	19.3%
1928	18.9%	1956	29.9%
1932	14.1%	1960	26.1%
1936	14.1%	1964	33.3%
1940	14.6%	1968	32.4%
1944	11.2%		

The figures show quite clearly that the proportion of split outcomes has been rising. Much of the increase is a consequence of recent ticket-splitting in the South. But there is an ascending curve for the North also; the values for the non-Confederate states have been higher in each of the last four elections than in any earlier election in the set.[66]

Again, the time series may be too short; one could write off the last few elections as exceptional. But there has probably been enough change here to allow speculation about what has been causing it. It may be that congressional incumbency, with the electoral services and other advan-

65. *Supra,* n. 53, p. 32. The 1968 figure was derived from material in "Complete Returns of the 1968 Elections by Congressional District," *Congressional Quarterly Weekly,* June 6, 1969, pp. 884–921. The percentages for 1920–1948 are based on data for incomplete sets of districts; presidential returns for this period are unavailable for from 13 to 91 districts.

66. Sectional proportions for elections from 1920 through 1964 are presented in *id.,* p. 34. In 1968, of the 329 non-Confederate districts 45 were simultaneously carried by Nixon and Democratic congressional candidates; 26 were carried by Humphrey and Republican candidates. "Complete Returns of the 1968 Elections by Congressional District," *Congressional Quarterly Weekly,* June 6, 1968, pp. 884–921.

tages it offers, has become a more potent political resource.[67] Possibly the coming of television has induced voters to rely more heavily upon candidate orientation than on party orientation in deciding how to mark their ballots. Or at the base of it may be a general weakening of party linkage—the product of media politics, efforts of reform movements, and the decay of party organizations. Individual states, on inspection, differ remarkably in their contributions to congressional partisan swings. Connecticut and Indiana, two of the heaviest contributors over the years, are also strongholds of traditional party regimes. The most laggard of the larger northern states is Massachusetts, in which only five districts have shifted from one party to the other since World War II (each only once, and one of them in the "wrong" direction in 1946) and in which party ties and party organizations are both exceedingly weak.[68]

Whatever the explanations may be for trends in the time series, it can be argued that propounders of congressional districting formulas for the 1970s should have an eye for partisan swings and their preconditions. If present trends continue, House members could reach a happy state in which they are almost completely insulated from partisan electoral currents. To achieve such an insulation would be to give belated realization to an original constitutional design. But it would also be to abandon a blunt but effective weapon that has been wielded by the electorate now for well over a century. It would elevate representation by reflection over representation by authorization and probably drain from the national government some of its power to govern.[69]

67. In a study of 1962 congressional elections in ten California districts, David A. Leuthold has estimated the value of federally supplied staff salaries, research facilities, franking privileges, etc., to be at least $25,000 per incumbent. *Electioneering in a Democracy* (New York: Wiley, 1968), p. 131. Beyond this are the advantages of name recognition, constituency contacts, and political experience.

68. A part of the explanation of turnover disparities among these states is that they use different ballot forms. The relation between ballot form and voter choice is explored in Cummings, *supra,* n. 53, pp. 172–183, and in Angus Campbell and Warren E. Miller, "The Motivational Basis of Straight and Split Ticket Voting," 51 *American Political Science Review* 293–312.

69. The Massachusetts state legislature offers a good example of a body in which representation is almost entirely by reflection. There is little apparent relation between partisan voting for governor and for legislators. Each legislative house has switched party control only three times in the last half-century. All the switches took place between 1948 and 1958; shifts in party balance have been a response to gradual changes in party identification rather than to fluctuations in sentiment on issues or statewide candidates. Former governors of the last half-century report a gradual diminution in the power to govern. Robert C. Wood and Bradbury Seasholes, "The Image of the Governor as a Public and Party Leader: The Disintegration of an Image—Reflections of Five Governors," in Robert R. Robbins, ed., *State Government and Public Responsibility 1961: The Role of the Governor in*

COMMUNITY. The third value that can be served in districting is community. The concern here is exclusively with representation by reflection and how it can best be effected. The problem of preserving ties between constituents and congressmen in an age of large metropolitan districts is not easily solved.[70] For three decades the proportion of adults who, when polled, could correctly identify their congressmen has hovered at or just below the 50 percent mark: 1942 (two readings), 50 percent and 51 percent; 1943, 49 percent; 1946 (two readings), 46 percent and 41 percent; 1947, 38 percent; 1965, 43 percent.[71] It is possible that urbanization, by weakening old community ties, has weakened ties between constituents and congressmen. In a breakdown of the 1942 figures by size of place, 67 percent of farmers and 61 percent of residents of towns under 10,000 could identify their congressmen, but only 23 percent of the residents of cities over 500,000 could do so.[72] In 1965, 62 percent of the college-educated gave the correct answers.[73] There may be a race here between rising educational standards, on the one hand, and urbanization and growing district size, on the other. The size of his district places the contemporary congressman in a decidedly ambiguous position; his constituency is too large to reach personally and, at least in the large metropolitan areas, too small to reach through television.[74]

Massachusetts (Medford, Mass.: Tufts University, Lincoln Filene Center, 1961), pp. 77–100. The governors have not found party an important resource in governing: "As a means to advance their executive objectives, the party seemed to them of little relevance in campaign, legislative maneuvering, or executive staffing. It appeared to be chiefly a convenient instrument for fund raising. Essentially, it was a more or less marginal resource—sometimes helpful, rarely vital." (p. 93.) The Massachusetts legislature is not highly esteemed by the public; one state opinion survey, taken five months after the 1968 election, turned up percentages of 35 who approved and 48 who disapproved the way it was "doing its job." The figures were almost identical for Democratic and Republican voters (Boston *Globe,* April 21, 1969, p. 1).

70. The original intention was that each congressional district contain about 30,000 persons, five or six thousand of them voters. U.S. Constitution, Art. I, Sec. 2; *The Federalist,* Edward G. Bourne, ed. (New York: M. Walter Dunne, 1901), No. 57, p. 393.

71. All results are from American Institute of Public Opinion surveys. The figures for 1942, 1943, and 1946 are reported in Hadley Cantril, ed., *Public Opinion, 1935–46* (Princeton, New Jersey: Princeton University Press, 1951), p. 133. The 1947 figure is in Jewell and Patterson, *supra,* n. 35, p. 340. The 1965 figure is reported in *Congressional Quarterly Weekly,* November 12, 1965, p. 2320.

72. Cantril, *Public Opinion,* p. 133.

73. *Congressional Quarterly Weekly,* November 12, 1965, p. 2320.

74. Consider the problem of the New York City congressman who must pay to beam his campaign messages to about thirty-five districts in order to reach his own.

One way to try to forge ties is to build constituencies that approximate communities. The argument is that congressmen can be more "reflective" if they serve districts that are in some sense communities than if they serve territories gathered together on a map by some other criterion. The reasons that this should be true are several: (a) a district that embraces a community has clearer interests than one that does not; (b) a congressman can insensately "embody" a constituency more effectively if it has a clear identity—that is, he can himself more easily be a representative sample of it; (c) a congressman can more accurately perceive the interests and attitudes of his district if it has a clear identity; and (d) the communications linkage between congressman and constituents will be better if constituents are bound together by local associational ties. These arguments are familiar; they supply a brief codified rationale for the Anglo-American tradition of local representation.[75]

To build congressional districts that approximate communities is not easy in an age of metropolitan sprawl, and the task is further complicated by the fact that "community" is impossible to define with precision. John Ladd argues that the term, with its long history of usage, is a practical concept rather than a theoretical concept, that "there is no single criterion of membership or specific practical consequence thereof which can be used to define 'community' in the general sense." [76] Even so, it is possible to give reasons why one collection of people looks more like a community than another. Philip E. Jacob and Henry Teune identify a "relationship of *community* among people within the same political entity" as one in which "they are held together by mutual ties of one kind or another which give the group a feeling of identity and self-awareness." [77]

The traditional shorthand method of drawing legislative districts that pay deference to community ties has been to follow the boundaries of local political units. Thus in the drawing of British parliamentary districts in the nineteenth century, county and borough boundaries were

75. Willmoore Kendall, writing a decade ago, contended a little optimistically that congressional constituencies in fact were communities: "[A]lthough the constituencies and states differ greatly in this regard, they all nevertheless approximate, in a way in which the national constituency cannot do, to *structured communities,* involving more or less endless series of face-to-face hierarchical relations among individuals . . ." 4 *Midwest Journal of Political Science* 340.

76. "The Concept of Community: A Logical Analysis," in Carl J. Friedrich, ed., *Community* (New York: Liberal Arts Press, 1959), pp. 272–273.

77. "The Integrative Process: Guidelines for Analysis of the Bases of Political Community," in Philip E. Jacob and James V. Toscano, eds., *The Integration of Political Communities* (Philadelphia: Lippincott, 1964), p. 4.

always respected.[78] British county lines are still "virtually inviolable." [79] American states have been comparably solicitous; in Maryland, for example, no congressional district had ever crossed a county line until the 1960s.[80] In grouping small counties and in building districts within large ones, American legislatures have commonly followed community criteria. Thus, there exist—or have existed until recently—districts embracing the Maryland Eastern Shore, Harlem, the Mississippi Delta, and the Little Dixie section of Missouri. In 1968 the New York state legislature intentionally drew a new district to serve Brooklyn Negroes; one explanation for the action was that "the Democratic county organization . . . lived up to a pledge to create a district embracing the Bedford-Stuyvesant area." [81] In early 1970 the New York legislature reached across three city boroughs to create a district "tailor-made" for a Puerto Rican congressional candidate.[82] Whether or not a district embraces a community is in some respects subject to quantitative measurement: Karl W. Deutsch and James V. Toscano have advocated the study of flows of various transactions among populations as indicators of levels of cohesion.[83]

Some efforts to draw districts of distinguishable character have put emphasis squarely on demographic homogeneity rather than on internal local ties. The term community may not apply here, except insofar as one can speak of the sum of district components as comprising a community of interest. In the British Redistribution Act of 1885, boundaries of parliamentary districts "were deliberately drawn with a view to separating 'the pursuits of the population.' " [84] "In the larger towns, divisions

78. D. E. Butler, *The Electoral System in Britain, 1918–1951* (Oxford, 1953), p. 206.

79. Vivian Vale, "*Reynolds* v. *Sims* Abroad: A Briton Compares Apportionment Criteria," 22 *Western Political Quarterly* 90. It might be added that there is something to be said for the British custom of assigning constituencies place names rather than numbers.

80. Dwynal B. Pettengill, "Maryland: Frustration of One Party Control," in Malcolm E. Jewell, ed., *The Politics of Reapportionment* (New York: Atherton Press, 1962), p. 213.

81. Clayton Knowles, "Bingham May Sue on Redistricting," New York *Times,* February 26, 1968, p. 58.

82. Richard Reeves, "Legislature Plan on Redistricting to Aid State G.O.P." New York *Times,* January 20, 1970, p. 1.

83. Karl W. Deutsch, "Transaction Flows as Indicators of Political Cohesion," and James V. Toscano, "Transaction Flow Analysis in Metropolitan Areas: Some Preliminary Explorations," in Jacob and Toscano, *supra,* n. 77.

84. Henry Pelling, *Social Geography of British Elections, 1885–1910* (New York: Macmillan, 1967), p. 3.

representing the business or middle-class residential interest were usually separated out from the working-class quarters; in the counties, the agricultural and industrial areas were given distinct representation, and thus the 'landed interest' was given a further lease of life." [85] By this standard it would be possible—if perhaps not desirable—to draw concentric sets of districts for some American metropolitan areas to match their concentrically arrayed social classes. One American city follows the plan; the Denver metropolitan area is divided into two congressional districts, one of them allotted to Denver, and the other, doughnut-shaped, allotted to the suburban counties surrounding it.

However community may be defined, efforts to realize it in districting are likely to produce conflict with other values. The more stringent the Court's equality standard, the more probable it is that districts will slice through communities rather than enclose them. More districts will have, in Lewis A. Dexter's terminology, "orphaned sections." [86] Emphasizing community can also violate the compactness standard. No natural law ordains that people with community ties live in areas of regular geometrical shape. The new Bedford-Stuyvesant district is relatively compact, but it is hard to see how the arguments for its creation would be any less persuasive if it had been built to look like a dragon or a centipede. [87] Drawing districts along community lines can also reduce partisan competition. The relationship is not a necessary one; the parties are likely to be matched rather evenly, for example, in districts centered in medium-sized cities like Flint, Madison, Akron, Chattanooga, Salt Lake City, and Syracuse. In most cases, however, an adherence to community criteria will probably produce safe districts. There is, in short, a trade-off between community and each of the other districting values. But, as long as representation by reflection remains an important form of political linkage, the claim for community ties will remain strong.

85. *Id.,* p. 9.

86. "Standards for Representative Selection and Apportionment," Pennock and Chapman, *supra,* n. 18, p. 159. It is possible to conceive of a situation in which the achievement of perfect population equality among a set of districts would produce a permanent lowering of the proportion of the population in the total set who could correctly identify their congressmen's names.

87. In Alexander M. Bickel's words, "Is it unnatural or otherwise forbidden so to gerrymander districts that a solid Negro or Puerto Rican vote is ensured, thus making certain that legislative bodies will contain members of those minority groups?" "The Durability of *Colegrove* v. *Green,*" 72 *Yale Law Journal* 43. There is, to be sure, the vexed question of whether drawing districts along racial lines is constitutional. *Wright* v. *Rockefeller,* 376 U.S. 52 (1964).

PRACTICES

To shift from districting theory to districting practice is to turn to a different realm, a realm of subtle bargaining, grand partisan deals, pursuit of political self-interest, secret map-making, and a multitude of other undertakings regularly condemned by the newspapers as outrageous. That politicians pursue their own interests can hardly be denied. A good many political theories, some of them expressed in rhapsodic tones, hinge on the assumption that politicians serve the public interest by serving their own. But whether they do or not is a matter for persistent examination.

To turn to practice is to introduce the subject of gerrymandering. The term has been variously defined;[88] perhaps it cannot be defined precisely without loss of shadings of its meaning. Let it here refer to the drawing of districts, usually of irregular shape, in such a fashion as to serve the interests of parties, other groups, or individual politicians. Attention will be given in the following pages to the consequences of gerrymandering. In a search for consequences it becomes advisable to break down congressional gerrymandering into three subcategories, each of them the outcome of a separate form of bargaining engaged in by politicians. The subcategories shade into each other, and they are not meant to be exhaustive. But it will serve a purpose to treat them as pure types. The spotlight will be on districting practices in the larger northern states; their size at once gives political cartographers greater leeway and the achievements of the cartographers greater national significance.

PARTISAN GERRYMANDERING. Gerrymandering in its most familiar form involves the dishing of one political party by another; the dominant party draws districts with an eye toward maximizing its holdings.[89] At least

88. To one author gerrymandering is the "adjusting of electoral boundaries so as to secure some other object besides equal representation" (W. J. M. Mackenzie, *Free Elections* [New York: Rinehart, 1958], p. 110). To another it is "the maneuvering of district boundaries for partisan advantage" (Andrew Hacker, *Congressional Districting: The Issue of Equal Representation* [Washington, D.C.: Brookings Institution, 1964], p. 60). Some definitions are broader. "Gerrymandering is discriminatory districting. It equally covers squiggles, multimember districting, or simple nonaction, where the result is racial or political malrepresentation." Dixon, *Democratic Representation,* p. 460. "In the broadest sense of the term, any reapportionment or redistricting smacking of political skullduggery may be termed a gerrymander." Neil Tabor, "The Gerrymandering of State and Federal Legislative Districts," 16 *Maryland Law Review* 278.

89. The best analysis of the logic of partisan gerrymandering strategies is presented in Hacker, *supra,* n. 88, chapter 3.

three conditions must be satisfied for partisan gerrymandering to occur: One party must have sufficient control of the instruments of government to be able to impose its will upon the other; the minority party must be large enough to supply a target for majority assault (it would be difficult to gerrymander against Louisiana Republicanism); and the majority party must be reasonably cohesive. The last requirement is needed to assure that bargaining will take place exclusively within the majority party, rather than between individuals across party lines. In bargaining within the majority party there is typically, but not necessarily, a fairly high degree of central coordination;[90] that is, party leaders have considerable influence over decisions. After reaching internal agreement on its districting plan, the majority party forthwith imposes it upon the minority.[91]

A good example of partisan gerrymandering is the activity of New York Republicans in 1961.[92] The state had lost two congressional seats in the national reapportionment and was therefore forced to redistrict. The incumbent congressional delegation was 22 to 21 Democratic. The governorship and both houses of the state legislature were Republican. In November 1961, after several months of intricate exercises in map-making, Republican leaders introduced and won quick enactment of a new districting plan geared to produce as many as 26 Republican congressmen. Three Democratic districts were abolished entirely, and four marginal Democratic districts were given transfusions of Republican voters. Two new Republican districts were drawn on Long Island, and three districts were rendered significantly more habitable for Republicans in New York City. A good many of the new districts were products of geometric artistry; one was said to resemble "a camel biting the tail of a barking dachshund," another "an X-ray of a badly-shattered elbow." [93] (Eight

90. There is a discussion of bargaining of this kind in Charles E. Lindblom, *The Intelligence of Democracy: Decision Making Through Mutual Adjustment* (New York: Free Press, 1965), chapter 7.

91. The above discussion can apply to actions by one group against another as well as to one party against another. In 1966, for example, the Mississippi legislature broke up the old Delta district in order to head off the election of a Negro congressman. "Special Report: Congressional Redistricting," *Congressional Quarterly Weekly*, September 16, 1966, pp. 2072–2074. The Delta district was the only one in the South with a substantial Negro majority. No Negro has been elected to Congress from a former Confederate state since 1898.

92. There are accounts in Hacker, *supra*, n. 88, pp. 62–65; in Gus Tyler and David I. Wells, "New York: 'Constitutionally Republican,'" in Jewell, *The Politics of Reapportionment*, chapter 13; and in Gus Tyler and David I. Wells, "Camel Bites Dachshund," *New Republic*, November 27, 1961, pp. 9–10.

93. Tyler and Wells, "Camel Bites Dachshund," p. 9.

years later *Wells* v. *Rockefeller* gave the state's Republicans a chance to strike again. As a "high Republican reapportionment expert" explained, "now it's just a question of slicing the salami, and the salami happens to be in our hands." [94] It was sliced early in 1970.)

The most striking aspect of the New York Republican effort in 1961 is that it proved not very successful; in the 1962 election the party carried only 21 seats out of 41. But comparable efforts have been resoundingly successful. After the 1950 census California Republicans drew new lines that increased their congressional margin from 13–10 to 19–11. A decade later California Democrats, then in control of the legislature, retaliated by converting a 16–14 Democratic advantage into a 25–13 advantage[95] (thereby precisely counterbalancing in 1962 an 18–6 Republican delegation elected in Ohio, the product of an earlier bout of gerrymandering). It is not difficult to believe that a party in control of most of the key state governments can invoke cartography to boost its congressional fortunes substantially. And until the 1960s the Republicans—habitual rulers of most of the northern legislatures—doubtless did so. There is no sure way to detect gerrymandering by examining election results; the most innocent districting plan will penalize a party whose voters are either inordinately concentrated (like Michigan Democrats) or inordinately dispersed (like Missouri Republicans). But the figures in Table 3 are highly suggestive. Table 3 gives popular vote totals and partisan seat distributions for congressional elections in 1952 and 1958 in the eight largest northern states. In the 1950s these states elected 196 congressmen —almost half the House. All eight used districting systems in whose construction the Republican interest had been exclusive or predominant. The 1952 and 1958 elections were, in a sense, mirror-image elections; the Republicans won 54 percent of the two-party vote in the eight states in 1952, and the Democrats won 53.5 percent in 1958. And yet the Republicans won 64.8 percent of the seats in 1952 (a bonus of 10.8 percent, or about twenty-one seats), and the Democrats won only 47.7 percent in 1958 (a negative bonus of 5.8 percent, or about eleven seats). Probably most of the disparity was a consequence of gerrymandering.[96] Indeed,

94. Sidney E. Zion, "State Republicans See a Gain of 6 to 8 House Seats," New York *Times,* April 8, 1969, p. 34.

95. The 1961 California redistricting did not meet the most exacting standards of majority party ruthlessness; the Democrats sought and won the support of a number of Republican incumbents in order to forestall a referendum challenge. There is an account in H. Frank Way, "California: 'Brutal Butchery of the Two-Party System'?" in Jewell, *Politics of Reapportionment, supra,* n. 80.

96. It should be noted that until the 1960s, there were few states outside the border and fringe South where the Democrats could engage in countervailing dis-

the 1952 Republican congressional victory (221 to 213) may have been an artifact of gerrymandering in two states alone; mostly by ingenious cartographic efforts, California and New York Republicans managed to convert a 1950 Republican margin of two in the two states into a 1952 margin of nineteen.

Partisan gerrymandering has another important consequence: *Of the three subcategories under review here, partisan gerrymandering is the best producer of marginal districts.* The reason is that parties with absolute control over districting tend to be too greedy. A controlling party normally concedes a minimum of very safe districts to the opposition and then tries to salvage as many as possible for its own adherents. In this latter effort there is a tendency to spread electoral resources too thinly —sometimes, to be sure, with the governing assumption that it is better to have a district that will vote with the dominant party some of the time than with the minority all the time. Again, the New York districting plan of 1961 offers a good example. The Republican intention was to create six districts (out of nineteen) in New York City that party members could contest with some hope of success. The result was to supply the city with swing districts. One of the six became safe for the Democrats, three others remained marginal throughout the decade, and another turned Democratic after the retirement of a Republican incumbent in 1968; only one voted Republican in four consecutive elections. Other good examples of districting plans in which party ambitions have produced marginality are the North Carolina Democratic plan of 1961 [97] and the New Jersey Democratic plan of 1965.[98] In some of the large states a kind of regression toward equity seems to occur over a decade as incumbents come and go and populations shift around; delicately woven partisan fabrics gradually become unraveled. Thus the congressional holdings of New York Republicans in the elections of 1952 through 1960 were 27 (out of 43), 26, 26, 24, and 21; of California Republicans in 1952 through 1960, 19 (out of 30), 19, 17, 14, and 14; and of California Democrats in 1962 through 1968, 25 (out of 38), 23, 21, and 21.

BIPARTISAN GERRYMANDERING. Of the eight large northern states discussed

---

crimination. Because of low voter turnout in Democratic southern and core-city constituencies, the Republican gerrymandering advantage did not manifest itself in disparities between the Republican proportion of the national popular congressional vote and the Republican proportion of the House membership.

97. Preston W. Edsell, "North Carolina: 'This Bill or Nothing,'" in Jewell, *supra*, n. 80.

98. "Special Report: Congressional Districting," *Congressional Quarterly Weekly,* September 16, 1966, pp. 2082–2085.

TABLE 3
Partisan Seat Distributions and Popular Vote Totals in the Eight Largest Northern States, House Elections of 1952 and 1958

	1952			1958		
	Republican percentage of House seats	Republican percentage of congressional two-party vote	Difference between seat and vote percentages	Democratic percentage of House seats	Democratic percentage of congressional two-party vote	Difference between seat and vote percentages
California	63.4	54.1	9.3	53.3	60.1	−6.8
Illinois	64.0	53.7	10.3	56.0	54.5	1.5
Massachusetts	57.2	53.2	4.0	57.2	57.7	−0.5
Michigan	72.3	52.6	19.7	38.9	53.1	−14.2
New Jersey	64.3	57.3	7.0	35.7	49.8	−14.1
New York	62.8	53.9	8.9	44.2	50.5	−6.3
Ohio	69.6	55.6	14.0	39.2	50.9	−11.7
Pennsylvania	63.4	52.3	11.1	53.3	51.1	2.2
Eight-state total	64.8	54.0	10.8	47.7	53.5	−5.8

above, only in Ohio did Republicans maintain sovereign control over congressional districting in the 1960s. Either as an indirect consequence of *Baker* v. *Carr* or as a direct consequence of gains in electoral strength, Democrats were in a position to take part in districting decisions at least once in each of the other seven. Democrats also won a share in decisions in a number of smaller northern states, including Connecticut, Indiana, and Iowa.

One consequence of rising Democratic fortunes has been a greater incidence of what can be called bipartisan gerrymandering. Two conditions must be satisfied for it to occur: control of the relevant instruments of state government must be divided between the two parties, and both parties must be hierarchically organized. Bargaining takes place within each party with a high degree of central coordination, and then between the parties with the respective party elites meeting as equals. Two casebook examples of bipartisan gerrymandering are the Illinois and Pennsylvania compacts of 1961 and 1962.[99] The states had lost, respectively, one and three congressmen in the 1960 reapportionment; both were thus forced to redistrict. In each of them the Democrats controlled the governorship and the lower house of the state legislature, but not the state senate. In each state a deal between the parties was therefore in order, and in each a deal was struck. The terms were about the same in each case; state congressional losses were absorbed in such a fashion as to cause minimal disruption in either party's House representation. Party elites played an important role; in both states the key bargainers on the Democratic side were the leaders of city machines—Congressman William Green of Philadelphia and Mayor Richard Daley of Chicago. Each party in Pennsylvania adeptly butchered one of its own incumbents in furthering its general cause.

The overall effect of bipartisan gerrymandering is the creation of a large number of safe seats for both parties; each party is allowed to reinforce its hold over its own districts. This probably helps to account for the fact that partisan congressional turnover was very low in both Illinois and Pennsylvania in the 1960s. But not all districts need be rendered safe. When hierarchical organizations bargain over territory, it sometimes makes sense to overcome conflict by creating "no man's lands." Thus, in 1944 Churchill and Stalin agreed that their interests were "50/50"

99. The discussion below draws from accounts in David W. Minar, "Equilibrium in Illinois: Frustration and Accommodation of the Parties," and Edward F. Cooke and William J. Keefe, "Pennsylvania: The Limits of Power in a Divided Government," in Jewell, *supra*, n. 80.

TABLE 4

Kinds of Gerrymandering Associated with Strength of State Party Organizations, Levels of State Party Competition, and Single-Party or Divided Control of State Government

	One-Party Control of State Government		Split Control of State Government	
	State party organizations strong	*State party organizations weak*	*State party organizations strong*	*State party organizations weak*
Generally competitive states	Partisan Gerrymandering (New York, 1961)	Partisan Gerrymandering (California, 1961)	Bipartisan Gerrymandering (Illinois, 1961) (Pennsylvania, 1962)	Individual Gerrymandering (Massachusetts, 1962) (California, 1968)
One-party states	a	Individual Gerrymandering (Texas, 1965)	a	a

a. Rare or nonexistent combinations of variables.

in Hungary and in Yugoslavia. In the Illinois and Pennsylvania compacts of 1961 and 1962 one district in each state was treated in precisely the same fashion. In Illinois, "the disposition of the twelfth Cook County seat was the final and most difficult question. It was solved by creation of a 'swing' district (Eleventh) in northwest Chicago. . . . The composition of this district was the main subject of the final and crucial committee negotiations, the problem being what constituted a swing district." [100] And in Pennsylvania, "each side submitted several plans for a 'swing district' in eastern Pennsylvania." [101] The final product was "about as evenly balanced between the parties as it was possible to make it—only 1,478 registrations in the new district separated the parties in 1961, only 1,989 votes separated the candidates in 1960." [102]

INDIVIDUAL GERRYMANDERING. In a third kind of gerrymandering the bargaining participants are individuals rather than parties. Like bipartisan gerrymandering it became more commonplace in the 1960s. Two conditions must be satisfied for it to occur: the party organizations of a state must be weak; and either the relevant instruments of state government must be divided between the parties or the state must be a one-party state. (With this final set of conditions now presented, Table 4 offers a schematization of conditions underlying each form of gerrymandering.) What happens in "individual gerrymandering" is that hierarchical party organizations disappear from the picture; bargaining with an element of central coordination gives way to bargaining among a number of equals. The equals are in most cases congressional incumbents guarding their own interests (or their local agents doing the guarding for them), but sometimes they are state legislators nurturing dreams of congressional careers.

Two paradigm examples of individual gerrymandering are the Massachusetts redistricting of 1962 and the California redistricting of 1967. (Another could as easily be the Texas redistricting of 1965.) Massachusetts and California, both models of successful Progressive reform, have very weak party organizations. Massachusetts was induced to redistrict in 1962 by the loss of two of its fourteen congressional seats in the 1960 reapportionment; California redrew in 1967 under court order. Massachusetts was ruled by a Democratic legislature and Republican governor in 1962; California enjoyed the same arrangement in 1967. The bargaining in Massachusetts went as follows: "The final redistricting plan was

100. Minar, *supra*, n. 99, p. 146.
101. Cooke and Keefe, *supra*, n. 99, p. 163.
102. *Id.*, p. 166.

the result of a March 19 flying visit to the State House in Boston by Reps. [Thomas P.] O'Neill (D), Edward P. Boland (D), Torbert H. Macdonald (D), Silvio O. Conte (R) and William H. Bates (R). The five Congressmen, in six hours of frantic lobbying, were able to convince the General Court [the legislature] to abandon the Democratic-sponsored redistricting plan which Republicans claimed was designed to give the Democrats a 10–2 edge in the Massachusetts U.S. House delegation, and to adopt the plan drawn up by the congressmen themselves, protecting the House seats of all incumbents except [Thomas] Lane and [Laurence] Curtis." [103] (Lane and Curtis were the two singled out as expendable.) It was reported that the final plan had the approval of the governor and also of the White House. But not everyone was happy. The president of the state senate likened the five congressmen to "vultures sweeping down over the State House to preserve their own jobs." [104]

About the same thing happened in California in 1967.[105] The thirty-eight incumbent congressmen "agreed on more than 50 shrewdly calculated transfers of territory among districts in order to cement themselves into office." Every marginal incumbent was strengthened. In one bargain, "two Los Angeles County Republicans, Reps. Charles Wiggins and Craig Hosmer, agreed to take over pieces of neighboring Orange County to help save Democrat Richard Hanna from creeping Republicanism. . . . Mr. Hanna gladly surrendered about 60,000 Orange Countians of Republican persuasion to Mr. Wiggins and about 25,000 to Mr. Hosmer; in return, the Democrat agreed to accept about 60,000 of Mr. Hosmer's Los Angeles County constituents in the Democratic-oriented community of Lakewood." To be sure, some partisan qualms had to be overcome. But overcome they were; in the words of one Democrat, "Earlier in the year it was hard to think of undercutting the comeback chances of Democratic colleagues who'd gone down last November. But as the '66 election got more distant and Democratic prospects for '68 kept looking worse, we all decided that the first law of politics is survival."

The goal of each participant in individual gerrymandering is the preservation of his own seat; if each is successful in his quest, the consequence is a complete stamping out of partisan turnover. Whether turn-

---

103. "Massachusetts—Two Seat Loss," *Congressional Quarterly Weekly*, May 11, 1961, p. 810.

104. *Ibid.*

105. The following account and quotations were taken from Joseph W. Sullivan, "Massive Gerrymander Mapped in California by 38 Congressmen," *Wall Street Journal*, November 9, 1967, p. 1.

over can in fact be completely abolished is doubtful, but a reasonable judgment would be that it can be effectively minimized; no Massachusetts incumbent has gone down in a November election since 1962, and all thirty-seven California incumbents who ran in 1968 were reelected—only three with less than 55 percent of the vote.[106] The Supreme Court's equality standard has allowed multilateral bargainers to plan their transactions with a new sophistication; it is now legitimate—even necessary—to weave districts back and forth across county lines. Looked at in one way, individual gerrymandering is a magnificent triumph of politicians over parties; it elevates individual goals over party goals. And the two are by no means identical. In the Pennsylvania redistricting of 1962, the four incumbent congressmen from Allegheny County—two Democrats and two Republicans—arranged a side-bargain designed to strengthen all four of them. Governor David Lawrence, his eye on eventual Democratic capture of one of the two Republican seats, was understandably quoted as being "furious." [107] Perhaps it is not surprising that individual legislators, if allowed to write the rulebook, will seek two of the main prerogatives of trade union membership: (a) rigid seniority rules (in the House, a consequence of the destruction of party leadership resources in 1910), and (b) lifetime tenure on the job.

In these discussions of the consequences of forms of gerrymandering, nothing has been said yet about serving the "community" value. And, indeed, not much can be said with precision. It is clear that parties and politicians often draw districts along community lines by intention; that is, as in the Bedford-Stuyvesant case, they pay deference to the community value themselves. It is also clear that, in all three forms of gerrymandering, community-oriented districts very often emerge as by-products of self-serving strategies; to segregate voters by party affiliation or by presumed allegiance to individual politicians is often to segregate them by community. But the by-products of strategy are occasionally districts of a different order. For example, the sixth Texas district created in 1965, a district incorporating slices of Dallas and Tarrant counties and then wending its way to within thirty miles of Houston,[108] arouses the suspicion that it was drawn to cement the incumbent in office by disburdening him

106. The Democrats thereby preserved their 21–17 edge in the California delegation despite a drop, between 1966 and 1968, from 46.8 to 44.8 percent of the state two-party congressional vote.

107. Cooke and Keefe, *supra*, n. 99, p. 164.

108. "Special Report: Congressional Redistricting," *Congressional Quarterly Weekly*, September 19, 1966, p. 2124.

of any coherent population center capable of generating an electoral challenger. There are a good many districts in California, New York, and elsewhere that satisfy no obvious community criteria.

CONCLUSION

For several decades the salient problem in American legislative districting has been the persistence of population disparities among districts. There was always in theory a simple mathematical remedy, and now the remedy has been successfully imposed. Hence it is easy to assume that solutions to lingering districting problems in the post-*Wesberry* era can be comparably simple and mathematical. A compactness standard may yet be enshrined in constitutional law. A lower federal court invoked compactness as an antiseptic against political line-drawing in its charge to the New York state legislature in 1967: "[L]et them divide the State into 41 substantially equal parts, provided they be reasonably compact and contiguous. Let them deliberate as free and independent legislators so long as they do not allow considerations of race, sex, economic status or politics to cross their minds." [109]

Compactness certainly offers an effective remedy against gerrymandering. But, like a prescription of castration to achieve birth control, it has the effect of foreclosing a range of other and less draconian options. And there are other options. The Supreme Court's equality decisions have come at a time when congressional districts are becoming ever larger and more urban and when partisan congressional turnover is declining. The first development raises questions about community roots, about representation by reflection. The second raises questions about the function of partisan swings, about representation by authorization. The Court, ironically, may have contributed to the second trend itself by legitimizing the crossing of county lines in building equal districts and by helping to create more favorable conditions for bipartisan and individual gerrymandering.

Down at the state level the debate over districting has remained sterile. It should not be surprising that legislatures flounder when their districting alternatives are ranged for them on a continuum between judicial purity and partisan lust. There is lacking a sense that districting can legitimately serve different values and that there are complex trade-offs among these values. In judging the California redistricting of 1967 it surely makes sense to ask whether the districts are roughly equal in popu-

109. *Wells* v. *Rockefeller,* 273 F. Supp. 991 (1967).

lation; it also makes sense to ask whether the districts display internal coherence and whether a state as large as California—soon to elect a tenth of the House—should be allowed to try to abolish partisan turnover. It makes sense, in short, to devote attention to representative linkages as well as to voter equality, to ask how the House can be rendered a more vital representative body rather than a body increasingly insulated from popular control.

*   *   *

COMMENTARY *by Allan P. Sindler*

From a public-policy viewpoint, it is a great pity that analyses of the reapportionment problem such as Professor Mayhew's (and other parts of this volume) were not characteristic of the literature available to the Court prior to its watershed decision in 1962 of *Baker* v. *Carr* and its subsequent implementation. To be sure, the Court itself must bear most of the responsibility for its increasingly rigid insistence on a single simple standard, mechanistically applied: defining and "solving" the problem of inequitable legislative apportionment in terms of quantitative equalitarianism. Yet political scientists and other specialists, by failing to promote and enrich a high-quality public dialogue on the issue, bear their share of the responsibility as well. This volume should serve to lay to rest any belief that the lopsidedness of public discourse on the reapportionment problem simply has reflected the fact that one side had all the compelling points and the other had no persuasive defense or caveats to offer.

That belief is understandable in light of the virtual monopoly in ideological warfare enjoyed by the opponents of malapportionment. Clothing themselves in the garments of the pleading or outraged aggrieved, they sought to offset their deficiency in actual power by dunning the conscience of America through exploitation of a favored symbol—citizen voter equality. As a practical complement to this moral posture, they held out the promise of great changes in policy outcomes at state and national levels as a consequence of equitable apportionment. Most political scientists shared and promoted these perspectives, and too many, unfortunately, permitted their preferences as citizens to subsume their role as careful professional analysts of politics and institutional arrangements. The quest for equitable representation thus became frozen in the mold of approximate mathematical equality of the number of persons per district.

Little was heard from the other side which, perhaps because it possessed the power, remained generally inarticulate or satisfied to allude vaguely to the preservation of community values through representation of area or of political units.

This lineup has changed drastically in the wake of judicial intervention and policy-making. The claim to citizen voting equality has been transformed from a challenger's plea to an accepted and enforced rule. That rule apparently is in the process of being extended to all levels of representation and of being applied to the virtual exclusion of other factors, except for such ostensibly related ones as compactness of districts. (It makes an interesting question, one not really probed in this volume, why legislatures and courts were willing and able to achieve rapid compliance in this politically sensitive area, to contrast to such other prickly matters as racial desegregation in education and religious activities in public schools.) The dissenters and claimants are now those who must argue the inadequacy or the danger of overreliance upon the emerging dogma of mathematical equalitarianism. In this context, this volume is a most welcome, if belated, stimulus to a proper examination, rather than a continued polemization, of the problem.

It now appears that the attribution of "revolution" to the anticipated effects of the Court's apportionment rule is yet another example of the badly inflated rhetoric of our time. Such mistaken expectations derive from more than neglect of the fact that suburbanites would gain more than urbanites in any redressing of the numerical inequalities of representation. They proceed more fundamentally from a truncated view of policy causation and from an unawareness of the extent to which the achievement of citizen voting equality provides no clear answers to other relevant dimensions of the problem of apportionment. Some recent students of comparative state politics have come up with findings which push in the direction of the relatively low influence of political-institutional factors—apportionment arrangements included—on policy outcomes, as compared to such factors as per-capita income, urbanism, and the like. One does not have to take the argument that far to acknowledge that the apportionment factor, taken alone and in abstraction from the complex policy-making process of a state or the nation, cannot be linked to policy consequences in any simple, direct, or unmediated way. Similarly, as Professor Mayhew's study cogently demonstrates, a host of critical questions about the nature of representation and its systemic consequences, relating both to theory and practice, remain untouched by tunnel-vision concentration on just the one dimension of citizen voting equality.

The true complexity of the apportionment/representation problem, illuminated by the articles in this volume, approximates the "thicket" Mr. Justice Frankfurter warned his brethren about in his vigorous dissent in *Baker* v. *Carr*. This need not mean, contrary to Justice Frankfurter's conclusion, that the Court should not enter at all, but it surely means that the Court's entry should be accompanied by a far greater caution and flexibility than has been shown to date. The reason why the effects of the Court's position have not been more basic and far-reaching is not that complex criteria have been sensitively applied, but that the primary criterion the Court has applied inflexibly has proved to be neither the catalyst nor the determinant of the cumulative change that its proponents assumed it would be.

If the judicial interpretation were to proceed no further than at present, presumably the political system could absorb and adjust to the new rule with no greater upset than was occasioned, say, by the establishment of suffrage for women. It is very likely, however, that we have seen but the beginning of judicial policy-making in this area. If so, studies like this volume will spur, it is to be hoped, the informed discussion that should precede and shape such a development, rather than follow it as an ineffectual postmortem of a fait accompli.

If I have read Professor Mayhew's article right, his stance is consistent with the drift of the last few paragraphs above. He is not much concerned with passing judgment on the wisdom of the Court's insistence that congressional districts adhere to the equal-population principle. True, he does note that the unforeseen effects might include an encouragement of district formation indifferent to the values of community and cutting through existing political subdivisions, thereby facilitating types of gerrymandering which would reduce the number of competitive districts. But his concern is circumscribed by the realization that the set of constraints on the drawing of district boundaries, including the requirement of equal populations, as yet still leaves to the authority and discretion of state governments—and not to the courts—the determination of very major options on representation. In short, the requirement that districts have equal populations has not created a new ball game for districting, much less a revolution; it has simply tightened up the rules, so that stealing bases has become somewhat more difficult.

Professor Mayhew's real concern, as I understand it, is that the perception of the apportionment/districting/representation problems held by the Court and others is incomplete and distorted. Hence, any extension of the Court's jurisdiction over facets of the problem beyond the mandate for districts of equal population is likely to be counterproductive, by virtue of its unanticipated effects on other important sectors of the political system. I would emphatically endorse Mayhew's argument that the theoretical and practical implications of apportionment and districting schemes are neither exhausted nor well understood by reliance on the standard of citizen equality or on a perspective which relates isolated individuals directly to government without mediation by parties, groups, community, and the like. Different electoral arrangements have different effects on the overall political system, on political parties, on group and community life. Those factors merit explicit inclusion and analysis, as in Mayhew's article, in any considered view of the problem.

When these factors are included in the analysis, a thicketlike complexity results. Even at the level of the individual district and without reference to systemic consequences, the several relevant values discussed by Mayhew often cannot be satisfied by any single districting arrangement; a choice must be made among competing values. What does one say about a carefully gerrymandered district, bizarrely shaped and the very antithesis of compactness, which promotes the values of an ethnic community? Or about creating districts which are homogeneous in class, in the name of community but at the expense of party competition? Or about emphasizing party competition, when that involves the neglect of the values of community and compactness? To require districts of equal population is to say nothing, necessarily, about any of these other vital dimensions of representation which are associated with the concept of effective—not merely nominal—citizen equality.

When the context is enlarged, as it must be, to include systemic factors and consequences, the thicket may well become impenetrable. We are fortunate that the problem at the level of national government is confined, in practical terms, to the House of Representatives, because parts of it logically apply to the Senate and to the presidency, as well. For example, the mere fact that states vary in the degree of competition within them between the major parties raises some of the problems examined by Mayhew. What proportion of politically safe and unsafe districts (states) should underly an optimally functioning Senate or the aggregated total of state electorates which decides a presidential election? How much turnover in seats and in party control is desirable, and how do the answers relate back to the structure of districting? It is economical, if somewhat deceitful, to avoid having to answer such questions by treating them as nonproblems for plausible reasons. For one thing, states certainly satisfy the values of community and compactness. More critically, states are the constitutionally mandated unit for Senate and presidential elections, and therefore, unlike House districts, they are not up for a possible redrawing of lines in the aftermath of each federal census. States and their fixed boundaries may be accepted, therefore, as givens in the situation in a way not true of the boundaries of House districts.

It would be misleading, however, to imply that the unit of the state bears the same relationship to senatorial as to presidential elections. The Senate is a multi-member body, composed of two representatives per state and intended to represent state electorates equally without regard to population differences. The presidency is a single-member post, intended to represent the national electorate, albeit through electoral procedures which use state electorates as basic units. The latter commitment requires an indirect election device, which, in turn, builds in the certainty that the arithmetical weight of a vote will be unequal—that is, it will vary with the state (and the state's political situation) in which it was cast. The argument of citizen voting inequality, when applied generally to the election of a single chief executive and particularly to the presidency of the nation, has been used with increasing appeal on behalf of the reform of direct popular election. That argument, together with anxiety about the possibility inherent in any indirect election scheme that a candidate not highest in national popular vote may win, seems likely to carry the day in the near future.

The relation of the House to the districting problems examined by Mayhew is more direct than the Senate's (because House district boundaries are not "natural" like the unit of the state itself and are subject to being redrawn) and is more diffuse than the presidency's (because the House is a multi-member body). The problems doubtless would appear in sharpened focus if the basic unit in presidential elections were intrastate districts whose boundaries were alterable by action of state legislatures and governors. (One reform of presidential election procedures has proposed precisely that: the creation of electoral districts, which presumably would serve as House districts also, in which the candidate who secured the largest popular vote would get the district's single electoral vote; the winner of the statewide popular vote would get the two electoral votes assigned to the state.) Would the present tolerance of gerrymandering or of large numbers of noncompetitive districts suddenly decrease? Would a constitutional issue emerge over effective citizen voter equality, going beyond the equal-population principle to plunge into the thicket described by Mayhew?

If the multi-member characteristic of the House serves to lower the visibility and urgency of the problem, it also serves to complicate greatly the search for solutions. A view of the problem from the standpoint of the individual district and its electorate is not easily reconcilable with a focus on the needs of the House as an effective participant in national governance. As a voter, I may strongly prefer composing districts so as to heighten inter-party competition, but how would a House made up of marginal-district congressmen function—and with what effects on the political system? (It might be noted in passing that the two-party system would be jeopardized and the single-member district system itself would come quickly under attack if the major parties lacked large numbers of safe districts which could withstand adverse national electoral tides.) Similarly, a preference for defining community in terms of homogeneous class, ethnic, or racial districts is not difficult to defend; but would the aggregate of such districts provide a suitable base for the operations of the House and its role in national government? Turning the problem around offers no easing of the difficulties. Suppose it could be determined that the House performed most effectively when about X percent of its members came from marginal districts or when about Y percent came from homogeneous districts or when about Z percent were freshmen. How could districting requirements be altered to bring about such results?

If these problems are solvable at all, the solutions are not likely to emerge without considerably more concentrated thought and research. It is to be hoped, therefore, that the Court is not headed inexorably and swiftly down the path feared by many of the contributors to this volume. Having cleaned up some of the underbrush, the Court may yet choose to depart from the thicket altogether. Or, penetrating further, it may be sensitive to the range of values—and the obstacles to reconciling them— so well presented by Mayhew. Yet the danger of action based on a truncated perspective on congressional apportionment and districting, whether by the Court or aroused publics, clearly remains, for ours is an age sworn to the quest of greater representativeness. It remains to be seen whether those in pursuit of that goal can be persuaded that citizen voter equality is not the only—and often not the most important—perspective on the matter.

SELECTED REFERENCES

Atleson, James B. "The Aftermath of Baker v. Carr: An Adventure in Judicial Experimentation." *California Law Review* 51 (1963): 535–572.

Auerbach, Carl A. "The Reapportionment Cases: One Person, One Vote—One Vote, One Value." *Supreme Court Review* 1964: 1–87.

Baker, Gordon E. *The Reapportionment Revolution*. New York: Random House, 1966.

Banzhaf, John F., III. "Multi-Member Electoral Districts—Do They Violate the 'One Man, One Vote' Principle?" *Yale Law Journal* 75 (1966): 1309–1338.

Boyd, William J. D. *Changing Patterns of Apportionment*. New York: National Municipal League, 1965.

Brady, David, and Edmonds, Douglas. "The Effects of Malapportionment on Policy Output in the United States." Mimeographed. Iowa City, Iowa: University of Iowa, Dept. of Political Science, 1966.

David, Paul T., and Eisenberg, Ralph. *Devaluation of the Urban and Suburban Vote, a Statistical Investigation of Long-Term Trends in State Legislative Representation*. Charlottesville: University of Virginia, Bureau of Public Administration, 1961.

———. *State Legislative Districting*. Chicago: Public Administration Service, 1962.

De Grazia, Alfred. *Essay on Apportionment and Representative Government*. Washington, D.C.: American Enterprise Institute, 1963.

Dixon, Robert G., Jr. *Democratic Representation: Reapportionment in Law and Politics*. New York: Oxford University Press, 1968.

Dixon, Robert G., Jr., et al. "Reapportionment Symposium." *Michigan Law Review* 63 (1964): 209–278.

Dixon, Robert G., Jr. "The Warren Court Crusade for the Holy Grail of 'One Man-One Vote.'" *Supreme Court Review* 1969: 219–270.

Dye, Thomas R. "Malapportionment and Public Policy in the States." *Journal of Politics* 27 (1965): 586–601.

Goldwin, Robert A., ed. *Representation and Misrepresentation: Legislative Reapportionment in Theory and Practice*. Chicago: Rand McNally, 1968.

Hacker, Andrew. *Congressional Districting: The Issue of Equal Representation*. Rev. ed. Washington, D.C.: Brookings Institution, 1964.

Hamilton, Howard D., ed. *Legislative Apportionment: Key to Power.* New York: Harper and Row, 1964.

——. *Reapportioning Legislatures: A Consideration of Criteria and Computers.* Columbus, Ohio: Charles E. Merrill Books, 1966.

Hanson, Royce. *The Political Thicket: Reapportionment and Constitutional Democracy.* Englewood Cliffs, N.J.: Prentice-Hall, 1966.

Hill, A. Spencer. "The Reapportionment Decisions: A Return to Dogma?" *Journal of Politics* 31 (1969): 186–213.

Hofferbert, Richard I. "The Relationship Between Public Policy and Some Structural and Environmental Variables in the American States." *American Political Science Review* 60 (1966): 73–82.

Irwin, William P. "Representation and Election: The Reapportionment Cases in Retrospect." *Michigan Law Review* 67 (1969): 729–754.

Jacob, Herbert. "The Consequences of Malapportionment: A Note of Caution." *Social Forces* (1964): 246–261.

Jewell, Malcolm E. *Legislative Representation in the Contemporary South.* Durham, N.C.: Duke University Press, 1967.

Jewell, Malcolm E., ed. *The Politics of Reapportionment.* New York: Atherton Press, 1962.

Lehne, Richard. "Shape of the Future; Suburbs Seen as Biggest Bloc in Congress for the First Time After 1970 Reapportionment." *National Civic Review* 58 (1969): 351–355.

McKay, Robert. "Political Thickets and Crazy Quilts: Reapportionment and Equal Protection." *Michigan Law Review* 61 (1963): 645–710.

——. *Reapportionment: The Law and Politics of Equal Representation.* New York: Twentieth Century Fund, 1965.

——. "The Problem of Malapportionment: A Symposium on Baker v. Carr." *Yale Law Journal* 72 (1962): 7–106.

Pulsipher, Allan G. and Weatherby, James L., Jr. "Malapportionment, Party Competition and the Functional Distribution of Governmental Expenditures." *American Political Science Review* 62 (1968): 1207–1219.

Schubert, Glendon. *Reapportionment.* New York: Charles Scribner's, 1965.

Schubert, Glendon and Press, Charles. "Measuring Malapportionment." *American Political Science Review* 58 (1964): 302–327.

"Symposium: One Man-One Vote and Local Government." *George Washington Law Review* 36 (1968): 689–823.

U.S. Advisory Commission on Intergovernmental Relations. "Apportionment of State Legislatures." Mimeographed. Report No. A-15. Washington, D.C.: Government Printing Office, 1962.

PREPARED BY DARWIN R. LEISTER

INDEX

Albert, Carl, 246

Apportionment: effect on state policies, 154–201; and equalitarian democracy, 91–92, 99–100; formula, 252; limits of, 100–104; patterns of, 151–152, 193–201; significance of, 144–146, 152–153. *See also* Gerrymandering

—as justiciable question, 60–77, 132, 134. See also *Baker* v. *Carr, Reynolds* v. *Sims*

Arithmetic absolutism: rule of, 2, 3, 8, 11, 12, 15–16, 21, 22, 24, 25, 28, 45–46, 92, 121–122, 140–146, 250, 251, 288. See also *Hadley* v. *Junior College District, Kirkpatrick* v. *Preisler, Wells* v. *Rockefeller, Wesberry* v. *Sanders*

Aspinall, Wayne N., 237

Avery v. *Midland County, Texas*, 12, 27 (n. 57), 82, 84–85

Bagehot, Walter, 31, 91–92

Baker v. *Carr*, 11, 14, 15, 32, 35, 44–45, 60–64, 67, 69, 74–75, 122, 124, 131, 132, 136, 144, 149, 156, 162, 164, 173, 185, 188, 196, 201, 208, 279, 287

Banzhaf, John F., III, 128, 129, 130

Bipartisan commissions, 3, 15, 30, 35–39, 45, 54, 148–149, 279–280

Birch, David L., 215

Black, Justice Hugo: mentioned, 16, 44, 49, 66, 68, 133; quoted, 18, 26, 27–28, 76, 85 (n. 39)

Blackmun, Justice Harry A., 24–25

Boundaries, drawing of, 1–2, 46–48, 70, 130–138, 142, 147–150, 171, 222–226. See also *Gomillion* v. *Lightfoot, Reynolds* v. *Sims, Wright* v. *Rockefeller*

Brady, David, 153–154, 155, 163, 172, 173, 174–175, 176, 179, 180–182, 186, 189, 191

Brennan, Justice William: mentioned, 20, 22, 64, 135–136, 140; quoted, 19, 33, 62, 87, 124–125

Brown v. *Board of Education*, 17

Burger, Justice Warren: mentioned, 24, 44, 53; quoted, 28

Burns v. *Richardson*, 80, 125

Calhoun, J. C., 92–93

Celler, Emanuel, 254

Census (1970), 2, 7, 90, 121, 137, 139, 140, 148, 157, 209, 210, 216, 217, 250

Chavis v. *Whitcomb*, 33–34, 51–52, 71, 79, 80, 126–127, 129–130

Citizen participation, 41–43, 115–118, 145

Clark, Joseph, 240

Clark, Justice Thomas, 44, 63

Colegrove v. *Green*, 74, 127, 131–132

Congress: effects of reapportionment on, 4, 209–248; electoral base of, 238–241

Congressional representation, 249–285

Connecticut Compromise, 4, 25

Conventions, nominating, 39–41

Councils of Government, 43–44

Cox, Archibald, 10

Dahl, Robert, 60

Danielson, Michael N., 234

Data, reliability of, 203–206

Daver, Manning J., 162–165, 166, 167, 170, 184–185

David, Paul T., 162–163, 165, 166, 167, 170, 179, 180–181, 183–186, 189–190

Davidson, Roger, 258

Decentralization, 42, 72–73, 83

Democracy, equalitarian: and reapportionment, 3, 91–92, 95, 98–104, 107; and representation, 9, 58, 60

Deutsch, Karl W., 272

Dexter, Lewis A., 114 n, 273